# Nature and Industrialization

An anthology edited by
ALASDAIR CLAYRE
at the Open University

OXFORD UNIVERSITY PRESS
in association with `
THE OPEN UNIVERSITY PRESS

*Oxford University Press, Walton Street, Oxford OX2 6DP*

*Oxford  New York  Toronto*
*Delhi  Bombay  Calcutta  Madras  Karachi*
*Kuala Lumpur  Singapore  Hong Kong  Tokyo*
*Nairobi  Dar es Salaam  Cape Town*
*Melbourne  Auckland*

*and associated companies in*
*Beirut  Berlin  Ibadan  Nicosia*

*Oxford is a trade mark of Oxford University Press*

CASEBOUND ISBN 0 19 871096 8
PAPERBACK ISBN 0 19 871097 6

*Selection and editorial material*
*copyright © The Open University 1977*

*First published 1977*
*Reprinted 1979, 1982, 1983, 1984, 1985*

*Printed in Hong Kong*

# Preface

Nature and industrialization are the themes of this anthology; and the period it covers is roughly that of the first industrial revolution in Britain, 1760–1860.

In the Open University's second Foundation Course in the Arts five disciplines—literature, music, history, philosophy, and the history of art—concentrate on this period. It is hoped that any general reader may also find in it a wide enough selection of the work of the period, in all the arts, to get some sense of what it was like to be alive at that time, and to enjoy the book for its own sake.

Anyone who likes to read the introduction may prefer to come to it after the text rather than before. The book is arranged in themes; there is a mainly chronological order within them and an order of development of a broader kind between them, so that the text can be read from start to finish without any need for commentary. However, in case any set of passages seems to need comment the introduction is arranged in the same order, and each theme is dealt with separately.

The five other authors particularly involved in the last part of the Open University's course have been Stuart Brown (Philosophy, chairman), Cicely Havely (Literature), Richard Middleton (Music), Christopher Harvie (History), and Stephen Bayley (History of Art). All have contributed most valuably to the anthology. Graham Martin and Nuala O'Faolain have also given help with the literature. More generally such an anthology would not have come into being without the Open University; several members of the Arts Faculty and the BBC who worked on this course and its predecessor have helped, as have a number of Open University students. The publishing department of the Open University and the editor and copyeditors at the Oxford University Press have put the book most kindly and efficiently through the press. Finally there is a special debt to two people who have done some of the work of organization and detailed research: Georgina Coleman at the Open University, and Emma Duncan, scholar of Wadham College, Oxford. I would like to thank them all. None is responsible for any faults that remain in either the detail or the conception of the whole: as the originator of the idea for this part of the Open University's course and the editor of the book, responsibility for both must fall solely on me.

A.C.

# Contents

'    ' *has been used for the original author's own title.*
"    " *has been used for a title taken from his/her words.*
*No inverted commas have been used where the anthology title does not occur in the original.*

# List of Illustrations

# Introduction

All centuries can claim to be 'centuries of change'; but perhaps the hundred years from 1760 have a stronger claim than any other. First the industrial system, which has since transformed both work and nature throughout the world, was developed in Britain in those years. In the arts, there was a dramatic change in almost every accepted form and canon of taste: 'romanticism' has no precise beginning and end, but its main development lies within this period. In political life, at least three great revolutions—1776, 1789, and 1848—changed the western world; while there were reforms, such as those of 1832 in Britain, scarcely less significant for the future. Finally, from the point of view of the five 'arts' that contribute to this anthology—literature, history, music, the history of art, and philosophy—this is a period of particular significance. Not only does the century see the development of more exact standards in the writing of history, and of new disciplines in the study of literature, music, and the fine arts: it is the period in which the sciences separate themselves from philosophy, and philosophy itself divides into two main streams, one owing allegiance to Locke and Hume and mainly British, the other, mainly continental, to Hegel and Marx. Thus many of the familiar divisions of modern life, both between the arts and the sciences and between different national traditions within them, are established in this period. One might almost say that it is the age in which the modern world and our ways of understanding it took shape together.

I   The debate about ecology may seem, like the word, a modern one: it can be a surprise to realize how far the question had been explored already in the mid-eighteenth century, even before the coming of industrialization. It is almost as if three movements gathered way together in later eighteenth-century life: first a quickening in the powers of economic production—the invention of the spinning jenny and the power-loom, the development of the steam engine, the growth of the factory system; at the same time a new confidence in those powers, visible both in the poetry of the time and in philosophy as it begins to give birth to economics in the 1770s; and thirdly a completely contrary movement of thought, one that criticizes the effects of civilization and technology on human life: the increased desires that seem to be the inescapable accompaniment of economic development, the effects of industrialization on the landscape, and mechanization and habits of commercial calculation on the inner life of men.

However, the anthology opens not with a piece of critical philosophy but in an optimistic mood, with a description of the weaving country round Halifax—an area that the woollen industry would transform a century later into a huge industrial centre—seen as it was well before the industrial revolution by the author of *Robinson Crusoe*. The countryside is tidy, populous, and prosperous in this traveller's vision. But in *The Adventurer* Dr. Johnson raises the question that many people will ask again in the century that follows: how far has industriousness really benefited the human race? Socrates is walking in the streets of Athens: 'How many things are here', he says, 'that I do not want!' Yet Johnson answers the question on the whole optimistically, 'sensibly', in favour of civilization; and Adam Smith, two decades later, will follow him with just the same argument (XII.2). The poorest artificer is better provided for in civilized society, than 'many an African king, the absolute master of the lives and liberties of ten thousand naked savages'.

This was not an idle comparison to be making at the time, for 'noble savages' were much in fashion when Adam Smith published *An Inquiry into the Nature and Causes of the Wealth of Nations* in 1776. A powerful voice had recently been raised on the side of nature, against civilization: that of Jean-Jacques Rousseau. The idea that civilization is a fall from nature and that the expansion of human desire is a loss, not a gain, since it deprives men of the possibility of satisfaction, was not new: Johnson could find an ancestry for it as far back as ancient Greece. But Rousseau developed it systematically, and in an appendix to his second major work, *On the Origin of Inequality among Men*, he attacked the whole fabric of civilization as a monstrous distortion of nature. From Rousseau many revolutionary ideas flowed: a new enthusiasm for equality, which was to find political expression in the French Revolution; a new concern—even more among his followers than in Rousseau himself—for 'the primitive man' or 'the savage' as the natural man, natural because uncorrupted by the complications of civilized life, without vanity, without conflicting duties and desires, independent of other men's help for the satisfaction of his simple needs; and a new love of nature itself—of mountains, woods, lakes, fields, the sea, the solitude in which man can rediscover his own inner life undisturbed by human society.

II  The second section of the anthology looks more closely at the way the countryside and country work were described in this period and before. Did the love of nature lead men to idealize country life, and suppose that the work of shepherds and farm-labourers was somehow idyllic in Britain? If so, did this idealization of nature and country work make the artists of the nineteenth century too eager to condemn industrialization, seeing it only as damaging? It destroyed their scenery; did they to some extent exaggerate the destructive effects it had on the work of ordinary people? For if country work before the industrial revolution was generally as hard as Crabbe in *The Village* implies, or as even the descriptive engravings of Pyne may suggest to a modern eye (Plate 21), then industrialization may have met an unfairly hostile response from the artists and intellectuals. Perhaps it replaced not an idyll but often cruelly heavy forms of labour, idealized by artists who saw them as beautiful from a distance or who invested them with their own intense inner vision, as Samuel Palmer does in his woodcuts (for example Plate 1).

This is a question which cannot be easily answered; perhaps it cannot be answered at all. Certainly there is idealization of country life in much of English poetry. Crabbe in 1783 complains of the use of classical models, conventions about shepherds in ancient Sicily or Italy, by the English poets of the earlier part of the century: he says it makes it hard for people to understand the real sufferings of the poor in his East Anglian parish. Perhaps the charge can be sustained—as the extract from Pope's Pastoral 'Winter' shows—for Pope explicitly modelled his verse on Virgil, and no real Thames-side shepherd said or did things like his Thyrsis and Lycidas. But then Pope didn't of course pretend they did: it is a little like complaining that a piece of music that evokes summer with a certain vibrancy in the strings, such as Vivaldi's *Seasons*, does not sound exactly like real bees or cicadas on a summer's day. But then men and bees are not equally parts of the scenery. Perhaps Crabbe has a case when he complains at the use of human beings and their expression as part of a decorative musical pattern, no matter how beautiful. However, the extract from *Windsor Forest* shows that pastoral convention is only one aspect of Pope's art: he can also describe winter scenes in a simple way, and enter into the life of a bird as freely as Keats, in his letter about the truth of the imagination, says he would 'take part in the existence' of a sparrow that came by his window (XIII.3) 'and pick about the gravel'.

One further point may perhaps be noted. Some of the most idyllic of all presentations of country life occur in the songs of working people themselves. The song quoted at the start of this section, 'The Merry Haymakers', originated as a printed ballad in the late seventeenth century, and it was probably composed in a city. Nevertheless it has been taken up by country people, and recovered from oral tradition in Sussex in the present century. Is this survival of the song merely compensation for hardship in fantasy? Is haymaking, like harvest, a specially privileged time enjoyed more than other seasons? Or to what extent have there always been deep feelings for nature in country working people just as much as in artists, poets, and romantic philosophers, that lead them to respond to this kind of imagery and sense that it fits their experience of summer at least? I do not know the answer, and doubt if a simple answer can be given. Even Stephen Duck the Thresher Poet, a real farm labourer who thought the pastoral convention was merely a sham, might have given an equivocal reply, as his account of the alternation of his feelings while haymaking suggests (II.4).

From the nineteenth century also some autobiographical accounts of country work survive. They confirm what Stephen Duck showed earlier: that even before machinery work could be monotonous, exhausting, and paced by the clock and the farmer's curse. In George Edwards's record of his early life on a farm, as with the account of women's work in the fields, there is plenty of hardship, and the compensations may well have been found more in home life and in rituals and games outside work, such as the crowning of the gleaning queen recorded at the end of the period, than in the experience of the work itself. For all we know, the loss of these may have been an equal source of deprivation, or a greater one than the changes that industrialization brought to the actual working day.

**III**  In the third section of the anthology two writers describe the contrast between nature and the work of men from the point of view of painting. William Gilpin in the 1790s sees nature almost as a series of arranged pictures, yet as superior to any actual picture; for a painting, like a city, is a human artefact, and so must be less beautiful than nature.

Ruskin, at the end of the period, has the whole industrial revolution between him and the green fields of his youth. He said once that he thought all the colours in nature had faded in the nineteenth century. Turner, the painter he loved and championed throughout his early life, is seen first exploring the London of his own childhood: and then suddenly finding the open sky and the green hill-sides, and discovering what nature is. The contrast for Ruskin, if not for the real Turner, is absolute.

Between the two is a letter of Constable's about nature and painting; while the plates give examples of his painting and drawing, and show something of the contrast between the ways he and Turner might paint a scene of water and sky (Plates 5, 6, 7). In the letter Constable describes painting as 'but another word for feeling'. However, distinctions which critics may make much of—such as the contrast between science and emotion—are always liable to be spanned by a practising artist: for elsewhere Constable writes equally unambiguously: 'Why then may not landscape be considered as a branch of natural philosophy? . . . Painting should be . . . considered as a pursuit *legitimate, scientific,* and *mechanical.*'

**IV** Even though the romantic poets are no doubt better read in their own editions than in any anthology, there can be some value in having even a short selection of their poems about nature in such a context. It may show something of the new genius that broke through at this moment, in the description of landscape, in the sense of communion with nature and in the feeling of close relationship with all other living beings. Coleridge's 'Frost at Midnight' is an outstanding example of their reconciliation; while Wordsworth too describes the old Cumberland beggar almost as if he were a natural phenomenon. His *Prelude*, which recounts the growth of a poet's imagination, has as its central theme the relation between man and nature: in the ascent of Snowdon, clouds and sea seem as vital as the climbers and their sheep-dog. And this is not merely vivid description. As he says in 'Tintern Abbey' Wordsworth believed in a spirit in the universe that was alive.

Byron, in the next generation, laughs at the kind of nature-poetry that Wordsworth and Coleridge wrote. His early poem *Childe Harold's Pilgrimage* uses mountain scenery to create a sense of isolated, pessimistic superiority, the 'Byronic' withdrawal from human contact which so many people seem to have found irresistibly attractive. There may be a hint of the Byronic hero in a number of figures to be encountered later in the period—including conceivably Liszt and Charlotte Bronte's Mr Rochester. The stanzas from *Don Juan* meanwhile are a reminder of another sense of the word 'nature' which Byron came to personify for the romantic imagination of the time: surrender to passionate impulse in love.

Walter Scott in *The Heart of Midlothian*, gives a vivid account of a less untamed lady than Byron's Haidee, who pursues the romantic sensations of wonder and awe, but goes too far. The idea of looking at waterfalls and precipices for pleasure was a comparatively recent one in 1818 when this novel was written: the enthusiasm for mountains owes something to the influence of Jean-Jacques Rousseau with his Swiss origins, as perhaps does the reference to the freedom and nobility of the Scottish 'savage's' gesture.

John Clare, like Stephen Duck earlier, in one sense knew nature from closer to than Wordsworth or Scott: he worked as a farm labourer and he knew the hard work associated with country life as well as the beauty of scenery. Yet he has an undiminished zest for the appearance of every aspect of nature: he is a reminder that a love of landscape cannot be assumed to be confined to those who see it from a distance with clean hands. As in Coleridge's 'Frost at Midnight' and Wordsworth's account of climbing Snowdon, attention to scenery and to spontaneous animal life seems to go here with a sharpened awareness of the lives of the village people, the gossips caught in the February sunlight or the shepherds 'croodling' against the 'whizzing storms'.

Clare, like Stephen Duck, is a rare poet in coming from a working village environment. A more 'literary' tradition develops out of Wordsworth and Coleridge, through Keats and then through Tennyson, preserving the reverence for nature that is so characteristic of the *Lyrical Ballads* and developing the more musical aspects of English verse by a revival of the richness of Spenser and the other Elizabethans. There is increasingly an archaic tone in English poetry from the early nineteenth century on; though even in a medieval setting Keats could note more brutal aspects of life than those he chose to write about in the odes, as the short extract from 'Isabella' shows, with its diver who goes 'all naked to the hungry shark', and its 'torched mines and noisy factories'.

V From the first years of the industrial revolution, and even earlier, some observers had noted what would be one of its deepest-lying problems, that of repetition and monotony. Adam Smith (see XII.2) raised it in 1776; in the nineteenth century, it became a topic for urgent debate. Factory hours, even if the work was physically lighter than the tasks it replaced, could induce extreme fatigue, especially in small children, because of the absence of play and the constant exercise of a limited number of muscles. The factory system was also attacked, particularly in its first years, on the grounds that it separated children from their parents, and that it reversed some 'natural' order of family life, deposing the father from his traditional authority. Often his wife and children could earn more in the factory than he could if he had retained his old calling as a hand-loom weaver.

Those who championed the new factory system were not all concerned merely with making profits. A reformer and early Socialist like Robert Owen (whose 'model village' is shown in Plate 9) could hold that factory discipline, when suitably tempered with humanity, could mould human character into desirable habits of method and order. But perhaps the most enthusiastic proponent of the factory system was the Scottish chemist Andrew Ure. His book *The Philosophy of Manufactures* provoked a response, in *The Curse of the Factory System*, from John Fielden, M.P. for Oldham, a mill-owner who had reduced hours in his own business, and who was later prominent in the Ten Hours movement. Fielden's observations of the effects of fatigue are close and perceptive, and the ideas in his book were echoed by another mill-owner in the next decade, Friedrich Engels (XVII.2) and by Engels's friend Karl Marx in his early writings.

In the work of his later years, *Das Kapital*, Karl Marx described the great change that had come about in industry when machines began to be invented that were capable of making other machines. He believed that the lot of the domestic outworker in this new industrialized world was even worse than that of the factory worker, and that the only way for men to free themselves from domination by machines was to learn to master many skills and trades, and to combine scientific and manual work. His reasons for believing this are to be found throughout his work but perhaps nowhere more fully than in the *Grundrisse*, written in the 1850s, from which a short extract is given below (XVII.4).

**VI** There is a pair of accounts of the changing system of transport in the 1830s and early 1840s: canal-building, then railway construction, in the same Yorkshire–Lancashire area. The painting of the Pont-y-Cysylltau Aqueduct (Plate 10) shows something of the impact that canal and railway construction could make on the landscape of that time (as Plate 9 shows the effect of new factories). It has become so familiar since, that this impact can easily be forgotten, in an age when even railways tend to be contrasted with motorways as more ancient and thus more 'natural' methods of transport. Perhaps sheep-tracks in their turn were once seen as disturbing signs of unnatural innovation in the Wiltshire hills

**VII** The anthology goes on to give some accounts of the woollen industry, as it began to transform northern Britain. The woollen industry is particularly significant in this book, not only because of its economic importance to Britain and the industrial revolution as a whole, but also because the areas to be examined in most detail include Haworth in the mill country of Yorkshire, the birthplace of Charlotte Bronte.

This anthology is designed to be read, at best, in conjunction with all the other elements of the study it forms part of, in particular a gramophone record which gives much of the music referred to at the end of this book, and one novel of the period, *Jane Eyre*. If history is expected to consist exclusively of those main features that one tends to pick out in any retrospective view—if the whole of the country in the 1840s and 1850s is expected to be seen caught up in a visible process of industrialization, violent urban growth, and concern about 'The Condition of England'—it can be helpful to note a novel, and a novelist, apparently oblivious of these movements, yet no less of their time than anything in this anthology.

**VIII** Wool mills tended to be built in steep river valleys with fast running water for power and for cleansing. The pattern of urbanization that the cotton mills typically gave rise to was different. Cotton was worked in factories powered by steam. They spread out over the areas where there were coalfields. Cotton flourished typically in the wet climate of Lancashire; wool, characteristically, in Yorkshire. Both created great trading cities: but Manchester in the west was the largest, and with its hinterland of mill towns it became a 'megalopolis', stretching out almost continuously from the Cheshire plain to the edges of the Pennines. It was, after London, perhaps before London, the capital of England in this period. The metal trades shaped a different kind of city again in Birmingham and the Black Country: there are many closely linked towns, full of small foundries and metal-work factories, with more skilled craftsmen, fewer 'factory hands' and probably less difference between richest and poorest than in Manchester. But London was still the biggest city of all, and growing frighteningly in extent as well as in density, as the two illustrations from the middle and end of the period show (Plates 11 and 12).

A number of descriptions of conditions in Manchester itself follow, in which Engels's stands out for some modern critics, for the courage with which it confronts an unprecedented reality. It must have been in some ways like the difficulty of describing the concentration camps when they were first opened in 1945: language has not evolved for these tasks, and words may literally fail a writer, or he may describe the new in terms of the old (factories as palaces, smoke clouds as serpents), or he may caricature it, as perhaps Dickens seems to be doing in his 'Coketown'. (The American critic, Steven Marcus, has argued this case most forcefully, in his *Engels, Manchester and the Working Class* (1974).) However, to avoid any easy assessment of Dickens's methods of description based on this example alone, an earlier passage, from *The Old Curiosity Shop*, follows; there is no exact location for the city Dickens here describes, whereas 'Coketown' is based mainly on his impressions of an actual northern town, Preston.

IX   What was to be done? Chadwick accounted for one of the chief sources of disease and mortality in cities in 1835, when he traced the spread of epidemics to insanitary conditions. He believed it was polluted air that spread disease; but even an attempt to deal with that mistaken diagnosis helped to solve some of the problems of infected water. The section concludes with two passages of Ruskin, one describing an industrial urban scene (at Rochdale, just north of Manchester) and contrasting it with medieval Pisa. He says he is not suggesting a return to the Middle Ages—though the medievalist influences such as Pugin's *Contrasts* can certainly be felt here. He believes modern reformers must take ideas from the Middle Ages, but make a new city that embodies them afresh, without copying them. His ideal of the tight city surrounded by green fields, that anyone can walk out of in a few minutes into open country, has had a strong influence since; not always on house-buyers at the edges of cities, it is true—perhaps more on those who have driven past them impatiently along arterial roads, and on those who have planned for the improvement of their environment. Today there is a swing back towards the kind of Victorian unplanned development that Ruskin attacked. The trouble is that when there are more than a few thousand people to be housed in a city, it has to go upwards if it cannot go outwards; Le Corbusier with his high buildings set among open parkland is one twentieth-century successor to Ruskin's vision, and few people can see much value in his ideas today, plagiarized as they have been by manufacturers of rectangular slabbed tower blocks set close together on asphalt. The problem Ruskin identified in the 1860s cannot be said to have been solved.

X  The next section continues the story of hard conditions with accounts of poverty and unemployment, and of protest. 'The Poor Cotton Weaver', though it may have been based originally on a semi-comic Lancashire ballad model, is perhaps the most desperate of all the folk-songs about work. It dates from the early years of the century, but this version may be from the 1840s. The fate of the poor when they fell out of work was exacerbated by the New Poor Law of 1834. The new workhouses in which conditions were designed to be less favourable than the worst obtaining in the outside world, so that no one should be tempted to enter a workhouse out of preference—was particularly appalling to working people. Workhouses were named 'Bastilles' and the vivid picture of a medieval castle still in use as a prison (Plate 13) for the incarceration of dissidents is a reminder of how highly charged the word 'Bastille' and the memory of the storming of the Bastille might still be.

Wordsworth's reflections on the New Poor Law—published at the end of the 1835–6 edition of the *Lyrical Ballads*—are an instance of the criticism he believed the poet could contribute to a public debate; they stress the nature of unemployed people as individuals, as neighbours or friends to whom the writer and reader are related, rather than as statistics or as mechanical models of desire and aversion. The utilitarian reformers whom he accuses of inhumane thinking frequently had the most humane intentions; and their systematic approach to problems, their reliance on statistics, and their mechanical conceptions of human motivation were in part an almost military response to the chaos of urban expansion. Wordsworth asks if they are attacking rather than serving the true interests of those whose lives they administer.

Further examples of poverty follow: including a description of families in the woollen districts, not far from the areas that Defoe had described in their pre-industrial prosperity. The country was creating wealth, yet leaving its individual workers to become poorer; this was the view that many thinkers came to hold in the 1840s, and it was the experience of many working people. One form that protest took was an attack on machinery. There had been machine-breaking since the eighteenth century (Plate 14 recalls the attack on John Kay for his invention of the fly shuttle). But in the 1840s the grievances of the working people were exacerbated by a series of poor harvests, and the People's Charter was signed—in many cases a humbly meant submission to draw the attention of Members of Parliament to a whole range of wrongs that they seemed to be unaware of. George Rhodes, or whoever was the author of the letter to the *Morning Star* (X.7), shows no undue deference towards Parliament or any other 'authority' of his time. He comes from that area that Mrs. Gaskell singled out for its independence of character in her *Life of Charlotte Bronte* (VII.3). Mrs. Gaskell was writing a book with a new kind of hero in the industrial workers of her novels *Mary Barton* and *North and South*; though her sympathies are clearly most of all with the women.

A few short descriptions of individual poor people follow while Plates 15 and 18 also show some individual working people as nineteenth-century artists saw them. There is a brief self-portrait by a scavenger in a London street described by Henry Mayhew, the chronicler of London poverty. Charles Dickens's 'A Walk in the Workhouse' by contrast with some other accounts, is not a simple attack on the harsh conditions. It is a reminder that there can be a danger, in any anthology, of concentrating only on instances of the striking inhumanities of industrialization and urbanization. For all the misery that it portrays, this account by Dickens may do something to suggest that there were other causes of suffering even in workhouses than the inhumane administration of ruthless laws.

**XI** To the poet James Thomson describing a harvest scene in the early eighteenth century, all this would have been strange. In his vision, human industry is a blessing. It is worth remembering, sometimes, that the word 'industry' had a use like this, before the factory city transformed its meaning and associated it with ugliness, with smoke, and with machine-paced labour.

Meanwhile Cowper in *The Task* 1784 is clearly aware of the hardness of hard agricultural work; but in an extraordinary image he relates human labour to the movement of the world itself, which, like man, can never be at rest. Both men's descriptions of cornfields and harvest are notable also as early instances of that sensitivity in the depiction of nature and of light that the romantic poets would develop in the following years.

But unlike Thomson and Cowper, it sometimes seems that the nineteenth-century poets were ready in advance with complaints about industry before the darkest industry had come to blacken the landscape, and against urbanization even before the vast cities of the later nineteenth century had grown. We may often be struck by the early date of many of the criticisms of industrialization in England: it is almost as if the case against it had been made in advance by poets and artists, as if the industrial revolution came on an aesthetic and philosophic world prepared for just the opposite at just that moment, for a return to nature, to solitude, and to simplicity. Once again we are left with a question: how far was this coincidence, and how far was the romantic case against industrial and urban life a response to the beginning of the industrial revolution itself, by men who were sensitive to the direction of change from the first?

**XII**  Adam Smith wrote before any serious industrialization had impinged on his world. He knew James Watt, the inventor of the steam engine, and knew of some spinning machinery in the cotton industry; but he did not take them seriously into account in his writings. Agriculture was for him the main source of wealth, and the division of labour in all trades, not mechanization, was the main means by which wealth would grow.

Already in his day many of the mercantile restrictions on trade that he attacked had virtually disappeared. Smith was optimistic about the present and future of Britain, and of America still more. His book appeared perhaps significantly in the year when the American colonies declared their independence of Britain. He gave a cheerful and lucid account of work and the economy in his day.

In one respect, however, his optimism was muted. He thought that repetitive and mechanical trades harmed the mental powers of those subjected to them. There was in fact a hidden cost in the division of labour. This qualification on so much enthusiasm for divided labour occurs very late in *The Wealth of Nations*, almost at the end. It crops up in a discussion of the need for public education, partly to counter these depressing mental and moral effects. Adam Smith did not accept the conventional estimate of the 'artisan' as more skilled than the farm labourer; he thought that agricultural labour was much more complex and demanding than most mechanical work. And it was farm labour that he expected to multiply most in the period that would follow his own. Nevertheless, it is significant that Smith noticed the effects of repetition without attributing to them the weight they were to have in the next century, when Fielden or Engels or Marx would write of this as an overwhelming problem for society. It is a problem not yet solved today.

The first generation to think of themselves as 'economists' in England were united in their enthusiasm for Adam Smith. Malthus with his famous law of population-growth outstripping natural resources, and Bentham, with his uncompromising views on the real meaning of labour—to be viewed with nothing but aversion, and done only for the sake of money and repose—stand here as examples of a group that included also Ricardo (Marx's main irritant and the starting-point for much of his economic theory) and James Mill, the father of John Stuart Mill. These, with Adam Smith, were 'the classical economists', as Marx called them, and it was mainly in their time, the early nineteenth century, that Adam Smith's ideas began to have an impact on the economy.

The thinking behind the New Poor Law was much influenced by the work of the economists. Jeremy Bentham had perhaps the widest influence in the generation after Adam Smith. Although himself a reformer who campaigned for the abolition of cruel and antiquated laws, he attracted odium for the exceptionally mechanical thinking in some of his ideas of human nature, and for the inhumane consequences which could arise from these theoretical simplifications.

**XIII**  Wordsworth, in the postscript to the third edition of the *Lyrical Ballads* pointed out some of them. In the earlier preface of 1802, he had spoken in more general terms of the role of the poet as opposed to the abstract thinker. Where poets could bring 'relationship and love' the economists seemed to represent much that was hideous in the new industrial system, with their habits of calculation and abstraction, and their tendency to isolate the pursuit of material gain as a dominant motive of human action. They provoked a violent reaction in their own generation and the next, from the poets above all. Blake with his *Jerusalem* is the most damning, attacking the whole structure of abstract thinking and scientific method as substituting a bloodless 'spectre' for the inner light and individuality in every human being.

Coleridge adds his own more metaphysical account of the antithesis between the 'organic' and the 'mechanical'. For Coleridge, as for Wordsworth and Shelley, poetry, philosophy, and politics were not confined within distinct areas of experience. Here the comments of Raymond Williams on this whole generation of poets (see Chapter II of *Culture and Society 1780–1950*) may be of particular interest.

**XIV**  Meanwhile, in case we take all these arguments with unflinching seriousness, it is worth interpolating some contemporary jokes on the subject: one again from Byron, and one from Thomas Love Peacock, caricaturing Shelley (though Peacock made fun of utilitarians and economists just as much).

**XV**   If the metaphysical champions of the organic and the poets were not always treated with respect, neither were politicians and 'men of the world', when young poets like Shelley came to write political satires in that period. Meanwhile in his own ironic way Dickens follows the romantic poets in laughing at the systematic thinkers. His Mr. Gradgrind is not so much a representative manufacturer as a caricature of someone like Bentham or James Mill, a believer in rigid intellectual order, in forced education, in strict economy and utility. This debate between the economists and their critics on these points is one that has not died out today.

**XVI**   The phrase that began to be used in the 1840s for the whole complex of problems created by industrial development, urbanization, poverty, the destruction of communities and of old beliefs, was 'the Condition of England' question. Here Carlyle and Macaulay prepare the case, and Carlyle states it again in 1843. Like Coleridge, Carlyle had studied German philosophy and imaginative writing. He had translated a play by the poet Schiller, whose *Letters on the Aesthetic Education of Man* were an influential source of anti-mechanistic ideas, and which had much impressed the young philosopher Hegel. Carlyle, like Schiller and Coleridge, contrasted the 'mechanical' with the 'organic' as death against life. Engels and Marx inherited this anti-mechanistic legacy from a number of sources, and it was the work of Marx's later years to reconcile it with his belief that in the future men must come to live with the machine, but as its master, not its victim.

**XVII**   How much of the problem was caused by the degradation of work? And is all work 'noble', or are only certain kinds of work worth doing? The debate was one that ran through much of the social thought of the last two decades of the period, and the conflicting arguments cannot be summarized briefly. Carlyle, at the height of the century's enthusiasm for 'the gospel of work', wrote that 'even cotton spinning is noble'. Engels, like John Fielden in *The Curse of the Factory System* (III.4), held that some work was unfit for human beings to do. Similar views were being worked out independently, from a philosophical standpoint, by Karl Marx in his *Economic–Philosophical Manuscripts* of 1844: notebooks which he did not himself publish, but which formed the basis for much of his subsequent thinking. The extract from a later work, the *Outline of a Critique of Political Economy* or *Grundrisse*, was also unpublished at the time of Marx's death, and in fact left uncompleted by him: as far as can be ascertained, he had originally planned it as a massive work of which his surviving book *Das Kapital* is only a fragment, approximately a twelfth of the whole. The extract

quoted here shows that even in his mature thought Marx is still wrestling with those ideas of Adam Smith about work and rest which had
appealed so strongly to Bentham, but had set Marx off in 1843–4 on his
life-long critique of what he thought of as 'bourgeois political economy'.

After these two quotations from Marx are two from his English contemporary John Ruskin. Ruskin was already, in the 1850s, deriving
social and philosophical ideas from this thinking about art. Increasingly
as he grew older, criticism of painting and architecture became for him
criticism of life, and particularly criticism of the way men were made to
work in nineteenth-century England. His praise of the methods of
Gothic craftsmen was not intended as a simple piece of nostalgic
medievalism, but as a contribution to the understanding of the nature
of all work, and to the establishment of a more human way of working
in the place of industrial mass-production. It is illustrated, in the original edition, by Ruskin's own drawings. Another one, reproduced as
Plate 8, shows the versatility of this writer–artist, who is neglected now
by contrast with Marx, but who had as great an influence on late
nineteenth-century working-class politics in Britain, as well as on thinking about art, as any other man of the time.

**XVIII** Did 'the Condition of England' call for reform or revolution?
In this period some classic formulations of the two paths of political
change can be found. Adam Smith and John Stuart Mill are both just
within the period, and they put the reformers' case; Marx and Engels,
the revolutionary one. The conditions that these men wrote of are now
long past, and their arguments cannot validly be thought of as independent of time and place. Marx might have been a 'reformist' in some
parts of the contemporary world, Mill conceivably a revolutionary in
others; nevertheless they are representative figures, to whom many
people look back today.

However, Marx is seen as an ancestor not only by some who are revo-
lutionaries, as he was, against capitalism, but by those who control the
state apparatus in certain powerful countries—including some where
other Marxists look for their revolutionary overthrow. Thus the spectrum
of meanings attached to the idea of Marxism is a wide one. Similarly,
John Stuart Mill is seen as a predecessor by many liberals today, but
'liberal' can mean a whole range of different things, from 'radical reformer' to a supporter of greater economic inequality in the name of market freedom, an attitude usually today associated with conservativism.
Adam Smith was not a supporter of greater inequality, any more than
Marx was of permanent State power: there is therefore no simple sense
in which it is accurate to see the political and economic systems of the
West and East today as founded on Adam Smith and Karl Marx

respectively. Yet each economy looks to one of these bodies of ideas for its legitimizing doctrine: much as a worldly Renaissance pope, who perhaps would have been more at home with Pontius Pilate than with Christ, may nevertheless have looked to Christian doctrine for the 'legitimation' of his office in his time.

When that has been said, it is true that we have in Adam Smith's early attack on 'the man of system' a particularly clear statement of the case for what is now called 'piecemeal reform'. Such arguments have been used not only against authoritarian centralized states, but also against revolutionary attempts to impose a single vision on the complexity of other people's lives. 'We can only see part of the world; others have their own view of it; so we should reform tentatively, a step at a time, constantly revising and improving plans in the light of other people's responses': this is the piecemeal reformer's case, and Adam Smith stated it in his own day in much these terms. Marx and Engels wrote their *Communist Manifesto* in anticipation of the revolution of 1848, which they hoped would be general throughout Europe. John Stuart Mill valued private property though he valued it as it might be, rather than as it was. But so fairly did he present the opposite case, for socialism or communism, that he converted at least one highly influential thinker—William Morris (XXV.4)—to socialism.

The battle that began in that period over these questions is clearly still being waged throughout the world today.

**XIX**   The first extract from Adam Smith in the next section is worth comparing with the ideas of Gilpin on the picturesque or with the romantic descriptions of nature by Wordsworth or Scott. If one of the aims of romantic art is to arouse wonder, to Adam Smith it appears that the object of classical philosophy is to still it. He clearly regards the sense of philosophical puzzlement at anything extraordinary in the universe as a kind of discomfort or even a dizziness, almost comparable perhaps to Lady Staunton's sensation later, on confronting the waterfall in *The Heart of Midlothian*. Philosophy's task is to reduce that discomfort by explaining the unusual phenomenon in terms of some universal law or intellectual system. The admiration that such systems arouse in the mind seems to Adam Smith akin to the pleasure given by 'a well-composed concerto of instrumental music' (see XXII.1).

In another of his early works, *The Theory of Moral Sentiments*, Adam Smith examines the connections between beauty and utility. We have already met the mid-eighteenth-century ambivalence about economic development in Dr. Johnson's *Adventurer*. He resolved it, after many arguments, in the end positively, and in favour of civilization. It may seem surprising to find a similar alternation of pro and con in Adam Smith's own writing: he is often thought of today as the founder or codifier of modern economics and an unquestioning exponent of the value of material wealth. Yet Smith was first a moral philosopher; and he came to political economy only in the course of developing his early ideas about the duty of the state to provide sustenance for its people (or, as he believed, to avoid impeding them from providing it for themselves). This early work *The Theory of Moral Sentiments* rehearses many philosophical doubts about the value of wealth. It might almost be Rousseau writing some of these words. Yet suddenly at the end, he dismisses the whole train of thought as 'splenetic'—the way we feel in a low mood. Instead, he says, when we are cheerful we pursue wealth; and the major work of the later part of his life, *The Wealth of Nations*, details the way in which men can best attain it. But he did not believe that the pursuit of riches or the accumulation of capital were the best things men could aim for; merely the practical, everyday means that most men looked to for improving their condition. When he died, Adam Smith was still thought of primarily as a moral philosopher, and he revised *The Theory of Moral Sentiments* shortly before his death, though it was afterwards largely eclipsed by the work of his friend Hume. Thus Adam Smith himself probably never expected his economic writings to be read in isolation from their context in moral philosophy as they were in the generation that followed.

Next Bentham sets out the principle of utility and, more briefly, his assumption of universal self-interest. Finally, John Stuart Mill examines the concept of nature from a philosophical point of view, and traces some of the confusions and fallacies that its use can give rise to. In particular, he offers a philosophical critique of the idea that what is 'natural' is in any sense to be identified with what is 'right'.

**XX** The short extracts about painters in the later part of the period, and two of the later paintings included here (Plates 16 and 17), show an increasing preoccupation with moral values in art. William Holman Hunt was a member of the Pre-Raphaelite Brotherhood, the group of mid-nineteenth-century painters in England who believed one should go back to the Middle Ages for models, before the Renaissance with its supposedly too polished techniques and its worldliness in morals had corrupted painting. Ruskin, whose allegiance to Turner remained strong, also favoured the Pre-Raphaelite Brotherhood in the middle years of his life. Ford Madox Brown, the painter of 'Work', was admired by the Pre-Raphaelites (XX.3). He derived his inspiration for 'Work' from the ideas of Carlyle (XVII.1), who is shown in the corner of the picture with F. D. Maurice, a Christian socialist reformer.

**XXI**   To show some examples of writing about nature in the later years of the period, a few poems have again been selected: Tennyson's 'Mariana' (1830) and the later 'Gareth and Lynette' (1859); a poem by Hartley Coleridge, the beginning of Arnold's 'Scholar Gipsy', and an early work by Gerard Manley Hopkins. In 'Gareth and Lynette' Tennyson shows something of the influence of medieval legend on the imagination of the mid-century artists; and he gives a strong feeling of the Pre-Raphaelite ideals of medieval architectural splendour, and of mystical feminine enchantment in the Lady of the Lake. In all these poems, as in the two Pre-Raphaelite paintings shown here, there is also perhaps a new attentiveness to very small detail in description, as if each object had been fixed in turn from close to by the eye of a precise draughtsman: the moss on the flower plots, the pear tree, the individual nail, each is evoked separately and with even attentiveness. This precise attention to detail can also be seen in Gerard Manley Hopkins. But Hopkins seems always to be looking behind surfaces for inner structure and rhythm. This is one of his early poems, which may stand as a contrast to the winter-pieces in other sections (II and IV), and the verse-form is not in itself unconventional; only perhaps the intensity of the description gives a hint of what was to come later, in the mature poems such as 'The Wreck of the Deutschland' or in even a short lyric like 'Binsey Poplars' (XXV.1), when he had evolved his own personal style and versification.

**XXII**   In the two extracts that follow about listening to music there is a clear contrast between two kinds of response to art. Adam Smith expects music to interest the whole man, his intellect as well as his senses. He values ordered complexity, and thinks of music much as he does of an abstract system of philosophical reasoning, both equally pleasurable and for not dissimilar reasons. Some critics dismiss the poem that follows as 'below Coleridge's best', but it does show how he values simplicity and is stirred by a folk-song more than by a rehearsed and elaborate form of art like opera. And in his own train of thought Coleridge seems to follow any spontaneous suggestion of the imagination, so that the poem ends on a note quite different from its beginning, and may well have been as unpredictable to the poet as it is to the reader. 'Classical' and 'romantic' are not simply words to define; but the contrast between these two passages may serve to illustrate some of the most striking aspects of the distinction.

**XXIII**   Because the main work of European composition in the period was not being done in Britain, music may at first appear to be out of place, compared with the other arts in this anthology; but it seems better to sacrifice strict 'unity of place' to quality of original composition. And only the composers themselves were foreign to Britain: Mendelssohn, like Liszt, was played in British concert halls in the period. And both were deeply concerned with the ideas and feelings that have been traced through this anthology.

Both looked for inspiration to the past, and Liszt in particular believed that 'natural' organic form in music was superior to 'mechanical' form, and that 'the people' and 'the gipsy' have a specially close relationship to nature, and hence to uncorrupted sources of traditional art. The impulse to collect folk music, and to correct Liszt's errors of detailed reasoning about gipsies, has continued well into the twentieth century, particularly in Eastern Europe, and has produced a controversy that can help the understanding of folk-music elsewhere.

XXIV   Some of the same concerns can be found in Britain too, and the tensions in popular music in this period between country and town, between farm work and factory work, between oral tradition, music-hall and printing press, are not yet resolved today. A number of extracts from the work of folk-song collectors and scholars, mostly looking back on the period of this anthology, consider these questions.

XXV   Finally, as a 'Retrospect', there are a few short extracts from later writers who continued to write about some of the main themes explored in the anthology, into our own century. Biographical notes about them and about all the main authors in the book are given at the back, and I think there is no need to introduce them further. I leave you to the author of *A Tour Through The Whole Island of Great Britain*, Daniel Defoe.

# I Prelude

DANIEL DEFOE                                                    I.1

## The weaving country round Halifax

from *A Tour through the Whole Island of Great Britain* 1724–6

From Blackstone Edge to Hallifax is eight miles, and all the way, except from Sorby to Hallifax, is thus up hill and down; so that, I suppose, we mounted to the clouds and descended to the water level about eight times, in that little part of the journey.

But now I must observe to you, that after having pass'd the second hill, and come down into the valley again, and so still the nearer we came to Hallifax, we found the houses thicker, and the villages greater in every bottom; and not only so, but the sides of the hills, which were very steep every way, were spread with houses, and that very thick; for the land being divided into small enclosures, that is to say, from two acres to six or seven acres each, seldom more; every three or four pieces of land had a house belonging to it.

Then it was I began to perceive the reason and nature of the thing, and found that this division of the land into small pieces, and scattering of the dwellings, was occasioned by, and done for the convenience of the business which the people were generally employ'd in, and that, as I said before, though we saw no people stirring without doors, yet they were all full within; for, in short, this whole country, however mountainous, and that no sooner we were down one hill but we mounted another, is yet infinitely full of people; those people all full of business; not a beggar, not an idle person to be seen, except here and there an alms-house, where people antient, decrepid, and past labour, might perhaps be found; for it is observable, that the people here, however laborious, generally live to a great age, a certain testimony to the goodness and wholesomeness of the country, which is, without doubt, as healthy as any part of England; nor is the health of the people lessen'd, but help'd and establish'd by their being constantly employ'd, and, as we call it, their working hard; so that they find a double advantage by their being always in business.

This business is the clothing trade, for the convenience of which the houses are thus scattered and spread upon the sides of the hills, as above, even from the bottom to the top; the reason is this; such has been the bounty of nature to this otherwise frightful country, that two things essential to the business, as well as to the ease of the people are found here, and that in a situation which I never saw the like of in any part of England; and, I believe, the like is not to be seen so contrived in any part of the world; I mean coals and running water upon the tops of the highest hills: This seems to have been directed by the wise hand of Providence for the very purpose which is now served by it, namely, the manufactures, which otherwise could not be carried on; neither indeed could one fifth part of the inhabitants be supported without them, for the land could not maintain them. After we had mounted the third hill, we found the country, in short, one continued village, tho' mountainous every way, as before; hardly a house standing out of a speaking distance from another, and (which soon told us their business) the day clearing up, and the sun shining, we could see that almost at every house there was a tenter, and almost on every tenter a piece of cloth, or kersie, or shalloon, for they are the three articles of that country's labour; from which the sun glancing, and, as I may say, shining (the white reflecting its rays) to us, I thought it was the most agreeable sight that I ever saw, for the hills, as I say, rising and falling so thick, and the vallies opening sometimes one way, sometimes another, so that sometimes we could see two or three miles this way, sometimes as far another; sometimes like the streets near St. Giles's, called the Seven Dials; we could see through the glades almost every way round us, yet look which way we would, high to the tops, and low to the bottoms, it was all the same; innumerable houses and tenters, and a white piece upon every tenter.

But to return to the reason of dispersing the houses, as above; I found, as our road pass'd among them, for indeed no road could do otherwise, wherever we pass'd any house we found a little rill or gutter of running water, if the house was above the road, it came from it, and cross'd the way to run to another; if the house was below us, it cross'd us from some other distant house above it, and at every considerable house was a manufactury or work-house, and as they could not do their business without water, the little streams were so parted and guided by gutters or pipes, and by turning and dividing the streams, that none of those houses were without a river, if I may call it so, running into and through their work-houses.

Again, as the dying-houses, scouring-shops and places where they used this water, emitted the water again, ting'd with the drugs of the dying fat, and with the oil, the soap, the tallow, and other ingredients used by the clothiers in dressing and scouring, &c. which then runs away thro' the lands to the next, the grounds are not only universally watered, how dry soever the season, but that water so ting'd and so fatten'd enriches the lands they run through, that 'tis hardly to be imagined how fertile and rich the soil is made by it.

2

Then, as every clothier must keep a horse, perhaps two, to fetch and carry for the use of his manufacture, (viz.) to fetch home his wooll and his provisions from the market, to carry his yarn to the spinners, his manufacture to the fulling mill, and, when finished, to the market to be sold, and the like; so every manufacturer generally keeps a cow or two, or more, for his family, and this employs the two, or three, or four pieces of enclosed land about his house, for they scarce sow corn enough for their cocks and hens; and this feeding their grounds still adds by the dung of the cattle, to enrich the soil.

But now, to speak of the bounty of nature again, which I but just mentioned; it is to be observed, that these hills are so furnished by nature with springs and mines, that not only on the sides, but even to the very tops, there is scarce a hill but you find, on the highest part of it, a spring of water, and a coal-pit. I doubt not but there are both springs and coal-pits lower in the hills, 'tis enough to say they are at the top; but, as I say, the hills are so full of springs, so the lower coal-pits may perhaps be too full of water, to work without dreins to carry it off, and the coals in the upper pits being easie to come at, they may chuse to work them, because the horses which fetch the coals, go light up the hill, and come loaden down.

Having thus fire and water at every dwelling, there is no need to enquire why they dwell thus dispers'd upon the highest hills, the convenience of the manufactures requiring it. Among the manufacturers houses are likewise scattered an infinite number of cottages or small dwellings, in which dwell the workmen which are employed, the women and children of whom, are always busy carding, spinning, &c. so that no hands being unemploy'd, all can gain their bread, even from the youngest to the antient; hardly any thing above four years old, but its hands are sufficient to it self.

This is the reason also why we saw so few people without doors; but if we knock'd at the door of any of the master manufacturers, we presently saw a house full of lusty fellows, some at the dye-fat, some dressing the cloths, some in the loom, some one thing, some another, all hard at work, and full employed upon the manufacture, and all seeming to have sufficient business.

# SAMUEL JOHNSON                                                    I.2
## "The plenty and ease of a great city"
from *The Adventurer*, 1753

> *Inventas—vitam excoluere per artes.*
> Virgil, Aeneid, vi, 663
> They polish life by useful arts.

That familiarity produces neglect, has been long observed. The effect of all external objects, however great or splendid, ceases with their novelty: the courtier stands without emotion in the royal presence; the rustic tramples under his foot the beauties of the spring, with little attention to their colour or their fragrance; and the inhabitant of the coast darts his eye upon the immense diffusion of waters, without awe, wonder or terror.

Those who have passed much of their lives in this great city, look upon its opulence and its multitudes, its extent and variety, with cold indifference; but an inhabitant of the remoter parts of the kingdom is immediately distinguished by a kind of dissipated curiosity, a busy endeavour to divide his attention amongst a thousand objects, and a wild confusion of astonishment and alarm.

The attention of a new-comer is generally first struck by the multiplicity of cries that stun him in the streets, and the variety of merchandise and manufactures which the shopkeepers expose on every hand; and he is apt, by unwary bursts of admiration, to excite the merriment and contempt of those, who mistake the use of their eyes for effects of their understanding, and confound accidental knowledge with just reasoning.

But, surely, these are subjects on which any man may without reproach employ his meditations: the innumerable occupations, among which the thousands that swarm in the streets of London are distributed, may furnish employment to minds of every cast, and capacities of every degree. He that contemplates the extent of this wonderful city, finds it difficult to conceive, by what method plenty is maintained in our markets, and how the inhabitants are regularly supplied with the necessaries of life; but when he examines the shops and warehouses, sees the immense stores of every kind of merchandise piled up for sale, and runs over all the manufactures of art and products of nature, which are everywhere attracting his eye and soliciting his purse, he will be inclined to conclude, that such quantities cannot easily be exhausted, and that part of mankind must soon stand still for want of employment, till the wares already provided shall be worn out and destroyed.

As Socrates was passing through the fair at Athens, and casting his eyes over the shops and customers, 'how many things are here', says he, 'that I do not want!' The same sentiment is every moment rising in the mind of him that walks the streets of London, however inferior in philosophy to Socrates: he beholds a thousand shops crowded with goods, of which he can scarcely tell the use, and which, therefore, he is apt to consider as of no value: and, indeed, many of the arts by which families are supported, and wealth is heaped together, are of that minute and superfluous kind, which nothing but experience could evince possible to be prosecuted with advantage, and which, as the world might easily want, it could scarcely be expected to encourage.

But so it is, that custom, curiosity, or wantonness, supplies every art with patrons, and finds purchasers for every manufacture; the world is so adjusted, that not only bread, but riches may be obtained without great abilities, or arduous performances: the most unskilful hand and unenlightened mind have sufficient incitements to industry; for he that is resolutely busy, can scarcely be in want. There is, indeed, no employment, however despicable, from which a man may not promise himself more than competence, when he sees thousands and myriads raised to dignity, by no other merit than that of contributing to supply their neighbours with the means of sucking smoke through a tube of clay; and others raising contributions upon those, whose elegance disdains the grossness of smoky luxury, by grinding the same materials into a powder, that may at once gratify and impair the smell.

Not only by these popular and modish trifles, but by a thousand unheeded and evanescent kinds of business, are the multitudes of this city preserved from idleness, and consequently from want. In the endless variety of tastes and circumstances that diversify mankind, nothing is so superfluous, but that some one desires it; or so common, but that some one is compelled to buy it. As nothing is useless but because it is in improper hands, what is thrown away by one is gathered up by another; and the refuse of part of mankind furnishes a subordinate class with the materials necessary to their support.

When I look round upon those who are thus variously exerting their qualifications, I cannot but admire the secret concatenation of society, that links together the great and the mean, the illustrious and the obscure; and consider with benevolent satisfaction, that no man, unless his body or mind be totally disabled, has need to suffer the mortification of seeing himself useless or burdensome to the community: he that will diligently labour, in whatever occupation, will deserve the sustenance which he obtains, and the protection which he enjoys; and may lie down every night with the pleasing consciousness, of having contributed something to the happiness of life.

Contempt and admiration are equally incident to narrow minds: he whose comprehension can take in the whole subordination of mankind, and whose perspicacity can pierce to the real state of things through the thin veils of fortune or of fashion, will discover meanness in the highest stations, and dignity in the meanest; and find that no man can become venerable but by virtue, or contemptible but by wickedness.

In the midst of this universal hurry, no man ought to be so little influenced by example, or so void of honest emulation, as to stand a lazy spectator of incessant labour; or please himself with the mean happiness of a drone, while the active swarms are buzzing about him: no man is without some quality, by the due application of which he

5

might deserve well of the world; and whoever he be that has but little in his power, should be in haste to do that little, lest he be confounded with him that can do nothing.

By this general concurrence of endeavours, arts of every kind have been so long cultivated, that all the wants of man may be immediately supplied; idleness can scarcely form a wish which she may not gratify by the toil of others, or curiosity dream of a toy which the shops are not ready to afford her.

Happiness is enjoyed only in proportion as it is known; and such is the state or folly of man, that it is known only by experience of its contrary: we who have long lived amidst the conveniences of a town immensely populous, have scarce an idea of a place where desire cannot be gratified by money. In order to have a just sense of this artificial plenty, it is necessary to have passed some time in a distant colony, or those parts of our island which are thinly inhabited: he that has once known how many trades every man in such situations is compelled to exercise, with how much labour the products of nature must be accommodated to human use, how long the loss or defect of any common utensil must be endured, or by what awkward expedients it must be supplied, how far men may wander with money in their hands before any can sell them what they wish to buy, will know how to rate at its proper value the plenty and ease of a great city.

But that the happiness of man may still remain imperfect, as wants in this place are easily supplied, new wants likewise are easily created: every man, in surveying the shops of London, sees numberless instruments and conveniences, of which, while he did not know them, he never felt the need; and yet, when use has made them familiar, wonders how life could be supported without them. Thus it comes to pass, that our desires always increase with our possessions; the knowledge that something remains yet unenjoyed, impairs our enjoyment of the good before us.

They who have been accustomed to the refinements of science, and multiplications of contrivance, soon lose their confidence in the unassisted powers of nature, forget the paucity of our real necessities, and overlook the easy methods by which they may be supplied. It were a speculation worthy of a philosophical mind, to examine how much is taken away from our native abilities, as well as added to them by artificial expedients. We are so accustomed to give and receive assistance, that each of us singly can do little for himself; and there is scarce any one amongst us, however contracted may be his form of life, who does not enjoy the labour of a thousand artists.

But a survey of the various nations that inhabit the earth will inform us, that life may be supported with less assistance, and that the dexterity, which practice enforced by necessity produces, is able to effect much by very scanty means. The nations of Mexico and Peru erected cities and temples without the use of iron, and at this day the rude Indian supplies himself with all the necessaries of life: sent like the rest of mankind naked into the world, as soon as his parents have nursed him up to strength, he is to provide by his own labour for his own support. His first care is to find a sharp flint among the rocks; with this he undertakes to fell the trees of the forest; he shapes his bow, heads his arrows, builds his cottage, and hollows his canoe, and from that time lives in a state of plenty and prosperity; he is sheltered from the storms, he is fortified against beasts of prey, he is enabled to pursue the fish of the sea, and the deer of the mountains; and as he does not know, does not envy the happiness of polished nations, where gold can supply the want of fortitude and skill, and he whose laborious ancestors have made him rich, may lie stretched upon a couch, and see all the treasures of all the elements poured down before him.

This picture of a savage life, if it shows how much individuals may perform, shows likewise how much society is to be desired. Though the perseverance and address of the Indian excite our admiration, they nevertheless cannot procure him the conveniences which are enjoyed by the vagrant beggar of a civilized country: he hunts like a wild beast to satisfy his hunger; and when he lies down to rest after a successful chase, cannot pronounce himself secure against the danger of perishing in a few days; he is, perhaps, content with his condition, because he knows not that a better is attainable by man; as he that is born blind does not long for the perception of light, because he cannot conceive the advantages which light would afford him: but hunger, wounds and weariness are real evils, though he believes them equally incident to all his fellow creatures; and when a tempest compels him to lie starving in his hut, he cannot justly be concluded equally happy with those whom art has exempted from the power of chance, and who make the foregoing year provide for the following.

To receive and to communicate assistance, constitutes the happiness of human life: man may indeed preserve his existence in solitude, but can enjoy it only in society: the greatest understanding of an individual doomed to procure food and clothing for himself, will barely supply him with expedients to keep off death from day to day; but as one of a large community performing only his share of the common business, he gains leisure for intellectual pleasures, and enjoys the happiness of reason and reflection.

# JEAN-JACQUES ROUSSEAU I.3
## Civilization as a 'fall' from nature

from *Discourse on the Origins of Inequality among Men*, 1754

Man has hardly any troubles except those he has given himself. . . . It is only with great effort that we have managed to make ourselves unhappy. When on the one hand one considers the immense works of man, so many sciences brought to perfection, so many arts invented, so many forces turned to use, abysses filled in, mountains raised, rocks broken, rivers made navigable, lands cleared, lakes dug out, marshes drained, enormous buildings reared on the earth, the sea covered with ships and sailors; and when on the other hand one looks with a little reflection for the real advantages resulting from all this for the happiness of the human race, one can only be struck by the astonishing disproportion between the two, and lament the blindness of man, who, to feed his pride and I know not what vain self-admiration, chases so eagerly after all the miseries he is prey to, which beneficent nature had taken care to keep from him.

Men are wicked; sad and continual experience supplies the place of proof; yet man is naturally good—I hope I have proved it. So what can have depraved him to this point, if not the alterations that have occurred in his constitution, the progress he has made, and the knowledge he has acquired? However much one admires human society, it will not be any the less true that it necessarily makes men hate each other in proportion as their interests cross, and makes them render each other apparent services while in fact doing each other all the harm imaginable. What is one to think of a relationship where the reason of each individual dictates private maxims directly contrary to those that public reason preaches to the body of society, and in which each one finds his profit in the unhappiness of others? Perhaps there is not one man living at ease whose heirs, often his own children, are not secretly wishing for his death, not one ship at sea whose shipwreck would not be good news to some merchant; not one house which a debtor would not like to see burn with all the papers it contains; not one people which does not rejoice in the disasters of its neighbours.

It is thus that we find our advantage in the misfortunes of our fellow-men and that one man's loss almost always makes another man's prosperity. But what is more dangerous still, public calamities become the expectation and the hope of a multitude of individuals. Some wish for epidemics, others for deaths, some for war, others for famine; I have seen abominable men weeping with grief at the appearance of a good harvest, and the huge and fatal fire of London which cost the life or the property of so many miserable people, made perhaps the fortune of more than ten thousand individuals.

'Primitive' man, when he has dined, is at peace with all peoples and the friend of all his fellows. If it is a question sometimes of fighting for his meal, he never comes to blows without having first compared the difficulty of winning with that of finding food elsewhere; and as pride is not involved in the fight, it ends with a few blows; the winner eats, the loser goes to take his chance elsewhere, and all is at peace again. But with man in society, it is quite different; first it is a question of acquiring what is necessary, then what is superfluous; then come luxuries, then immense riches; then subjects, and then slaves; he has not a moment's respite. Stranger still, the less his needs are natural and pressing, the more his passions grow, and, what is worse, the power of satisfying them grows too; so that after long prosperity, after having heaped up many treasures and pillaged many men, my hero ends by cutting every throat until he can be the sole master of the Universe. That is—in outline—the moral picture, if not of human life, at least of the secret pretensions in the heart of every civilized man.

# II Country Work: Contrasting Pictures

ANON

'The Merry Haymakers'

Ballad, 1695, and oral tradition

'Twas in the pleasant month of May
In the springtime of the year,
And down by yonder meadow
There runs a river clear.
See how the little fishes,
How they do sport and play,
Causing many a lad and many a lass
To go there a-making hay.

Then in comes that scytheman
That meadow to mow down,
With his old leathered bottle
And the ale that runs so brown.
There's many a stout and a labouring man
Goes there his skill to try,
He works, he mows, he sweats, he blows
And the grass cuts very dry.

Then in comes both Tom and Dick
With their pitchforks and their rakes,
And likewise Black-eyed Susan,
The hay all for to make.
There's a sweet, sweet, sweet and a jug, jug, jug,
How the harmless birds do sing
From the morning till the evening
As we were haymaking.

It was just at one evening
As the sun was a-going down,
We saw the jolly piper come
A-strolling through the town;
There he pulled out his tapering pipes

11

And he made the valleys ring.
So we all put down our rakes and forks
And we left the haymaking.

We called for a dance
And we tripped it along,
We danced all round the hay-cocks
Till the rising of the sun,
When the sun did shine such a glorious light
And the harmless birds did sing,
Each lad he took his lass in hand
And went back to his haymaking.

## ALEXANDER POPE                                                    II.2
### Winter

from *Windsor Forest*, 1704–13

To plains with well-breath'd beagles we repair,
And trace the mazes of the circling hare:
(Beasts, urged by us, their fellow beast pursue,
And learn of man each other to undo)
With slaughtering guns the unwearied fowler roves,
When frosts have whiten'd all the naked groves;
Where doves in flocks the leafless trees o'ershade,
And lonely woodcocks haunt the watery glade.
He lifts the tube, and levels with his eye;
Straight a short thunder breaks the frozen sky:
Oft, as in airy rings they skim the heath,
The clamorous lapwings feel the leaden death:
Oft, as the mounting larks their notes prepare,
They fall, and leave their little lives in air.

## ALEXANDER POPE                                                    II.3
### Shepherds' Lament

from 'Winter: The Fourth Pastoral', 1709

THYRSIS
    No more the mounting larks, while Daphne sings,
Shall, listening in mid-air, suspend their wings;
No more the birds shall imitate her lays,

Or, hush'd with wonder, hearken from the sprays:
No more the streams their murmurs shall forbear,
A sweeter music than their own to hear;
But tell the reeds, and tell the vocal shore,
Fair Daphne's dead, and music is no more!

. . .

LYCIDAS
   How all things listen, while thy Muse complains!
Such silence waits on Philomela's strains,
In some still evening, when the whispering breeze
Pants on the leaves, and dies upon the trees.
To thee, bright goddess, oft a lamb shall bleed,
If teeming ewes increase my fleecy breed.
While plants their shade, or flowers their odours give,
Thy name, thy honour, and thy praise shall live!

THYRSIS
   But see, Orion sheds unwholesome dews;
Arise, the pines a noxious shade diffuse;
Sharp Boreas blows, and Nature feels decay,
Time conquers all, and we must time obey.
Adieu, ye vales, ye mountains, streams, and groves;
Adieu, ye shepherds' rural lays and loves;
Adieu, my flocks; farewell, ye sylvan crew;
Daphne, farewell; and all the world adieu!

# STEPHEN DUCK                                          II.4

## "Week after Week"

from *The Thresher's Labour*, 1730

   The Eye beholds no pleasant Object here:
No chearful Sound diverts the list'ning Ear.
The Shepherd well may tune his Voice to sing,
Inspir'd by all the Beauties of the Spring:
No Fountains murmur here, no Lambkins play,
No Linets warble, and no Fields look gay;
'Tis all a dull and melancholy Scene,
Fit only to provoke the Muses Spleen.
When sooty Pease we thresh, you scarce can know
Our native Colour, as from Work we go;

The Sweat, and Dust, and suffocating Smoke,
Make us so much like *Ethiopians* look:
We scare our Wives, when Evening brings us home;
And frighted Infants think the Bug-bear come.
Week after Week we this dull Task pursue,
Unless when winnowing Days produce a new;
A new indeed, but frequently a worse,
The Threshall yields but to the Master's Curse:
He counts the Bushels, counts how much a Day,
Then swears we've idled half our Time away.
Why look ye, Rogues! D'ye think that this will do?
Your Neighbours thresh as much again as you.
Now in our Hands we wish our noisy Tools,
To drown the hated Names of Rogues and Fools;
But wanting those, we just like School-boys look,
When th'angry Master views the blotted Book:
They cry their Ink was faulty, and their Pen;
We, The Corn threshes bad, 'twas cut too green. . . .
But now the Winter hides his hoary Head,
And Nature's Face is with new Beauty spread;
The Spring appears, and kind Refreshing Showers
New clothe the Field with Grass, and deck with Flowers;
Next her, the ripening Summer presses on,
And *Sol* begins his longest Stage to run:
Before the Door our welcome Master stands,
And tells us the ripe Grass requires our Hands.
The long much-wish'd Intelligence imparts
Life to our Looks, and Spirit to our Hearts:
We wish the happy Season may be fair,
And joyful, long to breathe in opener Air.

When Morn does thro' the Eastern Windows peep,
Strait from our Beds we start, and shake off Sleep;
This new Employ with eager haste to prove,
This new Employ becomes so much our Love:
Alas! that human Joys shou'd change so soon,
Even this may bear another Face at Noon!
The Birds salute us as to Work we go,
And a new Life seems in our Breasts to glow. . . .

And now the Field design'd our Strength to try
Appears, and meets at last our longing Eye;
The Grass and Ground each chearfully surveys,
Willing to see which way th' Advantage lays.

As the best Man, each claims the foremost Place,
And our first Work seems but a sportive Race.
With rapid Force our well-whet Blades we drive,
Strain every Nerve, and Blow for Blow we give:
Tho' but this Eminence the Foremost gains,
Only t'excel the rest in Toil and Pains.
But when the scorching Sun is mounted high,
And no kind Barns with friendly Shades are nigh,
Our weary Scythes entangle in the Grass,
And Streams of Sweat run trickling down a-pace;
Our sportive Labour we too late lament,
And wish that Strength again, we vainly spent. . . .
With Heat and Labour tir'd, our Scythes we quit,
Search out a shady Tree, and down we sit;
From Scrip and Bottle hope new Strength to gain;
But Scrip and Bottle too are try'd in vain.
Down our parch'd Throats we scarce the Bread can get,
And quite o'er-spent with Toil, but faintly eat;
Nor can the Bottle only answer all,
Alas! the Bottle and the Beer's too small.
Our Time slides on, we move from off the Grass,
And each again betakes him to his Place.
Not eager now, as late, our Strength to prove,
But all contented regular to move:
Often we whet, as often view the Sun,
To see how near his tedious Race is run;
At length he vails his radiant Face from sight,
And bids the weary Traveller good-night:
Homewards we move, but so much spent with Toil,
We walk but slow, and rest at every Stile.
Our good expecting Wives, who think we stay,
Got to the Door, soon eye us in the way;
Then from the Pot the Dumpling's catch'd in haste,
And homely by its side the Bacon's plac'd.
Supper and Sleep by Morn new Strength supply,
And out we set again our Works to try:
But not so early quite, nor quite so fast,
As to our Cost we did the Morning past.

# GEORGE CRABBE

## "The poor laborious natives of the place"

from *The Village*, 1783

> Fled are those times, when, in harmonious strains,
> The rustic poet praised his native plains:
> No shepherds now, in smooth alternate verse,
> Their country's beauty or their nymphs' rehearse;
> Yet still for these we frame the tender strain,
> Still in our lays fond Corydons complain,
> And shepherds' boys their amorous pains reveal,
> The only pains, alas! they never feel. . . .
>
> I grant indeed that fields and flocks have charms
> For him that grazes or for him that farms;
> But when amid such pleasing scenes I trace
> The poor laborious natives of the place,
> And see the mid-day sun, with fervid ray,
> On their bare heads and dewy temples play;
> While some, with feebler heads and fainter hearts,
> Deplore their fortune, yet sustain their parts—
> Then shall I dare these real ills to hide
> In tinsel trappings of poetic pride?
> No; cast by Fortune on a frowning coast
> Which neither groves nor happy valleys boast;
> Where other cares than those the Muse relates,
> And other shepherds dwell with other mates;
> By such examples taught, I paint the Cot,
> As Truth will paint it, and as Bards will not: . . .
>
> Go then! and see them rising with the sun,
> Through a long course of daily toil to run;
> See them beneath the dog-star's raging heat,
> When the knees tremble and the temples beat; . . .
>
> Behold them, leaning on their scythes, look o'er
> The labour past, and toils to come explore;
> See them alternate suns and showers engage,
> And hoard up aches and anguish for their age;
> Through fens and marshy moors their steps pursue,
> When their warm pores imbibe the evening dew;
> Then own that labour may as fatal be
> To these thy slaves, as thine excess to thee.

Amid this tribe too oft a manly pride
Strives in strong toil the fainting heart to hide,
There may you see the youth of slender frame
Contend with weakness, weariness, and shame;
Yet, urged along, and proudly loth to yield,
He strives to join his fellows of the field:
Till long-contending nature droops at last,
Declining health rejects his poor repast,
His cheerless spouse the coming danger sees,
And mutual murmurs urge the slow disease.
    Yet grant them health, 'tis not for us to tell,
Though the head droops not, that the heart is well;
Or will you praise that homely, healthy fare,
Plenteous and plain, that happy peasants share!
Oh! trifle not with wants you cannot feel,
Nor mock the misery of a stinted meal;
Homely, not wholesome, plain, not plenteous, such
As you who praise would never deign to touch.
    Ye gentle souls, who dream of rural ease,
Whom the smooth stream and smoother sonnet please;
Go! if the peaceful cot your praises share,
Go look within, and ask if peace be there;
If peace be his—that drooping weary sire,
Or theirs, that offspring round their feeble fire;
Or hers, that matron pale, whose trembling hand
Turns on the wretched hearth th' expiring brand!
    Nor yet can Time itself obtain for these
Life's latest comforts, due respect and ease;
For yonder see that hoary swain, whose age
Can with no cares except its own engage;
Who, propt on that rude staff, looks up to see
The bare arms broken from the withering tree,
On which, a boy, he climb'd the loftiest bough,
Then his first joy, but his sad emblem now.
    He once was chief in all the rustic trade;
His steady hand the straightest furrow made;
Full many a prize he won, and still is proud
To find the triumphs of his youth allow'd; . . .

A transient pleasure sparkles in his eyes,
He hears and smiles, then thinks again and sighs:
For now he journeys to his grave in pain;
The rich disdain him; nay, the poor disdain;
Alternate masters now their slave command,

17

Urge the weak efforts of his feeble hand,
And, when his age attempts its task in vain,
With ruthless taunts, of lazy poor complain.
    Oft may you see him, when he tends the sheep,
His winter charge, beneath the hillock weep;
Oft hear him murmur to the winds that blow
O'er his white locks and bury them in snow,
When, roused by rage and muttering in the morn,
He mends the broken edge with icy thorn: . . .

# MRS BURROWS                                           II.6

## Work in the Fields

from 'A Childhood in the Fens, about 1850–60',
published 1931

On the day that I was eight years of age, I left school and began to
work fourteen hours a day in the fields, with forty to fifty children of
whom, even at that early age, I was the eldest. We were followed all day
long by an old man carrying a long whip in his hand which he did not
forget to use. A great many of the children were only five years of age.
You will think that I am exaggerating, but I am *not*; it is as true as the
Gospel. Thirty-five years ago is the time I speak of, and the place, Croyland in Lincolnshire, nine miles from Peterborough. I could even now
name several of the children who began at the age of five to work in the
gangs, and also the name of the ganger. We always left the town, summer and winter, the moment the old Abbey clock struck six. . . .

We had to walk a very long way to our work, never much less than
two miles each way, and very often five miles each way. The large farms
all lay a good distance from the town, and it was on those farms that
we worked. In the winter, by the time we reached our work, it was
light enough to begin, and of course we worked until it was dark and
then we had our long walk home. I never remembered to have reached
home sooner than six and more often seven, even in winter. In the summer, we did not leave the fields in the evening until the clock had
struck six, then of course we must walk home, and this walk was no
easy task for us children who had worked hard all day on the ploughed
fields. . . .

[I remember once] it was a most terrible day. The cold east wind (I
suppose it was an east wind, for surely no wind ever blew colder), the
sleet and snow which came every now and then in showers seemed almost to cut us to pieces. We were working upon a large farm that lay
half-way between Croyland and Peterborough. Had the snow and sleet

come continuously we should have been allowed to come home, but because it only came at intervals, of course we had to stay. I have been out in all sorts of weather but never remember a colder day. Well, the morning passed along somehow. The ganger did his best for us by letting us have a run in our turns, but that did not help us very much because we were all too numb with the cold to be able to run much. Dinner-time came, and we were preparing to sit down under a hedge and eat our cold dinner and drink our cold tea, when we saw the shepherd's wife coming towards us, and she said to our ganger, 'Bring these children into my house and let them eat their dinner there.' We went into that very small two-roomed cottage, and when we got into the largest room there was not standing room for us all, but this woman's heart was large, even if her house was small, and so she put her few chairs and table out into the garden, and then we all sat down in a ring upon the floor. She then placed in our midst a very large saucepan of hot boiled potatoes, and bade us help ourselves. Truly, although I have attended scores of grand parties and banquets since that time, not one of them has seemed half as good to me as that meal did.

# GEORGE EDWARDS                                    II.7

## "A wage-earner in the 1850s–60s"

from *From Crow-Scaring to Westminster*,
published 1922

It was in the year 1855 when I had my first experience of real distress. On my father's return home from work one night he was stopped by a policeman who searched his bag and took from it five turnips, which he was taking home to make his children an evening meal. There was no bread in the house. His wife and children were waiting for him to come home, but he was not allowed to do so.

He was arrested, taken before the magistrates next day, and committed to prison for fourteen days' hard labour for the crime of attempting to feed his children! The experience of that night I shall never forget.

The next morning we were taken into the workhouse, where we were kept all the winter. Although only five years old, I was not allowed to be with my mother.

On my father's release from prison he, of course, had also to come into the workhouse. Being branded as a thief, no farmer would employ him. But was he a thief? I say no, and a thousand times no! A nation that would not allow my father sufficient income to feed his children was responsible for any breach of the law he might have committed.

In the spring my father took us all out of the workhouse and we went back to our home. My father obtained work at brickmaking in the little village of Alby, about seven miles from Marsham. He was away from home all the week, and the pay for his work was 4s. per thousand bricks made, and he had to turn the clay with which the bricks were made three times. He was, however, by the assistance of one of my brothers, able to bring home to my mother about 13s. per week, which appeared almost a godsend. In the villages during the war hand-loom weaving was brought to a standstill, and thus my mother was unable to add to the family income by her own industry.

On coming out of the workhouse in March 1856 I secured my first job. It consisted of scaring crows from the fields of a farmer close to the house. I was then six years of age, and I was paid 1s. for a seven-day week. My first pay-day made me feel as proud as a duke. On receiving my wage I hastened home, made straight for my mother and gave her the whole shilling. To her I said:

'Mother, this is my money. Now we shall not want bread any more, and you will not have to cry again. You shall always have my money. I will always look after you.'

In my childish innocence I thought my shilling would be all she needed. It was not long, however, before I discovered my mistake, but my wage proved a little help to her. I am glad to recall in these days that I did keep my promise to her always to look after her, and my wife had the unspeakable pleasure of taking her to our home, and we looked after her for six years out of my 15s. a week, without receiving a penny from anyone, the Board of Guardians refusing to allow her anything in the nature of poor relief. My wife's mother also lived with us for sixteen years, and died at our house, and for twenty-two years of my married life I maintained these two old people.

My troubles began in the second week of my employment. Having to work long hours, I had to be up very early in the morning, soon after sunrise, and remain in the fields until after sunset. One day, being completely worn out, I unfortunately fell asleep. Equally unfortunately for me the crows were hungry, and they came on to the field and began to pick the corn. Soon after the farmer arrived on the scene and caught me asleep, and for this crime at six years of age he gave me a severe thrashing, and deducted 2d. from my wage at the end of the week. Thus I had only 10d. to take home to my mother that week. But my mother was too good to scold.

Having finished crow-scaring for that season, I was set looking after the cows, to see that they did not get out of the field, and take them home in the evening to be milked. This I continued to do all the summer.

In 1856, I entered upon my first harvest. During the wheat-cutting I made bonds for the binders. There were no reaping machines in those days, the corn all having to be cut by the scythe. Women were engaged to tie up the corn, and the little boys made bonds with which to tie the corn. For this work I received 3d. per day, or at the rate of 1s. 6d. per week.

When the wheat was carted I led the horse and shouted to the loaders to hold tight when the horse moved. When this work was finished and there was nothing further for me to do, I went gleaning with my mother. In those days it was the custom for the poor to glean the wheat-fields after they had been cleared. This was a help to the poor, for it often provided them with a little bread during the winter months, when they would not have had half enough to eat had it not been that they were allowed to glean. The men used to thresh the corn with a flail, dress it and clean it, and send it to the mill to be ground into meal. The rules for gleaning were very amusing. No one was allowed in the field while there was a sheaf of corn there, and at a given hour the farmer would open the gate and remove the sheaf, and shout 'All on.' If anyone went into the field before this was done the rest would 'shake' the corn she had gleaned.

This was a happy time for the women and children. At the conclusion of the harvest they would have what was called a gleaners' frolic. In the year to which I am referring, after harvest, I went keeping cows until the autumn, working for a farmer named Thomas Whighten. At the next wheat-sowing I was again put to scaring crows, and when this was finished I was set to work cleaning turnips, and what cold hands I had when the snow was on the ground! And what suffering from back-ache! Those who know anything about this class of work may judge how hard it was for a child of six and a half years. My mother did all she could to help me. She would get up in the morning and make a little fire over which to boil some water. With this she would soak a little bread and a small piece of butter. This would constitute my break-fast. For dinner I had, day after day for weeks, nothing but two slices of bread, a small piece of cheese, and an apple or an onion.

In the spring I left this employer and went with my father to work in the brickfield for a Mr. John Howlett, the leading farmer, who had about two years before put my father into prison for taking home tur-nips, but after a time had set him on again. This farmer used to have bricks made in the summer, and my father was set to make them, he having learned this trade when young. In fact, my family for genera-tions were brickmakers as well as agricultural labourers. Being then barely seven years of age, my daily task was made easier by my father, and I had not to go to work until after breakfast. My father, however, had to be up very early, as brickmaking in those days was very hard work. I was just man enough to wheel away eight bricks at a time. The summer being ended, I helped my father to feed bullocks. In the spring of 1858 I again went into the brickfield, and during the following

21

winter was set cleaning turnips by Mr. Howlett. By this time my wages were raised to 2s. per week. Well can I remember the many sore backs I had given me by the old steward, who never missed an opportunity to thrash me if I did not clean enough turnips. I might say I do not think I ever forgave this old tyrant for his cruelty to me. The treatment I received was no exception to the rule, all poor boys in those days were treated badly. One farmer I knew used to hang the poor boys up by the heels and thrash them on the slightest provocation, and the parents dare not say anything. Had my father complained of the treatment to his son he would have been discharged.

In the spring of 1859 I was set to work as a horseman. This was a new experience to me, but afterwards I was to become an efficient workman, having a liking for horses from the very first. My first job as a horseman was to lead the fore-horse in the drill, and many times the first day the horse trod on my feet. My next job was rolling, and I then thought I was a man, having for the first time a pair of reins in my hands. This change of work brought me another 6d. a week increase in my wages. By the next spring (1860) I was so far improved that I was set to plough, and on April 7th of that year something happened which caused me to change my employment. The old steward, to whom I have previously referred, rode up by the side of the horses and struck me on the knuckles because I was not ploughing straight enough. I at once swore at him and told him I would pay him out for that treatment when I became a man. He forthwith got down from his horse, took me on his knee, and thrashed me until I was black. I, however, got a little of my own back. I kicked him in the face until he was black, and then ran home and told my mother what had happened. She at once went after the steward, pulled his whiskers and slapped his face. For this she was summoned, and was fined 5s. and costs or fourteen days' hard labour. The fine was paid by a friend.

I soon found another job with a Mr. Charles Jones and rapidly improved in my work. I was kept using horses, taking a delight in my work, and soon became, although very young, quite an expert in ploughing. The head team-man was a nice fellow, and took a great interest in me, and taught me all he knew about horses. I worked for this man about four years, and then left because he would not pay me more than 2s. 9d. a week! I next went to work for three old bachelors by the names of Needham, William and James Watts, who lived together near to my home. I helped one of them to look after their team of five horses. They also took great interest in me, and here I was taught all kinds of skilled work on the farm, including drilling, stacking and thatching. I worked for them about three years, and by the time I left my wages had risen to about 6s. per week, mother taking 4s. for my board and allowing me 2s. with which to buy clothes and for pocket-money.

I might say by this time the condition of the family had very much improved. My elder brothers had grown up and left home. My mother by her hand-loom weaving had managed to clear off the debts which had been contracted while the children were small. It showed the honesty of these poor people.

## ANON                                                                    II.8

## Proclaiming the Queen of the Gleaners at Rempstone, Nottinghamshire

from letter in *The Nottinghamshire Guardian*, 1860.

The village crier having 'proclaimed the Queen', nearly 100 gleaners assembled at the end of the village. Women with their infant charges, boys with green boughs, and girls with flowers, the whole wearing gleaning-pockets; children's carriages and wheelbarrows, dressed in green and laden with babies, etc. were in requisition . . . [A] royal salute was shouted by the boys, and the crown brought out of its temporary depository. This part of the regalia was of simple make; its basis consisting of straw-coloured cloth surrounded with wheat, barley and oats of the present year. A streamer of straw-coloured ribbon, dependent on a bow at the crown, hung loosely down; a leaf of laurel was placed in front, while arching over the whole was a branch of jessamine, . . . The ceremony of crowning was now performed; after which the Queen, enthroned in an armchair decorated with flowers and branches, moved . . . [to] the 'first field to be gleaned'.

(Her Proclamation Speech was)

You have made me Queen of the Gleaners till the harvest is finished. I will try to rule by right and in kindness, and I trust to your obedience that I may not have to exercise my power. I will now tell you my laws, which shall farther be made known by the crier of the village.

1st. My attendant shall ring a bell each morning, when there are fields to be gleaned.

2nd. Half-past 8 o'clock shall be the hour of meeting, at the end of the village, and I will then accompany you to the field.

3rdly. Should any of my subjects enter an ungleaned field, without being led by me, their corn will be forfeited and it will be bestrewed.

# III Painting and Nature

WILLIAM GILPIN                                                    III.1

'On Picturesque Travel'

from *Three Essays*, 1792

. . . In treating of picturesque travel, we may consider first its *object*; and secondly its sources of *amusement*.

Its *object* is beauty of every kind, which either art, or nature can produce: but it is chiefly that species of *picturesque beauty*, which we have endeavoured to characterize in the preceding essay. This great object we pursue through the scenery of nature; and examine it by the rules of painting. We seek it among all the ingredients of landscape—trees — rocks — broken-grounds —woods—rivers—lakes—plains—vallies—mountains—and distances. These objects *in themselves* produce infinite variety. No two rocks, or trees are exactly the same. They are varied, a second time, by *combination*; and almost as much, a third time, by different *lights, and shades*, and other aerial effects. Sometimes we find among them the exhibition of *a whole*; but oftener we find only beautiful *parts*.

That we may examine picturesque objects with more ease, it may be useful to class them into the *sublime*; and the *beautiful*; tho, in fact, this distinction is rather inaccurate. *Sublimity alone* cannot make an object *picturesque*. However grand the mountain, or the rock may be, it has no claim to this epithet, unless its form, its colour, or its accompaniments have *some degree of beauty*. Nothing can be more sublime, than the ocean: but wholly unaccompanied, it has little of the picturesque. When we talk therefore of a sublime object, we always understand, that it is also beautiful: and we call it sublime, or beautiful, only as the ideas of sublimity, or of simple beauty prevail.

The *curious*, and *fantastic* forms of nature are by no means the favourite objects of the lovers of landscape. There may be beauty in a *curious* object; and so far it may be picturesque: but we cannot admire it merely for the sake of its curiosity. The *lusus naturae* is the naturalist's province, not the painter's. The spiry pinnacles of the mountain, and the castle-like arrangement of the rock, give no peculiar pleasure to the picturesque eye. It is fond of the simplicity of nature; and sees most beauty in her *most usual* forms. The *Giant's causeway* in Ireland may

25

strike it as a novelty; but the lake of Killarney attracts its attention. It would range with supreme delight among the sweet vales of Switzerland; but would view only with a transient glance, the Glaciers of Savoy. Scenes of this kind, as unusual, may please *once*; but the great works of nature, in her simplest and purest stile, open inexhausted springs of amusement.

But it is not only the *form*, and the *composition* of the objects of landscape, which the picturesque eye examines; it connects them with the atmosphere, and seeks for all those various effects, which are produced from that vast, and wonderful storehouse of nature. Nor is there in travelling a greater pleasure, than when a scene of grandeur bursts unexpectedly upon the eye, accompanied with some accidental circumstance of the atmosphere, which harmonizes with it, and gives it double value.

Besides the *inanimate* face of nature, its *living forms* fall under the picturesque eye, in the course of travel; and are often objects of great attention. The anatomical study of figures is not attended to: we regard them merely as the ornament of scenes. In the human figure we contemplate neither *exactness of form*; nor *expression*, any farther than it is shewn in *action*: we merely consider general shapes, dresses, groups, and occupations; which we often find *casually* in greater variety, and beauty, than any selection can procure.

In the same manner animals are the objects of our attention, whether we find them in the park, the forest, or the field. Here too we consider little more, than their general forms, actions, and combinations. Nor is the picturesque eye so fastidious as to despise even less considerable objects. A flight of birds has often a pleasing effect. In short, every form of life, and being has its use as a picturesque object, till it become too small for attention.

But the picturesque eye is not merely restricted to nature. It ranges through the limits of art. The picture, the statue, and the garden are all the objects of its attention. In the embellished pleasure-ground particularly, tho all is neat, and elegant—far too neat and elegant for the use of the pencil; yet, if it be well laid out, it exhibits the *lines*, and *principles* of landscape; and is well worth the study of the picturesque traveller. Nothing is wanting, but what his imagination can supply—a change from smooth to rough.

But among all the objects of art, the picturesque eye is perhaps most inquisitive after the elegant relics of ancient architecture; the ruined tower, the Gothic arch, the remains of castles, and abbeys. These are the richest legacies of art. They are consecrated by time; and almost deserve the veneration we pay to the works of nature itself.

Thus universal are the objects of picturesque travel. We pursue *beauty* in every shape; through nature, through art; and all its various arrangements in form, and colour; admiring it in the grandest objects, and not rejecting it in the humblest. . . .

The first source of amusement to the picturesque traveller, is the *pursuit* of his object—the expectation of new scenes continually opening, and arising to his view. We suppose the country to have been unexplored. Under this circumstance the mind is kept constantly in an agreeable suspence. The love of novelty is the foundation of this pleasure. Every distant horizon promises something new; and with this pleasing expectation we follow nature through all her walks. We pursue her from hill to dale; and hunt after those various beauties, with which she every where abounds.

The pleasures of the chase are universal. A hare started before dogs is enough to set a whole country in an uproar. The plough, and the spade are deserted. Care is left behind; and every human faculty is dilated with joy.

And shall we suppose it a greater pleasure to the sportsman to pursue a trivial animal, than it is to the man of taste to pursue the beauties of nature? to follow her through all her recesses? to obtain a sudden glance, as she flits past him in some airy shape? to trace her through the mazes of the cover? to wind after her along the vale? or along the reaches of the river?

After the pursuit we are gratified with the *attainment* of the object. Our amusement, on this head, arises from the employment of the mind in examining the beautiful scenes we have found. Sometimes we examine them under the idea of a *whole*: we admire the composition, the colouring, and the light, in one *comprehensive view*. When we are fortunate enough to fall in with scenes of this kind, we are highly delighted. But as we have less frequent opportunities of being thus gratified, we are more commonly employed in analyzing the *parts of scenes*; which may be exquisitely beautiful, tho unable to produce a whole. We examine what would amend the composition; how little is wanting to reduce it to the rules of our art; what a trifling circumstance sometimes forms the limit between beauty, and deformity. Or we compare the objects before us with other objects of the same kind:—or perhaps we compare them with the imitations of art. From all these operations of the mind results great amusement.

But it is not from this *scientifical* employment, that we derive our chief pleasure. We are most delighted, when some grand scene, tho perhaps of incorrect composition, rising before the eye, strikes us beyond the power of thought—when the *vox faucibus haeret*; and every mental operation is suspended. In this pause of intellect; this *deliquium* of the soul, an enthusiastic sensation of pleasure overspreads it, previous to any examination by the rules of art. The general idea of the scene makes an impression, before any appeal is made to the judgment. We rather *feel*, than *survey* it.

This high delight is generally indeed produced by the scenes of nature; yet sometimes by artificial objects. Here and there a capital picture will raise these emotions: but oftener the rough sketch of a capital master. This has sometimes an astonishing effect on the mind; giving the imagination an opening into all those glowing ideas, which inspired the artist; and which the imagination *only* can translate. In general however the works of art affect us coolly; and allow the eye to criticize at leisure. . . .

There is still another amusement arising from the correct knowledge of objects; and that is the power of creating, and representing *scenes of fancy*; which is still more a work of creation, than copying from nature. The imagination becomes a camera obscura, only with this difference, that the camera represents objects as they really are; while the imagination, impressed with the most beautiful scenes, and chastened by rules of art, forms its pictures, not only from the most admirable parts of nature; but in the best taste.

Some artists, when they give their imagination play, let it loose among uncommon scenes—such as perhaps never existed: whereas the nearer they approach the simple standard of nature, in its most beautiful forms, the more admirable their fictions will appear. It is thus in writing romances. The correct taste cannot bear those unnatural situations, in which heroes, and heroines are often placed: whereas a story, *naturally*, and of course *affectingly* told, either with a pen, or a pencil, tho known to be a fiction, is considered as a transcript from nature; and takes possession of the heart. The *marvellous* disgusts the sober imagination; which is gratified only with the pure characters of nature. . . .

We are, in some degree, also amused by the very visions of fancy itself. Often, when slumber has half-closed the eye, and shut out all the objects of sense, especially after the enjoyment of some splendid scene; the imagination, active, and alert, collects its scattered ideas, transposes, combines, and shifts them into a thousand forms, producing such exquisite scenes, such sublime arrangements, such glow, and harmony of colouring, such brilliant lights, such depth, and clearness of shadow, as equally foil description, and every attempt of artificial colouring.

It may perhaps be objected to the pleasureable circumstances, which are thus said to attend picturesque travel, that we meet as many disgusting, as pleasing objects; and the man of taste therefore will be as often offended, as amused.

But this is not the case. There are few parts of nature, which do not yield a picturesque eye some amusement. . . . It is true, when some large tract of barren country *interrupts* our expectation, wound up in quest of any particular scene of grandeur, or beauty, we are apt to be a little peevish; and to express our discontent in hasty exaggerated phrase. But when there is no disappointment in the case, even scenes the most barren of beauty, will furnish amusement.

Perhaps no part of England comes more under this description, than that tract of barren country, through which the great military road passes from Newcastle to Carlisle. It is a waste, with little interruption, through a space of forty miles. But even here, we have always something to amuse the eye. The interchangeable patches of heath, and green-sward make an agreeable variety. Often too on these vast tracts of intersecting grounds we see beautiful lights, softening off along the sides of hills: and often we see them adorned with cattle, flocks of sheep, heath-cocks, grouse, plover, and flights of other wild-fowl. A group of cattle, standing in the shade on the edge of a dark hill, and relieved by a lighter distance beyond them, will often make a compleat picture without any other accompaniment. . . .

But if we let the *imagination* loose, even scenes like these, administer great amusement. The imagination can plant hills; can form rivers, and lakes in vallies; can build castles, and abbeys; and if it find no other amusement, can dilate itself in vast ideas of space.

But altho the picturesque traveller is seldom disappointed with *pure nature*, however rude, yet we cannot deny, but he is often offended with the productions of art. He is disgusted with the formal separations of property—with houses, and towns, the haunts of men, which have much oftener a bad effect in landscape, than a good one. He is frequently disgusted also, when art aims more at beauty, than she ought. How flat, and insipid is often the garden-scene! how puerile, and absurd! the banks of the river how smooth, and parrallel! the lawn, and its boundaries, how unlike nature! Even in the capital collection of pictures, how seldom does he find *design, composition, expression, character*, or *harmony* either in *light*, or *colouring!* and how often does he drag through saloons, and rooms of state, only to hear a catalogue of the names of masters!

The more refined our taste grows from the *study of nature*, the more insipid are the *works of art*. Few of its efforts please. The idea of the great original is so strong, that the copy must be very pure, if it do not disgust. But the varieties of nature's charts are such, that, study them as we can, new varieties will always arise: and let our taste be ever so refined, her works, on which it is formed (at least when we consider them as *objects*,) must always go beyond it; and furnish fresh sources both of pleasure and amusement.

# JOHN CONSTABLE

III.2

## "Painting is but another word for feeling"

from Letter to Archdeacon John Fisher, 1821

Hampstead 23ᵈ Octʳ. 1821.

My dear Fisher

I trust you will pardon this delay of mine in replying to your last long and very kind letter. . . .

I have not been Idle and have made more particular and general study than I have ever done in one summer, but I am most anxious to get into my London painting room, for I do not consider myself at work without I am before a six foot canvas—I have done a good deal of skying—I am determined to conquer all dificulties and that most arduous one among the rest, and now talking of skies— . . .

It is quite amusing and interesting to us to see how admirably you fight their battles you certainly take the best possible ground for getting your friend out of a scrape—'(the examples of the great masters)'. That Landscape painter who does not make his skies a very material part of his composition—neglects to avail himself of one of his greatest aids. Sir Joshua Reynolds speaking of the 'Landscape' of Titian & Salvator & Claude—says *Even their skies seem to sympathise with the Subject*'. I have often been advised to consider my *Sky*—as a '*White Sheet drawn behind the Objects*'. Certainly if the Sky is *obtrusive*—(as mine are) it is bad, but if they are *evaded* (as mine are not) it is worse, they must and always shall with me make an effectual part of the composition. It will be difficult to name a class of Landscape, in which the sky is not the '*key note*', the *standard of 'Scale*', and the chief '*Organ of sentiment*'. You may conceive then what a '*white sheet*' would do for me, impressed as I am with these notions, and they cannot be Erroneous. The sky is the '*source of light*' in nature—and governs every thing. Even our common observations on the weather of every day, are suggested by them but it does not occur to us. Their difficulty in painting both as to composition and execution is very great, because with all their brilliancy and consequence, they ought not to come forward or be hardly thought about in a picture—any more than extreme distances are.

But these remarks do not apply to *phenomenon*—or what the painters call *accidental Effects of Sky*—because they always attract particularly.

I hope you will not think I am turned critic instead of painter. I say all this *to you* though you do not want to be told—that I know very well what I am about, & that my skies have not been neglected though they often failed in execution—and often no doubt from over anxiety

1. Samuel Palmer: A Rustic Scene (1825)

2. W. H. Pyne: Country Work (1808)

3. British School: Pithead (1830)

about them—which alone will destroy that Easy appearance which nature always has—in all her movements. . . .

How strange it is that we should prefer raising up all manner of difficulties in painting—to truth and common sense.

How much I can Imagine myself with you on your fishing excursion in the new forest, what River can it be. But the sound of water escaping from Mill dams, so do Willows, Old rotten Banks, slimy posts, & brickwork. I love such things—Shakespeare could make anything poetical—he mentions 'poor Tom's' haunts among *Sheep cots*—& *Mills*—the Water [mist] & the Hedge pig. As long as I do paint I shall never cease to paint such Places. They have always been my delight—& I should indeed have delighted in seeing what you describe in your company 'in the company of a man to whom nature does not spread her volume or utter her voice in vain'.

But I should paint my own places best—Painting is but another word for feeling. I associate my 'careless boyhood' to all that lies on the banks of the *Stour*. They made me a painter (& I am gratefull) that is I had often thought of pictures of them before I had ever touched a pencil, and your picture is one of the strongest instances I can recollect of it. But I will say no more—for I am fond of being an Egotist, in whatever relates to painting.

Does not the cathedral look very beautiful amongst the Golden foliage, its silvery grey must sparkle in it. Poor Read has sent me some copies made at Wilton, the Claude & a Van de Velde—they are very far from bad, and very much better than I expected. . . . I have requested the loan of the little Tenniers at the Miss Fishers for him to Copy. It is a Good Tone but rather too hot on the Right hand side.

My wife and children are now quite well, the former & my eldest boy having been great invalids. We sincerely hope Mrs. Fisher & all your Children and relations our good friends at Salisbury are well. . . . I long to get to work. I shall do another large Work of my Own, & Savile's picture—but that is a dead pall. He is not only a fool, but he is as Crazy as a fool can be.

My last year's work has got much *together*. This weather has blown & washed the *powder off*. I do not know what I shall do with it—but I love my children to[o] well to expose them to the taunts of the Ignorant —though they shall never flinch from honourable competition. I have just paper enough to say adieu—& add my Wife's (who is sitting by me) best regards to yourself and all your family. I am yours

John Constable

# JOHN RUSKIN

## Turner's Childhood

from *Modern Painters*, 1860

Near the south-west corner of Covent Garden, a square brick pit or well is formed by a close-set block of houses, to the back windows of which it admits a few rays of light. Access to the bottom of it is obtained out of Maiden Lane, through a low archway and an iron gate; and if you stand long enough under the archway to accustom your eyes to the darkness you may see on the left hand a narrow door, which formerly gave quiet access to a respectable barber's shop, of which the front window, looking into Maiden Lane, is still extant, filled, in this year (1860), with a row of bottles, connected, in some defunct manner, with a brewer's business. A more fashionable neighbourhood, it is said, eighty years ago than now—never certainly a cheerful one—wherein a boy being born on St. George's day, 1775, began soon after to take interest in the world of Covent Garden, and put to service such spectacles of life as it afforded.

No knights to be seen there, nor, I imagine, many beautiful ladies; their costume at least disadvantageous, depending much on incumbency of hat and feather, and short waists; the majesty of men founded similarly on shoebuckles and wigs;—impressive enough when Reynolds will do his best for it; but not suggestive of much ideal delight to a boy.

'Bello ovile dov' io dormii agnello'; of things beautiful, besides men and women, dusty sunbeams up or down the street on summer mornings; deep furrowed cabbage-leaves at the greengrocer's; magnificence of oranges in wheelbarrows round the corner; and Thames' shore within three minutes' race.

None of these things very glorious; the best, however, that England, it seems, was then able to provide for a boy of gift: who, such as they are, loves them—never, indeed, forgets them. The short waists modify to the last his visions of Greek ideal. His foregrounds had always a succulent cluster or two of greengrocery at the corners. Enchanted oranges gleam in Covent Gardens of the Hesperides; and great ships go to pieces in order to scatter chests of them on the waves. That mist of early sunbeams in the London dawn crosses, many and many a time, the clearness of Italian air; and by Thames's shore, with its stranded barges and glidings of red sail, dearer to us than Lucerne lake or Venetian lagoon,—by Thames's shore we will die.

With such circumstance round him in youth, let us note what necessary effects followed upon the boy. I assume him to have had Giorgione's sensibility (and more than Giorgione's, if that be possible) to colour and form. I tell you farther, and this fact you may receive trustfully, that his sensibility to human affection and distress was no less keen than even his sense for natural beauty—heart-sight deep as eyesight.

Consequently, he attaches himself with the faithfullest child-love to everything that bears an image of the place he was born in. No matter how ugly it is,—has it anything about it like Maiden Lane, or like Thames' shore? If so, it shall be painted for their sake. Hence, to the very close of life, Turner could endure ugliness which no one else, of the same sensibility, would have borne with for an instant. Dead brick walls, blank square windows, old clothes, market-womanly types of humanity—anything fishy and muddy, like Billingsgate or Hungerford Market, had great attraction for him; black barges, patched sails, and every possible condition of fog.

You will find these tolerations and affections guiding or sustaining him to the last hour of his life; the notablest of all such endurances being that of dirt. No Venetian ever draws anything foul; but Turner devoted picture after picture to the illustration of effects of dinginess, smoke, soot, dust, and dusty texture; old sides of boats, weedy road-side vegetation, dung-hills, straw-yards, and all the soilings and stains of every common labour.

And more than this, he not only could endure, but enjoyed and looked for *litter*, like Covent Garden wreck after the market. His pictures are often full of it, from side to side; their foregrounds differ from all others in the natural way that things have of lying about in them. Even his richest vegetation, in ideal work, is confused; and he delights in shingle, débris, and heaps of fallen stones. The last words he ever spoke to me about a picture were in gentle exultation about his St. Gothard: 'that *litter* of stones which I endeavoured to represent.'

The second great result of this Covent Garden training was, under-standing of and regard for the poor, whom the Venetians, we saw, despised; whom, contrarily, Turner loved, and more than loved—under-stood. He got no romantic sight of them, but an infallible one, as he prowled about the end of his lane, watching night effects in the wintry streets; nor sight of the poor alone, but of the poor in direct relations with the rich. He knew, in good and evil, what both classes thought of, and how they dealt with, each other.

Reynolds and Gainsborough, bred in country villages, learned there the country boy's reverential theory of 'the squire,' and kept it. They painted the squire and the squire's lady as centres of the movements of the universe, to the end of their lives. But Turner perceived the younger squire in other aspects about his lane, occurring prominently in its night scenery, as a dark figure, or one of two, against the moonlight. He saw also the working of city commerce, from endless warehouse, tower-ing over Thames, to the back shop in the lane, with its stale herrings—highly interesting these last; one of his father's best friends, whom he often afterwards visited affectionately at Bristol, being a fishmonger and glue-boiler; which gives us a friendly turn of mind towards herring-fishing, whaling, Calais poissardes, and many other of our choicest subjects in after-life; all this being connected with that mysterious forest below London Bridge on one side; and, on the other, with these masses of human power and national wealth which weigh upon us, at Covent Garden here, with strange compression, and crush us into narrow Hand Court.

'That mysterious forest below London Bridge' better for the boy than wood of pine, or grove of myrtle. How he must have tormented the watermen, beseeching them to let him crouch anywhere in the bows, quiet as a log, so only that he might get floated down there among the ships, and round and round the ships, and with the ships, and by the ships, and under the ships, staring, and clambering;—these the only quite beautiful things he can see in all the world, except the sky; but these, when the sun is on their sails, filling or falling, endlessly disordered by sway of tide and stress of anchorage, beautiful unspeakably; which ships also are inhabited by glorious creatures—red-faced sailors, with pipes, appearing over the gunwales, true knights, over their castle parapets—the most angelic beings in the whole compass of London world. And Trafalgar happening long before we can draw ships, we, nevertheless, coax all current stories out of the wounded sailors, do our best at present to show Nelson's funeral streaming up the Thames; and vow that Trafalgar shall have its tribute of memory some day. Which, accordingly, is accomplished—once, with all our might, for its death; twice, with all our might, for its victory; thrice, in pensive fairwell to the old *Téméraire*, and with it, to that order of things.

Now this fond companying with sailors must have divided his time, it appears to me, pretty equally between Covent Garden and Wapping (allowing for incidental excursions to Chelsea on one side, and Greenwich on the other), which time he would spend pleasantly, but not magnificently, being limited in pocket-money, and leading a kind of 'Poor Jack' life on the river.

In some respects, no life could be better for a lad. But it was not calculated to make his ear fine to the niceties of language, nor form his moralities on an entirely regular standard. Picking up his first scraps of vigorous English chiefly at Deptford and in the markets, and his first ideas of female tenderness and beauty among nymphs of the barge and the barrow,—another boy might, perhaps, have become what people usually term 'vulgar.' But the original make and frame of Turner's mind being not vulgar, but as nearly as possible a combination of the minds of Keats and Dante, joining capricious waywardness, and intense openness to every fine pleasure of sense, and hot defiance of formal precedent, with a quite infinite tenderness, generosity, and desire of justice

34

and truth—this kind of mind did not become vulgar, but very tolerant of vulgarity, even fond of it in some forms; and on the outside, visibly infected by it, deeply enough; the curious result, in its combination of elements, being to most people wholly incomprehensible. It was as if a cable had been woven of blood-crimson silk, and then tarred on the outside. People handled it, and the tar came off on their hands; red gleams were seen through the black underneath, at the places where it had been strained. Was it ochre?—said the world—or red lead? . . .

Under these influences pass away the first reflective hours of life, with such conclusion as they can reach. In consequence of a fit of illness, he was taken—I cannot ascertain in what year—to live with an aunt, at Brentford; and here, I believe, received some schooling, which he seems to have snatched vigorously; getting knowledge, at least by translation, of the more picturesque classical authors, which he turned presently to use, as we shall see. Hence also, walks about Putney and Twickenham in the summer time acquainted him with the look of English meadow-ground in its restricted states of paddock and park; and with some round-headed appearances of trees, and stately entrances to houses of mark. the avenue at Bushey, and the iron gates and carved pillars of Hampton, impressing him apparently with great awe and admiration; so that in after-life his little country house is,—of all places in the world,—at Twickenham! Of swans and reedy shores he now learns the soft motion and the green mystery, in a way not to be forgotten.

And at last fortune wills that the lad's true life shall begin; and one summer's evening, after various wonderful stage-coach experiences on the north road, which gave him a love of stage-coaches ever after, he finds himself sitting alone among the Yorkshire hills. For the first time, the silence of Nature round him, her freedom sealed to him, her glory opened to him. Peace at last; no roll of cart-wheel, nor mutter of sullen voices in the back shop; but curlew-cry in space of heaven, and welling of bell-toned streamlet by its shadowy rock. Freedom at last. Dead-wall, dark railing, fenced field, gated garden, all passed away like the dream of a prisoner; and behold, far as foot or eye can race or range, the moor, and cloud. Loveliness at last. It is here then, among these deserted vales! Not among men. Those pale, poverty-struck, or cruel faces;—that multitudinous, marred humanity—are not the only things that God has made. Here is something He has made which no one has marred. Pride of purple rocks, and river pools of blue, and tender wilderness of glittering trees, and misty lights of evening on immeasurable hills.

Beauty, and freedom, and peace; and yet another teacher, graver than these. Sound preaching at last here, in Kirkstall crypt, concerning fate and life. Here, where the dark pool reflects the chancel pillars, and the cattle lie in unhindered rest, the soft sunshine on their dappled bodies, instead of priests' vestments; their white furry hair ruffled a little, fitfully, by the evening wind deep-scented from the meadow thyme.

Consider deeply the import to him of this, his first sight of ruin, and compare it with the effect of the architecture that was around Giorgione. There were indeed aged buildings, at Venice, in his time, but none in decay. All ruin was removed, and its place filled as quickly as in our London; but filled always by architecture loftier and more wonderful than that whose place it took, the boy himself happy to work upon the walls of it; so that the idea of the passing away of the strength of men and beauty of their works never could occur to him sternly. Brighter and brighter the cities of Italy had been rising and broadening on hill and plain, for three hundred years. He saw only strength and immortality, could not but paint both; conceived the form of man as deathless, calm with power, and fiery with life.

Turner saw the exact reverse of this. In the present work of men, meanness, aimlessness, unsightliness: thin-walled, lath-divided, narrow-garreted houses of clay; booths of a darksome Vanity Fair, busily base.

But on Whitby Hill, and by Bolton Brook, remained traces of other handiwork. Men who could build had been there; and who also had wrought, not merely for their own days. But to what purpose? Strong faith, and steady hands, and patient souls—can this, then, be all you have left? this the sum of your doing on the earth;—a nest whence the night-owl may whimper to the brook, and a ribbed skeleton of consumed arches, looming above the bleak banks of mist, from its cliff to the sea?

As the strength of men to Giorgione, to Turner their weakness and vileness, were alone visible. They themselves, unworthy or ephemeral; their work, despicable, or decayed. In the Venetian's eyes, all beauty depended on man's presence and pride; in Turner's, on the solitude he had left, and the humiliation he had suffered.

And thus the fate and issue of all his work were determined at once. He must be a painter of the strength of nature, there was no beauty elsewhere than in that; he must paint also the labour and sorrow and passing away of men: this was the great human truth visible to him.

Their labour, their sorrow, and their death. Mark the three. Labour; by sea and land, in field and city, at forge and furnace, helm and plough. No pastoral indolence nor classic pride shall stand between him and the troubling of the world; still less between him and the toil of his country,—blind, tormented, unwearied, marvellous England.

Also their Sorrow; Ruin of all their glorious work, passing away of their thoughts and their honour, mirage of pleasure. . . .

And their Death. . . . This has to be looked upon, and in a more terrible shape than ever Salvator or Dürer saw it. . . . But the English death—the European death of the nineteenth century was of another range and power; more terrible a thousand-fold in its merely physical grasp and grief; more terrible, incalculably, in its mystery and shame. What were the robber's casual pang, or the range of the flying skirmish, compared to the work of the axe, and the sword, and the famine, which was done during this man's youth on all the hills and plains of the Christian earth, from Moscow to Gibraltar? He was eighteen years old when Napoleon came down on Arcola. Look on the map of Europe and count the blood-stains on it, between Arcola and Waterloo.

Not alone those blood-stains on the Alpine snow, and the blue of the Lombard plain. The English death was before his eyes also. No decent, calculable, consoled dying; no passing to rest like that of the aged burghers of Nuremberg town. No gentle processions to churchyards among the fields, the bronze crests bossed deep on the memorial tablets, and the skylark singing above them from among the corn. But the life trampled out in the slime of the street, crushed to dust amidst the roaring of the wheel, tossed countlessly away into howling winter wind along five hundred leagues of rock-fanged shore. Or, worst of all, rotted down to forgotten graves through years of ignorant patience, and vain seeking for help from man, for hope in God—infirm, imperfect yearning, as of motherless infants starving at the dawn; oppressed royalties of captive thought, vague ague-fits of bleak, amazed despair.

# IV Nature and Romantic Literature

SAMUEL TAYLOR COLERIDGE

'Frost at Midnight'

from *Lyrical Ballads*, 1798

The Frost performs its secret ministry,
Unhelped by any wind. The owlet's cry
Came loud—and hark, again! loud as before.
The inmates of my cottage, all at rest,
Have left me to that solitude, which suits
Abstruser musings: save that at my side
My cradled infant slumbers peacefully.
'Tis calm indeed! so calm, that it disturbs
And vexes meditation with its strange
And extreme silentness. Sea, hill, and wood,
This populous village! Sea, and hill, and wood,
With all the numberless goings-on of life,
Inaudible as dreams! the thin blue flame
Lies on my low-burnt fire, and quivers not;
Only that film, which fluttered on the grate,
Still flutters there, the sole unquiet thing.
Methinks, its motion in this hush of nature
Gives it dim sympathies with me who live,
Making it a companionable form,
Whose puny flaps and freaks the idling Spirit
By its own moods interprets, every where
Echo or mirror seeking of itself,
And makes a toy of Thought.
                                    But O! how oft,
How oft, at school, with most believing mind,
Presageful, have I gazed upon the bars,
To watch that fluttering *stranger*! and as oft
With unclosed lids, already had I dreamt
Of my sweet birth-place, and the old church-tower,
Whose bells, the poor man's only music, rang
From morn to evening, all the hot Fair-day,
So sweetly, that they stirred and haunted me

With a wild pleasure, falling on mine ear
Most like articulate sounds of things to come!
So gazed I, till the soothing things, I dreamt,
Lulled me to sleep, and sleep prolonged my dreams!
And so I brooded all the following morn,
Awed by the stern preceptor's face, mine eye
Fixed with mock study on my swimming book:
Save if the door half opened, and I snatched
A hasty glance, and still my heart leaped up,
For still I hoped to see the *stranger's* face,
Townsman, or aunt, or sister more beloved,
My play-mate when we both were clothed alike!

Dear Babe, that sleepest cradled by my side,
Whose gentle breathings, heard in this deep calm,
Fill up the intersperséd vacancies
And momentary pauses of the thought!
My babe so beautiful! it thrills my heart
With tender gladness, thus to look at thee,
And think that thou shalt learn far other lore,
And in far other scenes! For I was reared
In the great city, pent 'mid cloisters dim,
And saw nought lovely but the sky and stars.
But *thou*, my babe! shalt wander like a breeze
By lakes and sandy shores, beneath the crags
Of ancient mountain, and beneath the clouds,
Which image in their bulk both lakes and shores
And mountain crags: so shalt thou see and hear
The lovely shapes and sounds intelligible
Of that eternal language, which thy God
Utters, who from eternity doth teach
Himself in all, and all things in himself.
Great universal Teacher! he shall mould
Thy spirit, and by giving make it ask.

Therefore all seasons shall be sweet to thee,
Whether the summer clothe the general earth
With greenness, or the redbreast sit and sing
Betwixt the tufts of snow on the bare branch
Of mossy apple-tree, while the night thatch
Smokes in the sun-thaw; whether the eave-drops fall
Heard only in the trances of the blast,
Or if the secret ministry of frost
Shall hang them up in silent icicles,
Quietly shining to the quiet Moon.

# WILLIAM WORDSWORTH

## 'Above Tintern Abbey'

from *Lyrical Ballads*, 1798

Five years have past; five summers, with the length
Of five long winters! and again I hear
These waters, rolling from their mountain-springs
With a soft inland murmur.—Once again
Do I behold these steep and lofty cliffs,
That on a wild secluded scene impress
Thoughts of more deep seclusion; and connect
The landscape with the quiet of the sky.
The day is come when I again repose
Here, under this dark sycamore, and view
These plots of cottage-ground, these orchard-tufts,
Which at this season, with their unripe fruits,
Are clad in one green hue, and lose themselves
'Mid groves and copses. Once again I see
These hedge-rows, hardly hedge-rows, little lines
Of sportive wood run wild: these pastoral farms,
Green to the very door; and wreaths of smoke
Sent up, in silence, from among the trees!
With some uncertain notice, as might seem
Of vagrant dwellers in the houseless woods,
Or of some Hermit's cave, where by his fire
The Hermit sits alone.
                   These beauteous forms,
Through a long absence, have not been to me
As is a landscape to a blind man's eye:
But oft, in lonely rooms, and 'mid the din
Of towns and cities, I have owed to them,
In hours of weariness, sensations sweet,
Felt in the blood, and felt along the heart;
And passing even into my purer mind,
With tranquil restoration:—feelings too
Of unremembered pleasure: such, perhaps,
As have no slight or trivial influence
On that best portion of a good man's life,
His little, nameless, unremembered, acts
Of kindness and of love. Nor less, I trust,
To them I may have owed another gift,
Of aspect more sublime; that blessed mood,

In which the burthen of the mystery,
In which the heavy and the weary weight
Of all this unintelligible world,
Is lightened:—that serene and blessed mood,
In which the affections gently lead us on,—
Until, the breath of this corporeal frame
And even the motion of our human blood
Almost suspended, we are laid asleep
In body, and become a living soul:
While with an eye made quiet by the power
Of harmony, and the deep power of joy,
We see into the life of things.
                                    If this
Be but a vain belief, yet, oh! how oft—
In darkness and amid the many shapes
Of joyless daylight; when the fretful stir
Unprofitable, and the fever of the world,
Have hung upon the beatings of my heart—
How oft, in spirit, have I turned to thee,
O sylvan Wye! thou wanderer thro' the woods,
How often has my spirit turned to thee!
   And now, with gleams of half-extinguished thought,
With many recognitions dim and faint,
And somewhat of a sad perplexity,
The picture of the mind revives again:
While here I stand, not only with the sense
Of present pleasure, but with pleasing thoughts
That in this moment there is life and food
For future years. And so I dare to hope,
Though changed, no doubt, from what I was when first
I came among these hills; when like a roe
I bounded o'er the mountains, by the sides
Of the deep rivers, and the lonely streams.
Wherever nature led: more like a man
Flying from something that he dreads than one
Who sought the thing he loved. For nature then
(The coarser pleasures of my boyish days,
And their glad animal movements all gone by)
To me was all in all.—I cannot paint
What then I was. The sounding cataract
Haunted me like a passion: the tall rock,
The mountain, and the deep and gloomy wood,
Their colours and their forms, were then to me
An appetite; a feeling and a love,

That had no need of a remoter charm,
By thought supplied, nor any interest
Unborrowed from the eye.—That time is past,
And all its aching joys are now no more,
And all its dizzy raptures. Not for this
Faint I, nor mourn nor murmur; other gifts
Have followed; for such loss, I would believe,
Abundant recompense. For I have learned
To look on nature, not as in the hour
Of thoughtless youth; but hearing oftentimes
The still, sad music of humanity,
Nor harsh nor grating, though of ample power
To chasten and subdue. And I have felt
A presence that disturbs me with the joy
Of elevated thoughts; a sense sublime
Of something far more deeply interfused,
Whose dwelling is the light of setting suns,
And the round ocean and the living air,
And the blue sky, and in the mind of man:
A motion and a spirit, that impels
All thinking things, all objects of all thought,
And rolls through all things. Therefore am I still
A lover of the meadows and the woods,
And mountains; and of all that we behold
From this green earth; of all the mighty world
Of eye, and ear,—both what they half create,
And what perceive; well pleased to recognise
In nature and the language of the sense
The anchor of my purest thoughts, the nurse,
The guide, the guardian of my heart, and soul
Of all my moral being.
                          Nor perchance,
If I were not thus taught, should I the more
Suffer my genial spirits to decay:
For thou art with me here upon the banks
Of this fair river; thou my dearest Friend,
My dear, dear Friend; and in thy voice I catch
The language of my former heart, and read
My former pleasures in the shooting lights
Of thy wild eyes. Oh! yet a little while
May I behold in thee what I was once,
My dear, dear Sister! and this prayer I make,
Knowing that Nature never did betray
The heart that loved her; 'tis her privilege,

Through all the years of this our life, to lead
From joy to joy; for she can so inform
The mind that is within us, so impress
With quietness and beauty, and so feed
With lofty thoughts, that neither evil tongues,
Rash judgments, nor the sneers of selfish men,
Nor greetings where no kindness is, nor all
The dreary intercourse of daily life,
Shall e'er prevail against us, or disturb
Our cheerful faith, that all which we behold
Is full of blessings. Therefore let the moon
Shine on thee in thy solitary walk;
And let the misty mountain-winds be free
To blow against thee: and, in after years,
When these wild ecstasies shall be matured
Into a sober pleasure; when thy mind
Shall be a mansion for all lovely forms,
Thy memory be as a dwelling-place
For all sweet sounds and harmonies; oh! then,
If solitude, or fear, or pain, or grief,
Should be thy portion, with what healing thoughts
Of tender joy wilt thou remember me,
And these my exhortations! Nor, perchance—
If I should be where I no more can hear
Thy voice, nor catch from thy wild eyes these gleams
Of past existence—wilt thou then forget
That on the banks of this delightful stream
We stood together; and that I, so long
A worshipper of Nature, hither came
Unwearied in that service: rather say
With warmer love—oh! with far deeper zeal
Of holier love. Nor wilt thou then forget
That after many wanderings, many years
Of absence, these steep woods and lofty cliffs,
And this green pastoral landscape, were to me
More dear, both for themselves and for thy sake!

# WILLIAM WORDSWORTH                               IV.3
## 'The Old Cumberland Beggar'
from *Lyrical Ballads*, 1798

          . . . Then let him pass, a blessing on his head!
          And while, in that vast solitude to which

The tide of things has led him, he appears
To breathe and live but for himself alone,
Unblam'd, uninjur'd, let him bear about
The good which the benignant law of heaven
Has hung around him, and, while life is his,
Still let him prompt the unletter'd Villagers
To tender offices and pensive thoughts.
Then let him pass, a blessing on his head!
And, long as he can wander, let him breathe
The freshness of the vallies, let his blood
Struggle with frosty air and winter snows,
And let the charter'd wind that sweeps the heath
Beat his grey locks against his wither'd face.
Reverence the hope whose vital anxiousness
Gives the last human interest to his heart.
May never House, misnamed of industry,
Make him a captive; for that pent-up din,
Those life-consuming sounds that clog the air,
Be his the natural silence of old age.
Let him be free of mountain solitudes,
And have around him, whether heard or not,
The pleasant melody of woodland birds.
Few are his pleasures; if his eyes, which now
Have been so long familiar with the earth,
No more behold the horizontal sun
Rising or setting, let the light at least
Find a free entrance to their languid orbs.
And let him, *where* and *when* he will, sit down
Beneath the trees, or by the grassy bank
Of high-way side, and with the little birds
Share his chance-gather'd meal, and, finally,
As in the eye of Nature he has liv'd,
So in the eye of Nature let him die.

# WILLIAM WORDSWORTH                            IV.4

## Climbing Snowdon

from *The Prelude*, 1805

In one of these excursions, travelling then
Through Wales on foot, and with a youthful Friend,
I left Bethkelet's huts at couching-time,

And westward took my way to see the sun
Rise from the top of Snowdon. Having reach'd
The Cottage at the Mountain's foot, we there
Rouz'd up the Shepherd, who by ancient right
Of office is the Stranger's usual guide;
And after short refreshment sallied forth.

It was a Summer's night, a close warm night,
Wan, dull and glaring, with a dripping mist
Low-hung and thick that cover'd all the sky,
Half threatening storm and rain; but on we went
Uncheck'd, being full of heart and having faith
In our tried Pilot. Little could we see
Hemm'd round on every side with fog and damp,
And, after ordinary travellers' chat
With our Conductor, silently we sank
Each into commerce with his private thoughts:
Thus did we breast the ascent, and by myself
Was nothing either seen or heard the while
Which took me from my musings, save that once
The Shepherd's Cur did to his own great joy
Unearth a hedgehog in the mountain crags
Round which he made a barking turbulent.
This small adventure, for even such it seemed
In that wild place and at the dead of night,
Being over and forgotten, on we wound
In silence as before. With forehead bent
Earthward, as if in opposition set
Against an enemy, I panted up
With eager pace, and no less eager thoughts.
Thus might we wear perhaps an hour away,
Ascending at loose distance each from each,
And I, as chanced, the foremost of the Band;
When at my feet the ground appear'd to brighten,
And with a step or two seem'd brighter still;
Nor had I time to ask the cause of this,
For instantly a Light upon the turf
Fell like a flash: I looked about, and lo!
The Moon stood naked in the Heavens, at height
Immense above my head, and on the shore
I found myself of a huge sea of mist,
Which, meek and silent, rested at my feet:
A hundred hills their dusky backs upheaved
All over this still Ocean, and beyond,

Far, far beyond, the vapours shot themselves,
In headlands, tongues, and promontory shapes,
Into the Sea, the real Sea, that seem'd
To dwindle, and give up its majesty,
Usurp'd upon as far as sight could reach.
Meanwhile, the Moon look'd down upon this shew
In single glory, and we stood, the mist
Touching our very feet; and from the shore
At distance not the third part of a mile
Was a blue chasm; a fracture in the vapour,
A deep and gloomy breathing-place through which
Mounted the roar of waters, torrents, streams
Innumerable, roaring with one voice.
The universal spectacle throughout
Was shaped for admiration and delight,
Grand in itself alone, but in that breach
Through which the homeless voice of waters rose,
That dark deep thoroughfare had Nature lodg'd
The Soul, the Imagination of the whole.

# GEORGE GORDON, LORD BYRON     IV.5

## Solitude

from *Childe Harold's Pilgrimage*, 1816

Where rose the mountains, there to him were friends;
Where roll'd the ocean, thereon was his home;
Where a blue sky, and glowing clime, extends,
He had the passion and the power to roam;
The desert, forest, cavern, breaker's foam,
Were unto him companionship; they spake
A mutual language, clearer than the tome
Of his land's tongue, which he would oft forsake
For Nature's pages glass'd by sunbeams on the lake.

Like the Chaldean, he could watch the stars,
Till he had peopled them with beings bright
As their own beams; and earth, and earthborn jars,
And human frailties, were forgotten quite
Could he have kept his spirit to that flight,
He had been happy; but this clay will sink
Its spark immortal, envying it the light

47

To which it mounts, as if to break the link
That keeps us from yon heaven which woos us to its brink.

But in Man's dwellings he became a thing
Restless and worn, and stern and wearisome,
Droop'd as a wild-born falcon with clipt wing,
To whom the boundless air alone were home:
Then came his fit again, which to o'ercome,
As eagerly the barr'd-up bird will beat
His breast and beak against his wiry dome
Till the blood tinge his plumage, so the heat
Of his impeded soul would through his bosom eat.

Self-exiled Harold wanders forth again,
With nought of hope left, but with less of gloom;
The very knowledge that he lived in vain,
That all was over on this side the tomb,
Had made Despair a smilingness assume,
Which, though 'twere wild—as on the plunder'd wreck
When mariners would madly meet their doom
With draughts intemperate on the sinking deck—
Did yet inspire a cheer, which he forbore to check.

# GEORGE GORDON, LORD BYRON                        IV.6

## Haidee and the sea-caves

from *Don Juan*, 1818–20

They look'd up to the sky, whose floating glow
Spread like a rosy ocean, vast and bright:
They gazed upon the glittering sea below,
Whence the broad moon rose circling into sight;
They heard the waves splash, and the wind so low,
And saw each other's dark eyes darting light
Into each other—and, beholding this,
Their lips drew near, and clung into a kiss,

A long, long kiss, a kiss of youth and love,
And beauty, all concentrating like rays
Into one focus, kindled from above;
Such kisses as belong to early days,
Where heart, and soul, and sense in concert move,
And the blood's lava, and the pulse a blaze,.

Each kiss a heart-quake,—for a kiss's strength,
I think, it must be reckon'd by its length.

    By length I mean duration; theirs endured
    Heaven knows how long, no doubt they never reckon'd;
And if they had, they could not have secured
    The sum of their sensations to a second:
They had not spoken; but they felt allured,
    As if their souls and lips each other beckon'd,
Which, being join'd, like swarming bees they clung,
Their hearts the flowers from whence the honey sprung.

    They were alone, but not alone as they
    Who shut in chambers think it loneliness;
The silent ocean, and the starlight bay,
    The twilight glow, which momently grew less;
The voiceless sands, and dropping caves, that lay
    Around them, made them to each other press,
As if there were no life beneath the sky
Save theirs, and that their life could never die.

# WALTER SCOTT                               IV.7

## The Waterfall

from *The Heart of Midlothian*, 1818

There was one source . . . from which Lady Staunton derived a pure
degree of pleasure. Gifted in every particular with a higher degree of
imagination than that of her sister, she was an admirer of the beauties
of nature, a taste which compensates many evils to those who happen
to enjoy it. . . . With the two boys for her guides, she undertook long
and fatiguing walks among the neighbouring mountains to visit glens,
lakes, waterfalls, or whatever scenes of natural wonder or beauty lay
concealed among their recesses. It is Wordsworth, I think, who, talking
of an old man under difficulties, remarks, with a singular attention to
nature—

        —whether it was care that spurred him,
        God only knows; but to the very last,
        He had the lightest foot in Ennerdale.

In the same manner, languid, listless, and unhappy, within doors, at
times even indicating something which approached near to contempt of
the homely accommodations of her sister's house, . . . Lady Staunton

49

appeared to feel interest and energy while in the open air, and traversing the mountain landscapes in society with the two boys, whose ears she delighted with stories of what she had seen in other countries, and what she had to show them at Willingham Manor. And they, on the other hand, exerted themselves in doing the honours of Dumbartonshire to the lady who seemed so kind, insomuch that there was scarce a glen in the neighbouring hills to which they did not introduce her.

Upon one of these excursions, while Reuben was otherwise employed, David alone acted as Lady Staunton's guide, and promised to show her a cascade in the hills, grander and higher than any they had yet visited. It was a walk of five long miles, and over rough ground, varied, however, and cheered, by mountain views, and peeps now of the firth and its islands, now of distant lakes, now of rocks and precipices. The scene itself, too, when they reached it, amply rewarded the labour of the walk. A single shoot carried a considerable stream over the face of a black rock, which contrasted strongly in colour with the white foam of the cascade, and, at the depth of about twenty feet, another rock intercepted the view of the bottom of the fall. The water, wheeling out far beneath, swept round the crag, which thus bounded their view, and tumbled down the rocky glen in a torrent of foam. Those who love nature always desire to penetrate into its utmost recesses, and Lady Staunton asked David whether there was not some mode of gaining a view of the abyss at the foot of the fall. He said that he knew a station on a shelf on the farther side of the intercepting rock, from which the whole waterfall was visible, but that the road to it was steep and slippery and dangerous. Bent, however, on gratifying her curiosity, she desired him to lead the way; and accordingly he did so over crag and stone, anxiously pointing out to her the resting-places where she ought to step, for their mode of advancing soon ceased to be walking, and became scrambling.

In this manner, clinging like sea-birds to the face of the rock, they were enabled at length to turn round it, and came full in front of the fall, which here had a most tremendous aspect, boiling, roaring, and thundering with unceasing din, into a black cauldron, a hundred feet at least below them, which resembled the crater of a volcano. The noise, the dashing of the waters, which gave an unsteady appearance to all around them, the trembling even of the huge crag on which they stood, the precariousness of their footing, for there was scarce room for them to stand on the shelf of rock which they had thus attained, had so powerful an effect on the senses and imagination of Lady Staunton, that she called out to David she was falling, and would in fact have dropped from the crag had he not caught hold of her. The boy was bold and stout of his age—still he was but fourteen years old, and as his assistance gave no confidence to Lady Staunton, she felt her situation become really perilous. The chance was, that, in the appalling novelty of the circumstances, he might have caught the infection of her panic, in which case it is likely that both must have perished. She now screamed with terror, though without hope of calling any one to her assistance. To her amazement, the scream was answered by a whistle from above, of a tone so clear and shrill, that it was heard even amid the noise of the waterfall.

In this moment of terror and perplexity, a human face, black, and having grizzled hair hanging down over the forehead and cheeks, and mixing with mustaches and a beard of the same colour, and as much matted and tangled, looked down on them from a broken part of the rock above.

'It is The Enemy!' said the boy, who had very nearly become incapable of supporting Lady Staunton.

'No, no,' she exclaimed, inaccessible to supernatural terrors, and restored to the presence of mind of which she had been deprived by the danger of her situation, 'it is a man—For God's sake, my friend, help us!'

The face glared at them, but made no answer; in a second or two afterwards, another, that of a young lad, appeared beside the first, equally swart and begrimed, but having tangled black hair, descending in elf locks, which gave an air of wildness and ferocity to the whole expression of the countenance. Lady Staunton repeated her entreaties, clinging to the rock with more energy, as she found that, from the superstitious terror of her guide, he became incapable of supporting her. Her words were probably drowned in the roar of the falling stream, for, though she observed the lips of the younger being whom she supplicated move as he spoke in reply, not a word reached her ear.

A moment afterwards it appeared he had not mistaken the nature of her supplication, which, indeed, was easy to be understood from her situation and gestures. The younger apparition disappeared, and immediately after lowered a ladder of twisted osiers, about eight feet in length, and made signs to David to hold it fast while the lady ascended. Despair gives courage, and finding herself in this fearful predicament, Lady Staunton did not hesitate to risk the ascent by the precarious means which this accommodation afforded; and, carefully assisted by the person who had thus providentially come to her aid, she reached the summit in safety. She did not, however, even look around her until she saw her nephew lightly and actively follow her example, although there was now no one to hold the ladder fast. When she saw him safe she looked round, and could not help shuddering at the place and company in which she found herself.

They were on a sort of platform of rocks, surrounded on every side by precipices, or overhanging cliffs, and which it would have been scarce possible for any research to have discovered, as it did not seem to be commanded by any accessible position. It was partly covered by a huge fragment of stone, which, having fallen from the cliffs above, had been intercepted by others in its descent, and jammed so as to serve for a sloping roof to the farther part of the broad shelf or platform on which they stood. A quantity of withered moss and leaves, strewed beneath this rude and wretched shelter, showed the lairs,—they could not be termed the beds,—of those who dwelt in this eyry, for it deserved no other name. Of these, two were before Lady Staunton. One, the same who had afforded such timely assistance, stood upright before them, a tall, lathy young savage; his dress a tattered plaid and philabeg, no shoes, no stockings, no hat or bonnet, the place of the last being supplied by his hair, twisted and matted like the *glibbe* of the ancient wild Irish, and, like theirs, forming a natural thick-set, stout enough to bear off the cut of a sword. Yet the eyes of the lad were keen and sparkling; his gesture free and noble, like that of all savages. He took little notice of David Butler, but gazed with wonder on Lady Staunton, as a being different probably in dress, and superior in beauty, to anything he had ever beheld.

## JOHN CLARE                                              IV.8
### 'February: a Thaw'
from *The Shepherd's Calendar*, 1827

> The snow is gone from cottage tops
> The thatch moss glows in brighter green
> And eves in quick succession drops
> Where grinning icles once hath been
> Pit patting wi a pleasant noise
> In tubs set by the cottage door
> And ducks and geese wi happy joys
> Douse in the yard pond brimming oer
>
> The sun peeps thro the window pane
> Which childern mark wi laughing eye
> And in the wet street steal again
> To tell each other spring is nigh
> And as young hope the past recalls
> In playing groups will often draw
> Building beside the sunny walls
> Their spring-play-huts of sticks or straw

And oft in pleasures dreams they hie
Round homsteads by the village side
Scratting the hedgrow mosses bye
Where painted pooty shells abide
Mistaking oft the ivy spray
For leaves that come wi budding spring
And wondering in their search for play
Why birds delay to build and sing

The milkmaid singing leaves her bed
As glad as happy thoughts can be
While magpies chatter oer her head
As jocund in the change as she
Her cows around the closes stray
Nor lingering wait the foddering boy
Tossing the molehills in their play
And staring round in frolic joy

Ploughmen go whistling to their toils
And yoke again the rested plough
And mingling oer the mellow soils
Boys' shouts and whips are noising now
The shepherd now is often seen
By warm banks oer his work to bend
Or oer a gate or stile to lean
Chattering to a passing friend

Odd hive bees fancying winter oer
And dreaming in their combs of spring
Creeps on the slab beside their door
And strokes its legs upon its wing
While wild ones half asleep are humming
Round snowdrop bells a feeble note
And pigions coo of summer coming
Picking their feathers on the cote

The barking dogs by lane and wood
Drive sheep afield from foddering ground
And eccho in her summer mood
Briskly mocks the cheery sound
The flocks as from a prison broke
Shake their wet fleeces in the sun
While following fast a misty smoke
Reeks from the moist grass as they run

53

Nor more behind his masters heels
The dog creeps oer his winter pace
But cocks his tail and oer the fields
Runs many a wild and random chase
Following in spite of chiding calls
The startld cat wi harmless glee
Scaring her up the weed green walls
Or mossy mottld apple tree

As crows from morning perches flye
He barks and follows them in vain
Een larks will catch his nimble eye
And off he starts and barks again
Wi breathless haste and blinded guess
Oft following where the hare hath gone
Forgetting in his joys excess
His frolic puppy days are done

The gossips saunter in the sun
As at the spring from door to door
Of matters in the village done
And secret newsings mutterd oer
Young girls when they each other meet
Will stand their tales of love to tell
While going on errands down the street
Or fetching water from the well

A calm of pleasure listens round
And almost whispers winter bye
While fancy dreams of summer sounds
And quiet rapture fills the eye
The sun beams on the hedges lye
The south wind murmurs summer soft
And maids hang out white cloaths to dry
Around the eldern skirted croft

Each barns green thatch reeks in the sun
Its mate the happy sparrow calls
And as nest building spring begun
Peeps in the holes about the walls
The wren a sunny side the stack
Wi short tail ever on the strunt
Cockd gadding up above his back
Again for dancing gnats will hunt

The gladdend swine bolt from the sty
And round the yard in freedom run
Or stretching in their slumbers lye
Beside the cottage in the sun
The young horse whinneys to its mate
And sickens from the threshers door
Rubbing the straw yards banded gate
Longing for freedom on the moor

Hens leave their roosts wi cackling calls
To see the barn door free from snow
And cocks flye up the mossy walls
To clap their spangld wings and crow
About the steeples sunny top
The jackdaw flocks resemble spring
And in the stone archd windows pop
Wi summer noise and wanton wing

The small birds think their wants are oer
To see the snow hills fret again
And from the barns chaff litterd door
Betake them to the greening plain
The woodmans robin startles coy
Nor longer at his elbow comes
To peck wi hungers eager joy
Mong mossy stulps the litterd crumbs

Neath hedge and walls that screen the wind
The gnats for play will flock together
And een poor flyes odd hopes will find
To venture in the mocking weather
From out their hiding holes again
Wi feeble pace they often creep
Along the sun warmd window pane
Like dreaming things that walk in sleep

The mavis thrush wi wild delight
Upon the orchards dripping tree
Mutters to see the day so bright
Spring scraps of young hopes poesy
And oft dame stops her burring wheel
To hear the robins note once more
That tutles while he pecks his meal
From sweet briar hips beside the door

The hedghog from its hollow root
Sees the wood moss clear of snow
And hunts each hedge for fallen fruit
Crab hip and winter bitten sloe
And oft when checkd by sudden fears
As shepherd dog his haunt espies
He rolls up in a ball of spears
And all his barking rage defies

Thus nature of the spring will dream
While south winds thaw but soon again
Frost breaths upon the stiffening stream
And numbs it into ice—the plain
Soon wears its merry garb of white
And icicles that fret at noon
Will eke their icy tails at night
Beneath the chilly stars and moon

Nature soon sickens of her joys
And all is sad and dumb again
Save merry shouts of sliding boys
About the frozen furrowd plain
The foddering boy forgets his song
And silent goes wi folded arms
And croodling shepherds bend along
Crouching to the whizzing storms

# JOHN CLARE IV.9
## 'The Nightingale's Nest'
written 1825–30

Up this green woodland-ride let's softly rove,
And list the nightingale—she dwells just here.
Hush! let the wood-gate softly clap, for fear
The noise might drive her from her home of love;
For here I've heard her many a merry year—
At morn, at eve, nay, all the livelong day,
As though she lived on song. This very spot,
Just where that old man's beard all wildly trails
Rude arbours o'er the road and stops the way—
And where that child its bluebell flowers hath got,
Laughing and creeping through the mossy rails—

There have I hunted like a very boy,
Creeping on hands and knees through matted thorn
To find her nest and see her feed her young.
And vainly did I many hours employ:
All seemed as hidden as a thought unborn.
And where those crimping fern-leaves ramp among
The hazel's under-boughs, I've nestled down
And watch'd her while she sung; and her renown
Hath made me marvel that so famed a bird
Should have no better dress than russet brown.
Her wings would tremble in her ecstasy,
And feathers stand on end, as 'twere with joy,
And mouth wide open to release her heart
Of its out-sobbing songs. The happiest part
Of summer's fame she shared, for so to me
Did happy fancies shapen her employ;
But if I touched a bush or scarcely stirred,
All in a moment stopt. I watched in vain:
The timid bird had left the hazel bush,
And at a distance hid to sing again.
Lost in a wilderness of listening leaves,
Rich ecstasy would pour its luscious strain,
Till envy spurred the emulating thrush
To start less wild and scarce inferior songs;
For while of half the year care him bereaves,
To damp the ardour of his speckled breast,
The nightingale to summer's life belongs,
And naked trees and winter's nipping wrongs
Are strangers to her music and her rest.
Her joys are evergreen, her world is wide—
Hark! there she is as usual—let's be hush—
For in this blackthorn-clump, if rightly guessed,
Her curious house is hidden. Part aside
These hazel branches in a gentle way
And stoop right cautious 'neath the rustling boughs,
For we will have another search to-day
And hunt this fern-strewn thorn clump round and round;
And where this reeded wood-grass idly bows,
We'll wade right through, it is a likely nook:
In such like spots and often on the ground,
They'll build, where rude boys never think to look.
Ay, as I live! her secret nest is here,
Upon this whitethorn stump! I've searched about
For hours in vain. There! put that bramble by—

Nay, trample on its branches and get near.
How subtle is the bird! she started out,
And raised a plaintive note of danger nigh,
Ere we were past the brambles; and now, near
Her nest, she sudden stops—as choking fear
That might betray her home. So even now
We'll leave it as we found it: safety's guard
Of pathless solitudes shall keep it still.
See there! she's sitting on the old oak bough,
Mute in her fears; our presence doth retard
Her joys, and doubt turns every rapture chill.
Sing on, sweet bird! may no worse hap befall
Thy visions than the fear that now deceives.
We will not plunder music of its dower,
Nor turn this spot of happiness to thrall;
For melody seems hid in every flower
That blossoms near thy home. These harebells all
Seem bowing with the beautiful in song;
And gaping cuckoo, with its spotted leaves,
Seems blushing with the singing it has heard.
How curious is the nest! no other bird
Uses such loose materials, or weaves
Its dwelling in such spots: dead oaken leaves
Are placed without and velvet moss within,
And little scraps of grass, and—scant and spare,
Of what seem scarce materials—down and hair;
For from men's haunts she nothing seems to win.
Yet nature is the builder, and contrives
Homes for her children's comfort even here,
Where solitude's disciples spend their lives
Unseen, save when a wanderer passes near
Who loves such pleasant places. Deep adown
The nest is made, a hermit's mossy cell.
Snug lie her curious eggs in number five,
Of deadened green, or rather olive-brown;
And the old prickly thorn-bush guards them well.
So here we'll leave them, still unknown to wrong,
As the old woodland's legacy of song.

# JOHN KEATS

'To Autumn'

from 'Lamia' and other poems, 1820

Season of mists and mellow fruitfulness,
    Close bosom-friend of the maturing sun;
Conspiring with him how to load and bless
    With fruit the vines that round the thatch-eves run;
To bend with apples the moss'd cottage-trees,
    And fill all fruit with ripeness to the core;
        To swell the gourd, and plump the hazel shells
    With a sweet kernel; to set budding more,
And still more, later flowers for the bees,
Until they think warm days will never cease,
        For Summer has o'er-brimm'd their clammy cells.

Who hath not seen thee oft amid thy store?
    Sometimes whoever seeks abroad may find
Thee sitting careless on a granary floor,
    Thy hair soft-lifted by the winnowing wind;
Or on a half-reap'd furrow sound asleep,
    Drows'd with the fume of poppies, while thy hook
        Spares the next swath and all its twined flowers:
And sometimes like a gleaner thou dost keep
    Steady thy laden head across a brook;
    Or by a cyder-press, with patient look,
        Thou watchest the last oozings hours by hours.

Where are the songs of Spring? Ay, where are they?
    Think not of them, thou hast thy music too,—
While barred clouds bloom the soft-dying day,
    And touch the stubble-plains with rosy hue;
Then in a wailful choir the small gnats mourn
    Among the river sallows, borne aloft
        Or sinking as the light wind lives or dies;
And full-grown lambs loud bleat from hilly bourn;
    Hedge-crickets sing; and now with treble soft
    The red-breast whistles from a garden-croft;
        And gathering swallows twitter in the skies.

# JOHN KEATS IV.11
## The lovers and the merchant brothers
from 'Isabella or The Pot of Basil', 1820

> Parting they seem'd to tread upon the air,
>    Twin roses by the zephyr blown apart
> Only to meet again more close, and share
>    The inward fragrance of each other's heart.
> She, to her chamber gone, a ditty fair
>    Sang, of delicious love and honey'd dart;
> He with light steps went up a western hill,
> And bade the sun farewell, and joy'd his fill.
>
> All close they met again, before the dusk
>    Had taken from the stars its pleasant veil,
> All close they met, all eves, before the dusk
>    Had taken from the stars its pleasant veil,
> Close in a bower of hyacinth and musk,
>    Unknown of any, free from whispering tale.
> Ah! better had it been for ever so,
> Than idle ears should pleasure in their woe.
>
> . . .
>
> With her two brothers this fair lady dwelt,
>    Enriched from ancestral merchandise,
> And for them many a weary hand did swelt
>    In torchèd mines and noisy factories,
> And many once proud-quiver'd loins did melt
>    In blood from stinging whip; with hollow eyes
> Many all day in dazzling river stood,
> To take the rich-ored driftings of the flood.
>
> For them the Ceylon diver held his breath,
>    And went all naked to the hungry shark;
> For them his ears gush'd blood; for them in death
>    The seal on the cold ice with piteous bark
> Lay full of darts; for them alone did seethe
>    A thousand men in troubles wide and dark:
> Half-ignorant, they turn'd an easy wheel,
> That set sharp racks at work, to pinch and peel.
>
> Why were they proud? Because their marble founts
>    Gush'd with more pride than do a wretch's tears?

Why were they proud? Because fair orange-mounts
   Were of more soft ascent than lazar stairs!
Why were they proud? Because red-lined accounts
   Were richer than the songs of Grecian years?
Why were they proud? again we ask aloud,
Why in the name of Glory were they proud?

   . . .

How was it these same ledger-men could spy
   Fair Isabella in her downy nest?
How could they find out in Lorenzo's eye
   A straying from his toil? Hot Egypt's pest
Into their vision covetous and sly!
   How could these money-bags see east and west?
Yet so they did—and every dealer fair
Must see behind, as doth the hunted hare.

4. Richard Wilson: Snowdon (1774)

5. J. M. W. Turner: Buttermere Lake with part of Cromack (1798)

6. John Constable: Sketch for 'Hadleigh Castle' (1829)

7. John Constable: Root of a tree at Hampstead (1831)

8. John Ruskin: Study of Gneiss Rock, Glenfinlas (1853)

# V  The Factory System

HOUSE OF COMMONS SELECT COMMITTEE ON          V.1
THE WOOLLEN INDUSTRY
'The Factory System and the Domestic System'
from *Parliamentary Papers*, 1806

. . . it may be expedient for Your Committee to state that there are
three different modes of carrying on the Woollen Manufacture; that of
the Master Clothier of the West of England, the Factory, and, the
Domestic System.

In all the Western Counties as well as in the North, there are Factories, but the Master Clothier of the West of England buys his Wool
from the Importer, if it be Foreign, or in the Fleece, or of the Woolstapler, if it be of Domestic growth; after which, in all the different
processes through which it passes, he is under the necessity of employing as many distinct classes of persons; sometimes working in their own
houses, sometimes in those of the Master Clothier, but none of them
going out of their proper line. Each class of Workmen, however, acquires
great skill in performing its particular operation, and hence may have
arisen the acknowledged excellence, and, till of late, superiority, of the
Cloths of the West of England. It is however a remarkable fact, of
which Your Committee has been assured by one of its own Members,
that previously to the introduction of Machinery, it was very common,
and it is said sometimes to happen at this day, for the North Country-
man to come into the West of England, and, in the Clothing Districts
of that part of the Kingdom, to purchase his Wool; which he carries
home; where, having worked it up into Cloth, he brings it back again,
and sells it in its native District. This is supposed to arise from the
Northern Clothier being at liberty to work himself, and employ his
own family and others, in any way which his interest or convenience
may suggest.

In the Factory system, the Master Manufacturers, who sometimes
possess a very great capital, employ in one or more Buildings or Factories, under their own or their Superintendant's inspection, a number
of Workmen, more or fewer according to the extent of their Trade. This
system, it is obvious, admits in practice of local variations. But both in
the system of the West of England Clothier, and in the Factory system,
the work, generally speaking, is done by persons who have no property

in the goods they manufacture, for in this consists the essential distinction between the two former systems, and the Domestic.

In the last-mentioned, or Domestic system, which is that of Yorkshire, the Manufacture is conducted by a multitude of Master Manufacturers, generally possessing a very small, and scarcely ever any great extent of Capital. They buy the Wool of the Dealer; and, in their own houses, assisted by their wives and children, and from two or three to six or seven Journeymen, they dye it (when dying is necessary) and through all the different stages work it up into undressed Cloth.

Various processes however, the chief of which were formerly done by hand, under the Manufacturer's own roof, are now performed by Machinery, in public Mills, as they are called, which work for hire. There are several such Mills near every manufacturing Village, so that the Manufacturer, with little inconvenience or loss of time, carries thither his goods, and fetches them back again when the process is completed. When it has attained to the state of undressed Cloth, he carries it on the Market-day to a public Hall or Market, where the Merchants repair to purchase.

Several thousands of these small Master Manufacturers attend the Market of Leeds, where there are three Halls for the exposure and sale of their Cloths: and there are other similar Halls, where the same system of selling in public Market prevails, at Bradford, Halifax, and Huddersfield. The Halls consist of long walks or galleries, throughout the whole length of which the Master Manufacturers stand in a double row, each behind his own little division or stand, as it is termed, on which his goods are exposed to sale. In the interval between these rows the Merchants pass along, and make their purchases. At the end of an hour, on the ringing of a bell, the Market closes, and such Cloths as have been purchased are carried home to the Merchants houses; such Goods as remain unsold continuing in the Halls till they find a purchaser at some ensuing Market. It should however be remarked, that a practice has also obtained of late years, of Merchants giving out Samples to some Manufacturer whom they approve, which Goods are brought to the Merchant directly, without ever coming into the Halls. These however, no less than the others, are manufactured by him in his own family. The greater Merchants have their working-room, or, as it is termed, their Shop, in which their Workmen, or, as they are termed, Croppers, all work together. The Goods which, as it has been already stated, are bought in the undressed state, here undergo various processes, till, being completely finished, they are sent away for the use of the consumer, either in the Home or the Foreign Market; the Merchants sending them abroad directly without the intervention of any other Factor. Sometimes again the Goods are dressed at a stated rate by Dressers, who take them in for that purpose.

The greater part of the Domestic Clothiers live in Villages and detached houses, covering the whole face of a district of from 20 to 30 miles in length, and from 12 to 15 in breadth. Coal abounds throughout the whole of it; and a great proportion of the Manufacturers occupy a little Land, from 3 to 12 or 15 acres each. They often likewise keep a Horse, to carry their Cloth to the Fulling Mill and the Market.

Though the system which has been just described be that which has been generally established in the West Riding of Yorkshire, yet there have long been a few Factories in the neighbourhood of Halifax and Huddersfield; and four or five more, one however of which has been since discontinued, have been set on foot not many years ago in the neighbourhood of Leeds. These have for some time been objects of great jealousy to the Domestic Clothiers. The most serious apprehensions have been stated, by Witnesses who have given their evidence before Your Committee in behalf of the Domestic Manufacturers, lest the Factory system should gradually root out the Domestic; and lest the independent little Master Manufacturer, who works on his own account, should sink into a Journeyman working for hire.

Your Committee cannot wonder that the Domestic Clothiers of Yorkshire are warmly attached to their accustomed mode of carrying on the manufacture: It is not merely that they are *accustomed* to it—it obviously possesses many eminent advantages seldom found in a great manufacture.

It is one peculiar recommendation of the Domestic system of Manufacture, that, as it has been expressly stated to Your Committee, a young man of good character can always obtain credit for as much Wool as will enable him to set up as a little Master Manufacturer, and the public Mills, which are now established in all parts of the Clothing District, and which work for hire at an easy rate, enable him to command the use of very expensive and complicated Machines, the construction and necessary repairs of which would require a considerable capital. Thus, instances not unfrequently occur, wherein men rise from low beginnings, if not to excessive wealth, yet to a situation of comfort and independence.

It is another advantage of the Domestic system of Manufacture, and an advantage which is obviously not confined to the individuals who are engaged in it, but which, as well as other parts of this system, extends its benefits to the Landholder, that any sudden stoppage of a Foreign Market, any failure of a great House, or any other of those adverse shocks to which our Foreign Trade especially is liable, in its present extended state, has not the effect of throwing a great number of Workmen out of employ, as it often does, when the stroke falls on the capital of a single individual. In the Domestic system, the loss is spread over a large superficies; it affects the whole body of the

Manufacturers; and, though each little Master be a sufferer, yet few if any feel the blow so severely as to be altogether ruined. Moreover, it appears in evidence, that, in such cases as these, they seldom turn off any of their standing set of Journeymen, but keep them at work in hopes of better times.

On the whole, Your Committee feel no little satisfaction in bearing their testimony to the merits of the Domestic system of Manufacture; to the facilities it affords to men of steadiness and industry to establish themselves as little Master Manufacturers, and maintain their families in comfort by their own industry and frugality; and to the encouragement which it thus holds out to domestic habits and virtues. Neither can they omit to notice its favourable tendencies on the health and morals of a large and important class of the community.

On the whole, Your Committee do not wonder that the Domestic Clothiers are warmly attached to their peculiar system. This is a predilection in which the Committee participate; but at the same time they must declare, that they see at present no solid ground for the alarm which has gone forth, lest the Halls should be deserted, and the generality of Merchants should set up Factories. Your Committee, however, must not withhold the declaration, that if any such disposition had been perceived, it must have been their less pleasing duty to state, that it would by no means have followed, that it was a disposition to be counteracted by positive law.

The right of every man to employ the Capital he inherits, or has acquired, according to his own discretion, without molestation or obstruction, so long as he does not infringe on the rights or property of others, is one of those privileges which the free and happy Constitution of this Country has long accustomed every Briton to consider as his birthright; and it cannot therefore be necessary for Your Committee to enlarge on its value, or to illustrate its effects. These would be indubitably confirmed by an appeal to our own Commercial prosperity, no less than by the history of other trading nations, in which it has been ever found, that Commerce and Manufactures have flourished in free, and declined in despotic countries. But without recurring to principles, of which, even under different circumstances, Your Committee would be compelled to admit the force, Your Committee have the satisfaction of seeing, that the apprehensions entertained of Factories are not only vicious in principle, but that they are practically erroneous; to such a degree, that even the very opposite dispositions might be reasonably entertained; nor would it be difficult to prove, that the Factories, to a certain extent at least, and in the present day, seem absolutely necessary to the well-being of the Domestic system; supplying those very particulars wherein the Domestic system must be acknowledged to be inherently defective: for, it is obvious, that the little Master Manufacturers cannot afford, like the man who possesses considerable capital, to try the experiments which are requisite, and incur the risks, and even losses, which almost always occur, in inventing and perfecting new articles of manufacture, or in carrying to a state of greater perfection articles already established. He cannot learn, by personal inspection, the wants and habits, the arts, manufactures, and improvements of foreign countries; diligence, economy, and prudence are the requisites of his character, not invention, taste, and enterprize; nor would he be warranted in hazarding the loss of any part of his small capital: He walks in a sure road as long as he treads in the beaten track; but he must not deviate into the paths of speculation. The Owner of a Factory, on the contrary, being commonly possessed of a large capital, and having all his workmen employed under his own immediate superintendance, may make experiments, hazard speculation, invent shorter or better modes of performing old processes, may introduce new articles, and improve and perfect old ones, thus giving the range to his taste and fancy, and, thereby alone, enabling our Manufacturers to stand the competition with their commercial rivals in other Countries. Meanwhile, as is well worthy of remark (and experience abundantly warrants the assertion), many of these new fabrics and inventions, when their success is once established, become general among the whole body of Manufacturers: the Domestic Manufacturers themselves thus benefiting, in the end, from those very Factories which had been at first the objects of their jealousy. The history of almost all our other Manufactures, in which great improvements have been made of late years, in some cases at an immense expence, and after numbers of unsuccessful experiments, strikingly illustrates and enforces the above remarks. It is besides an acknowledged fact, that the Owners of Factories are often among the most extensive purchasers at the Halls, where they buy from the Domestic Clothier the established articles of Manufacture, or are able at once to answer a great and sudden order; while, at home, and under their own superintendance, they make their fancy goods, and any articles of a newer, more costly, or more delicate quality, to which they are enabled by the Domestic system to apply a much larger proportion of their capital. Thus, the two Systems, instead of rivalling, are mutual aids to each other; each supplying the other's defects, and promoting the other's prosperity.

## ANDREW URE V.2

### The Blessings of the Factory System

from *The Philosophy of Manufactures*, 1835

This island is pre-eminent among civilized nations for the prodigious development of its factory wealth, and has been therefore long viewed with a jealous admiration by foreign powers. This very pre-eminence, however, has been contemplated in a very different light by many influential members of our own community, and has been even denounced by them as the certain origin of innumerable evils to the people, and of revolutionary convulsions to the state. If the affairs of the kingdom be wisely administered, I believe such allegations and fears will prove to be groundless, and to proceed more from the envy of one ancient and powerful order of the commonwealth, towards another suddenly grown into political importance than from the nature of things.

In the recent discussions concerning our factories, no circumstance is so deserving of remark, as the gross ignorance evinced by our leading legislators and economists, gentlemen well informed in other respects, relative to the nature of those stupendous manufactures which have so long provided the rulers of the kingdom with the resources of war, and a great body of the people with comfortable subsistence; which have, in fact, made this island the arbiter of many nations, and the benefactor of the globe itself. Till this ignorance be dispelled, no sound legislation need be expected on manufacturing subjects. To effect this purpose, is a principal, but not the sole aim of the present volume, for it is intended also to convey specific information to the classes directly concerned in the manufactures, as well as general knowledge to the community at large, and particularly to young persons about to make the choice of a profession.

The blessings which physico-mechanical science has bestowed on society, and the means it has still in store for ameliorating the lot of mankind, has been too little dwelt upon; while, on the other hand, it has been accused of lending itself to the rich capitalists as an instrument for harassing the poor, and of exacting from the operative an accelerated rate of work. It has been said, for example, that the steam-engine now drives the powerlooms with such velocity as to urge on their attendant weavers at the same rapid pace; but the handweaver, not being subjected to this restless agent, can throw his shuttle and move his treddles as his convenience. There is, however, this difference in the two cases, that in the factory, every member of the loom is so adjusted, that the driving force leaves the attendant nearly nothing at all to do, certainly no muscular fatigue to sustain, while it procures for him good, unfailing wages, besides a healthy workshop gratis: whereas the non-factory weaver, having everything to execute by muscular exertion, finds the labour irksome, makes in consequence innumerable short pauses, separately of little account, but great when added together; earns therefore proportionally low wages, while he loses his health by poor diet and the dampness of his hovel. . . .

The constant aim and effect of scientific improvement in manufactures are philanthropic, as they tend to relieve the workmen either from niceties of adjustment which exhaust his mind and fatigue his eyes, or from painful repetition of effort which distort or wear out his frame. At every step of each manufacturing process described in this volume, the humanity of science will be manifest. . . .

Self-acting inventions . . . , however admirable as exercises of mechanical science, do nothing towards the supply of the physical necessities of society. Man stands in daily want of food, fuel, clothing, and shelter; and is bound to devote the powers of body and mind, of nature and art, in the first place to provide for himself and his dependents a sufficiency of these necessaries, without which there can be no comfort, nor leisure for the cultivation of the taste and intellect. To the production of food and domestic accommodation, not many automatic inventions have been applied, or seem to be extensively applicable; though, for modifying them to the purposes of luxury, many curious contrivances have been made. Machines, more or less automatic, are embodied in the coal-mines of Great Britain; but such combinations have been mainly directed, in this as well as other countries, to the materials of clothing. These chiefly consist of flexible fibres of vegetable or animal origin, twisted into smooth, tenacious threads, which are then woven into cloth by being decussated in a loom. Of the animal kingdom, silk, wool, and hair, are the principal textile products. The vegetable tribes furnish cotton, flax, hemp, besides several other fibrous substances of inferior importance. . . .

The term *Factory*, in technology, designates the combined operation of many orders of work-people, adult and young, in tending with assiduous skill a system of productive machines continuously impelled by a central power. This definition includes such organizations as cotton-mills, flax-mills, silk-mills, woollen-mills, and certain engineering works; but it excludes those in which the mechanisms do not form a connected series, nor are dependent on one prime mover. Of the latter class, examples occur in iron-works, dye-works, soap-works, brass-foundaries, &c. Some authors, indeed, have comprehended under the title *factory*, all extensive establishments wherein a number of people co-operate towards a com-purpose of art; and would therefore rank breweries, distilleries, as well as the workshops of carpenters, turners, coopers, &c., under the factory system. But I conceive that this title, in its strictest sense, involves the idea of a vast automaton, composed of various mechanical and intellectual organs, acting in uninterrupted concert for the production of a common object, all of them being subordinated to a self-regulated moving force. If the marshalling of human beings in systematic order for the execution of any technical enterprise were allowed to constitute a factory, this term might embrace every department of civil and military engineering; a latitude of application quite inadmissible. . . .

In my recent tour, continued during several months, through the manufacturing districts, I have seen tens of thousands of old, young, and middle-aged of both sexes, many of them too feeble to get their daily bread by any of the former modes of industry, earning abundant food, raiment, and domestic accommodation, without perspiring at a single pore, screened meanwhile from the summer's sun and the winter's frost, in apartments more airy and salubrious than those of the metropolis, in which our legislative and fashionable aristocracies assemble. In those spacious halls the benignant power of steam summons around him his myriads of willing menials, and assigns to each the regulated task, substituting for painful muscular effort on their part, the energies of his own gigantic arm, and demanding in return only attention and dexterity to correct such little aberrations as casually occur in his workmanship. The gentle docility of this moving force qualifies it for impelling the tiny bobbins of the lace-machine with a precision and speed inimitable by the most dexterous hands, directed by the sharpest eyes. Hence, under its auspices, and in obedience to Arkwright's polity, magnificent edifices, surpassing far in number, value, usefulness, and ingenuity of construction, the boasted monuments of Asiatic, Egyptian, and Roman despotism, have, within the short period of fifty years, risen up in this kingdom, to show to what extent, capital, industry, and science may augment the resources of a state, while they meliorate the condition of its citizens. Such is the factory system, replete with prodigies in mechanics and political economy, which promises, in its future growth, to become the great minister of civilization to the terraqueous globe, enabling this country, as its heart, to diffuse along with its commerce, the life-blood of science and religion to myriads of people still lying 'in the region and shadow of death.'

When Adam Smith wrote his immortal elements of economics, automatic machinery being hardly known, he was properly led to regard the division of labour as the grand principle of manufacturing improvement; and he showed, in the example of pinmaking, how each handicraftsman, being thereby enabled to perfect himself by practice in one point, became a quicker and cheaper workman. In each branch of manufacture he saw that some parts were, on that principle, of easy execution, like the cutting of pin wires into uniform lengths, and some were comparatively difficult, like the formation and fixation of their heads; and therefore he concluded that to each a workman of appropriate value and cost was naturally assigned. This appropriation forms the very essence of the division of labour, and has been constantly made since the origin of society. The ploughman, with powerful hand and skilful eye, has been always hired at high wages to form the furrow, and the ploughboy at low wages, to lead the team. But what was in Dr. Smith's

70

time a topic of useful illustration, cannot now be used without risk of misleading the public mind as to the right principle of manufacturing industry. In fact, the division, or rather adaptation of labour to the different talents of men, is little thought of in factory employment. On the contrary, wherever a process requires peculiar dexterity and steadiness of hand, it is withdrawn as soon as possible from the *cunning* workman, who is prone to irregularities of many kinds, and it is placed in charge of a peculiar mechanism, so self-regulating, that a child may superintend it.

The principle of the factory system then is, to substitute mechanical science for hand skill, and the partition of a process into its essential constituents, for the division or graduation of labour among artisans. On the handicraft plan, labour more or less skilled, was usually the most expensive element of production—*Materiam superabat opus*; but on the automatic plan, skilled labour gets progressively superseded, and will, eventually, be replaced by mere overlookers of machines. . . .

Steam-engines furnish the means not only of their support but of their multiplication. They create a vast demand for fuel; and, while they lend their powerful arms to drain the pits and to raise the coals, they call into employment multitudes of miners, engineers, shipbuilders, and sailors, and cause the construction of canals and railways: and, while they enable these rich fields of industry to be cultivated to the utmost, they leave thousands of fine arable fields free for the production of food to man, which must have been otherwise allotted to the food of horses. Steam-engines moreover, by the cheapness and steadiness of their action, fabricate cheap goods, and procure in their exchange a liberal supply of the necessaries and comforts of life, produced in foreign lands.

Improvements in machinery have a three-fold bearing:—

1st. They make it possible to fabricate some articles which, but for them, could not be fabricated at all.

2d. They enable an operative to turn out a greater quantity of work than he could before,—time, labour, and quality of work remaining constant.

3d. They effect a substitution of labour comparatively unskilled, for that which is more skilled. . . .

The attempts continually made to carry our implements and machines into foreign countries, and to tempt our artisans to settle and superintend them there, evince the high value set by other nations on our mechanical substitutes for hand labour; and as they cannot be directly counteracted, they should be rendered, as far as possible, unavailing, by introducing such successive improvements at home as may always keep us foremost in the career of construction. It would be therefore no less disastrous to the operative, than to the capitalist, were any extraneous obstacles thrown in their way, since any good machine suppressed, or rejected, in this country, would infallibly be received with open arms by some of our neighbours, and most readily by our mechanical rivals in France, Belgium, Germany, and the United States. . . .

It is one of the most important truths resulting from the analysis of manufacturing industry, that unions are conspiracies of workmen against the interests of their own order, and never fail to end in the suicide of the body corporate which forms them; an event the more speedy, the more coercive or the better organized the union is. The very name of union makes capital restive, and puts ingenuity on the alert to defeat its objects. When the stream of labour is suffered to glide on quietly within its banks, all goes well; when forcibly dammed up, it becomes unprofitably stagnant for a time, and then brings on a disastrous inundation. Were it not for unions, the vicissitudes of employment, and the substitution of automatic for hand work, would seldom be so abrupt as to distress the operative.

Some may imagine that the present work, which purposes to give a minute analysis and description of the several processes of manufacture, may prove injurious to the trade of this country, by putting foreigners in possession of much useful knowledge, now hardly within their reach. To this I reply, that knowledge is available just in proportion to the capacity and means of the persons who acquire it. Every invention and improvement relative to cotton fabrics is primarily attracted to Manchester as the surest and most productive scene of its development, where it can be most profitable to the inventor, because most profitable to the trade concentred there. Lancashire is the fertile and well-laboured soil in which the seed of factory knowledge will bring forth fruit one hundred fold, whereas abroad it can yield little more than a tenfold return.

# JOHN FIELDEN                                                    V.3
## The Effects of Repetition
from *The Curse of the Factory System*, 1836

As I have been personally and from an early age engaged in the operations connected with factory labour; that is to say, for about forty years, a short account of my own experience may not be useless in this place, as it is this experience which teaches me to scoff at the representations of those who speak of the labour of factories as 'very light,' and 'so easy, as to require no muscular exertion.' I well remember being set to work in my father's mill when I was little more than ten years old; my associates, too, in the labour and in recreation are fresh in my memory. Only a few of them are now alive; some dying very young, others living to become men and women; but many of those who lived, have died off before they had attained the age of fifty years, having the appearance of being much older, a premature appearance of age which I verily believe was caused by the nature of the employment in which they had been brought up. For several years after I began to work in the mill, the hours of labour at our works did not exceed *ten* in the day, winter and summer, and even with the labour of those hours, I shall never forget the fatigue I often felt before the day ended, and the anxiety of us all to be relieved from the unvarying and irksome toil we had gone through before we could obtain relief by such play and amusements as we resorted to when liberated from our work. I allude to this fact, because it is not uncommon for persons to infer, that, because the children who work in factories are seen to play like other children when they have time to do so, the labour is, therefore, light, and does not fatigue them. The reverse of this conclusion I know to be the truth. I know the effect which ten hours' labour had upon myself; I who had the attention of parents better able than those of my companions to allow me extraordinary occasional indulgence. And he knows very little of human nature who does not know, that, to a child, diversion is so essential, that it will undergo even exhaustion in its amusements. I protest, therefore, against the reasoning, that, because a child is not brought so low in spirit as to be incapable of enjoying the diversions of a child, it is not worked to the utmost that its feeble frame and constitution will bear.

I well know, too, from my own experience, that the labour now undergone in the factories is much greater than it used to be, owing to the greater attention and activity required by the greatly-increased speed which is given to the machinery that the children have to attend to, when we compare it with what it was thirty or forty years ago; and, therefore, I fully agree with the Government Commissioners, that a restriction to ten hours per day, is *not a sufficient protection to* children. . . .

Here, then, is the 'curse' of our factory-system: as improvements in machinery have gone on, the 'avarice of masters' has prompted many to exact more labour from their hands than they were fitted by nature to perform, and those who have wished for the hours of labour to be less for all ages than the legislature would even yet sanction, have had no alternative but to conform more or less to the prevailing practice, or abandon the trade altogether. This has been the case with regard to myself and my partners. . . .

The political economists in England, who everlastingly bellow out 'foreign competition,' and who, during these ten years, have been receiving *three* pieces of the English manufactured goods in return for their fixed incomes, where they ought to have received *one* piece only; these gentlemen, I have no doubt, know their watch-word to be a fallacy; and their anxiety to keep up the delusion among the manufacturers, is a convincing proof of it. A Dr. URE is, it seems, now amongst the most conspicuous of the agents of these philosophers, and is trying, not to get the manufacturers down to *ten* hours' labour a day, but to lengthen the period to *fifteen* or *sixteen* hours a day, by telling us that some of our competitors work that long time. . . .

The hand-loom weaver neither goes himself nor sends his child to a factory, when he can by any possibility avoid it. . . .

The reader should know, that the hand-loom weavers are a very large body in Lancashire, extremely poor, very laborious, and the makers of some of the most beautiful of our manufactures; but their dislike to the factories is such, that, if they could obtain work in them and get better wages, they (except a very few comparatively) will neither go into them, nor suffer their children to go. A committee of the House of Commons sat in the years 1834 and 1835 to consider their sufferings, and, before that Committee it was proved, that more than one-half of the borough of Bolton (containing 42,000 souls) consisted of hand-loom weavers; and that a large majority of them, with the families depending on them for support, lived upon the pittance of 2¾ (twopence threefarthings) per day! The members of that Committee, of which I myself was one, constantly put it to the weavers who appeared before it, why they did not go into the factories, when they knew they would get so much more money. Their answers were, that, in the first place, work in the factories was not so easily obtained as the members of the Committee seemed to suppose; and I myself knew this to be the case, for, before I came up to Parliament, I was applied to weekly by scores of hand-loom weavers, who were so pressed down in their condition as to be obliged to seek such work, and it gave me and my partners no small pain to have the applications, and be compelled to refuse work to the many who applied for it. They answered, in the next place, that the long hours, the congregating young persons together early and late, and the tragical accidents of the factories, prevented their doing so. One poor man, a silk-weaver in Manchester, who was examined, stated that his little son had succeeded, with some difficulty, in getting into a factory. I will quote his evidence from the Report of the Hand-loom Weavers' Committee, 1835, p. 185.

'Did you persevere in getting employment for that boy?—The boy was a very good lad, and he actually went against my will; I was disinclined to let him go to the factory, for I am averse to children going to factories.

Is he there still?—No: I am sorry to say he is not.

What reason have you to be sorry?—I will relate to the Committee the circumstance. He pressed me to let him go to work at a cotton-mill, and he did go: I was very reluctant to let him; he was not three days at work when he received a crush in his head, which ended his existence in twenty days.

Did he receive that hurt from the machinery?—Yes.'

The same witness spoke of the immoral tendency of congregating young people in the factories so early and so late as is practised, and gave all these as his reasons for coming to this conclusion: 'I have had seven boys, but if I had 77 I should never send one to a cotton factory!'

# KARL MARX                                                    V.4
## 'Machinery and Large-Scale Industry'
from *Capital* (*Das Kapital*), 1867

In manufacture, the revolution in the mode of production begins with the labour-power, in modern industry it begins with the instruments of labour. Our first inquiry then is, how the instruments of labour are converted from tools into machines, or what is the difference between a machine and the implements of a handicraft? We are only concerned here with striking and general characteristics; for epochs in the history of society are no more separated from each other by hard and fast lines of demarcation, than are geological epochs.

Mathematicians and mechanicians, and in this they are followed by a few English economists, call a tool a simple machine, and a machine a complex tool. They see no essential difference between them, and even give the name of machine to the simple mechanical powers, the lever, the inclined plane, the screw, the wedge, &c. . . . Another explanation of the difference between tool and machine is that in the case of a tool, man is the motive power, while the motive power of a machine is something different from man, is, for instance, an animal, water, wind, and so on. . . . (But) since the application of animal power is one of man's earliest inventions, production by machinery would have preceded production by handicrafts. When in 1735, John Wyalt brought out his spinning machine, and began the industrial revolution of the 18th century, not a word did he say about an ass driving it instead of a man, and yet this part fell to the ass. He described it as a machine 'to spin without fingers.'*

*Before his time, spinning machines, although very imperfect ones, had already been used, and Italy was probably the country of their first appearance. A critical history of technology would show how little any of the inventions of the 18th century are the work of a single individual. Hitherto there is no such book. Darwin has interested us in the history of Nature's Technology, *i.e.*, in the formation of the organs of plants and animals, which organs serve as instruments of production for sustaining life. Does not the history of the productive organs of man, of organs that are the material basis of all social organisation, deserve equal attention? . . .

The machine proper is . . . a mechanism that, after being set in motion, performs with its tools the same operations that were formerly done by the workman with similar tools. Whether the motive power is derived from man, or from some other machine, makes no difference in this respect. From the moment that the tool proper is taken from man, and fitted into a mechanism, a machine takes the place of a mere implement. The difference strikes one at once, even in those cases where man himself continues to be the prime mover. The number of implements that he himself can use simultaneously, is limited by the number of his own natural instruments of production, by the number of his bodily organs. In Germany, they tried at first to make one spinner work two spinning wheels, that is, to work simultaneously with both hands and both feet. This was too difficult. Later, a treddle spinning wheel with two spindles was invented, but adepts in spinning, who could spin two threads at once, were almost as scarce as two-headed men. The Jenny, on the other hand, even at its very birth, spun with 12–18 spindles, and the stocking-loom knits with many thousand needles at once. The number of tools that a machine can bring into play simultaneously, is from the very first emancipated from the organic limits that hedge in the tools of a handicraftsman.

In many manual implements the distinction between man as mere motive power, and man as the workman or operator properly so-called, is brought into striking contrast. For instance, the foot is merely the prime mover of the spinning wheel, while the hand, working with the spindle, and drawing and twisting, performs the real operation of spinning. It is this last part of the handicraftsman's implement that is first seized upon by the industrial revolution, leaving to the workman, in addition to his new labour of watching the machine with his eyes and correcting its mistakes with his hands, the merely mechanical part of being the moving power. On the other hand, implements, in regard to which man has always acted as a simple motive power, as, for instance, by turning the crank of a mill,* by pumping, by moving up and down the arm of a bellows, by pounding with a mortar, &c., such implements soon call for the application of animals, water,† and wind as motive powers. Here and there, long before the period of manufacture, and also, to some extent, during that period, these implements pass over into machines, but without creating any revolution in the mode of

*Moses says: 'Thou shalt not muzzle the ox that treads the corn.' The Christian philanthropists of Germany, on the contrary, fastened a wooden board round the necks of the serfs, whom they used as a motive power for grinding, in order to prevent them from putting flour into their mouths with their hands.

†It was partly the want of streams with a good fall on them, and partly their battles with superabundance of water in other respects, that compelled the Dutch to resort to wind as a motive power. The windmill itself they got from Germany, where its invention was the origin of a pretty squabble between the nobles, the priests, and the emperor, as to which of those three the wind 'belonged.'. . .

production. It becomes evident, in the period of Large-Scale Industry, that these implements, even under their form of manual tools, are already machines. For instance, the pumps with which the Dutch, in 1836–7, emptied the Lake of Harlem, were constructed on the principle of ordinary pumps; the only difference being, that their pistons were driven by cyclopean steam-engines, instead of by men. The common and very imperfect bellows of the blacksmith is, in England, occasionally converted into a blowing-engine, by connecting its arm with a steam-engine. The steam-engine itself, such as it was at its invention, during the manufacturing period at the close of the 17th century, and such as it continued to be down to 1780,* did not give rise to any industrial revolution. It was, on the contrary, the invention of machines that made a revolution in the form of steam-engines necessary. As soon as man, instead of working with an implement on the subject of his labour, becomes merely the motive power of an implement-machine, it is a mere accident that motive power takes the disguise of human muscle; and it may equally well take the form of wind, water or steam. . . .

The machine, which is the starting point of the industrial revolution, supersedes the workman, who handles a single tool, by a mechanism operating with a number of similar tools, and set in motion by a single motive power, whatever the form of that power may be. Here we have the machine, but only as an elementary factor of production by machinery.

Increase in the size of the machine, and in the number of its working tools, calls for a more massive mechanism to drive it; and this mechanism requires, in order to overcome its resistance, a mightier moving power than that of man, apart from the fact that man is a very imperfect instrument for producing uniform continued motion. But assuming that he is acting simply as a motor, that a machine has taken the place of his tool, it is evident that he can be replaced by natural forces. Of all the great motors handed down from the manufacturing period, horse-power is the worst, partly because a horse has a head of his own, partly because he is costly, and the extent to which he is applicable in factories is very restricted. Nevertheless the horse was extensively used during the infancy of Large-Scale Industry. This is proved, as well by the complaints of contemporary agriculturists, as by the term 'horse-power,' which has survived to this day as an expression for mechanical force.

Wind was too inconstant and uncontrollable, and besides, in England, the birthplace of Large-Scale Industry, the use of water-power preponderated even during the manufacturing period. In the 17th century attempts

*It was, indeed, very much improved by Watt's first so-called single acting engine; but, in this form, it continued to be a mere machine for raising water, and the liquor from salt mines.

77

had already been made to turn two pairs of millstones with a single water-wheel. But the increased size of the gearing was too much for the water-power, which had now become insufficient, and this was one of the circumstances that led to a more accurate investigation of the laws of friction. In the same way the irregularity caused by the motive power in mills that were put in motion by pushing and pulling a lever, led to the theory, and the application, of the fly-wheel, which afterwards plays so important a part in Large-Scale Industry. In this way, during the manufacturing period, were developed the first scientific and technical elements of Modern Mechanical Industry. Arkwright's throstle-spinning mill was from the very first turned by water. But for all that, the use of water, as the predominant motive power, was beset with difficulties. It could not be increased at will, it failed at certain seasons of the year, and, above all, it was essentially local.* Not till the invention of Watt's second and so called double-acting steam-engine, was a prime mover found, that begot its own force by the consumption of coal and water, whose power was entirely under man's control, that was mobile and a means of locomotion, that was urban and not, like the water-wheel, rural, that permitted production to be concentrated in towns instead of, like the water-wheels, being scattered up and down the country,† that was of universal technical application, and, relatively speaking, little affected in its choice of residence by local circumstances. The greatness of Watt's genius showed itself in the specification of the patent that he took out in April, 1784. In that specification his steam-engine is described, not as an invention for a specific purpose, but as an agent universally applicable in Mechanical Industry. In it he points out applications, many of which, as for instance, the steam-hammer, were not introduced till half a century later. Nevertheless he doubted the use of steam-engines in navigation. His successors, Boulton and Watt, sent to the exhibition of 1851 steam-engines of colossal size for ocean steamers.

As soon as tools had been converted from being manual implements of man into implements of a mechanical apparatus, of a machine, the motive mechanism also acquired an independent form, entirely emancipated from the restraints of human strength. Thereupon the individual

*The modern turbine frees the industrial exploitation of water-power from many of its former fetters.
†'In the early days of textile manufactures, the locality of the factory depended upon the existence of a stream having a sufficient fall to turn a water-wheel; and, although the establishment of the water mills was the commencement of the breaking up of the domestic system of manufacture, yet the mills necessarily situated upon streams, and frequently at considerable distances the one from the other, formed part of a rural, rather than an urban system; and it was not until the introduction of the steam-power as a substitute for the stream that factories were congregated in towns, and localities where the coal and water required for the production of steam were found in sufficient quantities. The steam-engine is the parent of manufacturing towns.' (A. Redgrave in 'Reports of the Insp. of Fact. 30th April, 1866,' p. 36.)

machine, that we have hitherto been considering, sinks into a mere factor in production by machinery. One motive mechanism was now able to drive many machines at once. The motive mechanism grows with the number of the machines that are turned simultaneously, and the transmitting mechanism becomes a widespreading apparatus. . . .

A real machinery system . . . does not take the place of . . . independent machines, until the subject of labour goes through a connected series of detail processes, that are carried out by a chain of machines of various kinds, the one supplementing the other. Here we have again the co-operation by division of labour that characterises Manufacture; only now, it is a combination of detail machines. . . . The process was previously made suitable to the workman. This subjective principle of the division of labour no longer exists in production by machinery. Here, the process as a whole is examined objectively, in itself, that is to say, without regard to the question of its execution by human hands, it is analysed into its constituent phases; and the problem, how to execute each detail process, and bind them all into a whole, is solved by the aid of machines, chemistry, &c.* But, of course, in this case also, theory must be perfected by accumulated experience on a large scale. Each detail machine supplies raw material to the machine next in order; and since they are all working at the same time, the product is always going through the various stages of its fabrication, and is also consistantly in a state of transition, from one phase to another. . . . In Manufacture the isolation of each detail process is a condition imposed by the nature of division of labour, but in the fully developed factory the continuity of those processes is, on the contrary, imperative. . . .

An organised system of machine, to which motion is communicated by the transmitting mechanism from a central automaton, is the most developed form of production by machinery. Here we have, in the place of the isolated machine, a mechanical monster whose body fills whole factories, and whose demon power, at first veiled under the slow and measured motions of his giant limbs, at length breaks out into the fast and furious whirl of his countless working organs.

There were mules and steam-engines before there were any labourers, whose exclusive occupation it was to make mules and steam-engines; just as men wore clothes before there were such people as tailors. The inventions of Vaucanson, Arkwright, Watt, and others, were, however, practicable, only because those inventors found ready to hand a considerable number of skilled mechanical workmen, placed at their disposal by the manufacturing period. Some of these workmen were independent handicraftsmen of various trades, others were grouped together

*'The principle of the factory system, then, is to substitute . . . the partition of a process into its essential constituents, for the division or graduation of labour among artisans.' (Andrew Ure: 'The Philosophy of Manufactures.' Lond., 1835, p. 20.)

79

in manufactures, in which, as before-mentioned, division of labour was strictly carried out. As inventions increased in number, and the demand for the newly discovered machines grew larger, the machine-making industry split up, more and more, into numerous independent branches, and division of labour in these manufactures was more and more developed. Here, then, we see in Manufacture the immediate technical foundation of Large-Scale Industry. Manufacture produced the machinery, by means of which Large-Scale Industry abolished the handicraft and manufacturing systems in those spheres of production that it first seized upon. The factory system was therefore raised, in the natural course of things, on an inadequate foundation. . . . Apart from the dearness of the machines made in this way, a circumstance that is ever present to the mind of the capitalist, the expansion of industries carried on by means of machinery, and the invasion by machinery of fresh branches of production, were dependent on the growth of a class of workmen, who, owing to the almost artistic nature of their employment, could increase their numbers only gradually, and not by leaps and bounds. But besides this, at a certain stage of its development, Large-Scale Industry became technologically incompatible with the basis furnished for it by handicraft and Manufacture. The increasing size of the prime movers, of the transmitting mechanism, and of the machines proper, the greater complication, multiformity and regularity of the details of these machines, as they more and more departed from the model of those originally made by manual labour, and acquired a form, untrammelled except by the conditions under which they worked, the perfecting of the automatic system, and the use, every day more unavoidable, of a more refractory material, such as iron instead of wood—the solution of all these problems, which sprang up by the force of circumstances, everywhere met with a stumbling-block in the personal restrictions, which even the collective labourer of Manufacture could not break through, except to a limited extent. Such machines as the modern hydraulic press, the modern powerloom, and the modern carding engine, could never have been furnished by Manufacture. . . .

Along with the development of the factory system and of the revolution in agriculture that accompanies it, production in all the other branches of industry not only extends, but alters its character. The principle, carried out in the factory system, of analysing the process of production into its constituent phases, and of solving the problems thus proposed by the application of mechanics, of industry, and of the whole range of the natural sciences, becomes the determining principle everywhere. Hence, machinery squeezes itself into the manufacturing industries first for one detail process, then for another. Thus the solid crystal of their organisation, based on the old division of labour, becomes dissolved, and makes way for constant changes. Independently of this, a radical change takes place in the composition of the collective labourer, a change of the persons working in combination. In contrast with the manufacturing period, the division of labour is thenceforth based, wherever possible, on the employment of women, of children of all ages, and of unskilled labourers, in one word, on cheap labour, as it is characteristically called in England. This is the case not only with all production on a large scale, whether employing machinery or not, but also with the so-called domestic industry, whether carried on in the houses of the workpeople or in small workshops. This modern so-called domestic industry has nothing, except the name, in common with the old-fashioned domestic industry, the existence of which presupposes independent urban handicrafts, independent peasant farming, and above all, a dwelling-house for the labourer and his family. That old-fashioned industry has now been converted into an outside department of the factory, the manufactory, or the warehouse. Besides the factory operatives, the manufacturing workmen and the handicrafts-men, whom it concentrates in large masses at one spot, and directly commands, capital also sets in motion, by means of invisible threads, another army; that of the workers in the domestic industries, who dwell in the large towns and are also scattered over the face of the country. An example: The shirt factory of Messrs. Tillie at Londonderry, which employs 1000 operatives in the factory itself, and 9000 people spread up and down the country and working in their own houses.

The exploitation of cheap and immature labour-power is carried out in a more shameless manner in modern Manufacture than in the factory proper. This is because the technical foundation of the factory system, namely, the substitution of machines for muscular power, and the light character of the labour, is almost entirely absent in Manufacture, and at the same time women and over-young children are subjected, in a most unconscionable way, to the influence of poisonous or injurious substances. This exploitation is more shameless in the so-called domestic industry than in manufactures, and that because the power of resistance in the labourers decreases with their dissemination; because a whole series of plundering parasites insinuate themselves between the employer and the workman; because a domestic industry has always to compete, either with the factory system, or with manufacturing in the same branch of production; because poverty robs the workman of the conditions most essential to his labour, of space, light and ventilation; because employment becomes more and more irregular; and, finally, because in these the last resorts of the masses made 'redundant' by Large-Scale Industry and Agriculture, competition for work attains its maximum.

# VI Transport

JOSEPH PRIESTLEY                                    VI.1
'The Aire and Calder Navigation'
from *Navigable Rivers and Canals*, 1831

The rendering these rivers applicable to the purposes of commerce forms one of the most important features in the history of our inland navigation, and as they were made navigable under an act of parliament, passed above fifty years prior to the date of any enactment for a canal navigation, a brief outline of this extensive and useful undertaking may not prove unacceptable to our readers. . . .

From Leeds the Aire continues in an easterly direction by Temple Newsam, the seat of the Marchioness of Hertford, and Swillington Hall, the seat of Sir John Lowther, Bart. to Castleford, where it unites with the Calder. The two rivers, after their junction, continue to bear the name of Aire, and passing by Fryston Hall, Ferrybridge, Knottingley, Beal, Haddlesey, Weeland, Snaith and Rawcliffe, join the Ouse a little below the village of Armin, at a short distance from the town of Howden. The authority of the first act extending only to Weeland, the subsequent continuation of the navigation to the Ouse River was under a second act, the title of which will be recited in its proper place. The Aire is not navigable above Leeds; the length of the navigation, from Leeds to the junction with the Calder, is about eleven miles and a quarter, in which distance there is a fall of 43¾ feet by six locks. From the junction of the two rivers to Weeland, the distance is eighteen miles and a quarter, with a fall of 34½ feet by four locks, making the total length of navigation from Leeds to Weeland near thirty miles. On this part of the line of navigation are several short canals, railroads, &c. the property of individuals, who have made them for the easier conveyance of the produce of their estates to the banks of the river; . . .

From the navigation warehouse, at Wakefield Bridge, the course of the Calder is by Heath, Newland Park, formerly a preceptory of Knights Templars, but now the seat of Sir Edward Dodsworth, Bart. and Methley, where the Earl of Mexborough has a seat, to its junction with the Aire near Castleford; meandering for the distance of twelve miles and a half through a fertile and delightful valley. The fall from Wakefield Bridge to the union of the two rivers is 28¼ feet by four locks, viz. at the Old Mills, Kirkthorpe, Lakes and Penbank. The total length of the navigation from Wakefield to Weeland is thirty-one miles and a half, and the total fall is 62¾ feet. . . .

Though the first act for making this navigation was passed in the year 1699, an attempt for the same purpose had been made long before, for on the 15th of March, 1625, the first year of Charles the First's reign, a bill was brought into the House of Commons, entitled, *'An Act for the making and maintaining the rivers of Ayre and Cawldes, in the West Riding of the countye of Yorke, navigable and passable for Boats, Barges, and other Vessels, &c.'*

This bill was rejected, after a long debate on the question of committing and engrossing; nor does it appear that any further attempt was made for more than seventy years, when Lord Fairfax introduced a similar bill into the House of Commons, on the 18th of January, 1698. Petitions in favour of this bill were presented from the mayor, aldermen, and inhabitants of Leeds, the borough of Retford, King's Lynn, Lincoln, Manchester, the magistrates at the Quarter Sessions at Doncaster, Boroughbridge, the magistrates assembled at Wakefield Quarter Sessions, the clothiers of the town of Rochdale, Rotherham, Halifax, Kendal, clothiers of Wakefield, Bradford and Gainsbro'; and against the bill, from the lord mayor and commonalty of York, also one from Francis Nevill, of Chevet, Esq. the owner of the Soke Mills, at Wakefield.

It was not till the 3rd of April, 1699, that an act passed the House of Lords, and which received the royal assent on the 4th of May following. As some interesting particulars are contained in the petitions presented to the house in respect to the bill of 1698, they are briefly noticed below.

In the Leeds petition it is stated 'that Leeds and *Wakefeild* are the principal trading towns in the north for cloth; that they are situated on the Rivers Ayre and Calder, which have been viewed, and are found capable to be made navigable, which, if effected, will very much redound to the preservation of the highways, and a great improvement of trade; the petitioners having no conveniency of water carriage within sixteen miles of them, which not only occasions a great expense, but many times great damage to their goods, and sometimes the roads are unpassable, &c. &c.'

The clothiers of *Ratchdale* state that they are 'forty miles from any water carriage.' The clothiers of *Hallifax*, in their petition, state 'that they have no water carriage within thirty miles, and much damage happens through the badness of the roads by the overturning of carriages.'

The clothiers of Wakefield state 'that the towns of Leeds and *Wakefeild* are the principal markets in the north for woollen cloth, &c. &c.; that it will be a great improvement of trade to all the trading towns of the north by reason of the conveniency of water carriage, for want of which the petitioners send their goods twenty-two miles by land carriage, (to Rawcliffe), the expense whereof is not only very chargeable, but they are forced to stay two months sometimes while the roads are passable to market, and many times the goods receive considerable damage, through the badness of the roads by overturning.'. . .

In order to carry into execution the powers granted by this act for making the rivers of Aire and Calder navigable, the undertakers immediately advanced about £12,000, to which, in the course of a few years, other sums, to the amount of about £16,000 were lent and advanced; these sums, with all the money which the tolls produced for the first twenty-four years, were laid out in completing the works of navigation. So small was the trade of the country, that in the year 1830, the whole navigation, together with all the property attached thereto, was rented at £2,000 per annum, upon condition that the *Undertakers* themselves should be at the risk of keeping all dams, on the said rivers, good against any accidents. . . .

The tolls on this navigation were very materially reduced by the second act, viz. from ten shillings per ton in summer, and sixteen shillings per ton in winter, on all articles, for the whole line, to the following rates (see overleaf):—

In the year 1817, and again in 1818, a project was brought forward by a few landholders in that district, for making a canal from Knottingley, down the valley of the Went, to fall into the River Don, a little above New Bridge; and for extending a branch from the same at Norton, to Doncaster, which threatened serious injury to the trade upon the lower part of the Aire and Calder Navigation: but the hopes of the projectors were totally annihilated, by the undertakers of the Aire and Calder Navigation applying, in the year 1819, to parliament, for an act, to enable them to cut a canal from Knottingley to Goole, (now called the Goole Canal), . . .

In consequence of an application to parliament, by the projectors of another line of communication from Wakefield to Ferrybridge, the undertakers of the Aire and Calder called in Mr. Telford, who surveyed the country and made an estimate for shortening and improving the navigation between those two places, and also between Leeds and Castleford; and on the 19th of June, 1828, their projected improvements were sanctioned by an act, entitled, '*An Act to enable the Undertakers of the Navigation of the Rivers Aire and Calder, in the West Riding of the county of York, to make certain Cuts and Canals, and to improve the said Navigation.*' The estimate for this work, including £135,350, for extending the docks at the port of Goole, exclusive of land there, amounted to £462,120, and parliament granted a power to the undertakers to borrow at interest the sum of £750,000. This work

*Scale of Tolls authorized to be taken under the Act of 1774.*

| DESCRIPTION OF GOODS. | RATE. | | HOW CHARGED. |
|---|---|---|---|
| | s. | d. | |
| Dung or Stable Manure, Coals, Cinders, Slack, Culm, and Charcoal, any sum not exceeding. . . } | 0 | ½ | per Ton,   per Mile. |
| Pigeon Dung and Rape Dust. . . . . . . . . . . . . | 0 | 1 | ditto.         ditto. |
| Lime, if carried up the Rivers or Cuts . . . . . . . . | 0 | ¾ | ditto.         ditto. |
| Ditto if carried down the same . . . . . . . . . | 0 | ½ | ditto.         ditto. |
| Pack, Sheet, or Bag of Wool, Pelts or Spetches, not exceeding 312lbs. including Sheet . . . . . . } | 0 | 10½ | |
| For every Quarter of Wheat, Rye, Beans, Oats, Barley and other Grain . . . . . . . . . . . . . . . . {Of Eight Bushels Winchester Malt, Rape, Mustard and Linseed . . . Measure.} | 0 | 6 | From Leeds or Wakefield to Selby or Weeland, or *vice versa* —and so in proportion for any greater or less quantity than a Pack, Quarter, Thirty-two Pecks, or a Ton, or for any less Distance than the whole. |
| Apples, Pears, Onions and Potatoes, for every Thirty two Pecks . . . . . . . . . . } | 0 | 9 | |
| Chalk, Fuller's Earth, Pig-iron, Kelp, Flints, Pipe-Clay, Calais-Sand, and other Sands, (except got in the River) Stone, Bricks, Whiting, Rags and Old Ropes, Lead, Plaister, Alum, Slate, Old Iron, Tiles, Straw, Hay, and British Timber, per Ton . . . . . . . . . . . . . . . . . . . . | 3 | 0 | |
| Fir, Timber, Deals, Battens, Pipe Staves, Foreign Oak, Mahogany and Beech Logs, per Ton . . } | 3 | 6 | |
| Flour, Copperas, Wood, Tallow and Ashes, per Ton | 4 | 0 | |
| Bad Butter or Grease, per Ton. . . . . . . . . . . . | 4 | 3 | |
| Soap, per Ton . . . . . . . . . . . . . . . . . . . . | 5 | 4 | |
| Bar Iron, per Ton . . . . . . . . . . . . . . . . . . | 5 | 6 | |
| Cheese, per Ton . . . . . . . . . . . . . . . . . . . | 6 | 0 | |
| Powder Sugar, Currants, Prunes, Brass and Copper, Argol or Tartar, per Ton . . . . . . . . } | 4 | 8 | |
| Treacle, per Ton. . . . . . . . . . . . . . . . . . . | 5 | 9 | |
| Madder, per Ton . . . . . . . . . . . . . . . . . . | 6 | 0 | |
| Cloth Bales, and all other Goods, Wares and Merchandize, per Ton. . . . . . . . . . . . . . . . } | 7 | 0 | |

is already in execution, and when completed, the navigation will be
some miles shorter, and the depth of water will be sufficient to admit
vessels of one hundred tons burthen up to the towns of Leeds and
Wakefield; and will enable vessels from Leeds and Wakefield to reach
Goole in eight hours, and from Manchester within forty-five hours;
these vessels are expedited by a steam tug. An elegant steam packet
runs daily from Castleford to Goole for the Conveyance of passengers.

# FRANCIS WHISHAW                                    VI.2

## 'The Manchester and Leeds Railway'

from *Railways of Great Britain and Ireland*, 1842

If the population of a district through which a railway is carried afford any adequate notion of the extent of traffic that may be expected upon its entire opening, then may the proprietary of the Manchester and Leeds Railway look forward almost with certainty, to an ample return for their outlay, notwithstanding the enormously increased expenditure above the original estimate. According to the census of 1831, the population within three miles on either side of the line amounted to about 664,920 souls, or about 1847 per square mile; whereas the average population throughout the whole of England was found to be at the rate of only 260 individuals per square mile.

Our opinion, already expressed in another work, as to the importance of the Manchester and Leeds Railway, remains unaltered. We consider it one of the principal lines of railway throughout the kingdom, forming, as it does, the main link in the great transverse chain between Liverpool and Hull.

The manufactures of cotton, woollen, worsted, silk, and linen, are carried on to an amazing extent in the district traversed by this railway. Cotton, which is chiefly imported to Liverpool in its raw state, is sent from thence to the different factories to undergo the necessary course of preparation, from whence it is conveyed to Manchester either for home sale or for exportation.

A great proportion of the cotton manufactured in Great Britain, and intended for continental markets, is sent from Manchester to the ports of Hull and Goole; and the woollens and worsted manufactured in the West Riding of Yorkshire are, to a great extent, transmitted to Liverpool to be exported to the East and West Indies, to Canada and the United States, to South America, and to other parts of the globe.

We need, however, dwell no longer on the importance of this line to the particular district through which it passes. It must, it will, confer incalculable benefits, not only on the particular districts, but also on the community at large.

In an engineering point of view, it is equally important; and if completed throughout, in the way in which those parts already opened to the public afford so many excellent specimens, it will redound to the credit of GEORGE STEPHENSON more than all his other works put together. The line is literally studded with engineering difficulties from end to end, and those of no ordinary magnitude.

It must be a source of high gratification to those who, under Mr. Stephenson, have been engaged in carrying out this great work, to think that the formidable difficulties which beset their path at almost every turn are so nearly surmounted; and we must not omit to record in this page the name of the fortunate individual who has had the immediate superintendence of this stupendous work. It is Thomas Longridge Gooch, a pupil of the engineer-in-chief, and who had acquired considerable experience on the London and Birmingham Railway.

ACTS OF PARLIAMENT, &c.—The Act for the incorporation of the Manchester and Leeds Railway Company received the royal assent on the 4th July, 1836, and authorised a capital to be raised in joint-stock of 1,300,000*l*., and by loan 433,000*l*. additional. A second Act was passed in 1839, which received the royal assent on the 1st July of that year, authorising the sum of 866,000*l*. to be raised for the purpose of constructing the Oldham and Halifax branches, for making a diversion in the railway at Kirkthorpe, for enlarging the present station in Lees Street, and for constructing the line to Hunt's Bank, to join the Liverpool and Manchester proposed extension. The whole amount thus authorised to be raised is 2,599,000*l*.

The number of original shares is 13,000 of 100*l*. each, and of new shares also 13,000 of 50*l*. each, making the joint-stock capital equal to 1,950,000*l*.

The total amount received up to the 30th June, 1840, on account of calls, mortgages, bonds, &c. was 2,116,519*l*. 15*s*. 3*d*.; and the total expenditure to the same date was 2,113,988*l*. 15*s*. 7*d*. . . .

The intermediate stations are situate at Mill Hills, Blue Pits, Rochdale, Littleborough, Todmorden, Hebden Bridge, Sowerby Bridge, Brig-house, Dewsbury, Horbury, and Wakefield. At Normanton a temporary office is erected for the joint use of this Company and that of the North Midland Railway. . . .

CARRIAGE DEPARTMENT.—The carriages consist of first class, second class, and third class or Stanhopes.

The first-class carriages are in three compartments, and fitted up in the usual way. The weight of a first-class carriage is 8100 lbs.

The second-class are also in three compartments, and are open at the sides; but have wooden sliding-shutters instead of glass sashes. The space between the seats is inconveniently narrow. The weight of a second-class carriage is 6150 lbs.

The third-class, or Stanhopes, are 17 feet in extreme length, and 8 feet 8 inches in extreme width; at each end, for a length of 18 inches, the width is decreased to 5 feet. There are four entrances; and the whole is divided into four compartments by a wooden bar down the middle, and another across intersecting the first at right angles. The weight of this contrivance is 5050 lbs.; and the number of passengers it will contain depends on the bulk of the respective stanhopers. It has been stated that this description of carriage was put on the line merely as an experiment; but the scheme had already been tried on other lines, and found not to answer, so far as the railway-proprietors are concerned. It is quite proper to accommodate the poorest class of passengers; but surely the conveyance should be provided with seats, to distinguish them from the brute beasts which perish.

Besides the above, there is another description of carriage, similar to those used on the Scotch lines, which is mixed; the middle compartment being for first-class, and each of the end-compartments for second-class passengers respectively.

The carriages are all mounted on four wheels, and are hung on springs in the usual way. A perforated iron footboard, running the whole length of carriage, is substituted for the lower tier of steps, as in the railway-carriages of the North of England and Scotland.

The coke and cattle-trucks weigh each from 56 cwt. 3 qrs. to 60 cwt. 2 qrs. . . .

TRAFFIC, FARES, &c.—The line was opened to the public from Manchester as far as Littleborough on the 4th July, 1839; and between Normanton and Hebden Bridge on the 12th October, 1840.

The number of passengers conveyed by the trains from the opening on the 4th July, 1839, to February 3d, 1840, inclusive, amounted to 388,627, or at the rate, on an average, of 1807·56 per diem. The number of third to first-class passengers was as 28¼ to 1; of third to second, nearly as 5 to 1; and of second to first, rather more than 5 to 1.

The fare for a first-class passenger between Manchester and Little-borough, 13½ miles, is 4s.; for a second-class passenger, 2s. 6d.; and for a third-class passenger, 1s. 6d.; or at the rates of 3·555d., 2·222d., and 1·333d. per mile respectively. . . .

RECEIPTS AND EXPENDITURE.—The revenue from passengers, &c from 4th July, 1939, to 30th June, 1840, amounted to 35,080l. 2s. 8d.; and for goods and parcels to 5,219l. 10s. 9d.; together, 40,299l. 13s. 5d. Thus the receipts for passengers amounted to 96l. 12s. 9·47d.; and for goods and parcels to 14l. 7s. 6·93d. per diem respectively.

The expenditure for the same period amounted to 20,606l. 19s. 4d., which is equal to 51·13l. per cent on the gross revenue; but during this period there was no charge for maintenance of way.

The following shews the various items of expenditure from the 14th November, 1835, to 30th June, 1840:—

| | | | |
|---|---:|---:|---:|
| Parliamentary expenses. | £ 48,107 | 8 | 9 |
| Engineering | 33,048 | 2 | 3 |
| Land and compensation, and attendant expenses. | 277,628 | 17 | 8 |
| Works. | 1,446,494 | 0 | 3 |
| Stations, on account | 105,244 | 17 | 11 |
| Direction. | 9,600 | 0 | 0 |
| Travelling expenses | 2,913 | 5 | 8 |
| Advertising, printing, &c. | 1,171 | 16 | 7 |
| Secretary's office-expenses, including salaries, taxes, books, stationery, &c. | 3,887 | 18 | 2 |
| Law-charges for general business. | 6,345 | 17 | 4 |
| Stores. | 3,188 | 7 | 5 |
| Locomotive engines. | 38,694 | 2 | 1 |

| | | | |
|---|---:|---:|---:|
| Carriages . . . . . . . . . . . . . . . . . . . . . . . . . . . . . . . . | 21,387 | 7 | 2 |
| Wagons, &c. . . . . . . . . . . . . . . . . . . . . . . . . . . . . . . . | 4,649 | 12 | 3 |
| Mortgage and bond-stamps, interest on mortgages, and interest on bonds . . . . . . . . . . . . . . . . . . . . . . . . . . . . . . | 42,179 | 3 | 1 |
| Surplus land and materials, &c. which are available for resale . . | 29,730 | 3 | 8 |

|  | £ 2,071,651 | 0 | 3 |
|---|---:|---:|---:|
| Disbursements on account of land, &c. for the extension to Hunt's Bank including the expenses of Act No. 3 . . . . . . | 42,337 | 15 | 4 |

|  | £ 2,113,988 | 15 | 7 |
|---|---:|---:|---:|

The parliamentary estimate for this railway included the following items, and presents a strange contrast with the actual cost:—

| | |
|---|---:|
| Earthworks . . . . . . . . . . . . . . . . . . . . . . . . . . . . . . . | £ 360,570 |
| Masonry . . . . . . . . . . . . . . . . . . . . . . . . . . . . . . . . . | 226,579 |
| Stations. . . . . . . . . . . . . . . . . . . . . . . . . . . . . . . . . | 10,000 ! |
| Culverts. . . . . . . . . . . . . . . . . . . . . . . . . . . . . . . . . | 18,231 |
| Alterations to roads and streams. . . . . . . . . . . . . . . . . . . | 4,626 |
| Tunnels. . . . . . . . . . . . . . . . . . . . . . . . . . . . . . . . . | 74,255 ! |
| Fencing. . . . . . . . . . . . . . . . . . . . . . . . . . . . . . . . . | 21,340 |
| Formation of way, including rails, chairs, keys and pins, felt, blocks, sleepers, and ballasting. . . . . . . . . . . . . . . . . . . | 268,875 |
| Contingencies, nearly 12 per cent. . . . . . . . . . . . . . . . . . . . | 115,518 |

| | |
|---|---:|
| | 1,100,000 |
| Land and buildings . . . . . . . . . . . . . . . . . . . . . . . . . . . | 200,000 |

| | |
|---|---:|
| | £ 1,300,000 |

Thus the cost per mile (for the above included the whole distance to Leeds) was at the rate of about 21,443*l*. Up to the 30th June, 1840, the disbursements on account of the main line amounted to 2,071,651*l*., or at the rate of 41,474*l*. 9*s*. 10·67*d*. per mile; and according to the directors' report, 100,000*l*. additional will yet be required to complete the arrangements throughout.

# VII Yorkshire and the Woollen Industry

THE YORKSHIRE DIRECTORY, 1823
Haworth in 1823

Haworth, in the parish of Bradford, wapentake of Morley, and honour of Pontefract; 4 miles S. of Keighley. Population 4663.

Bronte, Rev. Patrick, curate
Oddy, Rev. Miles
Balfield, John, gentleman
Ackroyd, Thomas, victualler, Sun (Inn)
Andrew, Thomas, surgeon
Barraclough, George, ironmonger and watch maker
Bottomley, George, stone mason
Corlake, George, vict. Old King's Arms
Craven and Murgatroyd, corn mill millers
Harnett, Wm. vict. White Lion
Hartley, Wm. brazier and tinner
Jowitt, Jonathan, whitesmith
Midgely, Wm., vict. Fleece
Ramsden and Co., plasterers
Thomas, Wm., spirit merchant
Townsend, G. and W., worsted spinners
Wilkinson, Abraham, victualler, Black Bull
Wood, John, plumber and glazier
Wright, Wm., vict., Hope and Anchor
Wright, Nathaniel, worsted yarn mfcturer.
Wright and Newsome, cotton spinners and manufacturers

*Butchers*
Midgley, Robert
Rushforth, Abraham
Storey, John
Thomas, Wm
Thomas, John

*Cabinet makers*
Greenwood, John
Soper, John
Sugden, Abm.

*Confectioners*
Kaye, David
Rushforth, Abm.

*Grocers, etc.*
Atkinson, Henry
Barraclough, Jas.
Barraclough, Fra.
Driver, Jas.
Hartley, John
Hartley, Timothy
Lambert, Tobias
Pickles, William
Thomas, John
Wood, John
Wright, James

*Woolstaplers*
Eccles, William
Sutcliffe, Joseph
Townend, W. J. and J.

Pickles, Robert
Sugden and Heaton
Townend, E. and W.

*Worsted mfrs.*
Feather Brothers
Greenwood, James

*Worsted top mfrs.*
Craven, Uriah
Staincliffe, Wm.

# THE YORKSHIRE DIRECTORY, 1848          VII.2
Haworth in 1848

HAWORTH, a large old village, 4 miles S. by W. of Keighley, embosomed in the high moorlands, has in its township and chapelry the hamlets of STANBURY, 1 mile W.; and NEAR and FAR OXENHOPE, from 1 to 3 miles south of Haworth; and many scattered houses, &c. The township contains 6848 souls, and 10,540 acres of land, stretching westward to the borders of Lancashire, and nearly half of it in uncultivated heaths and commons. The MANORS and their owners are—*Haworth*, W. B. Ferrand, Esq.; *Oxenhope*, Joseph Greenwood, Esq.; and *Stanbury*, the Misses Rawson. Two *cattle fairs* are held at Haworth, on Easter Monday and the Monday after Old Michaelmas day. *Haworth Church* (St. Michael) was rebuilt in the reign of Henry VIII., and enlarged in 1755. The perpetual curacy, valued at £170, is in the gift of the vicar of Bradford, and incumbency of the Rev. P. Bronte, B.A. *Oxenhope Church* (St. Mary) was built in 1849, at the cost of £1500, and is a perpetual curacy, valued at £150, in the alternate patronage of the Crown and the Bishop of Ripon. *Stanbury Curacy*, valued at £100, is in the gift of the incumbent of Haworth. The Wesleyans have three, the Primitive Methodists one, and the Baptists two chapels, in the township. The *Free School at Haworth* is endowed with about £90, and that at *Stanbury* with about £30 a year.

POST OFFICES, at Wm. Hartley's, *Haworth*; Wm. Whitaker's, *Far Oxenhope*; and Abm. Sunderland's, *Stanbury*. Letters despatched 3 aft. *via* Keighley.

*Marked* 1, *reside at Near Oxenhope;* 2, *Far Oxenhope;* 3, *Stanbury; & the rest in Haworth.*
Akroyd, Jonathan, woolstapler
2 Bankroft Timothy, surveyor, &c.
Barraclough Zbbl. ironmonger
Bronte Rev Patrick, B.A. incumbent of Haworth

Crabtree Jph. & 2 Jonth. shuttle mkrs
Cranmer Rev James Stuart, B.D. master of the Grammar School
3 Craven Wm. flock dlr. & E. dress mkr
Firth J. cooper ‖ Brown J. sexton
Grant Rev Jph. B., B.A., incumbent of Oxenhope
Greenwood Wm. mfr. *Oxenhope Hs*
Hartley Wm. tinner & brazier, P.O.
Hudson John, painter, &c
Hughes Rev Geo. (Wes.) West lane
1 Lambert Robert, druggist
Lambert Thomas, plumber & glazier
Merrall Edwin, mfr.; h *Ebor House*, and Hartley; h *Cook gate*
Murgatroyd John & Rd. corn millers
Nicholls Rev. A. B. curate
2 Ogden Jas. asst. overseer & regr
Parker Thomas, temperance hotel
Pickles Mr Michl. & John, toll colr
Redman Joseph, church clerk, &c
3 Taylor George, Esq. & Mrs Mary
Thomas James & Rd. P. wine and spirit merchants
Townend John, woolstapler
Wadsworth John, hairdresser
Whalley Mr J. ‖ 2 Whitehead Wm.
Wood Humphrey, painter & glazier
2 Wright Jonathan, Wm. & Lupton, spinners

### INNS AND TAVERNS.

2 Bay Horse, James Roberts
Black Bull, John Sugden
3 Cross Inn, Joseph Greenwood
Fleece, Hannah Stancliffe
3 Friendly Inn, Wm. Robinson
King's Arms, Wilson Greenwood
2 Lamb, John Horsfall
3 New Inn, Joshua Sunderland
2 New Inn, Robert Pickles
Shoulder of Mutton, Far Oxhope
Sun, Robert Stoney, West lane
Waggoners' Inn, George Whitaker
White Lion, Joseph Sharp

### ACADEMIES.

Smith John B.
Sumerscale Wm.
3 Sunderland A.

### BEERHOUSES.

Greenwood J.
Marshall J.
Parker Wm.

### BLACKSMITHS
Gledhill Henry
Lund John
Moore Wm.
3 Scarborough J.
Whitaker James

### BOOKSELLERS, &c.
Greenwood John
Leighton Archbd.

### BOOT & SHOEMKS.
Akroyd Jonathan
2 Beaver John
3 Craven Joseph
1 Dawson Joseph
Hird Squire
Holt Joseph
Hudson Henry
Hudson Isaac
Hudson Isc. jun.
Newell Wm.
Roper Abraham
3 Scarborough Jns
Thornton Wm.
Taylor Joseph
3 Wilman Holmes
Whitham Wm.

### BUTCHERS.
2 Feather James
Garnett Wm.
Greenwood Wilsn
Holmes John
Holmes Joseph
Moore John
2 Roberts James
3 Sharp J.
2 Stoney Thomas
2 Whitaker J.
3 Wignall John

### CLOGGERS.
3 Craven Joseph
Fearnside Joseph
Hartley John
Helliwell Wm.
Mosley John

Murgatroyd Jph.
Sugden John

### FARMERS.
2 Akroyd James
Bankroft Abm.
Binns John
1 Boocock C.
1 Brooksbank Wm
Butterfield Abm.
Cousin James
Crabtree James
Dawson John
Dawson Joseph
Dean Joseph
3 Dugdale John
2 Dyson David
2 Foster Jonas
Garnett Wm.
3 Gott Joseph
Greenwood James
Halstead Wm.
Hartley Joseph
Hartley Wm.
Heaton Michael
Heaton Robert
Helliwell Thos.
3 Hey James
3 Holdsworth Jas.
Holdsworth Rt.
1 Hoyle Wm.
3 Hudson Eml.
Murgatroyd Rt.
Murgatroyd Ths.
1 Parker David
Pickles Michael
Ratcliff J.
1 Rushworth Wm.
3 Shakleton Benj.
3 Spencer Fredk.
Sunderland Jph.
Sutcliffe Holmes
Taylor George
Terry John
2 Whitaker Jtn.

GROCERS, &c.

Appleyard J.
2 Bankroft Timy.
Brown Robert
Brown Wm.
3 Craven John
Driver James
Firth Elizabeth
Firth Dnl. *draper*
3 Greenwood Jph
3 Greenwood Sus.
Greenwood John
Hartley (Hanb.) & Thomas (B.)
3 Hartley James
Hartley Betty
Hartley John
Hartley Timothy
Helliwell Betty
Hird John
Holmes Wm.
3 Hudson Emanl.
Hudson James
Hudson John
3 Hudson Saml.
Lambert John
Leighton Archbd.
Moore John
Newell John, *dpr.*
3 Redman John
Roper Wm.
3 Rushworth Ths.
Shackleton Jph.
Sugden Wm.
West Thomas
2 Whitaker John
Whitham Wm.
Wood Joseph
Wright Edward
Wright Grace
Wright Mary

JOINERS, &c.
* *are Cabt. Mks.;*
& † *Wheelwrights.*
*Charnock Jas.

*Hartley James
†Murgatroyd Noh
*Roper James
3 Rushworth Geo.
†Sutcliffe John
*Wood Robert
*Wood Wm.
†Wright Pickles
*Wright Robert

PLASTERERS

Greenwood John
Ingham Emanuel
Kendall John
Moore John

STONE MASONS.

Barstow David
Binns Wm.
Bottomley Thos.
2 Crabtree Wm.
Gregson James
2 Shackleton Wm.
3 Shackleton Wm.
Walmsley Wm.

SURGEONS.

Hall Edw. South
Ingham Amos

TAILORS.

Binns Benj.
Binns Wm.
Greenwood John
3 Holmes Jonas
2 Overend Isaac
Pickles Joseph O.
Redhough Joseph
Sugden Jonathan
Turner Wm.
Wood Greenwood

WORSTED SPINRS.
& MANFRS.

2 Akroyd John O.
Butterfield Bros.
Craven John and Joseph
2 Feather (John)
   & Speck (John)

95

1 Greenwood Wm.
Hartley J. *Sutton*
Kershaw Brothers
Lambert James
Merrall Brothers, *Ebor Mill*
Mitchell James
2 Pickles Rt. & Co.
Sugden Jonas & Brothers
Thomas Wm. jun
2 Watson Robert
2 Wright J. & Bros

**OMNIBUS**
*To Bradford and*
*Halifax on market*
*days; and to meet*
*trains at Keighley*
Whitaker Jonth.

CARRIERS.
Hartley Robert
Pickles Michael
Todd Wm.
Witham James

## MRS ELIZABETH GASKELL VII.3

Haworth and the people of the West Riding

from *The Life of Charlotte Brontë*, 1856

The Leeds and Skipton railway runs along a deep valley of the Aire; a slow and sluggish stream, compared to the neighbouring river of Wharfe. Keighley station is on this line of railway, about a quarter of a mile from the town of the same name. The number of inhabitants and the importance of Keighley have been very greatly increased during the last twenty years, owing to the rapidly extended market for worsted manufactures, a branch of industry that mainly employs the factory population of this part of Yorkshire, which has Bradford for its centre and metropolis.

Keighley is in process of transformation from a populous, old-fashioned village, into a still more populous and flourishing town. It is evident to the stranger, that as the gable-ended houses, which obtrude themselves corner-wise on the widening street, fall vacant, they are pulled down to allow of greater space for traffic, and a more modern style of architecture. The quaint and narrow shop-windows of fifty years ago, are giving way to large panes and plate-glass. Nearly every dwelling seems devoted to some branch of commerce. In passing hastily through the town, one hardly perceives where the necessary lawyer and doctor can live, so little appearance is there of any dwellings of the professional middle-class, such as abound in our old cathedral towns. In fact nothing can be more opposed than the state of society, the modes of thinking, the standards of reference on all points of morality, manners, and even politics and religion, in such a new manufacturing place as Keighley in the north, and any stately, sleepy, picturesque cathedral town in the south. Yet the aspect of Keighley promises well for future stateliness, if not picturesqueness. Grey stone abounds; and the rows of houses built of it have a kind of solid grandeur connected with their uniform and enduring lines. The framework of the doors, and the lintels of the windows, even in the smallest dwellings, are made of blocks of stone. There is no painted wood to require continual beautifying, or else present a shabby aspect; and the stone is kept scrupulously clean by the notable Yorkshire housewives. Such glimpses into the interior as a passer-by obtains, reveal a rough abundance of the means of living, and diligent and active habits in the women. But the voices of the people are hard, and their tones discordant, promising little of the musical taste that distinguishes the district, and which has already furnished a Carrodus to the musical world. The names over the shops (of which the one just given is a sample) seem strange even to an inhabitant of the neighbouring county, and have a peculiar smack and flavour of the place.

The town of Keighley never quite melts into country on the road to Haworth, although the houses become more sparse as the traveller journeys upwards to the grey round hills that seem to bound his journey in a westerly direction. First come some villas; just sufficiently retired from the road to show that they can scarcely belong to any one liable to be summoned in a hurry, at the call of suffering or danger, from his comfortable fireside; the lawyer, the doctor, and the clergyman live at hand, and hardly in the suburbs, with a screen of shrubs for concealment.

In a town one does not look for vivid colouring; what there may be of this is furnished by the wares in the shops, not by foliage or atmospheric effects; but in the country some brilliancy and vividness seems to be instinctively expected, and there is consequently a slight feeling of disappointment at the grey neutral tint of every object, near or far off, on the way from Keighley to Haworth. The distance is about four miles; and, as I have said, what with villas, great worsted factories, rows of workmen's houses, with here and there an old-fashioned farm-house and outbuildings, it can hardly be called 'country' any part of the way. For two miles the road passes over tolerably level ground, distant hills on the left, a 'beck' flowing through meadows on the right, and furnishing water power, at certain points, to the factories built on its banks. The air is dim and lightless with the smoke from all these habitations and places of business. The soil in the valley (or 'bottom,' to use the local term) is rich; but, as the road begins to ascend, the vegetation becomes poorer; it does not flourish, it merely exists; and, instead of trees, there are only bushes and shrubs about the dwellings. Stone dykes are everywhere used in place of hedges; and what crops there are, on the patches of arable land, consist of pale, hungry-looking, grey-green oats. Right before the traveller on this road rises Haworth village; he can see it for two miles before he arrives, for it is situated on the side of a pretty steep hill, with a background of dun and purple moors, rising and sweeping away yet higher than the church, which is built at the very summit of the long narrow street. All round the horizon there is this same line of sinuous wave-like hills; the scoops into which they fall only revealing other hills beyond, of similar colour and shape, crowned with wild, bleak moors—grand, from the ideas of solitude and loneliness which they suggest, or oppressive from the feeling which they give of being pent-up by some monotonous and illimitable barrier, according to the mood of mind in which the spectator may be. . . .

For a right understanding of the life of my dear friend, Charlotte Brontë, it appears to me more necessary in her case than in most others, that the reader should be made acquainted with the peculiar forms of population and society amidst which her earliest years were passed, and from which both her own and her sisters' first impressions of human life must have been received. I shall endeavour, therefore, before proceeding further with my work, to present some idea of the character of the people of Haworth, and the surrounding districts.

Even an inhabitant of the neighbouring county of Lancaster is struck by the peculiar force of character which the Yorkshiremen display. This makes them interesting as a race; while, at the same time, as individuals, the remarkable degree of self-sufficiency they possess gives them an air of independence rather apt to repel a stranger. I use this expression 'self-sufficiency' in the largest sense. Conscious of the strong sagacity and the dogged power of will which seem almost the birthright of the natives of the West Riding, each man relies upon himself, and seeks no help at the hands of his neighbour. From rarely requiring the assistance of others, he comes to doubt the power of bestowing it: from the general success of his efforts, he grows to depend upon them, and to over-esteem his own energy and power. He belongs to that keen, yet short-sighted class, who consider suspicion of all whose honesty is not proved as a sign of wisdom. The practical qualities of a man are held in great respect; but the want of faith in strangers and untried modes of action, extends itself even to the manner in which the virtues are regarded; and if they produce no immediate and tangible result, they are rather put aside as unfit for this busy, striving world; especially if they are more of a passive than an active character. The affections are strong and their foundations lie deep: but they are not—such affections seldom are—widespreading; nor do they show themselves on the surface. Indeed, there is little display of the amenities of life among this wild, rough population. Their accost is curt; their accent and tone of speech blunt and harsh. Something of this may, probably, be attributed to the freedom of mountain air and of isolated hill-side life; something be derived from their rough Norse ancestry. They have a quick perception of character, and a keen sense of humour; the dwellers among them must be prepared for certain uncomplimentary, though most likely true, observations, pithily expressed. Their feelings are not easily roused, but their duration is lasting. Hence there is much close friendship and faithful service; and for a correct exemplification of the form in which the latter frequently appears, I need only refer the reader of *Wuthering Heights* to the character of 'Joseph.'

From the same cause come also enduring grudges, in some cases amounting to hatred, which occasionally has been bequeathed from generation to generation. I remember Miss Brontë once telling me that it was a saying round about Haworth, 'Keep a stone in thy pocket seven year; turn it, and keep it seven year longer, that it may be ever ready to thine hand when thine enemy draws near.'

The West Riding men are sleuth-hounds in pursuit of money. Miss Brontë related to my husband a curious instance illustrative of this eager desire for riches. A man that she knew, who was a small manufacturer, had engaged in many local speculations which had always turned out well, and thereby rendered him a person of some wealth. He was rather past middle age, when he bethought him of insuring his life; and he had only just taken out his policy, when he fell ill of an acute disease which was certain to end fatally in a very few days. The doctor, half-hesitatingly, revealed to him his hopeless state. 'By jingo!' cried he, rousing up at once into the old energy, 'I shall *do* the insurance company! I always was a lucky fellow!'

These men are keen and shrewd; faithful and persevering in following out a good purpose, fell in tracking an evil one. They are not emotional; they are not easily made into either friends or enemies; but once lovers or haters, it is difficult to change their feeling. . . .

The injury done by James and Charles to the trade by which they gained their bread, made the great majority of them Commonwealth men. I shall have occasion afterwards to give one or two instances of the warm feelings and extensive knowledge on subjects of both home and foreign politics existing at the present day in the villages lying west and east of the mountainous ridge that separates Yorkshire and Lancashire; the inhabitants of which are of the same race and possess the same quality of character.

The descendants of many who served under Cromwell at Dunbar, live on the same lands as their ancestors occupied then; and perhaps there is no part of England where the traditional and fond recollections of the Commonwealth have lingered so long as in that inhabited by the woollen manufacturing population of the West Riding, who had the restrictions taken off their trade by the Protector's admirable commercial policy. I have it on good authority that, not thirty years ago, the phrase, 'in Oliver's days,' was in common use to denote a time of unusual prosperity. The class of Christian names prevalent in a district is one indication of the direction in which its tide of hero-worship sets. Grave enthusiasts in politics or religion perceive not the ludicrous side of those which they give to their children; and some are to be found, still in their infancy, not a dozen miles from Haworth, that will have to go through life as Lamartine, Kossuth, and Dembinsky. And so there is a testimony to what I have said, of the traditional feeling of the district, in the fact that the Old Testament names in general use among the Puritans are yet the prevalent appellations in most Yorkshire families of middle or humble rank, whatever their religious persuasion may be. There are numerous records, too, that show the kindly way in which the ejected ministers were received by the gentry, as well as by the poorer part of the inhabitants, during the persecuting days of Charles II. These little facts all testify to the old hereditary spirit of independence, ready ever to resist authority which was conceived to be unjustly exercised, that distinguishes the people of the West Riding to the present day.

The parish of Halifax touches that of Bradford, in which the chapelry of Haworth is included; and the nature of the ground in the two parishes is much of the same wild and hilly description. The abundance of coal and the number of mountain streams in the district, make it highly favourable to manufactures; and accordingly, as I stated, the inhabitants have for centuries been engaged in making cloth, as well as in agricultural pursuits. But the intercourse of trade failed, for a long time, to bring amenity and civilization into these outlying hamlets, or widely scattered dwellings. Mr. Hunter, in his *Life of Oliver Heywood*, quotes a sentence out of a memorial of one James Rither, living in the reign of Elizabeth, which is partially true to this day:—

'They have no superior to court, no civilities to practise: a sour and sturdy humour is the consequence, so that a stranger is shocked by a tone of defiance in every voice, and an air of fierceness in every countenance.'

Even now, a stranger can hardly ask a question without receiving some crusty reply, if, indeed, he receive any at all. Sometimes the sour rudeness amounts to positive insult. Yet, if the 'foreigner' takes all this churlishness good-humouredly, or as a matter of course, and makes good any claim upon their latent kindliness and hospitality, they are faithful and generous, and thoroughly to be relied upon. . . .

Forest customs, existing in the fringes of dark wood, which clothed the declivity of the hills on either side, tended to brutalize the population until the middle of the seventeenth century. Execution by beheading was performed in a summary way upon either men or women who were guilty of but very slight crimes; and a dogged, yet in some cases fine, indifference to human life was thus generated. The roads were so notoriously bad, even up to the last thirty years, that there was little communication between one village and another; if the product of industry could be conveyed at stated times to the cloth market of the district, it was all that could be done; and in lonely houses on the distant hill-side, or by the small magnates of secluded hamlets, crimes might be committed almost unknown, certainly without any great uprising of popular indignation calculated to bring down the strong arm of the law. It must be remembered that in those days there was no rural constabulary; and the few magistrates left to themselves, and generally related to one another, were most of them inclined to tolerate eccentricity, and to wink at faults too much like their own.

Men hardly past middle life talk of the days of their youth, spent in this part of the country, when, during the winter months, they rode up to the saddle-girths in mud; when absolute business was the only reason for stirring beyond the precincts of home; and when that business was conducted under a pressure of difficulties which they themselves, borne along to Bradford market in a swift first-class carriage, can hardly believe to have been possible. For instance, one woollen manufacturer says that, not five and twenty years ago, he had to rise betimes to set off on a winter's morning in order to be at Bradford with the great waggon-load of goods manufactured by his father; this load was packed over-night, but in the morning there was a great gathering around it, and flashing of lanterns, and examination of horses' feet, before the ponderous waggon got under way; and then someone had to go groping here and there, on hands and knees, and always sounding with a staff down the long, steep, slippery brow, to find where the horses might tread safely, until they reached the comparative easy-going of the deep-rutted main road. People went on horseback over the upland moors, following the tracks of the packhorses that carried the parcels, baggage, or goods from one town to another, between which there did not happen to be a highway. . . .

The amusements of the lower classes could hardly be expected to be more humane than those of the wealthy and better educated. The gentleman, who has kindly furnished me with some of the particulars I have given, remembers the bull-baitings at Rochdale, not thirty years ago. The bull was fastened by a chain or rope to a post in the river. To increase the amount of water, as well as to give their workpeople the opportunity of savage delight, the masters were accustomed to stop their mills on the day when the sport took place. The bull would sometimes wheel suddenly round, so that the rope by which he was fastened swept those who had been careless enough to come within its range down into the water, and the good people of Rochdale had the excitement of seeing one or two of their neighbours drowned, as well as of witnessing the bull baited, and the dogs torn and tossed.

The people of Haworth were not less strong and full of character than their neighbours on either side of the hills. The village lies embedded in the moors, between the two counties, on the old road between Keighley and Colne. About the middle of the last century, it became famous in the religious world as the scene of the ministrations of the Rev. William Grimshaw, curate of Haworth for twenty years. Before this time, it is probable that the curates were of the same order as one Mr. Nicholls, a Yorkshire clergyman, in the days immediately succeeding the Reformation, who was 'much addicted to drinking and company-keeping,' and used to say to his companions, 'You must not heed me but when I am got three feet above the earth,' that was, into the pulpit.

Mr. Grimshaw's life was written by Newton, Cowper's friend; and from it may be gathered some curious particulars of the manner in which a rough population were swayed and governed by a man of deep convictions, and strong earnestness of purpose. It seems that he had not been in any way remarkable for religious zeal, though he had led a moral life, and been conscientious in fulfilling his parochial duties, until a certain Sunday in September, 1744, when the servant, rising at five, found her master already engaged in prayer; she stated that, after remaining in his chamber for some time, he went to engage in religious exercises in the house of a parishioner, then home again to pray; thence, still fasting, to the church, where, as he was reading the second lesson, he fell down, and, on his partial recovery, had to be led from the church. As he went out, he spoke to the congregation, and told them not to disperse, as he had something to say to them, and would return presently. He was taken to the clerk's house, and again became insensible. His servant rubbed him, to restore the circulation; and when he was brought to himself 'he seemed in a great rapture,' and the first words he uttered were, 'I have had a glorious vision from the third heaven.' He did not say what he had seen, but returned into the church, and began the service again, at two in the afternoon, and went on until seven.

From this time he devoted himself, with the fervour of a Wesley, and something of the fanaticism of a Whitfield, to calling out a religious life among his parishioners. They had been in the habit of playing at football on Sunday, using stones for this purpose; and giving and receiving challenges from other parishes. There were horse-races held on the moors just above the village, which were periodical sources of drunkenness and profligacy. Scarcely a wedding took place without the rough amusement of foot-races, where the half-naked runners were a scandal to all decent strangers. The old custom of 'arvills,' or funeral feasts, led to frequent pitched battles between the drunken mourners. Such customs were the outward signs of the kind of people with whom Mr. Grimshaw had to deal. But, by various means, some of the most practical kind, he wrought a great change in his parish. In his preaching he was occasionally assisted by Wesley and Whitfield, and at such times the little church proved much too small to hold the throng that poured in from distant villages, or lonely moorland hamlets; and frequently they were obliged to meet in the open air; indeed, there was not room enough in the church even for the communicants. Mr. Whitfield was once preaching in Haworth, and made use of some such expression, as that he hoped there was no need to say much to this congregation, as they had sat under so pious and godly a minister for so many years; 'whereupon Mr. Grimshaw stood up in his place, and said with a loud voice, "Oh, sir! for God's sake do not speak so. I pray you do not flatter them. I fear the greater part of them are going to hell with their eyes open." ' But if they were so bound, it was not for want of exertion on Mr. Grimshaw's part to prevent them. He used to preach twenty or thirty times a week in private houses. If he perceived anyone inattentive to his prayers, he would stop and rebuke the offender, and not go on till he saw every one on their knees. He was very earnest in enforcing the strict observance of Sunday; and would not even allow his parishioners to walk in the fields between services. He sometimes gave out a very long Psalm (tradition says the 119th), and while it was being sung, he left the reading-desk, and taking a horsewhip went into the public-houses, and flogged the loiterers into church. They were swift who could escape the lash of the parson by sneaking out the back way. He had strong health and an active body, and rode far and wide over the hills, 'awakening' those who had previously had no sense of religion. To save time, and be no charge to the families at whose houses he held his prayer-meetings, he carried his provisions with him; all the food he took in the day on such occasions consisting simply of a piece of bread and butter, or dry bread and a raw onion.

The horse-races were justly objectionable to Mr. Grimshaw; they attracted numbers of profligate people to Haworth, and brought a match to the combustible materials of the place, only too ready to blaze out into wickedness. The story is, that he tried all means of persuasion, and even intimidation, to have the races discontinued, but in vain. At length, in despair, he prayed with such fervour of earnestness that the rain came down in torrents, and deluged the ground, so that there was no footing for man or beast, even if the multitude had been willing to stand such a flood let down from above. And so Haworth races were stopped, and have never been resumed to this day. Even now the memory of this good man is held in reverence, and his faithful ministrations and real virtues are one of the boasts of the parish.

ANGUS BETHUNE REACH                                          VII.4

'The Rural Cloth-Workers of Yorkshire:
Saddleworth'

from *The Morning Chronicle*, 1849

The name of Saddleworth is applied to a range of wild and hilly country, about seven miles long and five broad, lying on the western confines of Yorkshire, and including one spot from which a walk of ten
minutes will carry the visitor across the boundaries of four counties,
into Lancashire, Cheshire, Derbyshire, and Yorkshire. To all intents and
purposes, however, Saddleworth lies in the latter county, its heathery
hills and deep valleys dividing the woollen from the cotton cities, and
being themselves peopled by a hardy, industrious, and primitive race,
engaged in the manufacture of flannel and cloth—sometimes in mills,
sometimes by their own hearths; in which latter case the business of
a dairy farmer is often added to that of a manufacturer, and the same
hands ply the shuttle and milk the cows. Saddleworth is now intersec-
ted by the Leeds and Huddersfield Railway, and, as a consequence, is
beginning to lose much of those primitive characteristics for which it
was long renowned. Until recently there was no regular means of tran-
sit from many of its valleys to the more open parts of the country.
Goods were conveyed by the Manchester and Huddersfield Canal; and
many a small manufacturer and comfortable farmer grew grey amid the
hills, without ever having journeyed further than Oldham and Staleybridge on the one hand, and perhaps Huddersfield, or at furthest Leeds,
upon the other. The rail has, however, thrown open the wilds of Saddleworth to the world. Mills, driven by water and steam, are rising on
every hand, and the old-fashioned domestic industry, carried on in the
field and the loom shop, is gradually dying away. . . .
    The appearance of a cloth-weaving room is very different from that
of a cotton 'shed'. The looms are larger, heavier, and clumsier in appearance, and the shuttle traverses the twelve or fourteen feet, which it has
frequently to cover, with a far more deliberate motion than the
glancing jerks of the cotton shuttle, flying through the fast growing
webs of calico. The stuff having been woven, is subjected to the action
of steaming hot water and the 'fulling' hammers, which cause it to
shrivel up almost to one half of its former dimensions. The wages
earned by the artisans who labour in the steaming atmosphere of the
fulling mill are from eighteen to twenty-one shillings. The next process
is exclusively performed by women. It is called 'birling', and consists
of picking out of the cloth, with a sort of tweezers, all the little knots
and inequalities which may be apparent upon the face of the fabric. In
the country this operation is very generally performed at home. In

towns it is executed in the mills, the cloth being spread upon a wooden frame placed at an obtuse angle to the window, and three or four women, closely jammed together, being seated on benches before each frame. This is almost the only department of the trade in which married women are extensively employed away from their homes. In the birling room of a Huddersfield mill, I heard more giggling, and saw more symptoms denoting a relaxed state of discipline, than I had previously observed in any department in any of the textile industries. It was clear, from the atmosphere, that some of the women had been smoking, but the pipes were, of course, instantly smuggled away on our entrance. . . .

From the mill I proceeded to visit some of the cottages of the workpeople. Without a single exception, I found them neat, warm, comfortable, and clean. They consisted almost universally of a common room, serving as a parlour and kitchen, a scullery behind it, and two more bedrooms up-stairs. The main rooms were, I think, as a general rule, larger than those I have lately been accustomed to see. The floors were stone-flagged, nicely sanded. Samplers and pictures uniformly ornamented the walls, and the furniture was massive and old-fashioned; the chairs with rush bottoms and high, well-polished backs. One characteristic feature of these cottages was universal. It consisted of a sort of net stretched under the ceiling, and filled with crisp oat cakes. These formerly constituted almost the only bread consumed in the district, but home-baked wheaten loaves are now coming into general use. Indeed, almost every family in Saddleworth bakes its own bread and brews its own ale—a capital nutty-flavoured beverage it is. The composition of the oat cakes is, however, held to require a particular genius, and when a matron gets a reputation in that way, she frequently bakes for half a village. In the first cottage I entered I found a rosy-cheeked girl occupied in 'birling'. Her father worked in the mill; her mother had her household to attend to, and did a little 'birling' besides. The matron, upon her appearance, informed me that the house had five rooms, and that the weekly rent which they paid for it was three shillings and four-pence. The girl could, by devoting the whole of her time to the work, make seven or eight shillings per week by 'birling'. It was common for married women to birl enough to pay the rent, which they could do, and get ample time to attend to their families. Very few married worked in the mills. They found no difficulty in getting as much work as they wanted at home. In the second house which I saw there were also five rooms, and the rent was three shillings and one penny per week. Besides this the occupants paid sixpence a week for gas, which they could keep alight until half-after ten, and on Saturdays and Sundays as long as they pleased. The woman of the house was a fine, fat, hearty-looking dame of sixty, the very picture of health and matronly enjoyment. There was a bed, with curtains, in a corner of the room.

Who the occupant was I do not know—he did not think proper to show himself; but ever and anon a voice from amid the blankets joined vigorously in the conversation. The old lady corroborated the statement I had heard as to the small proportion of married women who preferred working in the mills to 'birling' at home. The use of oat cake, she said, was gradually decreasing, and she produced a substantial home-made wheaten loaf as a specimen of the bread coming into favour. She could remember when the people ate nothing but oat cakes. These were then made four times as thick as now. The people used to eat a great deal of cheese. Indeed, they used to live on cheese, oat cake, porridge, and butter milk; but now-a-days nothing but tea and coffee would do for them. They took a good deal of porridge yet, however, for breakfast; but generally they had some meat for dinner, perhaps some bacon, perhaps some beef. At all events, they had plenty of porridge and bread and potatoes. The price of meat was a little dearer than when she was a girl. Good mutton could not be had now under sixpence a pound, but she thought, on the whole, that people lived just as well now as they did forty years ago. . . .

From this place we proceeded by a steep path up the hill-side to a cluster of old-fashioned houses called Saddleworth-fold, and which were the first, or amongst the first, stone buildings erected in the district. They are occupied by several families, who are at once spinners, weavers, and farmers. The hamlet was a curious irregular clump of old-fashioned houses, looking as if they had been flung accidentally together up and down a little group of knolls. Over the small latticed windows were carved mullions of stone, and in a little garden grew a few box-wood trees, clipped into the quaint shapes which we associated with French and Dutch gardening. The man whose establishment we had come to see was a splendid specimen of humanity—tall, stalwart, with a grip like a vice, and a back as upright as a pump-bolt, although he was between seventy and eighty years of age. We entered the principal room of his house; it was a chamber which a novelist would love to paint—so thoroughly, yet comfortably, old-fashioned, with its nicely sanded floor, its great rough beams hung with goodly flitches of bacon, its quaint latticed windows, its high mantlepiece, reaching almost to the roof, over the roaring coal fire; its ancient, yet strong and substantial furniture, the chests of drawers and cupboards of polished oak, and the chairs so low-seated and so high-backed. An old woman, the wife of the proprietor, sat by the chimney-corner with a grandchild in her lap. Her daughter was engaged in some household work beside her. In this room the whole family, journeymen and all, took their meals together. Porridge and milk was the usual breakfast. For dinner they had potatoes and bacon, or sometimes beef, with plenty of oat bread; and for supper, 'butter-cake', or porridge again. The old man had never travelled further than Derby. He had thought of going to London once, but his heart failed him, and he had given up the idea. He did not at all approve of the new-fangled mill system, and liked the old-fashioned way of joining weaving and farming much better. He could just remember the building of the newest house in Saddleworth-fold. He thought the seasons had somehow changed in Saddleworth, for snow never lay upon the ground as it used to do, and the scanty crops of oats here and there sown did not ripen so well. The daughter having in the meantime placed oat cake and milk before me, the patriarch observed that until he was twenty he had never tasted wheaten bread, except when his mother lay in. In the room above us were two or three looms, and as many spinning jennies. They produced flannel and doeskin. Weaving and spinning formed the chief occupation of his family; they attended to the cows, of which he had four, and to the dairy, in their leisure time. He paid his sons no regular wages, but gave them board, lodging, and clothing, and 'anything reasonable', if they wanted to go to a hunt or a fair or 'soochloike'.

I may as well state here that the country weavers of Saddleworth are, like Nimrod, mighty hunters. Every third or fourth man keeps his beagle or his brace of beagles, and the gentlemen who subscribe to the district hunt pay the taxes on the dogs. There are no foxes in Saddleworth—the country, indeed, is too bare for them to pick up a living; but hares abound, and occasionally the people have 'trail' hunts—the quarry being a herring or a bit of rag dipped in oil, dragged across the country by an active runner, with an hour's law. A few, but only a very few, pursue the sport on horseback; the weavers, who form the great majority of the hunt, trusting to their own sound lungs and well-strung sinews to keep within sight of the dogs. Even the discipline of the mills is as yet in many instances insufficient to check this inherent passion for the chase. My informant, himself a millowner, told me that he had recently arranged a hunt to try the mettle of some dogs from another part of Yorkshire against the native breed. He had tried to keep the matter as quiet as he could; but it somehow leaked out, and the result was, that several mills were left standing, and that more than 500 carders, slubbers, spinners, and weavers formed the field. The masters, however, are often too keen sportsmen themselves to grudge their hands an occasional holiday of the sort. The Saddleworth weavers must be excellent fellows to run. A year or two ago, a gentleman, resident there, purchased a fox at Huddersfield, and turned him loose at Upper Mill, a spot almost in the centre of the hills. There started on the trail upwards of 300 sportsmen on foot. Reynard led the chase nearly to Manchester, a distance of about twenty miles, and then doubled back almost to the place where he was unbagged, favouring his pursuers with an additional score of miles' amusement. Of the 300 starters, upwards

107

of twenty-five were in at the death. My informant had reason to remember the chase, for it cost him the bursting of a blood-vessel. In passing through the little village of Dubcross I observed a quaint tavern sign, illustrative of the ruling passion. On the board was inscribed, 'Hark to bounty—hark!'

From Upper Mill I proceeded to a village called Delph, where there are only a very few mills, and round which is scattered a thick population of small farmers and hand-loom weavers. The cottages of many of these people are perched far up among the hills, on the very edge of the moors. As a general rule, the houses are inferior, both in construction and cleanliness, to those nearer the mills; and I should say, although the accounts I received were often most puzzlingly contradictory, that the run of wages is decidedly lower. In several of these remote dwellings I found beds of no inviting appearance in the loom room; and broken windows were often patched with old hats and dirty clothes. The hand-jenny spinners, when in employment, earn, as a pretty general rule, about eight shillings a week. The weavers, as I have said, may, and often do, make fifteen and seventeen shillings per week; but, taking the year round, and the good webs with the bad ones, ten shillings in many parts of Yorkshire would be too high an average. . . .

Another weaver, a very intelligent man—much more so, indeed, than most of his class, for he had travelled much, and had been twice in America—gave me some curious information. He confirmed what the old man at Saddleworth-fold had stated as to the non-ripening of the oats sown now-a-days, and spoke sensibly enough about machinery. 'Machinery,' he said, 'had been a great advantage to the weaver as long as it was pretty simple and cheap, for then he could use it for his own behoof.' His mother had told him that in her young days the distaff was the only drawing implement in Saddleworth. The carding was performed by the women with a rude instrument placed upon their knees, and the old-fashioned wheel, with its single spindle, was the only spinning apparatus known. 'Look, sir,' he continued, 'at that yarn. It was stretched out by the road-side today. In those days it would have taken a dozen of people, with a dozen of wheels, more than a week to spin it. Now my mistress can make it with the hand-jenny in two days and a half, and a power mule could spin it in a forenoon.' He feared that it was but natural that the power mule would supplant the hand mule, just as the hand mule had supplanted the spinning wheel. It was during the time that machinery was in the medium state, when any industrious man could obtain it, that the weavers of Saddleworth flourished most. At one time he had paid a journeyman £35 a year, besides his board, lodging, clothing, and washing, and they did not use in those times to work more than five or six hours a day. They were too often out following the hounds. Now his average wages were not above ten shillings a week, although he could sometimes make nearer twenty shillings. His wife worked the hand-jenny, and could make, when in full work, about fifteen pence a day. Thirty years ago she could have easily earned eighteen shillings a week. He kept a cow, and paid £7 10s of rent for the requisite land. His family consumed most of the dairy produce, selling very little. The ordinary price of buttermilk was about one penny for three quarts; of blue or skim-milk, one penny for three pints; and of new milk, about twopence a quart. Milk of all kinds was sent down during the summer time, in great quantities, by many of his neighbours, who kept donkeys to carry it to Staleybridge, Oldham, and other cotton towns, where the factory hands consumed it as fast as it could be sent in.

Adverting to the work and food question, I asked him whether the high prices a year and a half ago had exercised much influence in his trade. He answered nearly as follows:

'Did they not, indeed? Why, when corn is very dear, we have next to no trade at all. It stands to reason. The fabrics we make be mostly for the home market—the best and most nat'ral of all markets, sir; and if the poor people have to spend all they earn to pay for their food and to keep the roofs over them, why, they can't buy no good warm clothing. Two years ago flour was three shillings and sixpence a stone, and oatmeal was three shillings and twopence, and potatoes were selling as high as two shillings and sixpence a score. Then, sir, there was next to no work. I was better off than many, but even in our house it was hard living, I assure you; and a great lot of the weavers had to go work along with t'navvies on the railroad.'

I am happy to say that this honest man appeared to be in better case when I saw him. His house was beautifully clean, and his wife was preparing a comfortable stew for dinner. One of his children was recovering from scarlet fever, and two plump fowls were being boiled down to make chicken broth for the invalid. They had had fifteen fowls, of which ten had been thus used up, and they expected every day to get a fresh supply of poultry.

Comfort such as this must, however, by no means be taken as the rule. The weavers in the upland districts who have no farms, and those in the lower grounds who, although they possess no land, have got advantages of a particular class from the vicinity of the country mills— these two classes are generally decently off, and live wholesome and tolerably agreeable lives. But there are districts, principally in the neighbourhood of the large towns, where competition keeps the wages miserably low, and where hard labour brings in but a hard and scanty substance.

# EDWARD BAINES

## Woollen and Worsted Fabric

from *Account of the Woollen Manufacture of England*, 1858

It will conduce to the understanding of important points in the economy of the manufacture, to explain in the first place the difference between the woollen and the worsted fabrics. The raw material of both is sheep's wool. It would formerly have been sufficient to say that woollens were made of short wool, and worsted goods of long wool; but owing to the improvement in the worsted spinning machinery, much short wool, both English and colonial, is now used in that manufacture. Wool intended for woollens is prepared for spinning by the carding machine; whilst wool intended for worsted goods, being generally of a longer staple, is prepared for spinning by the metallic comb. But the essential distinction of woollens from worsted, cotton, linen, and every other textile fabric is, that they depend upon that peculiar property of sheep's wool, its disposition to *felt*; that is, under pressure and warm moisture, to *interlock its fibres* as by strong mutual attraction, and thus to *run up* into a compact substance not easily separable. Wools differ in the degree of this felting property; but, generally speaking, the long wools possess it in a lower degree than the short wools, and the wools which felt best are the best adapted for making woollen cloth. For worsted stuffs the felting property is not required; and not only have the wools used for this purpose less of the felting property, but they are so treated in the spinning and manufacture as almost entirely to destroy it.

In every other textile fabric, when the material is spun into yarn and woven into a web, the fabric is complete. But in woollen cloth, after the process of spinning and weaving comes the essential process of felting, by means of heavy pressure with soap and warm water; and so efficacious is this process, that a piece of cloth under it often shrinks up to two-thirds its original length and little more than half its width. The process is called milling or fulling, and some of the oldest traces of the woollen manufacture found in ancient records are in the mention of fulling mills on certain streams or estates. Before the milling, the web of the woollen cloth, when held up to the day, admits the light through its crossed threads; but after the milling, every fibre in the piece having laid hold of the neighbouring fibres, and all having firmly interlaced themselves together, the cloth becomes thick and opaque; of course it is made stouter, warmer, and more enduring in the wear; and if torn, it will be found that its tenacity has consisted not so much in the strength of the warp and weft as in the firm adhesion of all the fibres, so that it does not unravel like cotton or linen cloth.

After the cloth has been milled it undergoes the various processes of dressing or finishing, which consist mainly in these two—first, raising up all the fibres of the wool which can be detached by violent and long-continued brushing of the cloth with teazles, so as to make a nap on the surface; and then, secondly, shearing off that nap in a cutting machine, so clean and smooth as to give a soft and almost velvety appearance and feel to the cloth. This nap, more or less closely cut, distinguishes woollen cloth from nearly all other fabrics; it is one of its two essential characters; and, combined with the felting, it makes superfine broad cloth one of the finest, warmest, richest, most useful, and most enduring of all tissues.

But in order to produce these two principal characteristics of woollen cloth, the *felting* and the *nap*, it will easily be seen that woollen yarn, both for the warp and weft, is spun into a much feebler, looser, and less twisted thread, than other kinds of yarn. But this feebleness of the yarn constitutes a principal difficulty in applying the power-loom to the woollen manufacture. The threads are more liable to break by the passing of the shuttle through them, and the weaving is consequently more difficult. This difficulty is increased by the great width of the web, which in broad cloth, before it is milled, is nine feet. Owing to these combined causes, the power-loom in the woollen manufacture works much more slowly than in the worsted manufacture; in the latter, on the average, the shuttle flies at the rate of 160 picks per minute, whilst the power-loom in weaving broad cloth only makes 40 to 48 picks per minute—that is, just the same as the hand-loom. The weaving of woollen cloth by hand is a man's work, whereas the weaving of cotton, linen, or silk cloth by hand was a woman's or a child's work. Hence the hand-loom weaver in the woollen manufacture has never been reduced to the miserable wages paid to the same class of operatives in other manufactures, and hence he maintains a more equal competition with the steam-loom. It is to this cause that we must principally ascribe *the continued existence of the system of domestic manufacture in the woollen trade*; and to the same cause we must ascribe the slower advances made in the woollen than in those manufactures *where all the processes can be more advantageously carried on in factories, by one vast system of machinery, under a single eye, and by the power of great capital*. Whether for good or for evil, or for a combination of both, such are the economical results which may be traced in a great measure to the peculiarities in woollen yarn and cloth. . . .

But the economist may inquire—how is it that the worsted manufacture has of late years increased so much more rapidly than the woollen, seeing that it uses the same raw material, sheep's wool? I may briefly say, that it is to be ascribed in part to very remarkable improvements made within these few years in the process of Combing, which is now performed by machinery, instead of by hand, reducing the cost of the process almost to nothing; in part to the greater simplicity of the other processes, admitting of their being carried on almost entirely in large factories; but more than all to the introduction of cotton warps into the manufacture, which has not only cheapened the raw material, but has introduced a vast variety of new descriptions of goods, light, beautiful, cheap, and adapted both for dress and furniture.

I am informed by a Bradford merchant of great knowledge, that 'out of 100 pieces of worsted goods manufactured, at least 95 are made with cotton warps; and a rough estimate of the cotton contained would be, that if a piece weighed 3 lbs., one pound weight would be cotton and the rest wool.' There is still, therefore, a greater weight of wool than of cotton in those goods; but as cotton warps are stronger than woollen, owing to their being harder spun, even when their weight is less, the cloth may be made altogether much lighter than worsted goods were formerly made, and thus the material is economized.

If we look to the factory return made by the factory inspectors in 1856, and printed by the House of Commons in 1857, we shall find that in Yorkshire there were 445 worsted factories and 806 woollen factories; but the number of operatives was 78,994 in the former, and only 42,982 in the latter. The average number of operatives in the worsted factories therefore was 177, whilst in the woollen factories it was only 53. The whole number of operatives returned in the census of 1851, as employed in these two manufactures in the county of York, was 97,147 in the worsted manufacture, and 81,128 in the woollen. Four-fifths of all the hands employed in the worsted trade are in factories, whilst only about half of those in the woollen trade are in factories.

Everything tends to show that the worsted manufacture, like those of cotton and linen, has become an employment carried on by the machinery of large factories; and as mechanical improvements are constantly speeding the power-loom and the spindle,—so that in worsted factories the power-loom has increased 67 per cent. in speed within the last ten years, and the spindle 114 per cent.—manufactures thus situated must advance more rapidly than those which, like the woollen, are more dependent on manual labour.

## ANON VII.6

## 'A Bradford mill-hand looks back'

from *The Voice of the People*, 1858

Eh lad! it grieves me to think on't. Ha me, an my woife an barns used to sit us daan an get a guid supper, an drink a jug o' wur awn drink, after't days wark. An sometimes t'owd meastur wod cum in an sup wi us, an get one o't barns on tul his knee, an fotch a doll aat o' his pocket for't little un. But poor good man. They sed he wur a bankrup, an he dee'd sooin after, broken-hearted. Na then, aftur he wur deead, an a lot moor o't good owd stamp wur driven aat o't field, Braffurth streets began to stink o' cigars an Germans, an I hed to work for less than hauf 't wages I gat afore. T'lasses and lads gat wed, an t'owd woife an me wur left to oursens, an wen I gat to be sixty yir owd, they gee'd me t'sack, as they reckoned young folk cud du more wark nur me. T'poor lads an lasses wod a help'd me, but their wage war'nt eniff to keep theirsels; an I woddent go to't parish, so we sould our stuff, bit an bit. T'owd wife dee'd wi frettin wen she saw t'creddle in which aar barns was rock'd sell'd to buy some havver-meal; an I dee'd t'varry day t'Bumbaillies war comin to strip t'hoyle for a quarter's rent, altho' I'd lived thirty yir i't haas and ollus paid t'rent regular. But I's glad I *did* dee at t'time, for there as bin sich carryin on since wi poor folk, as is war than deeath, an, as far as I's consarned, I'd rather be e this Church-yard, removed from all the power o'grindin Jewish fops than live e the state o'wretchedness that the bulk o'poor folk suffer. But, as tha says tha has been lookin thrif their caantin haases—'Pay-hoyles'—we used to caw em. Let me hear what tha's seen.

Eh, lad! Ye'd be capp'd to see what I bin forced to glowre at. Caantin haase na are nout like th' 'Pay-Hoyles' you've seen. Whoy, if tha wor to see 't'Hall-Ings' na, ye'd be capp'd. It's moor loike Regent-Street e Lunnon, or a lump o' Squires' country-seats, than owt else. Ye nivver saw owt like it. Dost t'knaw wear them owd haases wur by't turnstile? Whoy, jest there, thear's a wareas as big as t'owd church, an twice as grand an a gurt Music Hall close tull it, for't rich folk to hear furrin singers. An ov a neet when they hev a Grand Concert, tha'd brust the-seln we laffin to see't sons o' swab dyers, and colliers dress'd up like dolls, and tryin to play't fine gentalmun. When yo wor alive young chaps used ta think theirselves grand if they'd a clean check brat on; but na, they rekkon nout of onny-boddy that hes'nt a gurt goold chain across his belly, and a shirt-collar touchin his hat. Then, all daan t'Leeds Road, there's nout to be seen but grand palaces. They look fust-rate grand *aatside*, but if tha wor to peep *inside*, an watch their carryins on,—chaps at sits at desk look like dummies at Moses & Son put their slop coats on, an are nout but mere writin machines, without soul or animation. They durs'nt look raand, flaid of t'meastur gie'en em t'seck, an hev to keep their fingers movin, as if they wor fiddlin wi blind Jim for a wager. The conceit an puppyism of these poor things would mak a pig stare; as, *wen t'meastur's aat*, they are sure to insult onny poor man that has 'casion to call at t'place. But in't *private* raam—eh mun,

113

that's t'shop! Sichna stink o' cigars an brandy. Whoy, some o't lot spend as mich as a hunnerd paand i't year on nout but cigars, not to rekkon o' t'brandy an wine they are ollus agate on. An there's summut else carried on war than that. I durs'nt tell thee in plain talk; but some o't fine dress'd women that goes to't market on Mondays and Thursdays, wi a market-basket jist big eniff ta hod their gloves, could tell you summut.

Na then, stop, I'm fair stall'd o'hearin the. It's no wonner that poor folk are pined as they are. I's go and see for myself t'next week. But, tha sed tha'd bin to some factories. Let's hear wat tha's seen there.

Eh! bless tha; factories na are neut like they used to be. There's one chap, caw'd Tim Pepper, at used to keep a little hoyle back o't Braan Caa, as has belt a gurt pleace aat o't taan that caps all ivver wor. Whoy, it's a taan in itsel. But talking o' pride an ambishon, that's t'chap for a show-off. He cuddant oppen t'mill withaat gettin up a gurt stir, and sendin for a real live Lord to tak t'chair; an after t'dinner, some fooil ov a slave, who caws hissen a po ït, spaated some verses in wich he caw'd Tim a King an a Prince. Eniff to mak Tim go crazed wi conceit. But po ïts are alla'ad gurt license, an we sud allus mak alla'ance for a silly 'STOREY.' Well, wen t'miln wor reddy for't 'hands', as human beeins are na caw'd, some means mun be ta'en to git um through Braffurth an other spots. Tim gav gooid wage an paid th'Railway for't 'hands', an lots o' weavin lasses an pieceners wur pleased at Punch wi't ride an guid wage. Then Tim belt a lot o'haases and kersen'd em 'Peppertaan,' an famlees flitted tul um as fast as they wur reddy; espeshly as Betty Byles kept saandin t'trumpet an beatin t'gong, like a chap e 'front ov a show-box, abaat the gurt liberality ov Tim. Weel, wen t'haases wur stock'd wi't poor dupes, an t'gurt miln full o' 'hands', it wur time fur Tim to think abaat hissen; but afore he'd start reight, he thout he'd hev a moniment erected to his honour an glory, for beeldin a miln *for his own benefit*. So th' ovverlookers got agate, an 'collected' brass through t'miln—some poor lasses *volluntary (?)* givin a *week's wage*, for to pay an artis for a marrable likeness o' their liberal meastur— Some o'th best an gurtest benefacturs o'mankind ha moniments ereckted wen they're deead: but Tim wanted his put up while he wur wick. Wen all wur reddy, a gurt stir wor made, an bans o'musick played i' front, an t'Busk o' Tim wur exhibited e San George's Hall, fur wot reason nobbudy cud tell, as they cud see Tim hisseln onny day. Owd Betty's peaper wur nearly full o't stuff abaat it; but as varry few reads her dreary sarmuns, it did'nt matter mich. Na then, Tim thout 'twar time he gat back t'brass he ligg'd aat e plessur trips an sturs, so he began dockin t'wage, an pokin t'high wage chaps to mak low wage uns tak their places; an for flaid 't'hands' sud'nt du wark eniff, he got pieces o' wood made, an gev em to't ovverlookers, an nobuddy cud go to't privvy withaat assin

114

t'ovverlooker fur a pass, as he mud knaw ha long they'd bin; so if a boddy wur poorly, an stopp't o'er long, they wur e danger o' gettin t'seck.

Drop it! Drop it! I cannot bide to hear sich stuff. I cannot believe it.

Eh! but it's true as ye an me are ghooasts. Ass onny o'th miln hands, they'll tell the' all abaat it. But, I hev'nt dun yet. If onny on em gets a pint or two o' ale at neet after wark, they get poak'd. A chap wur poak'd a fortnit sin, far that crime. Another chap has flitted there wi his wauf an two lasses, an gat fifty shillin i't week atween em, dus'nt get thirty na now near it, for all fower on em, an three-an-sixpence i't week aat o' that for rent; an they ar'nt alla'ad to sell ought if they live in a cottage haase; they mun tak a shop at a he rent to du that. This is t'chap as wur caw'd a King. He's na showin wat sooart 'na King or law-giver a factory meastur wud mak wen he gits pa'er. But Tim is no waur than monny moor on em. There's a chap up Bowlin Loin waur nor him. He used ta go abaat Bowlin once ov a day, wen he wur nobbut a poor coomber, wi slovven clogs, an baat stockins, an spent Sunday long leakin at ceards, as mucky as a pig; but na, he's a Manufacturer, an a bonny fellow he is. He pawses poor barnes abaat as it they wur nout but lumber in his gate; an he's bin hed up afore t'Magistrates for fellin women an barnes wi his kneives. An mich waur than that. No wed woman or young lass is safe wi him. He's a real brute. But he tried it on once too often latly, an't Magistrates, to their honner, sent t'brute to t'Hause o'Correction fur three munths, to kooil him daan a bit.

Na then, tha *mun* drop it! I's fair sick. Eh, dear! Ha thenkful I am that I dee'd wen I did. Whoy mun, wat tha's bin tellin is war than deeath.

We must'nt tak up too mich raam i't 'VOICE O'T PEOPLE' this week, but I's gie him a bit mysel t'next week. Guid neet!

115

# VIII  The North and the Big City

ALEXIS DE TOCQUEVILLE                                         VIII.1

Manchester

from *Journeys to England and Ireland*, 1835

An undulating plain, or rather a collection of little hills. Below the hills
a narrow river (the Irwell), which flows slowly to the Irish sea. Two
streams (the Meddlock and the Irk) wind through the uneven ground
and after a thousand bends, flow into the river. Three canals made by
man unite their tranquil, lazy waters at the same point. On this watery
land, which nature and art have contributed to keep damp, are scattered palaces and hovels. Everything in the exterior appearance of the
city attests the individual powers of man; nothing the directing power
of society. At every turn human liberty shows its capricious creative
force. There is no trace of the slow continuous action of government.
   Thirty or forty factories rise on the tops of the hills I have just
described. Their six stories tower up; their huge enclosures give notice
from afar of the centralisation of industry. The wretched dwellings of
the poor are scattered haphazard around them. Round them stretches
land uncultivated but without the charm of rustic nature, and still without the amenities of a town. The soil has been taken away, scratched
and torn up in a thousand places, but it is not yet covered with the
habitations of men. The land is given over to industry's use. The roads
which connect the still-disjointed limbs of the great city show, like the
rest, every sign of hurried and unfinished work; the incidental activity
of a population bent on gain, which seeks to amass gold so as to have
everything else all at once, and, in the interval, mistrusts all the niceties
of life. Some of these roads are paved, but most of them are full of ruts
and puddles into which foot or carriage wheel sinks deep. Heaps of
dung, rubble from buildings, putrid, stagnant pools are found here and
there among the houses and over the bumpy, pitted surfaces of the public places. No trace of surveyor's rod or spirit level. Amid this noisome
labyrinth, this great sombre stretch of brickwork, from time to time
one is astonished at the sight of fine stone buildings with Corinthian
columns. It might be a medieval town with the marvels of the nineteenth century in the middle of it. But who could describe the interiors
of these quarters set apart, home of vice and poverty, which surround

117

the huge palaces of industry and clasp them in their hideous folds. On ground below the level of the river and overshadowed on every side by immense workshops, stretches marshy land which widely spaced ditches can neither drain nor cleanse. Narrow, twisting roads lead down to it. They are lined with one-story houses whose ill-fitting planks and broken windows show them up, even from a distance, as the last refuge a man might find between poverty and death. None-the-less the wretched people living in them can still inspire jealousy of their fellow-beings. Below some of their miserable dwellings is a row of cellars to which a sunken corridor leads. Twelve to fifteen human beings are crowded pell-mell into each of these damp, repulsive holes.

The fetid, muddy waters, stained with a thousand colours by the factories they pass, of one of the streams I mentioned before, wander slowly round this refuge of poverty. They are nowhere kept in place by quays: houses are built haphazard on their banks. Often from the top of one of their steep banks one sees an attempt at a road opening out through the debris of earth, and the foundations of some houses or the debris of others. It is the Styx of this new Hades. Look up and all around this place and you will see the huge palaces of industry. You will hear the noise of furnaces, the whistle of steam. These vast structures keep air and light out of the human habitations which they dominate; they envelope them in perpetual fog; here is the slave, there the master; there is the wealth of some, here the poverty of most; there the organised efforts of thousands produce, to the profit of one man, what society has not yet learnt to give. Here the weakness of the individual seems more feeble and helpless even than in the middle of a wilderness.

A sort of black smoke covers the city. The sun seen through it is a disc without rays. Under this half-daylight 300,000 human beings are ceaselessly at work. A thousand noises disturb this dark, damp labyrinth, but they are not at all the ordinary sounds one hears in great cities.

The footsteps of a busy crowd, the crunching wheels of machinery, the shriek of steam from boilers, the regular beat of the looms, the heavy rumble of carts, those are the noises from which you can never escape in the sombre half-light of these streets. You will never hear the clatter of hoofs as the rich man drives back home or out on expeditions of pleasure. Never the gay shouts of people amusing themselves, or music heralding a holiday. You will never see smart folk strolling at leisure in the streets, or going out on innocent pleasure parties in the surrounding country. Crowds are ever hurrying this way and that in the Manchester streets, but their footsteps are brisk, their looks preoccupied, and their appearance sombre and harsh. . . .

From this foul drain the greatest stream of human industry flows out to fertilise the whole world. From this filthy sewer pure gold flows.

Here humanity attains its most complete development and its most brutish; here civilization makes it miracles, and civilised man is turned back almost into a savage.

# ANON

## 'Manchester's improving daily'

Broadside ballad, between 1830 and 1850

This Manchester's a rare fine place,
    For trade and other such like movements;
What town can keep up such a race,
    As ours has done for prime improvements
For of late what sights of alterations,
Both streets and buildings changing stations,
That country folks, as they observe us,
Cry out, 'Laws! pickle and presarve us!'
       Sing hey, sing ho, sing hey down, gaily,
       Manchester's improving daily.

Once Oldham Jone, in his smock frock,
    I'th' town stop'd late one afternoon, sir,
And staring at th' infirmary clock,
    Said, Wounds, that must be th' harvest moon, sir;
And ecod, it's fix'd fast up i'th' place there,
And stands behind that nice clock-face there:
Well, this caps aw, for I'll be bound, sir,
They mak' it shine there aw th' year round, sir.
       Sing hey, etc.

Our fine town hall, that cost such cash,
    Is to all buildings quite a sample;
And they say, sir, that, to make a dash,
    'Twas copied from Grecan temple:
But sure in Greece none e'er could view, sir,
Such a place built slanting on a brow, sir!
But Cross-Street, when there brass to spare is,
Must be rais'd and called the Town-Hall Terrace.
       Sing hey, etc.

Once Market-Street was called a lane,
    Old Toad-Lane too, a pretty pair, sir;
While Dangerous-Corner did remain,

119

There was hardly room for a sedan chair, sir:
But now they both are open'd wide, sir,
And dashing shops plac'd on each side, sir:
And to keep up making old things new, sir,
They talk of levelling th' Mill-Brew, sir.
     Sing hey, etc.

Steam coaches soon will run from here
    To Liverpool and other place;
And their quicker rate and cheaper fare
    Will make some folks pull curious faces:
But though steam-dealers may be winners,
'Twill blow up all the whip-cord spinners;
And stable boys may grieve and weep, sir,
For horse-flesh soon will be dog cheap, sir.
     Sing hey, etc.

With bumping stones our streets wur paved,
    From earth like large peck-loaves up rising:
All jolts and shakings now are saved
    The town they're now McAdamizing:
And so smooth and soft is Cannon-Street, sir,
It suits the corns on tender feet sir:
And hookers-in, when times a'n't good there,
May fish about for eels i'th' mud there.
     Sing hey, etc.

. . .

A powerful large steam-engine's bought,
    And plac'd beneath a'r owd church steeple,
To warm up th' church, and soon it's thought
    'Twill play the deuce wi' single people:
For a clever chap's fun eawt a scheme, sir,
To tie the marriage-knot by steam, sir;
And there's no doubt, when they begin it,
They'll wed above a score a minute.
     Sing hey, etc.

## ANON      VIII.3

### 'Oldham Workshops'

Broadside ballad, between 1830 and 1850

When I'd finished off my work last Saturday at neet,
Wi' new hat and Sunday cloas I dressed myself complete;

I took leof o' my mother wi' a very woeful face,
And started off for Owdhum soon, that famous, thriving place,
*Chorus*
With my whack row di dow dow, tal la la di ral di;
Whack row di dow dow, tal de ral de ral.

When I geet to Coppy Nook, it pleased me very well;
I seed all th'town afore me of which i'm goin' to tell.
There wur coaches, carts and coal pits as throng as yo'd desire
And coal enough they'd getten up to set th'whole town o'fire.

I coom up by th' Owd Church, and I seed th' New Market Hall;
It looked so queer a building, I couldn't help but call.
One part of it they'd setten out wi' very pratty shops,
They'n lined it wi' cast iron and they'n built it up o' props.

To Hibbert and Platts shop then I went i'th'Lackey Moor,
And fun no little trouble to get in the lodge door;
And then, by gum, so busy, they wur at it left and right,
Un stripped in all their shirts, too, I thought they're goin' to
    fight.

Some chaps ot they cawd smiths, great bellows they had got,
Like foo's they blowed cowd wind to make the iron hot;
But then owd Neddy engine, I think he beats the whole,
He's fond o' summut warm, sure, for they feed him up
    o' coal.

The moulders among sand, they were making things complete,
Fro' a shaftin' or a fly wheel to a handsome fire grate;
Cast iron's very dear now, or it would be nowt wrong,
To make a scoldin' woman a new cast iron tongue.

I went to Barnes's next un just looked through some rooms,
Where sum wur making' spring frames and others power looms;
Some tunin' and some filin' un screwin' bolts to beams:
I reckon soon both sun and moon they'll make to go by steam.

I went into a weavin' shad and such a clatter there,
Wi' looms un wheels aw goin' so fast, I hardly durst go near.
Then the lasses were si busy shiftin' templets, shuttlin' cops,
One shuttle had like to given me a devilish slop i'th' chops.

I went to lots o' factories to see what they're about;

121

I couldn't get to see much there because they'd all turned out.
They would not gie um brass enough, as far as I could learn,
Un so th'turnouts were goin' about a-lookin' for th'short turn.

If th' work folk would be reasonable un th' masters be but just,
The turnouts will turn in and prosper all things must;
For your lasses are all pratty, your workmen rare and clever,
So success to Owdham Town and trade and th'working folk for
    ever.

## FRIEDRICH ENGELS                                    VIII.4
## Manchester

from *The Condition of the Working Class in
England*, 1844–5

Manchester lies at the foot of the southern slope of a range of hills,
which stretch hither from Oldham, their last peak, Kersallmoor, being
at once the racecourse and the Mons Sacer of Manchester. Manchester
proper lies on the left bank of the Irwell, between that stream and the
two smaller ones, the Irk and the Medlock, which here empty into the
Irwell. On the right bank of the Irwell, bounded by a sharp curve of the
river, lies Salford, and farther westward Pendleton; northward from the
Irwell lie Upper and Lower Broughton; northward of the Irk, Cheetham
Hill; south of the Medlock lies Hulme; farther east Chorlton on Medlock; still farther, pretty well to the east of Manchester, Ardwick. The
whole assemblage of buildings is commonly called Manchester, and contains about four hundred thousand inhabitants, rather more than less.
The town itself is peculiarly built, so that a person may live in it for
years, and go in and out daily without coming into contact with a
working-people's quarter or even with workers, that is, so long as he
confines himself to his business or to pleasure walks. This arises chiefly
from the fact, that by unconscious tacit agreement, as well as with out-
spoken conscious determination, the working-people's quarters are
sharply separated from the sections of the city reserved for the middle-
class; or, if this does not succeed, they are concealed with the cloak of
charity. Manchester contains, at its heart, a rather extended commercial
district, perhaps half a mile long and about as broad, and consisting
almost wholly of offices and warehouses. Nearly the whole district is
abandoned by dwellers, and is lonely and deserted at night, only
watchmen and policemen traverse its narrow lanes with their dark
lanterns. This district is cut through by certain main thoroughfares
upon which the vast traffic concentrates, and in which the ground level is

lined with brilliant shops. In these streets the upper floors are occupied, here and there, and there is a good deal of life upon them until late at night. With the exception of this commercial district, all Manchester proper, all Salford and Hulme, a great part of Pendleton and Chorlton, two-thirds of Ardwick, and single stretches of Cheetham Hill and Broughton are all unmixed working-people's quarters, stretching like a girdle, averaging a mile and a half in breadth, around the commercial district. Outside, beyond this girdle, lives the upper and middle bourgeoisie, the middle bourgeoisie in regularly laid out streets in the vicinity of the working quarters, especially in Chorlton and the lower lying portions of Cheetham Hill; the upper bourgeoisie in remoter villas with gardens in Chorlton and Ardwick, or on the breezy heights of Cheetham Hill, Broughton, and Pendleton, in free, wholesome country air, in fine, comfortable homes, passed once every half or quarter hour by omnibuses going into the city. And the finest part of the arrangement is this, that the members of this money aristocracy can take the shortest road through the middle of all the labouring districts to their places of business, without ever seeing that they are in the midst of the grimy misery that lurks to the right and the left. . . .

The south bank of the Irk is . . . very steep and between fifteen and thirty feet high. On this declivitous hillside there are planted three rows of houses, of which the lowest rise directly out of the river, while the front walls of the highest stand on the crest of the hill in Long Millgate. Among them are mills on the river, in short, the method of construction is as crowded and disorderly here as in the lower part of Long Millgate. Right and left a multitude of covered passages lead from the main street into numerous courts, and he who turns in thither gets into a filth and disgusting grime, the equal of which is not to be found—especially in the courts which lead down to the Irk, and which contain unqualifiedly the most horrible dwellings which I have yet beheld. In one of these courts there stands directly at the entrance, at the end of the covered passage, a privy without a door, so dirty that the inhabitants can pass into and out of the court only by passing through foul pools of stagnant urine and excrement. This is the first court on the Irk above Ducie Bridge—in case any one should care to look into it. Below it on the river there are several tanneries which fill the whole neighbourhood with the stench of animal putrefaction. Below Ducie Bridge the only entrance to most of the houses is by means of narrow, dirty stairs and over heaps of refuse and filth. The first court below Ducie Bridge, known as Allen's Court, was in such a state at the time of the cholera that the sanitary police ordered it evacuated, swept, and disinfected with chloride of lime. Dr. Kay gives a terrible description of the state of this court at that time. Since then, it seems to have been partially torn away and rebuilt; at least looking down from Ducie Bridge, the passer-by sees

123

several ruined walls and heaps of *débris* with some newer houses. The view from this bridge, mercifully concealed from mortals of small stature by a parapet as high as a man, is characteristic for the whole district. At the bottom flows, or rather stagnates, the Irk, a narrow, coal-black, foul-smelling stream, full of *débris* and refuse, which it deposits on the shallower right bank. In dry weather, a long string of the most disgusting, blackish-green, slime pools are left standing on this bank, from the depths of which bubbles of miasmatic gas constantly arise and give forth a stench unendurable even on the bridge forty or fifty feet above the surface of the stream. But besides this, the stream itself is checked every few paces by high weirs, behind which slime and refuse accumulate and rot in thick masses. Above the bridge are tanneries, bone mills, and gasworks, from which all drains and refuse find their way into the Irk, which receives further the contents of all the neighbouring sewers and privies. It may be easily imagined, therefore, what sort of residue the stream deposits. Below the bridge you look upon the piles of *débris*, the refuse, filth, and offal from the courts on the steep left bank; here each house is packed close behind its neighbour and a piece of each is visible, all black, smoky, crumbling, ancient, with broken panes and window-frames. The background is furnished by old barrack-like factory buildings. On the lower right bank stands a long row of houses and mills; the second house being a ruin without a roof, piled with *débris*; the third stands so low that the lowest floor is uninhabitable, and therefore without windows or doors. Here the background embraces the pauper burial-ground, the station of the Liverpool and Leeds railway, and, in the rear of this, the Workhouse, the 'Poor-Law Bastille' of Manchester, which, like a citadel, looks threateningly down from behind its high walls and parapets on the hilltop, upon the working-people's quarter below.

# CHARLES DICKENS                                          VIII.5

## "Coketown"

from *Hard Times*, 1854

Coketown, to which Messrs Bounderby and Gradgrind now walked, was a triumph of fact; it had no greater taint of fancy in it than Mrs Gradgrind herself. Let us strike the keynote, Coketown, before pursuing our tune.

It was a town of red brick, or of brick that would have been red if the smoke and ashes had allowed it; but as matters stood it was a town of unnatural red and black like the painted face of a savage. It was a town of machinery and tall chimneys, out of which interminable serpents of smoke trailed themselves for ever and ever, and never got uncoiled. It had a black canal in it, and a river that ran purple with ill-smelling dye, and vast piles of buildings full of windows where there was a rattling and a trembling all day long, and where the piston of the steam-engine worked monotonously up and down like the head of an elephant in a state of melancholy madness. It contained several large streets all very like one another, and many small streets still more like one another, inhabited by people equally like one another, who all went in and out at the same hours, with the same sound upon the same pavements, to do the same work, and to whom every day was the same as yesterday and to-morrow, and every year the counterpart of the last and the next.

These attributes of Coketown were in the main inseparable from the work by which it was sustained; against them were to be set off, comforts of life which found their way all over the world, and elegancies of life which made, we will not ask how much of the fine lady, who could scarcely bear to hear the place mentioned. The rest of its features were voluntary, and they were these.

You saw nothing in Coketown but what was severely workful. If the members of a religious persuasion built a chapel there—as the members of eighteen religious persuasions had done—they made it a pious warehouse of red brick, with sometimes (but this is only in highly ornamented examples) a bell in a birdcage on the top of it. The solitary exception was the New Church; a stuccoed edifice with a square steeple over the door, terminating in four short pinnacles like florid wooden legs. All the public inscriptions in the town were painted alike, in severe characters of black and white. The jail might have been the infirmary, the infirmary might have been the jail, the town-hall might have been either, or both, or anything else, for anything that appeared to the contrary in the graces of their construction. Fact, fact, fact, everywhere in the material aspect of the town; fact, fact, fact, everywhere in the immaterial. The M'Choakumchild school was all fact, and the school of design was all fact, and the relations between master and man were all fact, and everything was fact between the lying-in hospital and the cemetery, and what you couldn't state in figures, or show to be purchaseable in the cheapest market and saleable in the dearest, was not, and never should be, world without end, Amen. . . .

A sunny midsummer day. There was such a thing sometimes, even in Coketown.

Seen from a distance in such weather, Coketown lay shrouded in a haze of its own, which appeared impervious to the sun's rays. You only knew the town was there, because you knew there could have been no such sulky blotch upon the prospect without a town. A blur of soot and smoke, now confusedly tending this way, now that way, now

125

aspiring to the vault of Heaven, now murkily creeping along the earth, as the wind rose and fell, or changed its quarter: a dense formless jumble, with sheets of cross light in it, that showed nothing but masses of darkness:—Coketown in the distance suggestive of itself, though not a brick of it could be seen.

The wonder was, it was there at all. It had been ruined so often, that it was amazing how it had borne so many shocks. Surely there never was such fragile china-ware as that of which the millers of Coketown were made. Handle them never so lightly and they fell to pieces with such ease that you might suspect them of having been flawed before. They were ruined, when they were required to send labouring children to school; they were ruined when inspectors were appointed to look into their works; they were ruined, when such inspectors considered it doubtful whether they were quite justified in chopping people up with their machinery; they were utterly undone, when it was hinted that perhaps they need not always make quite so much smoke. Besides Mr Bounderby's gold spoon which was generally received in Coketown, another prevalent fiction was very popular there. It took the form of a threat. Whenever a Coketowner felt he was ill-used—that is to say, whenever he was not left entirely alone, and it was proposed to hold him accountable for the consequences of any of his acts—he was sure to come out with the awful menace, that he would 'sooner pitch his property into the Atlantic.' This had terrified the Home Secretary within an inch of his life, on several occasions.

However, the Coketowners were so patriotic after all, that they never had pitched their property into the Atlantic yet, but, on the contrary, had been kind enough to take mighty good care of it. So there it was, in the haze yonder; and it increased and multiplied.

The streets were hot and dusty on the summer day, and the sun was so bright that it even shone through the heavy vapour drooping over Coketown, and could not be looked at steadily. Stokers emerged from low underground doorways into factory yards, and sat on steps, and posts, and palings, wiping their swarthy visages, and contemplating coals. The whole town seemed to be frying in oil. There was a stifling smell of hot oil everywhere. The steam-engines shone with it, the dresses of the Hands were soiled with it, the mills throughout their many stories oozed and trickled it. The atmosphere of those Fairy palaces was like the breath of the simoom: and their inhabitants, wasting with heat, toiled languidly in the desert. But no temperature made the melancholy mad elephants more mad or more sane. Their wearisome heads went up and down at the same rate, in hot weather and cold, wet weather and dry, fair weather and foul. The measured motion of their shadows on the walls, was the substitute Coketown had to show for the shadows of rustling woods; while, for the summer hum

126

of insects, it could offer, all the year round, from the dawn of Monday to the night of Saturday, the whirr of shafts and wheels.

Drowsily they whirred all through this sunny day, making the passenger more sleepy and more hot as he passed the humming walls of the mills. Sun-blinds, and sprinklings of water, a little cooled the main streets and the shops; but the mills, and the courts and alleys, baked at a fierce heat. Down upon the river that was black and thick with dye, some Coketown boys who were at large—a rare sight there—rowed a crazy boat, which made a spumous track upon the water as it jogged along, while every dip of an oar stirred up vile smells. But the sun itself, however beneficent, generally, was less kind to Coketown than hard frost, and rarely looked intently into any of its closer regions without engendering more death than life.

## CHARLES DICKENS                                      VIII.6
### "Evening came on"
from *The Old Curiosity Shop*, 1841

Evening came on. They were still wandering up and down, with fewer people about them, but with the same sense of solitude in their own breasts, and the same indifference from all around. The lights in the streets and shops made them feel yet more desolate, for with their help, night and darkness seemed to come on faster. Shivering with the cold and damp, ill in body, and sick to death at heart, the child needed her utmost firmness and resolution even to creep along.

Why had they ever come to this noisy town, when there were peaceful country places, in which, at least, they might have hungered and thirsted, with less suffering than in its squalid strife? They were but an atom, here, in a mountain-heap of misery, the very sight of which increased their hopelessness and suffering. . . .

'Ah! poor, houseless, wandering, motherless child!' cried the old man, clasping his hands and gazing as if for the first time upon her anxious face, her travel-stained dress, and bruised and swollen feet; 'has all my agony of care brought her to this at last? Was I a happy man once, and have I lost happiness and all I had, for this?'

'If we were in the country now,' said the child, with assumed cheerfulness, as they walked on looking about them for a shelter, 'we should find some good old tree, stretching out his green arms as if he loved us, and nodding and rustling as if he would have us fall asleep, thinking of him while he watched. Please God, we shall be there soon—to-morrow or next day at the farthest—and in the meantime let us think, dear, that it was a good thing we came here; for we are lost in the crowd and hurry of this place, and if any cruel people should pursue us, they could surely never trace us further. There's comfort in that. And here's a deep old doorway—very dark, but quite dry, and warm too, for the wind don't blow in here—What's that?'

Uttering a half shriek, she recoiled from a black figure which came suddenly out of the dark recess in which they were about to take refuge, and stood still, looking at them.

'Speak again,' it said; 'do I know the voice?'

'No,' replied the child timidly; 'we are strangers, and having no money for a night's lodging, were going to rest here.'

There was a feeble lamp at no great distance; the only one in the place, which was a kind of square yard, but sufficient to show how poor and mean it was. To this the figure beckoned them; at the same time drawing within its rays, as if to show that it had no desire to conceal itself or take them at an advantage.

The form was that of a man, miserably clad and begrimed with smoke, which, perhaps by its contrast with the natural colour of his skin, made him look paler than he really was. That he was naturally of a very wan and pallid aspect, however, his hollow cheeks, sharp features, and sunken eyes, no less than a certain look of patient endurance, sufficiently testified. His voice was harsh by nature, but not brutal; and though his face, besides possessing the characteristics already mentioned, was overshadowed by a quantity of long dark hair, its expression was neither ferocious nor bad.

'How came you to think of resting there?' he said. 'Or how,' he added, looking more attentively at the child, 'do you come to want a place of rest at this time of night?'

'Our misfortunes,' the grandfather answered, 'are the cause.'

'Do you know,' said the man, looking still more earnestly at Nell, 'how wet she is, and that the damp streets are not a place for her?'

'I know it well, God help me,' he replied. 'What can I do?'

The man looked at Nell again, and gently touched her garments, from which the rain was running off in little streams. 'I can give you warmth,' he said, after a pause; 'nothing else. . . . The fire is in a rough place, but you can pass the night beside it safely, if you'll trust yourselves to me. You see that red light yonder?'

They raised their eyes, and saw a lurid glare hanging in the dark sky; the dull reflection of some distant fire.

'It's not far,' said the man. 'Shall I take you there? You were going to sleep upon cold bricks; I can give you a bed of warm ashes—nothing better.'

Without waiting for any further reply than he saw in their looks, he took Nell in his arms, and bade the old man follow. . . .

'This is the place,' he said, pausing at a door to put Nell down and take her hand. 'Don't be afraid. There's nobody here will harm you.'

It needed a strong confidence in this assurance to induce them to enter, and what they saw inside did not diminish their apprehension and alarm. In a large and lofty building, supported by pillars of iron, with great black apertures in the upper walls, open to the external air; echoing to the roof with the beating of hammers and roar of furnaces, mingled with the hissing of red-hot metal plunged in water, and a hundred strange unearthly noises never heard elsewhere; in this gloomy place, moving like demons among the flame and smoke, dimly and fitfully seen, flushed and tormented by the burning fires, and wielding great weapons, a faulty blow from any one of which must have crushed some workman's skull, a number of men laboured like giants. Others, reposing upon heaps of coals or ashes, with their faces turned to the black vault above, slept or rested from their toil. Others again, opening the white-hot furnace-doors, cast fuel on the flames, which came rushing and roaring forth to meet it, and licked it up like oil. Others drew forth, with clashing noise, upon the ground, great sheets of glowing steel, emitting an insupportable heat, and a dull deep light like that which reddens in the eyes of savage beasts.

Through these bewildering sights and deafening sounds, their conductor led them to where, in a dark portion of the building, one furnace burnt by night and day—so, at least, they gathered from the motion of his lips, for as yet they could only see him speak: not hear him. The man who had been watching this fire, and whose task was ended for the present, gladly withdrew, and left them with their friend, who, spreading Nell's little cloak upon a heap of ashes, and showing her where she could hang her outer clothes to dry, signed to her and the old man to lie down and sleep. For himself, he took his station on a rugged mat before the furnace-door, and resting his chin upon his hands, watched the flame as it shone through the iron chinks, and the white ashes as they fell into their bright hot grave below.

The warmth of her bed, hard and humble as it was, combined with the great fatigue she had undergone, soon caused the tumult of the place to fall with a gentler sound upon the child's tired ears, and was not long in lulling her to sleep. The old man was stretched beside her, and with her hand upon his neck she lay and dreamed.

It was yet night when she awoke, nor did she know how long, or for how short a time, she had slept. But she found herself protected, both from any cold air that might find its way into the building, and from the scorching heat, by some of the workmen's clothes; and glancing at their friend saw that he sat in exactly the same attitude, looking with a fixed earnestness of attention towards the fire, and keeping so very still that he did not even seem to breathe. She lay in the state between sleeping and waking, looking so long at his motionless figure that at length she almost feared he had died as he sat there; and softly rising and drawing close to him, ventured to whisper in his ear.

He moved, and glancing from her to the place she had lately occupied, as if to assure himself that it was really the child so near him, looked inquiringly into her face.

'I feared you were ill,' she said. 'The other men are all in motion, and you are so very quiet.'

'They leave me to myself.' he replied. 'They know my humour. They laugh at me, but don't harm me in it. See yonder there—that's *my* friend.'

'The fire?' said the child.

'It has been alive as long as I have,' the man made answer. 'We talk and think together all night long.'

The child glanced quickly at him in her surprise, but he had turned his eyes in their former direction, and was musing as before.

'It's like a book to me,' he said—'the only book I ever learned to read; and many an old story it tells me. It's music, for I should know its voice among a thousand, and there are other voices in its roar. It has its pictures too. You don't know how many strange faces and different scenes I trace in the red-hot coals. It's my memory, that fire, and shows me all my life.'

The child, bending down to listen to his words, could not help remarking with what brightened eyes he continued to speak and muse.

'Yes,' he said, with a faint smile, 'it was the same when I was quite a baby, and crawled about it, till I fell asleep. My father watched it then.'

'Had you no mother?' asked the child.

'No, she was dead. Women work hard in these parts. She worked herself to death, they told me, and, as they said so then, the fire has gone on saying the same thing ever since. I suppose it was true. I have always believed it.'

'Were you brought up here, then?' said the child.

'Summer and winter,' he replied. 'Secretly at first, but when they found it out, they let him keep me here. So the fire nursed me—the same fire. It has never gone out.'

'You are fond of it?' said the child.

'Of course I am. He died before it. I saw him fall down—just there, where those ashes are burning now—and wondered, I remember, why it didn't help him.'

'Have you been here ever since?' asked the child.

'Ever since I came to watch it; but there was a while between, and a very cold dreary while it was. It burned all the time though, and roared and leaped when I came back, as it used to do in our play days. You may guess, from looking at me, what kind of child I was, but for all the difference between us I *was* a child, and when I saw you in the street to-night, you put me in mind of myself, as I was after he died, and made me wish to bring you to the fire. I thought of those old times again, when I saw you sleeping by it. You should be sleeping now. Lie down again, poor child, lie down again!'. . .

When she awoke again, broad day was shining through the lofty openings in the walls, and, stealing in slanting rays but midway down, seemed to make the building darker than it had been at night. The clang and tumult were still going on, and the remorseless fires were burning fiercely as before; for few changes of night and day brought rest or quiet there.

Her friend parted his breakfast—a scanty mess of coffee and some coarse bread—with the child and her grandfather, and inquired whither they were going. She told him that they sought some distant country place remote from towns or even other villages, and with a faltering tongue inquired what road they would do best to take.

'I know little of the country,' he said, shaking his head, 'for such as I, pass all our lives before our furnace doors, and seldom go forth to breathe. But there *are* such places yonder.'

'And far from here?' said Nell.

'Aye, surely. How could they be near us, and be green and fresh? The road lies, too, through miles and miles, all lighted up by fires like ours—a strange black road, and one that would frighten you by night.'

'We are here and must go on,' said the child boldly; for she saw that the old man listened with anxious ears to this account.

'Rough people—paths never made for little feet like yours—a dismal blighted way—is there no turning back, my child?'

'There is none,' cried Nell, pressing forward.

# IX Reform of the City

EDWIN CHADWICK

What is to be done?

from 'Report on the Sanitary Condition of the
Labouring Population', *Parliamentary Papers*, 1842

After as careful an examination of the evidence collected as I have been
able to make, I beg leave to recapitulate the chief conclusions which
that evidence appears to me to establish.

*First, as to the extent and operation of the evils which are the sub-
ject of the inquiry*:—

That the various forms of epidemic, endemic, and other disease
caused, or aggravated, or propagated chiefly amongst the labouring
classes by atmospheric impurities produced by decomposing animal and
vegetable substances, by damp and filth, and close and overcrowded
dwellings prevail amongst the population in every part of the kingdom,
whether dwelling in separate houses, in rural villages, in small towns, in
the larger towns—as they have been found to prevail in the lowest districts of the metropolis.

That such disease, wherever its attacks are frequent, is always found
in connexion with the physical circumstances above specified, and that
where those circumstances are removed by drainage, proper cleansing,
better ventilation, and other means of diminishing atmospheric impurity, the frequency and intensity of such disease is abated; and where
the removal of the noxious agencies appears to be complete, such
disease almost entirely disappears.

That high prosperity in respect to employment and wages, and various
and abundant food, have afforded to the labouring classes no exemp-
tions from attacks of epidemic disease, which have been as frequent and
as fatal in periods of commercial and manufacturing prosperity than in
any others.

That the formation of all habits of cleanliness is obstructed by defective supplies of water.

That the annual loss of life from filth and bad ventilation is greater
than the loss from death and wounds in any wars in which the country
has been engaged in modern times.

That of the 43,000 cases of widowhood, and 112,000 cases of

destitute orphanage relieved from the poor's rates in England and Wales alone, it appears that the greatest proportion of deaths of the heads of families occurred from the above specified and other removable causes; that their ages were under 45 years; that is to say, 13 years below the natural probabilities of life as shown by the experience of the whole population of Sweden.

That the public loss from the premature deaths of the heads of families is greater than can be represented by any enumeration of the pecuniary burdens consequent upon their sickness and death.

That, measuring the loss of working ability amongst large classes by the instances of gain, even from incomplete arrangements for the removal of noxious influences from places of work or from abodes, that this loss cannot be less than eight or ten years.

That the ravages of epidemics and other diseases do not diminish but tend to increase the pressure of population.

That in the districts where the mortality is the greatest the births are not only sufficient to replace the numbers removed by death, but to add to the population.

That the younger population, bred up under noxious physical agencies, is inferior in physical organisation and general health to a population preserved from the presence of such agencies.

That the population so exposed is less susceptible of moral influences, and the effects of education are more transient than with a healthy population.

That these adverse circumstances tend to produce an adult population short-lived, improvident, reckless, and intemperate, and with habitual avidity for sensual gratification.

That these habits lead to the abandonment of all the conveniences and decencies of life, and especially lead to the overcrowding of their homes, which is destructive to the morality as well as the health of large classes of both sexes.

That defective town cleansing fosters habits of the most abject degradation and tends to the demoralisation of large numbers of human beings, who subsist by means of what they find amidst the noxious filth accumulated in neglected streets and bye-places.

That the expenses of local public works are in general unequally and unfairly assessed, oppressively and uneconomically collected, by separate collections, wastefully expended in separate and inefficient operations by unskilled and practically irresponsible officers.

That the existing law for the protection of the public health and the constitutional machinery for reclaiming its execution, such as the Courts Leet, have fallen into desuetude, and are in the state indicated by the prevalence of the evils they were intended to prevent.

*Secondly, as to the means by which the present sanitary condition of the labouring classes may be improved:—*

The primary and most important measures, and at the same time the most practicable, and within the recognized province of public administration, are drainage, the removal of all refuse of habitations, streets, and roads, and the improvement of the supplies of water.

That the chief obstacles to the immediate removal of decomposing refuse of towns and habitations have been the expense and annoyance of the hand labour and cartage requisite for the purpose.

That this expense may be reduced to one-twentieth or to one-thirtieth, or rendered inconsiderable, by the use of water and self-acting means of removal by improved and cheaper sewers and drains.

That refuse when thus held in suspension in water may be most cheaply and innoxiously conveyed to any distance out of towns, and also in the best form for productive use, and that the loss and injury by the pollution of natural streams may be avoided.

That for all these purposes, as well as for domestic use, better supplies of water are absolutely necessary.

That for successful and economical drainage the adoption of geological areas as the basis of operations is requisite.

That appropriate scientific arrangements for public drainage would afford important facilities for private land-drainage, which is important for the health as well as sustenance of the labouring classes.

That for the protection of the labouring classes and of the ratepayers against inefficiency and waste in all new structural arrangements for the protection of the public health, and to ensure public confidence that the expenditure will be beneficial, securities should be taken that all local public works are devised and conducted by responsible officers qualified by the possession of the science and the skill of civil engineers.

That the oppressiveness and injustice of levies for the whole immediate outlay on such works upon persons who have only short interests in the benefits may be avoided by care in spreading the expense over periods coincident with the benefits.

That by appropriate arrangements, 10 or 15 per cent. on the ordinary outlay for drainage might be saved, which on an estimate of the expense of the necessary structural alterations of one-third only of the existing tenements would be a saving of one million and a half sterling, besides the reduction of the future expenses of management.

That for the prevention of the disease occasioned by defective ventilation, and other causes of impurity in places of work and other places in which large numbers are assembled, and for the general promotion of the means necessary to prevent disease, it would be good economy to appoint a district medical officer independent of private practice, and with the securities of special qualifications and

135

responsibilities to initiate sanitary measures and reclaim the execution of the law.

That by the combinations of all these arrangements, it is probable that the full ensurable period of life indicated by the Swedish tables; that is, an increase of 13 years at least, may be extended to the whole of the labouring classes.

That the attainment of these and the other collateral advantages of reducing existing charges and expenditure are within the power of the legislature, and are dependent mainly on the securities taken for the application of practical science, skill and economy in the direction of public works.

And that the removal of noxious physical circumstances, and the promotion of civic, household, and personal cleanliness, are necessary to the improvement of the moral condition of the population; for that sound morality and refinement in manners and health are not long found co-existent with filthy habits amongst any class of the community.

## JOHN RUSKIN IX.2
### Rochdale and Pisa

from 'Modern Manufacture and Design', 1859

The changes in the state of this country are now so rapid, that it would be wholly absurd to endeavour to lay down laws of art education for it under its present aspect and circumstances; and therefore I must necessarily ask, how much of it do you seriously intend within the next fifty years to be coal-pit, brick-field, or quarry? For the sake of distinctness of conclusion, I will suppose your success absolute: that from shore to shore the whole of the island is to be set as thick with chimneys as the masts stand in the docks of Liverpool: that there shall be no meadows in it; no trees; no gardens; only a little corn grown upon the house-tops, reaped and threshed by steam: that you do not leave even room for roads, but travel either over the roofs of your mills, on viaducts; or under their floors, in tunnels: that, the smoke having rendered the light of the sun unserviceable, you work always by the light of your own gas: that no acre of English ground shall be without its shaft and its engine; and therefore, no spot of English ground left, on which it shall be possible to stand, without a definite and calculable chance of being blown off it, at any moment, into small pieces.

Under these circumstances, (if this is to be the future of England,) no designing or any other development of beautiful art will be possible. Do not vex your minds, nor waste your money with any thought or effort in the matter. Beautiful art can only be produced by people who have beautiful things about them, and leisure to look at them, and unless you provide some elements of beauty for your workmen to be surrounded by, you will find that no elements of beauty can be invented by them.

I was struck forcibly by the bearing of this great fact upon our modern efforts at ornamentation in an afternoon walk, last week, in the suburbs of one of our large manufacturing towns. I was thinking of the difference in the effect upon the designer's mind, between the scene which I then came upon, and the scene which would have presented itself to the eyes of any designer of the Middle Ages, when he left his workshop. Just outside the town I came upon an old English cottage, or mansion, I hardly know which to call it, set close under the hill, and beside the river, perhaps built somewhere in the Charleses' times, with mullioned windows and a low arched porch; round which, in the little triangular garden, one can imagine the family as they used to sit in old summer times, the ripple of the river heard faintly through the sweet-briar hedge, and the sheep on the far-off wolds shining in the evening sunlight. There, uninhabited for many and many a year, it had been left in unregarded havoc of ruin; the garden-gate still swung loose to its latch; the garden, blighted utterly into a field of ashes, not even a weed taking root there; the roof torn into shapeless rents; the shutters hanging about the windows in rags of rotten wood; before its gate, the stream which had gladdened it now soaking slowly by, black as ebony and thick with curdling scum; the bank above it trodden into unctuous, sooty slime: far in front of it, between it and the old hills, the furnaces of the city foaming forth perpetual plague of sulphurous darkness; the volumes of their storm clouds coiling low over a waste of grassless fields, fenced from each other, not by hedges, but by slabs of square stones, riveted together with iron.

That was your scene for the designer's contemplation in his afternoon walk at Rochdale. Now fancy what was the scene which presented itself, in his afternoon walk, to a designer of the Gothic school of Pisa—Nino Pisano, or any of his men.

On each side of a bright river he saw rise a line of brighter palaces, arched and pillared, and inlaid with deep red porphyry, and with serpentine; along the quays before their gates were riding troops of knights, noble in face and form, dazzling in crest and shield; horse and man one labyrinth of quaint colour and gleaming light—the purple, and silver, and scarlet fringes flowing over the strong limbs and clashing mail, like sea-waves over rocks at sunset. Opening on each side from the river were gardens, courts, and cloisters; long successions of white pillars among wreaths of vine; leaping of fountains through buds of pomegranate and orange: and still along the garden paths, and under

137

and through the crimson of the pomegranate shadows, moving slowly, groups of the fairest women that Italy ever saw—fairest, because purest and thoughtfullest; trained in all high knowledge, as in all courteous art —in dance, in song, in sweet wit, in lofty learning, in loftier courage, in loftiest love—able alike to cheer, to enchant, or save, the souls of men. Above all this scenery of perfect human life, rose dome and bell-tower, burning with white alabaster and gold: beyond dome and bell-tower the slopes of mighty hills, hoary with olive; far in the north, above a purple sea of peaks of solemn Apennine, the clear, sharp-cloven Carrara mountains sent up their steadfast flames of marble summit into amber sky; the great sea itself, scorching with expanse of light, stretching from their feet to the Gorgonian isles; and over all these, ever present, near or far—seen through the leaves of vine, or imaged with all its march of clouds in the Arno's stream, or set with its depth of blue close against the golden hair and burning cheek of lady and knight,—the untroubled and sacred sky, which was to all men, in those days of innocent faith, indeed the unquestioned abode of spirits, as the earth was of men; and which opened straight through its gates of cloud and veils of dew into the awfulness of the eternal world;—a heaven in which every cloud that passed was literally the chariot of an angel, and every ray of its Evening and Morning streamed from the throne of God.

What think you of that for a school of design?

I do not bring this contrast before you as a ground of hopelessness in our task; neither do I look for any possible renovation of the Republic of Pisa, at Bradford, in the nineteenth century; but I put it before you in order that you may be aware precisely of the kind of difficulty you have to meet, and may then consider with yourselves how far you can meet it. To men surrounded by the depressing and monotonous circumstances of English manufacturing life, depend upon it, design is simply impossible. This is the most distinct of all the experiences I have had in dealing with the modern workman. He is intelligent and ingenious in the highest degree—subtle in touch and keen in sight: but he is, generally speaking, wholly destitute of designing power. And if you want to give him the power, you must give him the materials, and put him in the circumstances for it. Design is not the offspring of idle fancy: it is the studied result of accumulative observation and delightful habit. Without observation and experience, no design—without peace and pleasurableness in occupation, no design—and all the lecturings, and teachings, and prizes, and principles of art, in the world, are of no use, so long as you don't surround your men with happy influences and beautiful things. It is impossible for them to have right ideas about colour, unless they see the lovely colours of nature unspoiled; impossible for them to supply beautiful incident and action in their ornament, unless they see beautiful incident and action in the world about them.

138

Inform their minds, refine their habits, and you form and refine their designs; but keep them illiterate, uncomfortable, and in the midst of unbeautiful things, and whatever they do will still be spurious, vulgar, and valueless.

I repeat, that I do not ask you nor wish you to build a new Pisa for them. We don't want either the life or the decorations of the thirteenth century back again; and the circumstances with which you must surround your workmen are those simply of happy modern English life, because the designs you have now to ask for from your workmen are such as will make modern English life beautiful. All that gorgeousness of the Middle Ages, beautiful as it sounds in description, noble as in many respects it was in reality, had, nevertheless, for foundation and for end, nothing but the pride of life—the pride of the so-called superior classes; a pride which supported itself by violence and robbery, and led in the end to the destruction both of the arts themselves and the States in which they flourished.

# JOHN RUSKIN IX.3

## A city as it might be

from 'The Mystery of Life and its Arts', 1868

. . . Whatever our station in life may be, at this crisis, those of us who mean to fulfil our duty ought first to live on as little as we can; and, secondly, to do all the wholesome work for it we can, and to spend all we can spare in doing all the sure good we can.

And sure good is, first in feeding people, then in dressing people, then in lodging people, and lastly in rightly pleasing people, with arts, or sciences, or any other subject of thought. . . .

Lodging people, which you may think should have been put first, . . . I put . . . third, because we must feed and clothe people where we find them, and lodge them afterwards. And providing lodgment for them means a great deal of vigorous legislature, and cutting down of vested interests that stand in the way, and after that, or before that, so far as we can get it, thorough sanitary and remedial action in the houses that we have; and then the building of more, strongly, beautifully, and in groups of limited extent, kept in proportion to their streams, and walled round, so that there may be no festering and wretched suburb anywhere, but clean and busy street within, and the open country without, with a belt of beautiful garden and orchard round the walls, so that from any part of the city perfectly fresh air and grass, and sight of far horizon, might be reachable in a few minutes' walk. This the final aim; but in immediate action every minor and possible good to be instantly done, when, and as, we can; roofs mended that have holes in them—fences patched that have gaps in them—walls buttressed that totter—and floors propped that shake; cleanliness and order enforced with our own hands and eyes, till we are breathless, every day. And all the fine arts will healthily follow. I myself have washed a flight of stone stairs all down, with bucket and broom, in a Savoy inn, where they hadn't washed their stairs since they first went up them; and I never made a better sketch than that afternoon.

# X Poverty, Unemployment, and Protest

WILLIAM WORDSWORTH                X.1

'The Last of the Flock'

from *Lyrical Ballads*, 1798

> In distant countries I have been,
> And yet I have not often seen
> A healthy man, a man full grown
> Weep in the public roads alone.
> But such a one, on English ground,
> And in the broad high-way, I met;
> Along the broad high way he came,
> His cheeks with tears were wet.
> Sturdy he seemed, though he was sad;
> And in his arms a lamb he had.
>
> He saw me, and he turned aside,
> As if he wished himself to hide:
> Then with his coat he made essay
> To wipe those briny tears away.
> I follow'd him, and said, 'My friend
> 'What ails you? wherefore weep you so?'
> —'Shame on me, Sir! this lusty lamb,
> He makes my tears to flow.
> To-day I fetched him from the rock;
> He is the last of all my flock.
>
> When I was young, a single man,
> And after youthful follies ran,
> Though little given to care and thought,
> Yet, so it was, a ewe I bought;
> And other sheep from her I raised,
> As healthy sheep as you might see,
> And then I married, and was rich
> As I could wish to be;
> Of sheep I number'd a full score,
> And every year encreas'd my store.

Year after year my stock it grew,
And from this one, this single ewe,
Full fifty comely sheep I raised,
As sweet a flock as ever grazed!
Upon the mountain did they feed;
They throve, and we at home did thrive.
—This lusty lamb of all my store
Is all that is alive:
And now I care not if we die,
And perish all of poverty.

Ten children, Sir! had I to feed,
Hard labour in a time of need!
My pride was tamed, and in our grief
I of the parish ask'd relief.
They said I was a wealthy man;
My sheep upon the mountain fed,
And it was fit that thence I took
Whereof to buy us bread:'
'Do this; how can we give to you,'
They cried, 'what to the poor is due?'

I sold a sheep as they had said,
And bought my little children bread,
And they were healthy with their food;
For me it never did me good.
A woeful time it was for me,
To see the end of all my gains,
The pretty flock which I had reared
With all my care and pains,
To see it melt like snow away!
For me it was a woeful day.

Another still! and still another!
A little lamb, and then its mother!
It was a vein that never stopp'd,
Like blood-drops from my heart they dropp'd.
Till thirty were not left alive
They dwindled, dwindled, one by one,
And I may say that many a time
I wished they all were gone:
They dwindled one by one away;
For me it was a woeful day.

To wicked deeds I was inclined,
And wicked fancies cross'd my mind,
And every man I chanc'd to see,
I thought he knew some ill of me.
No peace, no comfort could I find,
No ease, within doors or without,
And crazily, and wearily,
I went my work about.
Oft-times I thought to run away;
For me it was a woeful day.

Sir! 'twas a precious flock to me,
As dear as my own children be;
For daily with my growing store
I loved my children more and more.
Alas! it was an evil time;
God cursed me in my sore distress,
I prayed, yet every day I thought
I loved my children less;
And every week, and every day,
My flock, it seemed to melt away.

They dwindled, Sir, sad sight to see!
From ten to five, from five to three,
A lamb, a weather, and a ewe;
And then at last, from three to two;
And of my fifty, yesterday
I had but only one,
And here it lies upon my arm,
Alas! and I have none;
To-day I fetched it from the rock
It is the last of all my flock.'

# ANON

## 'The Poor Cotton Weaver'

Ballad, early 19th Century

I'm a poor cotton weaver as many one knows,
I've nowt to eat i'th house an I've worn out my cloas,
You'd hardly give sixpence for all I have on,
My clogs they are brossen and stockings I've none,
You'd think it wur hard to be sent into th' world,
    To clem and do th' best ot you con.

Our church parson kept telling us long,
We should have better times if we'd hold our tongues,
I've houden my tongue till I can hardly draw breath,
I think i' my heart he means to clem me to death;
I know he lives weel by backbiting the de'il,
      But he never picked o'er in his life.


I tarried six week an thought every day wur t'last,
I tarried and shifted till now I'm quite fast;
I lived on nettles while nettles were good,
An Waterloo porridge were best of my food;
I'm telling you true I can find folks enew,
      That are living no better than me.


Old Bill o' Dan's sent bailiffs one day,
For a shop score I owed him that I could not pay,
But he wur too late for old Bill o' Bent,
Had sent tit and cart and taen goods for rent,
We had nou bur a stoo, that wur a seat for two,
      And on it cowered Margit and me.


The bailiffs looked round assly as a mouse,
When they saw aw things were taen out of house,
Says one to the other all's gone thou may see,
Aw sed lads never fret you're welcome to me;
They made no more ado, but nipp'd up th' owd stoo,
      And we both went wack upoth flags.


I geet howd of Margit for hoo wur strucken sick,
Hoo sed hoo ne'er had such a bang sin hoo wur wick
The bailiffs scoured off with owd stoo on their backs,
They would not have cared had they brook our necks,
They're mad at owd Bent cos he's taen goods for rent,
      And wur ready to flee us alive.


I sed to our Margit as we lay upoth floor,
We shall never be lower in this world I'm sure,
But if we alter I'm sure we mun amend,
For I think in my heart we are both at far end,
For meat we have none nor looms to weave on,
      Egad they're as weel lost as found.


144

Then I geet up my piece and I took it em back
I scarcely dare speak mester looked so black,
He said you wur o'erpaid last time you coom,
I said if I wur 'twas for weaving bout loom,
In a mind as I'm in I'll ne'er pick o'er again,
    For I've woven myself thoth' fur end.

Then aw coom out and left him to chew that,
When aw thought again aw wur vext till aw sweat,
To think that we mun work to keep them and awth set,
All the day o' my life and still be in their debt;
So I'll give o'er trade an work with a spade,
    Or go and break stones upoth road.

Our Margit declared if hoo'd cloas to put on,
Hoo'd go up to Lundun an see the big mon
An if things didn't alter when hoo had been,
Hoo swears hoo'd feight blood up toth e'en,
Hoo's nought again th' Queen but likes a fair thing,
    An hoo says hoo can tell when hoo's hurt.

## HOUSE OF COMMONS COMMITTEE ON CHILD LABOUR      X.3

## Richard Oastler's evidence

from *Parliamentary Papers*, 1832

*Richard Oastler*, appearing before the Committee, when asked, 'Has your mind been latterly directed to the consideration of the condition of children and young persons engaged in the mills and factories', made answer:

The immediate circumstance which led my attention to the facts was a communication made to me by a very opulent spinner [Mr John Wood, of Horton Hall, Bradford], that it was the regular custom to work children in factories 13 hours a day, and only allow them half an hour for dinner, and that in many factories they were worked considerably more. . . . From that moment, which was the 29th of September 1830, I have never ceased to use every legal means, which I had it in my power to use, for the purpose of emancipating these innocent slaves. The very day on which the fact was communicated to me, I addressed a letter to the public, in the *Leeds Mercury*, upon the subject. I have since that had many opponents to contend against; but not one single fact which I have communicated has ever been contradicted, or ever can be. . . .

The demoralizing effects of the system are as bad, I know it, as the demoralizing effects of slavery in the West Indies. I know that there are instances and scenes of the grossest prostitution amongst the poor creatures who are the victims of the system, and in some cases are the objects of the cruelty and rapacity and sensuality of their masters. These things I never dared to publish, but the cruelties which are inflicted personally upon the little children, not to mention the immensely long hours which they are subject to work, are such as I am very sure would disgrace a West Indian plantation.

On one occasion . . . I was in the company of a West India slave master and three Bradford spinners; they brought the two systems into fair comparison, and the spinners were obliged to be silent when the slave-owner said, 'Well, I have always thought myself disgraced by being the owner of black slaves, but we never, in the West Indies, thought it was possible for any human being to be so cruel as to require a child of nine years old to work twelve and a half hours a day; and that, you acknowledge, is your regular practice. . . .'

In the West Riding of Yorkshire when I was a boy it was the custom for the children to mix learning their trades with other instruction and with amusement, and they learned their trades or their occupations, not by being put into places, to stop there from morning to night, but by having a little work to do, and then some time for instruction, and they were generally under the immediate care of their parents; the villages about Leeds and Huddersfield were occupied by respectable little clothiers, who could manufacture a piece of cloth or two in the week, or three or four or five pieces, and always had their family at home: and they could at that time make a good profit by what they sold; there were filial affection and parental feeling, and not over-labour.

But that race of manufacturers has been almost completely destroyed; there are scarcely any of the old-fashioned domestic manufacturers left, and the villages are composed of one or two, or in some cases of three or four, mill-owners, and the rest, poor creatures who are reduced and ground down to want, and in general are compelled to live upon the labour of their little ones. It is almost the general system for the little children in these manufacturing villages to know nothing of their parents at all excepting that in the morning very early, at 5 o'clock, very often before 4, they are awaked by a human being that they are told is their father, and are pulled out of bed (I have heard many a score of them give an account of it) when they are almost asleep, and lesser children are absolutely carried on the backs of the older children asleep to the mill, and they see no more of their parents, generally speaking, till they go home at night, and are sent to bed.

Now that system must necessarily prevent the growth of filial affection.

146

It destroys the happiness in the cottage family, and leads both parents and children not to regard each other in the way that Providence designed they should. . . . With regard to the fathers, I have heard many of them declare that it is such a pain to them to think that they are kept by their little children, and that their little children are subjected to so many inconveniences, that they scarcely know how to bear their lives; and I have heard many of them declare that they would much rather be transported than be compelled to submit to it. I have heard mothers, more than on ten or eleven occasions, absolutely say that they would rather that their lives were ended than that they should live to be subjected to such misery. The general effect of the system is this, and they know it, to place a bonus upon crimes; because their little children, and their parents too, know that if they only commit theft and break the laws, they will be taken up and put into the House of Correction, and there they will not have to work more than 6 or 7 hours a day. . . .

## POOR LAW COMMISSION X.4

### Conclusions and Principles of Legislation

from *Parliamentary Papers*, 1834

If, while the general administration of the Poor Laws were allowed to remain on its present footing, such occasional or partial relief as that which is available to the settled labourers of a parish were rendered equally available to the unsettled labourers, we cannot doubt that such a proceeding would demoralize and depress this respectable and valuable class to the level of the settled and pauperized labourers. This is ample reason against assimilating the condition of the unsettled to that of the settled labourers, but none against placing the settled on the same footing as the unsettled. The present practice, as to unsettled labourers, is almost exactly that which we propose to make the rule for all classes, both settled and unsettled.

The non-parishioner has no right to partial relief; to occasional relief; to relief in aid of wages, or to any out-door relief whatever from the parish in which he resides; and yet the assurance which we propose to preserve to every one, that he shall not perish on the failure of his ability to procure subsistence, is preserved to him. If that ability actually fail him, he is assured that he can immediately obtain food until he can be passed home to his own parish, where he will be saved from perishing and be maintained at the public charge. By this course, however, he would be taken wholly out of employment, and reduced to the condition of a permanent pauper; and that condition being less eligible to him than the condition of an independent labourer, he struggles with all the occasional difficulties from which, if he were a parishioner and improvident, the usual administration of the Poor Laws would relieve him. Relief is accessible to him whenever a case of necessity occurs; it is indeed accessible to him whenever he chooses to avail himself of it; it is simply *ineligible* to him so long as he can subsist by his own industry. The ordinary workhouse of his own distant parish, with the inconveniences of removal superadded, produces on him effects of the same description as those which we find produced on parishioners by a well-regulated workhouse.

We attach much importance to the general superiority of the conduct and condition of the non-parishioners, the unsettled labourers. Although the evidence afforded from the dispauperized parishes appears to us to be conclusive as to the effects which may be anticipated from a similar change of system throughout the country, it is still liable to the objection, however unreasonable, that these parishes are individual and scattered instances, too few to establish a general conclusion; but the evidence afforded by the character and condition of the unsettled labourers pervades the whole country. Every body of labourers resident and labouring within a parish of which they are not parishioners, and where the distance of their own parishes and the administration of the poor's rates does not render partial relief available, may be referred to in proof of the general effects which would follow an improved system of administering relief. These labourers make no complaints of their having no right to partial relief, and we have not met with an instance of their having suffered from the want of it. The fact of the non-settled labourers maintaining an independent condition, whilst they have a right by law to return at the public expense to their own parishes and claim parochial aid proves that they themselves consider their present condition more advantageous than that of paupers, and that so considering it they are anxious to retain it.

From the above evidence it appears that wherever the principle which we have thus stated has been carried into effect, either wholly or partially, its introduction has been beneficial to the class for whose benefit poor laws exist. We have seen that in every instance in which the able-bodied labourers have been rendered independent of partial relief or of relief otherwise than in a well-regulated workhouse:

1. Their industry has been restored and improved.
2. Frugal habits have been created or strengthened.
3. The permanent demand for their labour has increased.
4. And the increase has been such, that their wages, so far from being depressed by the increased amount of labour in the market, have in general advanced.
5. The number of improvident and wretched marriages has diminished.

6. Their discontent has been abated, and their moral and social condition in every way improved.

### [PRINCIPLE OF LEGISLATION]

Results so important would, even with a view to the interest of that class exclusively, afford sufficient ground for the general introduction of the principle of administration under which those results have been produced. Considering the extensive benefits to be anticipated from the adoption of measures founded on principles already tried and found beneficial, and warned at every part of the inquiry by the failure of previous legislation, we shall, in the suggestion of specific remedies, endeavour not to depart from the firm ground of actual experience.

*We therefore submit, as the general principle of legislation on this subject, in the present condition of the country:*

*That those modes of administering relief which have been tried wholly or partially, and have produced beneficial effects in some districts, be introduced, with modifications according to local circumstances, and carried into complete execution in all.*

The chief specific measures which we recommend for effecting these purposes, are—

FIRST, THAT EXCEPT AS TO MEDICAL ATTENDANCE, AND SUBJECT TO THE EXCEPTION RESPECTING APPRENTICESHIP HEREIN AFTER STATED, ALL RELIEF WHATEVER TO ABLE-BODIED PERSONS OR TO THEIR FAMILIES, OTHER THAN IN WELL-REGULATED WORKHOUSES (i.e., PLACES WHERE THEY MAY BE SET TO WORK ACCORDING TO THE SPIRIT AND INTENTION OF THE 43 ELIZABETH) SHALL BE DECLARED UNLAWFUL, AND SHALL CEASE, IN MANNER AND AT PERIODS HEREAFTER SPECIFIED; AND THAT ALL RELIEF AFFORDED IN RESPECT OF CHILDREN UNDER THE AGE OF SIXTEEN SHALL BE CONSIDERED AS AFFORDED TO THEIR PARENTS.

It is true that nothing is necessary to arrest the progress of pauperism except that all who receive relief from the parish should work for the parish exclusively, as hard and for less wages than independent labourers work for individual employers, and we believe that in most districts useful work, which will not interfere with the ordinary demand for labour, may be obtained in greater quantity than is usually conceived. Cases, however, will occur where such work cannot be obtained in sufficient quantity to meet an immediate demand; and when obtained, the labour, by negligence, connivance, or otherwise, may be made merely formal, and thus the provisions of the legislature may be evaded more easily than in a workhouse. A well-regulated workhouse meets all cases and appears to be the only means by which the intention of the Statute of Elizabeth, that all the able-bodied shall be set to work, can be carried into execution.

149

The out-door relief of which we have recommended the abolition is in general partial relief, which, as we have intimated, is at variance with the spirit of the 43 Elizabeth, for the framers of that act could scarcely have intended that the overseers should 'take order for setting to work' those who have work and are engaged in work: nor could they by the words 'all persons using *no* ordinary and daily trade of life to get their living by', have intended to describe persons 'who *do* use an ordinary and daily trade of life'.

Wherever the language of the legislature is uncertain, the principle of administration, as well as of legal construction, is to select the course which will aid the remedy; and with regard to the able-bodied, the remedy set forth in the statute is to make the indolent industrious. In proposing further remedial measures we shall keep that object steadily in view.

And although we admit that able-bodied persons in the receipt of out-door allowances and partial relief may be, and in some are, placed in a condition less eligible than that of the independent labourer of the lowest class; yet to persons so situated, relief in a well-regulated work-house would not be a hardship: and even if it be in some rare cases a hardship, it appears from the evidence that it is a hardship to which the good of society requires the applicant to submit. The express or implied ground of his application is, that he is in danger of perishing from want. Requesting to be rescued from that danger out of the property of others, he must accept assistance on the terms, whatever they may be, which the common welfare requires. The bane of all pauper legislation has been the legislating for extreme cases. Every exception, every violation of the general rule to meet a real case of unusual hardship, lets in a whole class of fraudulent cases by which that rule must in time be destroyed. Where cases of real hardship occur, the remedy must be applied by individual charity, a virtue for which no system of compulsory relief can be or ought to be a substitute.

### [FURTHER EFFECTS OF PROPOSED ADMINISTRATION]

The preceding evidence as to the actual operation of remedial measures relates principally to rural parishes. We shall now show, from portions of the evidence as to the administration of relief upon a correct principle in towns, that by an uniform application of the principle which we recommend, or, in other words, by a recurrence to the original intention of the Poor Laws, other evils produced by the present system of partial relief to the able-bodied will be remedied. The principal of the further evils which it would extirpate is the tendency of that system to constant and indefinite increase, independently of any legitimate causes, a tendency which we have shown to arise from the irresistible temptations to fraud on the part of the claimants. These temptations we have seen are afforded—

first, by the want of adequate means, or of diligence and ability, even where the means exist, to ascertain the truth of the statements on which claims to relief are founded:

secondly, by the absence of the check of shame, owing to the want of a broad line of distinction between the class of independent labourers and the class of paupers, and the degradation of the former by confounding them with the latter:

thirdly, by the personal situation, connections, interests, and want of appropriate knowledge on the part of the rate distributors, which render the exercise of discretion in the administration of all relief, and especially of out-door relief, obnoxious to the influence of intimidation, of local partialities, and of local fears, and to corrupt profusion, for the sake of popularity or of pecuniary gain.


# WILLIAM WORDSWORTH                                         X.5

## On the Poor Laws

from Postscript to *Lyrical Ballads*, edition of
1835–6


. . . Among the many objects of general concern, and the changes going forward, which I have glanced at in verse, are some especially affecting the lower orders of society; in reference to these, I wish here to add a few words in plain prose. . . .

It is . . . not impossible that the state of mind which some of the foregoing poems may have produced in the reader, will dispose him to receive more readily the impression which I desire to make, and to admit the conclusions I would establish.

I. The first thing that presses upon my attention is the Poor-Law Amendment Act. . . . The point to which I wish to draw the reader's attention is, that *all* persons who cannot find employment, or procure wages sufficient to support the body in health and strength, are entitled to a maintenance by law.

This dictate of humanity is acknowledged in the Report of the Commissioners; but is there not room for apprehension that some of the regulations of the new act have a tendency to render the principle nugatory by difficulties thrown in the way of applying it? If this be so, persons will not be wanting to show it, by examining the provisions of the act in detail,—an attempt which would be quite out of place here; but it will not, therefore, be deemed unbecoming in one who fears that the prudence of the head may, in framing some of those provisions, have supplanted the wisdom of the heart, to enforce a principle which cannot be violated without infringing upon one of the most precious

151

rights of the English people, and opposing one of the most sacred claims of civilized humanity.

There can be no greater error, in this department of legislation, than the belief that this principle does by necessity operate for the degradation of those who claim, or are so circumstanced as to make it likely they may claim, through laws founded upon it, relief or assistance. The direct contrary is the truth: it may be unanswerably maintained that its tendency is to raise, not to depress; by stamping a value upon life, which can belong to it only where the laws have placed men who are willing to work, and yet cannot find employment, above the necessity of looking for protection against hunger and other natural evils, either to individual and casual charity, to despair and death, or to the breach of law by theft, or violence.

And here, as in the Report of the Commissioners the fundamental principle has been recognised, I am not at issue with them any farther than I am compelled to believe that their 'remedial measures' obstruct the application of it more than the interests of society require.

And, calling to mind the doctrines of political economy which are now prevalent, I cannot forbear to enforce the justice of the principle, and to insist upon its salutary operation.

And first for its justice: If self-preservation be the first law of our nature, would not every one in a state of nature be morally justified in taking to himself that which is indispensable to such preservation, where, by so doing, he would not rob another of that which might be equally indispensable to *his* preservation? And if the value of life be regarded in a right point of view, may it not be questioned whether this right of preserving life, at any expense short of endangering the life of another, does not survive man's entering into the social state; whether this right can be surrendered or forfeited, except when it opposes the divine law, upon any supposition of a social compact, or of any convention for the protection of mere rights of property?

But, if it be not safe to touch the abstract question of man's right in a social state to help himself even in the last extremity, may we not still contend for the duty of a christian government, standing *in loco parentis* towards all its subjects, to make such effectual provision, that no one shall be in danger of perishing either through the neglect or harshness of its legislation? Or, waiving this, is it not indisputable that the claim of the state to the allegiance, involves the protection, of the subject? And, as all rights in one party impose a correlative duty upon another, it follows that the right of the state to require the services of its members, even to the jeoparding of their lives in the common defence, establishes a right in the people (not to be gainsaid by utilitarians and economists) to public support when, from any cause, they may be unable to support themselves.

Let us now consider the salutary and benign operation of this principle. Here we must have recourse to elementary feelings of human nature, and to truths which from their very obviousness are apt to be slighted, till they are forced upon our notice by our own sufferings or those of others. In the Paradise Lost, Milton represents Adam, after the Fall, as exclaiming, in the anguish of his soul—

> 'Did I request Thee, Maker, from my clay
> To mould me man; did I solicit Thee
> From darkness to promote me?
> .    .    .    .    .    .    .    .    .    My will
> Concurred not to my being.'*

Under how many various pressures of misery have men been driven thus, in a strain touching upon impiety, to expostulate with the Creator! and under few so afflictive as when the source and origin of earthly existence have been brought back to the mind by its impending close in the pangs of destitution. But as long as, in our legislation, due weight shall be given to this principle, no man will be forced to bewail the gift of life in hopeless want of the necessaries of life.

Englishmen have, therefore, by the progress of civilisation among them, been placed in circumstances more favourable to piety and resignation to the divine will, than the inhabitants of other countries, where a like provision has not been established. And as Providence, in this care of our countrymen, acts through a human medium, the objects of that care must, in like manner, be more inclined towards a grateful love of their fellow-men. Thus, also, do stronger ties attach the people to their country, whether while they tread its soil, or, at a distance, think of their native land as an indulgent parent, to whose arms, even they who have been imprudent and undeserving may, like the prodigal son, betake themselves, without fear of being rejected.

Such is the view of the case that would first present itself to a reflective mind; and it is in vain to show, by appeals to experience, in contrast with this view, that provisions founded upon the principle have promoted profaneness of life, and dispositions the reverse of philanthropic, by spreading idleness, selfishness, and rapacity: for these evils have arisen, not as an inevitable consequence of the principle, but for want of judgment in framing laws based upon it; and, above all, from faults in the mode of administering the law. The mischief that has grown to such a height from granting relief in cases where proper vigilance would have shown that it was not required, or in bestowing it in undue measure, will be urged by no truly enlightened statesman, as a sufficient reason for banishing the principle itself from legislation.

Let us recur to the miserable states of consciousness that it precludes.

*Paradise Lost x. 743–7.

There is a story told, by a traveller in Spain, of a female who, by a sudden shock of domestic calamity, was driven out of her senses, and ever after looked up incessantly to the sky, feeling that her fellow-creatures could do nothing for her relief. Can there be Englishmen who, with a good end in view, would, upon system, expose their brother Englishmen to a like necessity of looking upwards only; or downwards to the earth, after it shall contain no spot where the destitute can demand, by civil right, what by right of nature they are entitled to?

Suppose the objects of our sympathy not sunk into this blank despair, but wandering about as strangers in streets and ways, with the hope of succour from casual charity; what have we gained by such a change of scene? Woeful is the condition of the famished Northern Indian, dependent, among winter snows, upon the chance-passage of a herd of deer, from which one, if brought down by his rifle-gun, may be made the means of keeping him and his companions alive. As miserable is that of some savage Islander, who, when the land has ceased to afford him sustenance, watches for food which the waves may cast up, or in vain endeavours to extract it from the inexplorable deep. But neither of these is in a state of wretchedness comparable to that, which is so often endured in civilised society: multitudes, in all ages, have known it, of whom may be said:—

> 'Homeless, near a thousand homes they stood,
> And near a thousand tables pined, and wanted food.'*

Justly might I be accused of wasting time in an uncalled-for attempt to excite the feelings of the reader, if systems of political economy, widely spread, did not impugn the principle, and if the safeguards against such extremities were left unimpaired. It is broadly asserted by many, that every man who endeavours to find work, *may* find it: were this assertion capable of being verified, there still would remain a question, what kind of work, and how far may the labourer be fit for it? For if sedentary work is to be exchanged for standing; and some light and nice exercise of the fingers, to which an artisan has been accustomed all his life, for severe labour of the arms; the best efforts would turn to little account, and occasion would be given for the unthinking and the unfeeling unwarrantably to reproach those who are put upon such employment, as idle, froward, and unworthy of relief, either by law or in any other way! Were this statement correct, there would indeed be an end of the argument, the principle here maintained would be superseded. But, alas! it is far otherwise. That principle, applicable to the benefit of all countries, is indispensable for England, upon whose coast families are perpetually deprived of their support by shipwreck, and where large masses of men are so liable to be thrown out of their

*Wordsworth, *Guilt and Sorrow*, 368–9.

154

ordinary means of gaining bread, by changes in commercial intercourse, subject mainly or solely to the will of foreign powers, by new discoveries in arts and manufactures; and by reckless laws, in conformity with theories of political economy, which, whether right or wrong in the abstract, have proved a scourge to tens of thousands, by the abruptness with which they have been carried into practice.

But it is urged,—refuse altogether compulsory relief to the able-bodied, and the number of those who stand in need of relief will steadily diminish through a conviction of an absolute necessity for greater fore-thought, and more prudent care of a man's earnings. Undoubtedly it would, but so also would it, and in a much greater degree, if the legislative provisions were retained, and parochial relief administered under the care of the upper classes, as it ought to be. For it has been invariably found, that wherever the funds have been raised and applied under the superintendence of gentlemen and substantial proprietors, acting in vestries, and as overseers, pauperism has diminished accordingly. Proper care in that quarter would effectually check what is felt in some districts to be one of the worst evils in the poor law system, viz. the readiness of small and needy proprietors to join in imposing rates that seemingly subject them to great hardships, while, in fact, this is done with a mutual understanding, that the relief each is ready to bestow upon his still poorer neighbours will be granted to himself, or his relatives, should it hereafter be applied for.

But let us look to inner sentiments of a nobler quality, in order to know what we have to build upon. Affecting proofs occur in every one's experience, who is acquainted with the unfortunate and the indigent, of their unwillingness to derive their subsistence from aught but their own funds or labour, or to be indebted to parochial assistance for the attainment of any object, however dear to them. A case was reported, the other day, from a coroner's inquest, of a pair who, through the space of four years, had carried about their dead infant from house to house, and from lodging to lodging, as their necessities drove them, rather than ask the parish to bear the expense of its interment:—the poor creatures lived in the hope of one day being able to bury their child at their own cost. It must have been heart-rending to see and hear the mother, who had been called upon to account for the state in which the body was found, make this deposition. By some, judging coldly, if not harshly, this conduct might be imputed to an unwarrantable pride, as she and her husband had, it is true, been once in prosperity. But examples, where the spirit of independence works with equal strength, though not with like miserable accompaniments, are frequently to be found even yet among the humblest peasantry and mechanics. There is not, then, sufficient cause for doubting that a like sense of honour may be revived among the people, and their ancient habits of independence restored, without resorting to those severities which the new Poor Law Act has introduced.

## ANGUS BETHUNE REACH X.6
### Poor People in Bradford
from *The Morning Chronicle*, 1849

In an architectural point of view, the best features of Bradford consist of numerous ranges of handsome warehouses. The streets have none of the old-fashioned picturesqueness of those of Halifax. The best of them are muddy, and not too often swept. Mills abound in great plenty, and their number is daily increasing, while the town itself extends in like proportion. Bradford is, as I have said, essentially a new town. Half a century ago it was a mere cluster of huts; now the district of which it is the heart contains upwards of 132,000 inhabitants. The value of life is about one in forty. Fortunes have been made in Bradford with a rapidity almost unequalled even in the manufacturing districts. In half a dozen years men have risen from the loom to possess mills and villas. At present, stuff manufacturers are daily pouring into the town from Leeds; while a vast proportion of the wool-combing of the empire seems, as it were, to have concentrated itself in Bradford. I was struck by the accent in which many of the woolcombers addressed me; and, in answer to my inquiries, I had frequently a roomfull of workmen exclaiming, 'I'm from Leicestershire!'—'I'm from Devonshire!'—'I'm from Cornwall!'—'I'm from Mount Mellick, in Queen's County!'. . .

During my investigations at Bradford I had more than one opportunity of seeing how the parochial authorities in agricultural districts pack their paupers off to the manufacturing regions. I select two cases. The first was that of a widow from a purely rural part of Yorkshire. She had a large young family. Her husband had been an agricultural labourer at fifteen shillings a week in summer, and in winter he broke stones on the road for fifteenpence a day. On his death the family became chargeable. The parish immediately offered to pay the expense of removal, and gave the family £1 1s. if they would go to Bradford. They consented, and several of the children being sickly and subject to fits, so as to be unable to work in the mills, they have been mainly supported by Bradford ever since. The woman who told me these particulars said that she knew many families who had been sent to Bradford from the same locality in the same way.

The other case is that of a poor Irishwoman, one of the cleanest, tidiest, and best specimens of her country people, in that walk of life, I have ever seen. Having heard of her case, she came out of the mill to

156

speak to me, and conducted me to her chamber. A poorer one, and yet a cleaner one I never saw; the deal table had been scoured until it shone again; there was a faded bit of carpeting on the floor, and not a speck of dust from wall to wall. I had never witnessed a more striking instance of cleanliness taking away all the squalor of poverty. In the room were three children. The eldest, a girl of seven, was rocking the cradle of the youngest, and attending to the proceedings of her other little sister.

'This is my housekeeper,' said the mother, 'and I can trust her, and feel easy about the younger ones when I am at my work.' The story of the family I shall relate nearly in the mother's words:

'My husband and me lived at Minstun (an agricultural district of Yorkshire). He was a hand-loom weaver. Wages were very low, and times were very hard with us. We were at Minstun ten months, and in that time we tasted flesh twice. My poor husband had a consumption on him, and little by little he was forced to give up work. The farmers and the neighbours were very hard-hearted to us. They never sent as much as a ha'p'orth of milk, even to the dying man. When he was gone, the parish offered me and my four children one shilling to pay the rent every week, and one shilling to live on. If we didn't like that, they said we might go to Bradford and they would give us thirty shillings, but they gave us twenty-nine shillings, and we came here. If they had only given us three shillings a week I would have stayed. I have a little boy, and I brought him to the mill, and told them all about us. The people at the mill were very kind much kinder than the farmers. They took the little boy, and set him to easy work, and gave him two shillings a week. Then the manager said I might come to the mill and see him, and try if I couldn't learn to do something myself. So I got to know how to pick lumps out of the slubbings, and first I got five shillings and sixpence, and last week I was raised to six shillings; so we have now eight shillings a week. Well, first I lived in a room belonging to the mill, with an outside stair, and I paid one shilling rent. But I was afraid of the children breaking their necks there. The only other place I could get near the mill was this. There are two rooms here, and the rent is two shillings. I know it's too much for the like of me to pay; but think of the children. Well, sir, the parish are very good to me, and give me three shillings a week—two shillings for the rent and one shilling for coals—and we live and clothe ourselves on the other eight shillings. We live chiefly on bread. I get a stone and a half of flour every week, and I bake it on Sundays. Then we have a little tea and coffee, and sometimes we have a little offal meat, because it's cheap. A good gentleman gave me the furniture I have, and the bed in the other room. It cost altogether fifteen shillings. Everybody has been very kind to me, and the neighbours come in often to look after the children when I'm at work. I was born in Shandon parish, in Cork; and oh! I wish there were mills there for the poor to work in. It would be a blessing to them indeed.'

## ANON X.7

Draft letter to *Northern Star*

MS., Saddleworth, *c.* 1847–8

Sir,

    I have been a reader of the *Star* ever since its first establishment, and for thirty years previous to that time, I have been a radical reformer; and as to the Charter, I am an advocate for that, with one exception, I have my doubts on the question of universal suffrage. I am of the opinion, that household suffrage would give us all we want; and if, as a body, the Chartists would consent to alter the Charter in that one point, and no other observe, in that case, I believe that Millions, who now stand aloofe, would join our ranks, and we should soon become invincible. As to giving the vote to every young man of 21 years of age, I can see no good likely to result from it; that is, if the young men of my parish are to be taken as a fair sample. On this head I have heard it observed, 'I have my misgiving allway, when I see hundreds of them collected together to see a footrace, a trail hunt; a cock fight, a pigeon flying or other such gatherings of the very scum and dregs of an uneducated mob.—I for one can see no remedy for this deplorable state of society, but a national system of secular education, totally apart from the sleek and canting, whineing black coated tribes of all creeds what-ever.'

    But turning our attention to the case of householders generally, I think I can perceive a more cheering picture. When a man becomes a housekeeper, he finds his case a much altered one, he finds himself loaded with cares and anxieties he before knew nothing of. Poverty begets reflection, and on mature reflection, he soon learns the cause of this poverty. He becomes a reader, and soon learns the a.b.c. of radicalism, but, alas, he finds to his sorrow, that he has no power. I live in the mountains that separate Lankashire from Yorkshire, and i had the mortification to witness the last Oldham election, and to see John Fielden hauled out his seat in Parliament, by a most infamous coalition of corn-law repealer, and the scum and dregs of the tory faction in that town, and this to put in what? nay I blush to tell it, a none-descript an corn-law repealer an thing of eternal twaddle; a thing that would vote for a coertion bill for ireland; a thing that could, to pleas little Jonny and his like, twaddle away for an hour about leting a rich jew perch in the stinking hole;—which was of about as much importance, as whether or not a parrot should perch beside the chairman.

158

Now in my opinion is this, had there been household suffrage in Old-ham, John Fielding would have been returned by four to one—And I hesitate not to say the same of Jones and Halifax—of Harney and Tiver-ton—of Grath and Derby and the same of twenty other towns which I could name. Now all this supposes the protection of the ballot, without which the Charter would not be worth a groat. I have never approved of that standing motto in the starr, 'The Charter and No Surrender.' I do not like this bull-dog propensity. Rather, say I, meet the man of scruples half-way; when by doing so, you gain his assistance—The fact of the case is this, in my opinion we need not the assistance of these hair-brained young men; except it comes loggerheads, and even then we are secure, for they would do as their fathers bid them—in 19 cases out of 20. Therefore my motto is, household suffrage and the charter. In my opinion we are approaching a national crisis; like the crew in a crazy ship, without masts and ruder, and in the dark, driven by a hurrycane, on an unknown shore. If you can find a quiet corner for this, it would please an old radical, and I would much like George Julian Harney to make reply to it, And I beg him to accept my thanks for his shewing up of that old fiend of Waterloo He seems to long for the smell of gun-powder again—pity, but he had it, mixed up with his own b——.

# HENRY MAYHEW                                           X.8

## The London Scavenger

from *London Labour and the London Poor*, 1851

'I don't know how old I am and I can't see what that consarns any one, as I's old enough to have a jolly rough beard, and so can take care of myself. . . .

'I likes to hear the paper read well enough, if I's resting; but old Bill, as often wolunteers to read, has to spell the hard words so, that one can't tell what the devil he's reading about. I never heers anything about books. . . . I don't know much good that ever anybody as I knows ever got out of books; they're fittest for idle people. . . .

'I never goes to any church or chapel. . . . I was once in a church but felt queer, as one does in them strange places, and never went again. They're fittest for rich people. Yes, I've heered about religion and about God Almighty. *What* religion have I heered on? Why, the regular religion. I'm satisfied with what I knows and feels about it, and that's enough about it. . . . I cares nothing about politics neither; but I'm a chartist.

'I'm not a married man. I was a-going to be married to a young woman as lived with me a goodish bit as my housekeeper' (this he said

159

very demurely); 'but she went to the hopping to yarn a few shillings for herself, and never came back. I heered that she'd taken up with an Irish Hawker, but I can't say as to the rights on it. Did I fret about her? Perhaps not; but I was wexed.'

'I'm sure I can't say what I spends my wages in. I sometimes makes 12s. 6d a week, and sometimes better than 21s. with night-work. I suppose grub costs 1s. a day, and beer 6d.; but I keeps no accounts. I buy ready-cooked meat; often cold b'iled beef, and eats it at any tap room. I have meat every day; mostly more than once a day. Wegetables I don't care about, only ingans and cabbage, if you can get it smoking hot, with plenty of pepper. The rest of my tin goes for rent and baccy and togs, and a little drop of gin now and then.'


# CHARLES DICKENS                                                    X.9
## 'A Walk in the Workhouse'
from *Household Words*, 1850


On a certain Sunday, I formed one of the congregation assembled in the chapel of a large metropolitan Workhouse. With the exception of the clergyman and clerk, and a very few officials, there were none but paupers present. The children sat in the galleries; the women in the body of the chapel, and in one of the side aisles; the men in the remaining aisle. The service was decorously performed, though the sermon might have been much better adapted to the comprehension and to the circumstances of the hearers. The usual supplications were offered, with more than the usual significancy in such a place, for the fatherless children and widows, for all sick persons and young children, for all that were desolate and oppressed, for the comforting and helping of the weak-hearted, for the raising-up of them that had fallen; for all that were in danger, necessity, and tribulation. The prayers of the congregation were desired 'for several persons in the various wards dangerously ill;' and others who were recovering returned their thanks to Heaven.

Among this congregation, were some evil-looking young women, and beetle-browed young men; but not many—perhaps that kind of characters kept away. Generally, the faces (those of the children excepted) were depressed and subdued, and wanted colour. Aged people were there, in every variety. Mumbling, blear-eyed, spectacled, stupid, deaf, lame; vacantly winking in the gleams of sun that now and then crept in through the open doors, from the paved yard; shading their listening ears, or blinking eyes, with their withered hands; poring over their books, leering at nothing, going to sleep, crouching and drooping in corners. There were weird old women, all skeleton within, all bonnet and cloak without, continually wiping their eyes with dirty dusters of pocket handkerchiefs; and there were ugly old crones, both male and female, with a ghastly kind of contentment upon them which was not at all comforting to see. Upon the whole, it was the dragon, Pauperism, in a very weak and impotent condition; toothless, fangless, drawing his breath heavily enough, and hardly worth chaining up.

When the service was over, I walked with the humane and conscientious gentleman whose duty it was to take that walk, that Sunday morning, through the little world of poverty enclosed within the workhouse walls. It was inhabited by a population of some fifteen hundred or two thousand paupers, ranging from the infant newly born or not yet come into the pauper world, to the old man dying on his bed. . . .

Groves of babies in arms; groves of mothers and other sick women in bed; groves of lunatics; jungles of men in stone-paved down-stairs day-rooms, waiting for their dinners; longer and longer groves of old people in up-stairs Infirmary wards, wearing out life, God knows how—this was the scenery through which the walk lay, for two hours. In some of these latter chambers, there were pictures stuck against the wall, and a neat display of crockery and pewter on a kind of sideboard; now and then it was a treat to see a plant or two; in almost every ward there was a cat.

In all of these Long Walks of aged and infirm, some old people were bedridden, and had been for a long time; some were sitting on their beds half-naked; some dying in their beds; some out of bed, and sitting at a table near the fire. A sullen or lethargic indifference to what was asked, a blunted sensibility to everything but warmth and food, a moody absence of complaint as being of no use, a dogged silence and resentful desire to be left alone again, I thought were generally apparent. On our walking into the midst of one of these dreary perspectives of old men, nearly the following little dialogue took place, the nurse not being immediately at hand:

'All well here?'

No answer. An old man in a Scotch cap sitting among others on a form at the table, eating out of a tin porringer, pushes back his cap a little to look at us, claps it down on his forehead again with the palm of his hand, and goes on eating.

'All well here?' (repeated.)

No answer. Another old man sitting on his bed, paralytically peeling a boiled potato lifts his head and stares.

'Enough to eat?'

No answer. Another old man, in bed, turns himself and coughs.

'How are you to-day?' To the last old man.

That old man says nothing; but another old man, a tall old man of very good address, speaking with perfect correctness, comes forward

161

from somewhere, and volunteers an answer. The reply almost always proceeds from a volunteer, and not from the person looked at or spoken to.

'We are very old, sir,' in a mild, distinct voice. 'We can't expect to be well, most of us.'

'Are you comfortable?'

'I have no complaint to make, sir.' With a half shake of his head, a half shrug of his shoulders, and a kind of apologetic smile.

'Enough to eat?'

'Why, sir, I have but a poor appetite,' with the same air as before; 'and yet I get through my allowance very easily.'

'But,' showing a porringer with a Sunday dinner in it; 'here is a portion of mutton, and three potatoes. You can't starve on that?'

'Oh dear no, sir,' with the same apologetic air. 'Not starve.'

'What do you want?'

'We have very little bread, sir. It's an exceedingly small quantity of bread.'

The nurse, who is now rubbing her hands at the questioner's elbow, interferes with, 'It ain't much raly, sir. You see they've only six ounces a day, and when they've took their breakfast, there *can* only be a little left for night, sir.'

Another old man, hitherto invisible, rises out of his bed-clothes, as out of a grave, and looks on.

'You have tea at night?' The questioner is still addressing the well-spoken old man.

'Yes, sir, we have tea at night.'

'And you can save what bread you can from the morning, to eat with it?'

'Yes, sir—if we can save any.'

'And you want more to eat with it?'

'Yes, sir.' With a very anxious face.

The questioner, in the kindness of his heart, appears a little discomposed, and changes the subject.

'What has become of the old man who used to lie in that bed in the corner?'

The nurse don't remember what old man is referred to. There has been such a many old men. The well-spoken old man is doubtful. The spectral old man who has come to life in bed, says, 'Billy Stevens.' Another old man who has previously had his head in the fire-place, pipes out,

'Charley Walters.'

Something like a feeble interest is awakened. I suppose Charley Walters had conversation in him.

'He's dead,' says the piping old man.

Another old man, with one eye screwed up, hastily displaces the piping old man, and says·

'Yes! Charley Walters died in that bed, and—and—'

'Billy Stevens,' persists the spectral old man.

'No, no! and Johnny Rogers died in that bed, and—and—they're both on 'em dead—and Sam'l Bowyer;' this seems very extraordinary to him; 'he went out!'

With this he subsides, and all the old men (having had quite enough of it) subside, and the spectral old man goes into his grave again, and takes the shade of Billy Stevens with him.

As we turn to go out at the door, another previously invisible old man, a hoarse old man in a flannel gown, is standing there, as if he had just come up through the floor.

'I beg your pardon, sir, could I take the liberty of saying a word?'

'Yes; what is it?'

'I am greatly better in my health, sir; but what I want, to get me quite round,' with his hand on his throat, 'is a little fresh air, sir. It has always done my complaint so much good, sir. The regular leave for going out, comes round so seldom, that if the gentlemen, next Friday, would give me leave to go out walking, now and then—for only an hour or so, sir!—'

Who could wonder, looking through those weary vistas of bed and infirmity, that it should do him good to meet with some other scenes, and assure himself that there was something else on earth? Who could help wondering why the old men lived on as they did; what grasp they had on life; what crumbs of interest or occupation they could pick up from its bare board; whether Charley Walters had ever described to them the days when he kept company with some old pauper woman in the bud, or Billy Stevens ever told them of the time when he was a dweller in the far-off foreign land called Home!

The morsel of burnt child, lying in another room, so patiently, in bed, wrapped in lint, and looking stedfastly at us with his bright quiet eyes when we spoke to him kindly, looked as if the knowledge of these things, and of all the tender things there are to think about, might have been in his mind—as if he thought, with us, that there was a fellow-feeling in the pauper nurses which appeared to make them more kind to their charges than the race of common nurses in the hospitals—as if he mused upon the Future of some older children lying around him in the same place, and thought it best, perhaps, all things considered, that he should die—as if he knew, without fear, of those many coffins, made and unmade, piled up in the store below—and of his unknown friend, 'the dropped child,' calm upon the box lid covered with a cloth. But there was something wistful and appealing, too, in his tiny face, as if, in the midst of all the hard necessities and incongruities he pondered on,

163

he pleaded, in behalf of the helpless and the aged poor, for a little more liberty—and a little more bread.

## MRS ELIZABETH GASKELL                                     X.10
### 'What is a Strike?'

from *North and South*, 1855

Margaret . . . began to take notice, instead of having her thoughts turned so exclusively inward. She saw unusual loiterers in the streets: men with their hands in their pockets sauntering along; loud-laughing and loud-spoken girls clustered together, apparently excited to high spirits, and a boisterous independence of temper and behaviour. The more ill-looking of the men—the discreditable minority—hung about on the steps of the beer-houses and gin-shops, smoking, and commenting pretty freely on every passer-by. Margaret disliked the prospect of the long walk through these streets, before she came to the fields which she had planned to reach. Instead, she would go and see Bessy Higgins. It would not be so refreshing as a quiet country walk, but still it would perhaps be doing the kinder thing.

Nicholas Higgins was sitting by the fire smoking, as she went in. Bessy was rocking herself on the other side.

Nicholas took the pipe out of his mouth, and standing up, pushed his chair towards Margaret; he leant against the chimneypiece in a lounging attitude, while she asked Bessy how she was.

'Hoo's rather down i' the' mouth in regard to spirits, but hoo's better in health. Hoo doesn't like this strike. Hoo's a deal too much set on peace and quietness at any price.'

'This is th' third strike I've seen,' said she, sighing, as if that was answer and explanation enough.

'Well, third time pays for all. See if we don't dang th' masters this time. See if they don't come, and beg us to come back at our own price. That's all. We've missed it afore time, I grant yo'; but this time we'n laid our plans desperate deep.'

'Why do you strike?' asked Margaret. 'Striking is leaving off work till you get your own rate of wages, is it not? You must not wonder at my ignorance; where I come from I never heard of a strike.'

'I wish I were there,' said Bessy, wearily. 'But it's not for me to get sick and tired o' strikes. This is the last I'll see. Before it's ended I shall be in the Great City—the Holy Jerusalem.'

'Hoo's so full of th' life to come, hoo cannot think of th' present. Now I, yo' see, am bound to do the best I can here. I think a bird i' th' hand is worth two i' the' bush. So them's the different views we take on th' strike question.'

'But,' said Margaret, 'if the people struck, as you call it, where I come from, as they are mostly all field labourers, the seed would not be sown, the hay got in, the corn reaped.'

'Well?' said he. He had resumed his pipe, and put his 'well' in the form of an interrogation.

'Why,' she went on, 'what would become of the farmers?'

He puffed away. 'I reckon, they'd have either to give up their farms, or to give fair rate of wage.'

'Suppose they could not, or would not do the last; they could not give up their farms all in a minute, however much they might wish to do so; but they would have no hay, nor corn to sell that year; and where would the money come from to pay the labourers' wages the next?'

Still puffing away. At last he said:

'I know nought of your ways down South. I have heerd they're a pack of spiritless, down-trodden men; welly clemmed to death; too much dazed wi' clemming to know when they're put upon. Now, it's not so here. We know when we're put upon; and we'en too much blood in us to stand it. We just take our hands fro' our looms, and say, "Yo' may clem us, but yo'll not put upon us, my masters!" And be danged to 'em, they shan't this time!'

'I wish I lived down South,' said Bessy.

'There's a deal to bear there,' said Margaret. 'There are sorrows to bear everywhere. There is very hard bodily labour to be gone through, with very little food to give strength.'

'But it's out of doors,' said Bessy. 'And away from the endless, endless noise, and sickening heat.'

'It's sometimes in heavy rain, and sometimes in bitter cold. A young person can stand it; but an old man gets racked with rheumatism, and bent and withered before his time; yet he must just work on the same, or else go to the workhouse.'

'I thought yo' were so taken wi' the ways of the South country.'

'So I am,' said Margaret, smiling a little, as she found herself thus caught. 'I only mean, Bessy, there's good and bad in everything in this world; and as you felt the bad up here, I thought it was but fair you should know the bad down there.'

'And yo' say they never strike down there?' asked Nicholas, abruptly.

'No!' said Margaret; 'I think they have too much sense.'

'An' I think,' replied he, dashing the ashes out of his pipe with so much vehemence that it broke, 'it's not that they've too much sense, but that they've too little spirit.'

'Oh, father!' said Bessy, 'what have ye gained by striking? Think of that first strike when mother died—how we all had to clem—you the worst of all; and yet many a one went in every week at the same wage, till all were gone in that there was work for; and some went beggars all their lives at after.'

'Ay,' said he. 'That there strike was badly managed. Folk got into th' management of it, as were either fools or not true men. Yo'll see, it'll be different this time.'

'But all this time you've not told me what you're striking for,' said Margaret, again.

'Why yo' see, there's five or six masters who have set themselves again paying the wages they've been paying these two years past, and flourishing upon, and getting richer upon. And now they come to us, and say we're to take less. And we won't. We'll just clem to death first; and see who'll work for 'em then. They'll have killed the goose that laid 'em the golden eggs, I reckon.'

'And so you plan dying, in order to be revenged upon them!'

'No,' said he, 'I dunnot. I just look forward to the chance of dying at my post sooner than yield. That's what folk call fine and honourable in a soldier, and why not in a poor weaver-chap?' '

'But,' said Margaret, 'a soldier dies in the cause of the Nation—in the cause of others.'

He laughed grimly. 'My lass,' said he, 'yo're but a young wench, but don't yo' think I can keep three people—that's Bessy, and Mary, and me —on sixteen shilling a week? Dun yo' think it's for mysel' I'm striking work at this time? It's just as much in the cause of others as yon soldier —only, m'appen, the cause he dies for it's just that of somebody he never clapt eyes on, nor heerd on all his born days, while I take up John Boucher's cause, as lives next door but one, wi' a sickly wife, and eight childer, none on 'em factory age; and I don't take up his cause only, though he's a poor good-for-nought, as can only manage two looms at a time, but I take up th' cause o' justice. Why are we to have less wage now, I ask, than two year ago?'

'Don't ask me,' said Margaret; 'I am very ignorant. Ask some of your masters. Surely they will give you a reason for it. It is not merely an arbitrary decision of theirs, come to without reason.'

'Yo're just a foreigner, and nothing more,' said he contemptuously. 'Much yo' know about it. Ask th' masters! They'd tell us to mind our own business, and they'd mind theirs. Our business being, yo' understand, to take the bated wage, and be thankful; and their business to bate us down to clemming point, to swell their profits. That's what it is.'

'But,' said Margaret, determined not to give way, although she saw she was irritating him, 'the state of trade may be such as not to enable them to give you the same remuneration.'

'State o' trade! That's just a piece o' masters' humbug. It's rate o' wages I was talking of. Th' masters keep th' state o' trade in their own hands; and just walk it forward like a black bug-a-boo, to frighten naughty children with into being good. I'll tell yo' it's their part,—their cue, as some folks call it,—to beat us down, to swell their fortunes; and it's ours to stand up and fight hard,—not for ourselves alone, but for them round about us—for justice and fair play. We help to make their profits, and we ought to help spend 'em. It's not that we want their brass so much this time, as we've done many a time afore. We'n gotten money laid by; and we're resolved to stand and fall together; not a man on us will go in for less wage than th' Union says is our due. So I say, "hooray for the strike," and let Thornton, and Slickson, and Hamper, and their set look to it!'. . .

'Poor Bessy!' said Margaret, turning round to her. 'You sigh over it all. You don't like struggling and fighting as your father does, do you?'

'No!' said she heavily. 'I'm sick on it. I could have wished to have had other talk about me in my latter days, than just the clashing and clanging and clattering that has wearied a' my life long, about work and wages, and masters, and hands, and knobsticks '

'Pooh, wench! latter days be farred! Thou'rt looking a sight better already for a little stir and change. Beside, I shall be a deal here to make it more lively for thee.'

'Tobacco-smoke chokes me!' said she, querulously.

'Then I'll never smoke no more i' th' house!' he replied, tenderly. 'But why did'st thou not tell me afore, thou foolish wench?'

She did not speak for a while, and then so low that only Margaret heard her:

'I reckon, he'll want a' the comfort he can get out o' either pipe or drink afore he's done.'

Her father went out of doors, evidently to finish his pipe.

Bessy said passionately,

'Now am not I a fool,—am I not, miss?—there, I knew I ought for to keep father at home, and away fro' the folk that are always ready for to tempt a man, in time o' strike, to go drink,—and there my tongue must needs quarrel with this pipe o' his'n,—and he'll go off, I know he will,—as often as he wants to smoke—and nobody knows where it'll end. I wish I'd letten myself be choked first.'

'But does your father drink?' said Margaret.

'No—not to say drink,' replied she, still in the same wild excited tone. 'But what win ye have? There are days wi' you as wi' other folk, I suppose, when yo' get up and go through th' hours, just longing for a bit of a change—a bit of a fillip, as it were. I know I ha' gone and bought a four-pounder out o' another baker's shop to common on such days, just because I sickened at the thought of going on for ever wi' the same sight in my eyes, and the same sound in my ears, and the same taste i' my mouth, and the same thought (or no thought, for that matter) in my head, day after day, for ever. I've longed for to be a man to go spreeing, even if it were only a tramp to some new place in search o' work. And father—all men—have it stronger in 'em than me to get tired o' sameness and work for ever. And what is 'em to do? It's little blame to them if they do go into th' gin-shop for to make their blood flow quicker, and more lively, and see things they never see at no other time—pictures, and looking-glass, and such like. But father never was a drunkard, though maybe, he's got worse for drink, now and then. Only yo' see,' and now her voice took a mournful, pleading tone, 'at times o' strike there's much to knock a man down, for all they start so hopefully; and where's the comfort to come fro'? He'll get angry and mad—they all do—and then they get tired out wi' being angry and mad, and maybe ha' done things in their passion they'd be glad to forget. Bless yo'r sweet pitiful face! but yo' dunnot know what a strike is yet.'

ANON                                                                      X.11

'The Cotton Lords of Preston'

Ballad, 1853

> Have you not heard the news of late
> About some mighty men so great?
> I mean the swells of Fishergate,
> The Cotton Lords of Preston.
> They are a set of stingy blades,
> They've locked up all their mills and shades.
> So now we've nothing else to do
> But come a-singing songs to you.
> So with our ballads we've come out
> To tramp the country round about,
> And try if we cannot live without
> The Cotton Lords of Preston.
>
> *Chorus*
> Everybody's crying shame
> On these gentlemen by name.
> Don't you think they're much to blame,
> The Cotton Lords of Preston?
>
> The working people such as we
> Pass their time in misery,

While they live in luxury,
The Cotton Lords of Preston
They're making money every way
And building factories every day,
Yet when we ask them for more pay,
They had the impudence to say:
'To your demands we'll not consent;
You get enough, so be content'—
But we will have the ten per cent
From the Cotton Lords of Preston.

Our masters say they're very sure
That a strike we can't endure;
They all assert we're very poor,
The Cotton Lords of Preston.
But we've determined every one
With them we will not be done,
And we will not be content
Until we get the ten per cent.
The Cotton Lords are sure to fall,
Both ugly, handsome, short and tall;
For we intend to conquer all
The Cotton Lords of Preston.

So men and women, all of you,
Come and buy a song or two,
And assist us to subdue
The Cotton Lords of Preston.
We'll conquer them and no mistake,
Whatever laws they seem to make,
And when we get the ten per cent
Then we'll live happy and content.
Oh then we'll dance and sing with glee
And thank you all right heartily,
When we gain the victory
And beat the Lords of Preston.

# XI  Poets on Work and Civilization

## The Development of Civilization

from 'Autumn', 1726–30

     When the bright Virgin gives the beauteous days,
And Libra weighs in equal scales the year,
From heaven's high cope the fierce effulgence shook
Of parting Summer, a serener blue,
With golden light enlivened, wide invests
The happy world. Attempered suns arise
Sweet-beamed, and shedding oft through lucid clouds
A pleasing calm; while broad and brown, below,
Extensive harvests hang the heavy head.
Rich, silent, deep they stand; for not a gale
Rolls its light billows o'er the bending plain;
A calm of plenty! till the ruffled air
Falls from its poise, and gives the breeze to blow.
Rent is the fleecy mantle of the sky;
The clouds fly different; and the sudden sun
By fits effulgent gilds the illumined field,
And black by fits the shadows sweep along—
A gaily chequered, heart-expanding view,
Far as the circling eye can shoot around,
Unbounded tossing in a flood of corn.
   These are thy blessings, Industry, rough power!
Whom labour still attends, and sweat, and pain;
Yet the kind source of every gentle art
And all the soft civility of life:
Raiser of human kind! by Nature cast
Naked and helpless out amid the woods
And wilds to rude inclement elements;
With various seeds of art deep in the mind
Implanted, and profusely poured around
Materials infinite; but idle all,
Still unexerted, in the unconscious breast
Slept the lethargic powers; Corruption still
Voracious swallowed what the liberal hand

171

Of Bounty scattered o'er the savage year.
And still the sad barbarian roving mixed
With beasts of prey; or for his acorn meal
Fought the fierce tusky boar—a shivering wretch!
Aghast and comfortless when the bleak north,
With winter charged, let the mixed tempest fly,
Hail, rain, and snow, and bitter-breathing frost.
Then to the shelter of the hut he fled,
And the wild season, sordid, pined away;
For home he had not: home is the resort
Of love, of joy, of peace and plenty, where,
Supporting and supported, polished friends
And dear relations mingle into bliss.
But this the rugged savage never felt,
Even desolate in crowds; and thus his days
Rolled heavy, dark, and unenjoyed along—
A waste of time! till Industry approached,
And roused him from his miserable sloth;
His faculties unfolded; pointed out
Where lavish Nature the directing hand
Of Art demanded; showed him how to raise
His feeble force by the mechanic powers,
To dig the mineral from the vaulted earth,
On what to turn the piercing rage of fire,
On what the torrent, and the gathered blast;
Gave the tall ancient forest to his axe;
Taught him to chip the wood, and hew the stone,
Till by degrees the finished fabric rose;
Tore from his limbs the blood-polluted fur,
And wrapped them in the woolly vestment warm,
Or bright in glossy silk, and flowing lawn;
With wholesome viands filled his table, poured
The generous glass around, inspired to wake
The life-refining soul of decent wit;
Nor stopped at barren bare necessity;
But, still advancing bolder, led him on
To pomp, to pleasure, elegance, and grace;
And, breathing high ambition through his soul,
Set science, wisdom, glory in his view,
And bade him be the lord of all below.
    Then gathering men their natural powers combined,
And formed a public; to the general good
Submitting, aiming, and conducting all.
For this the patriot-council met, the full,
The free, and fairly represented whole;

For this they planned the holy guardian laws,
Distinguished orders, animated arts,
And, with joint force Oppression chaining, set
Imperial Justice at the helm, yet still
To them accountable: nor slavish dreamed
That toiling millions must resign their weal
And all the honey of their search to such
As for themselves alone themselves have raised.
　　Hence every form of cultivated life
In order set, protected, and inspired
Into perfection wrought. Uniting all,
Society grew numerous, high, polite,
And happy. Nurse of art, the city reared
In beauteous pride her tower-encircled head;
And, stretching street on street, by thousands drew,
From twining woody haunts, or the tough yew
To bows strong-straining, her aspiring sons.
　　Then Commerce brought into the public walk
The busy merchant; the big warehouse built;
Raised the strong crane; choked up the loaded street
With foreign plenty; and thy stream, O Thames,
Large, gentle, deep, majestic, king of floods!
Chose for his grand resort. On either hand,
Like a long wintry forest, groves of masts
Shot up their spires; the bellying sheet between
Possessed the breezy void; the sooty hulk
Steered sluggish on; the splendid barge along
Rowed regular to harmony; around,
The boat light-skimming stretched its oary wings;
While deep the various voice of fervent toil
From bank to bank increased; whence, ribbed with oak
To bear the British thunder, black, and bold,
The roaring vessel rushed into the main.
　　Then too the pillared dome magnific heaved
Its ample roof; and Luxury within
Poured out her glittering stores. The canvas smooth,
With glowing life protuberant, to the view
Embodied rose; the statue seemed to breathe
And soften into flesh beneath the touch
Of forming art, imagination-flushed.
　　All is the gift of Industry,—whate'er
Exalts, embellishes, and renders life
Delightful. Pensive Winter, cheered by him,
Sits at the social fire, and happy hears
The excluded tempest idly rave along;

173

His hardened fingers deck the gaudy Spring;
Without him Summer were an arid waste;
Nor to the Autumnal months could thus transmit
Those full, mature, immeasurable stores
That, waving round, recall my wandering song.


## WILLIAM COWPER                                        XI.2

Work and the movement of the earth

from *The Task*, 1784

Ye fallen avenues! once more I mourn
Your fate unmerited, once more rejoice
That yet a remnant of your race survives.
How airy and how light the graceful arch,
Yet awful as the consecrated roof
Re-echoing pious anthems! while beneath
The chequer'd earth seems restless as a flood
Brush'd by the wind. So sportive is the light
Shot through the boughs, it dances as they dance,
Shadow and sunshine intermingling quick,
And darkening and enlightening, as the leaves
Play wanton, every moment, every spot.
    And now, with nerves new braced, and spirits cheer'd,
We tread the wilderness, whose well-roll'd walks,
With curvature of slow and easy sweep—
Deception innocent—give ample space
To narrow bounds. The grove receives us next;
Between the upright shafts of whose tall elms
We may discern the thresher at his task.
Thump after thump resounds the constant flail,
That seems to swing uncertain, and yet falls
Full on the destined ear. Wide flies the chaff;
The rustling straw sends up a frequent mist
Of atoms, sparkling in the noonday beam.
Come hither, ye that press your beds of down
And sleep not; see him sweating o'er his bread
Before he eats it.—'Tis the primal curse,
But soften'd into mercy; made the pledge
Of cheerful days, and nights without a groan.
    By ceaseless action all that is subsists.
Constant rotation of the unwearied wheel
That Nature rides upon maintains her health,

Her beauty, her fertility. She dreads
An instant's pause, and lives but while she moves.
Its own revolvency upholds the world.
Winds from all quarters agitate the air,
And fit the limpid element for use,
Else noxious: oceans, rivers, lakes and streams,
All feel the freshening impulse, and are cleansed
By restless undulation: . . .

# WILLIAM WORDSWORTH                                    XI.3

## "Outrage done to Nature"

from *The Excursion*, 1814

'Meanwhile, at social Industry's command,
How quick, how vast an increase. From the germ
Of some poor hamlet, rapidly produced
Here a huge town, continuous and compact,
Hiding the face of earth for leagues—and there,
Where not a habitation stood before,
Abodes of men irregularly massed
Like trees in forests,—spread through spacious tracts,
O'er which the smoke of unremitting fires
Hangs permanent, and plentiful as wreaths
Of vapour glittering in the morning sun.
And, wheresoe'er the traveller turns his steps,
He sees the barren wilderness erased,
Or disappearing; triumph that proclaims
How much the mild Directress of the plough
Owes to alliance with these new-born arts!
—Hence is the wide sea peopled,—hence the shores
Of Britain are resorted to by ships
Freighted from every climate of the world
With the world's choicest produce. Hence that sum
Of keels that rest within her crowded ports,
Or ride at anchor in her sounds and bays;
That animating spectacle of sails
That, through her inland regions, to and fro
Pass with the respirations of the tide,
Perpetual, multitudinous! . . .

. . . I grieve, when on the darker side
Of this great change I look; and there behold

175

Such outrage done to nature as compels
The indignant power to justify herself;
Yea, to avenge her violated rights,
For England's bane.—When soothing darkness spreads
O'er hill and vale,' the Wanderer thus expressed
His recollections, 'and the punctual stars,
While all things else are gathering to their homes,
Advance, and in the firmament of heaven
Glitter—but undisturbing, undisturbed;
As if their silent company were charged
With peaceful admonitions for the heart
Of all-beholding Man, earth's thoughtful lord;
Then, in full many a region, once like this
The assured domain of calm simplicity
And pensive quiet, an unnatural light
Prepared for never-resting Labour's eyes
Breaks from a many-windowed fabric huge;
And at the appointed hour a bell is heard,
Of harsher import than the curfew-knoll
That spake the Norman Conqueror's stern behest—
A local summons to unceasing toil!
Disgorged are now the ministers of day;
And, as they issue from the illumined pile,
A fresh band meets them, at the crowded door—
And in the courts—and where the rumbling stream,
That turns the multitude of dizzy wheels,
Glares, like a troubled spirit, in its bed
Among the rocks below. Men, maidens, youths,
Mother and little children, boys and girls,
Enter, and each the wonted task resumes
Within this temple, where is offered up
To Gain, the master idol of the realm,
Perpetual sacrifice. Even thus of old
Our ancestors, within the still domain
Of vast cathedral or conventual church,
Their vigils kept; where tapers day and night
On the dim altar burned continually,
In token that the House was evermore
Watching to God. Religious men were they;
Nor would their reason, tutored to aspire
Above this transitory world, allow
That there should pass a moment of the year,
When in their land the Almighty's service ceased.

'Triumph who will in these profaner rites
Which we, a generation self-extolled,
As zealously perform! I cannot share
His proud complacency:—yet do I exult,
Casting reserve away, exult to see
An intellectual mastery exercised
O'er the blind elements; a purpose given,
A perseverance fed; almost a soul
Imparted—to brute matter. I rejoice,
Measuring the force of those gigantic powers
That, by the thinking mind, have been compelled
To serve the will of feeble-bodied Man.
For with the sense of admiration blends
The animating hope that time may come
When, strengthened, yet not dazzled, by the might
Of this dominion over nature gained,
Men of all lands shall exercise the same
In due proportion to their country's need;
Learning, though late, that all true glory rests,
All praise, all safety, and all happiness,
Upon the moral law.

# XII Early Ideas of Work and the Economy

ADAM SMITH                                                          XII.1

"A mercenary exchange of good offices according
to agreed valuation"

from *The Theory of Moral Sentiments*, 1759

. . . All the members of human society stand in need of each other's
assistance, and are likewise exposed to mutual injuries. Where the necessary assistance is reciprocally afforded from love, from gratitude, from
friendship, and esteem, the society flourishes and is happy. All the different members of it are bound together by the agreeable bands of love
and affection, and are, as it were, drawn to one common centre of
mutual good offices.

But though the necessary assistance should not be afforded from
such generous and disinterested motives, though among the different
members of the society there should be no mutual love and affection,
the society, though less happy and agreeable, will not necessarily be dissolved. Society may subsist among different men, as among different
merchants, from a sense of its utility, without any mutual love or affection; and though no man in it should owe any obligation, or be bound
in gratitude to any other, it may still be upheld by a mercenary exchange of good offices according to an agreed valuation.

Society, however, cannot subsist among those who are at all times
ready to hurt and injure one another. The moment that injury begins,
the moment that mutual resentment and animosity take place, all the
bands of it are broken asunder, and the different members of which it
consisted, are, as it were, dissipated and scattered abroad by the violence and opposition of their discordant affections. If there is any
society among robbers and murderers, they must at least, according to
the trite observation, abstain from robbing and murdering one another.
Beneficence, therefore, is less essential to the existence of society than
justice. Society may subsist, though not in the most comfortable state,
without beneficence; but the prevalence of injustice must utterly
destroy it.

Though nature, therefore, exhorts mankind to acts of beneficence,
by the pleasing consciousness of deserved reward, she has not thought
it necessary to guard and enforce the practice of it by the terrors of

merited punishment in case it should be neglected. It is the ornament which embellishes, not the foundation which supports the building, and which it was, therefore, sufficient to recommend, but by no means necessary to impose. Justice, on the contrary, is the main pillar that upholds the whole edifice. If it is removed, the great, the immense fabric of human society, that fabric which, to raise and support, seems, in this world, if I may say so, to have been the peculiar and darling care of nature, must in a moment crumble into atoms. In order to enforce the observation of justice, therefore, nature has implanted in the human breast that consciousness of ill desert, those terrors of merited punishment, which attend upon its violation, as the great safeguards of the association of mankind, to protect the weak, to curb the violent, and to chastise the guilty. Men, though naturally sympathetic, feel so little for an other, with whom they have no particular connection, in comparison of what they feel for themselves; the misery of one, who is merely their fellow-creature, is of so little importance to them in comparison even of a small conveniency of their own; they have it so much in their power to hurt him, and may have so many temptations to do so, that if this principle did not stand up within them in his defence, and overawe them into a respect for his innocence, they would, like wild beasts, be at all times ready to fly upon him; and a man would enter an assembly of men as he enters a den of lions.

# ADAM SMITH                                                   XII.2
## Work and its effects

from *An Inquiry into the Nature and Causes of the Wealth of Nations*, 1776

(a) 'Of the Division of Labour.'

The greatest improvement in the productive powers of labour, and the greater part of the skill, dexterity, and judgment with which it is anywhere directed, or applied, seem to have been the effects of the division of labour.

The effects of the division of labour, in the general business of society, will be more easily understood by considering in what manner it operates in some particular manufactures. It is commonly supposed to be carried furthest in some very trifling ones; not perhaps that it really is carried further in them than in others of more importance; but in those trifling manufactures which are destined to supply the small wants of but a small number of people, the whole number of workmen must necessarily be small; and those employed in every different branch of the work can often be collected into the same workhouse, and placed at once under the view of the spectator. In those great manufactures, on the contrary, which are destined to supply the great wants of the great body of the people, every different branch of the work employs so great a number of workmen that it is impossible to collect them all into the same workhouse. We can seldom see more, at one time, than those employed in one single branch. Though in such manufactures, therefore, the work may really be divided into a much greater number of parts than in those of a more trifling nature, the division is not near so obvious, and has accordingly been much less observed.

To take an example, therefore, from a very trifling manufacture: but one in which the division of labour has been very often taken notice of, the trade of the pin-maker; a workman not educated to this business (which the division of labour has rendered a distinct trade), nor acquainted with the use of the machinery employed in it (to the invention of which the same division of labour has probably given occasion), could scarce, perhaps, with his utmost industry, make one pin in a day, and certainly could not make twenty. But in the way in which this business is now carried on, not only the whole work is a peculiar trade, but it is divided into a number of branches, of which the greater part are likewise peculiar trades. One man draws out the wire, another straights it, a third cuts it, a fourth points it, a fifth grinds it at the top for receiving the head; to make the head requires two or three distinct operations; to put it on is a peculiar business, to whiten the pins is another; it is even a trade by itself to put them into the paper; and the important business of making a pin is, in this manner, divided into about eighteen distinct operations, which, in some manufactories, are all performed by distinct hands, though in others the same man will sometimes perform two or three of them. I have seen a small manufactory of this kind where ten men only were employed, and where some of them consequently performed two or three distinct operations. But though they were very poor, and therefore but indifferently accommodated with the necessary machinery, they could, when they exerted themselves, make among them about twelve pounds of pins in a day. There are in a pound upwards of four thousand pins of a middling size. Those ten persons, therefore, could make among them upwards of forty-eight thousand pins in a day. Each person, therefore, making a tenth part of forty-eight thousand pins, might be considered as making four thousand eight hundred pins in a day. But if they had all wrought separately and independently, and without any of them having been educated to this peculiar business, they certainly could not each of them have made twenty, perhaps not one pin in a day; that is, certainly, not the two hundred and fortieth, perhaps not the four thousand eight hundredth part of what they are at present capable of performing, in consequence of a proper division and combination of their different operations.

181

In every other art and manufacture, the effects of the division of labour are similar to what they are in this very trifling one; though, in many of them, the labour can neither be so much subdivided, nor reduced to so great a simplicity of operation. The division of labour, however, so far as it can be introduced, occasions, in every art, a proportionable increase of the productive powers of labour. The separation of different trades and employments from one another seems to have taken place in consequence of this advantage. This separation, too, is generally carried furthest in those countries which enjoy the highest degree of industry and improvement; what is the work of one man in a rude state of society being generally that of several in an improved one. In every improved society, the farmer is generally nothing but a farmer; the manufacturer, nothing but a manufacturer. . . .

This great increase of the quantity of work which, in consequence of the division of labour, the same number of people are capable of performing, is owing to three different circumstances; first, to the increase of dexterity in every particular workman; secondly, to the saving of the time which is commonly lost in passing from one species of work to another; and lastly, to the invention of a great number of machines which facilitate and abridge labour, and enable one man to do the work of many.

First, the improvement of the dexterity of the workman necessarily increases the quantity of the work he can perform; and the division of labour, by reducing every man's business to some one simple operation, and by making this operation the sole employment of his life, necessarily increases very much the dexterity of the workman. . . .

Secondly, the advantage which is gained by saving the time commonly lost in passing from one sort of work to another is much greater than we should at first view be apt to imagine it. It is impossible to pass very quickly from one kind of work to another that is carried on in a different place and with quite different tools. A country weaver, who cultivates a small farm, must lose a good deal of time in passing from his loom to the field, and from the field to his loom. When the two trades can be carried on in the same workhouse, the loss of time is no doubt much less. It is even in this case, however, very considerable. A man commonly saunters a little in turning his hand from one sort of employment to another. When he first begins the new work he is seldom very keen and hearty; his mind, as they say, does not go to it, and for some time he rather trifles than applies to good purpose. The habit of sauntering and of indolent careless application, which is naturally, or rather necessarily acquired by every country workman who is obliged to change his work and his tools every half hour, and to apply his hand in twenty different ways almost every day of his life, renders him almost always slothful and lazy, and incapable of any vigorous application even on the most pressing occasions. Independent, therefore, of his deficiency in point of dexterity, this cause alone must always reduce considerably the quantity of work which he is capable of performing.

Thirdly, and lastly, everybody must be sensible how much labour is facilitated and abridged by the application of proper machinery. . . .

Whoever has been much accustomed to visit such manufactures must frequently have been shown very pretty machines, which were the inventions of such workmen in order to facilitate and quicken their own particular part of the work. In the first fire-engines, a boy was constantly employed to open and shut alternately the communication between the boiler and the cylinder, according as the piston either ascended or descended. One of those boys, who loved to play with his companions, observed that, by tying a string from the handle of the valve which opened this communication to another part of the machine, the valve would open and shut without his assistance, and leave him at liberty to divert himself with his playfellows. One of the greatest improvements that has been made upon this machine, since it was first invented, was in this manner the discovery of a boy who wanted to save his own labour.

All the improvements in machinery, however, have by no means been the inventions of those who had occasion to use the machines. Many improvements have been made by the ingenuity of the makers of the machines, when to make them became the business of a peculiar trade; and some by that of those who are called philosophers or men of speculation, whose trade it is not to do anything, but to observe everything; and who, upon that account, are often capable of combining together the powers of the most distant and dissimilar objects. In the progress of society, philosophy or speculation becomes, like every other employment, the principal or sole trade and occupation of a particular class of citizens. Like every other employment too, it is subdivided into a great number of different branches, each of which affords occupation to a peculiar tribe or class of philosophers; and this subdivision of employment in philosophy, as well as in every other business, improves dexterity, and saves time. Each individual becomes more expert in his own peculiar branch, more work is done upon the whole, and the quantity of science is considerably increased by it.

It is the great multiplication of the productions of all the different arts, in consequence of the division of labour, which occasions, in a well-governed society, that universal opulence which extends itself to the lowest ranks of the people. Every workman has a great quantity of his own work to dispose of beyond what he himself has occasion for; and every other workman being exactly in the same situation, he is enabled to exchange a great quantity of his own goods for a great quantity, or, what comes to the same thing, for the price of a great quantity of theirs. He supplies them abundantly with what they have occasion for, and they accommodate him as amply with what he has occasion for, and a general plenty diffuses itself through all the different ranks of the society. . . .

Observe the accommodation of the most common artificer or day-labourer in a civilized and thriving country, and you will perceive that the number of people of whose industry a part, though but a small part, has been employed in procuring him this accommodation, exceeds all computation. The woollen coat, for example, which covers the day-labourer, as coarse and rough as it may appear, is the produce of the joint labour of a great multitude of workmen. The shepherd, the sorter of the wool, the wool-comber or carder, the dyer, the scribbler, the spinner, the weaver, the fuller, the dresser, with many others, must all join their different arts in order to complete even this homely produc-tion. How many merchants and carriers, besides, must have been em-ployed in transporting the material from some of those workmen to others who often live in a very distant part of the country! how much commerce and navigation in particular, how many ship-builders, sailors, sail-makers, rope-makers, must have been employed in order to bring together the different drugs made use of by the dyer, which often come from the remotest corners of the world! What a variety of labour too is necessary in order to produce the tools of the meanest of those work-men! To say nothing of such complicated machines as the ship of the sailor, the mill of the fuller, or even the loom of the weaver, let us con-sider only what a variety of labour is requisite in order to form that very simple machine, the shears with which the shepherd clips the wool. The miner, the builder of the furnace for smelting the ore, the feller of the timber, the burner of the charcoal to be made use of in the smelting-house, the brick-maker, the brick-layer, the workmen who attend the furnace, the mill-wright, the forger, the smith, must all of them join their different arts in order to produce them. Were we to examine, in the same manner, all the different parts of his dress and household fur-niture, the coarse linen shirt which he wears next his skin, the shoes which cover his feet, the bed which he lies on, and all the different parts which compose it, the kitchen-grate at which he prepares his vic-tuals, the coals which he makes use of for that purpose, dug from the bowels of the earth, and brought to him perhaps by a long sea and a long land carriage, all the other utensils of his kitchen, all the furniture of his table, the knives and forks, the earthen or pewter plates upon which he serves up and divides his victuals, the different hands employed in preparing his bread and his beer, the glass window which lets in the heat and the light, and keeps out the wind and the rain, with all the knowledge and art requisite for preparing that beautiful and happy in-vention, without which these northern parts of the world could scarce have afforded a very comfortable habitation, together with the tools of all the different workmen employed in producing those different conveniencies; if we examine, I say, all these things, and consider what a variety of labour is employed about each of them, we shall be sensible that without the assistance and co-operation of many thousands, the very meanest person in a civilized country could not be provided, even according to, what we very falsely imagine, the easy and simple manner in which he is commonly accommodated. Compared, indeed, with the more extravagant luxury of the great, his accommodation must no doubt appear extremely simple and easy; and yet it may be true, perhaps, that the accommodation of an European prince does not always so much exceed that of an industrious and frugal peasant, as the accommodation of the latter exceeds that of many an African king, the absolute master of the lives and liberties of ten thousand naked savages.

(b) 'The real price of everything . . . is the toil and trouble of acquiring it.'

Every man is rich or poor according to the degree in which he can afford to enjoy the necessaries, conveniences, and amusements of human life. But after the division of labour has once thoroughly taken place, it is but a very small part of these with which a man's own labour can supply him. The far greater part of them he must derive from the labour of other people, and he must be rich or poor according to the quantity of that labour which he can command, or which he can afford to purchase. The value of any commodity, therefore, to the person who possesses it, and who means not to use or consume it himself, but to exchange it for other commodities, is equal to the quantity of labour which it enables him to purchase or command. Labour, therefore, is the real measure of the exchangeable value of all commodities.

The real price of every thing, what every thing really costs to the man who wants to acquire it, is the toil and trouble of acquiring it. What every thing is really worth to the man who has acquired it, and who wants to dispose of it or exchange it for something else, is the toil and trouble which it can save to himself, and which it can impose upon other people. What is bought with money or with goods is purchased by labour, as much as what we acquire by the toil of our own body. That money or those goods indeed save us this toil. They contain the value of a certain quantity of labour which we exchange for what is supposed at the time to contain the value of an equal quantity. Labour was the first price, the original purchase-money that was paid for all things. It was not by gold or by silver, but by labour, that all the wealth of the world was originally purchased; and its value, to those who possess it, and who want to exchange it for some new productions, is precisely equal to the quantity of labour which it can enable them to purchase or command.

Wealth, as Mr. Hobbes says, is power. But the person who either acquires, or succeeds to a great fortune, does not necessarily acquire or succeed to any political power, either civil or military. His fortune may, perhaps, afford him the means of acquiring both, but the mere possession of that fortune does not necessarily convey to him either. The power which that possession immediately and directly conveys to him, is the power of purchasing; a certain command over all the labour, or over all the produce of labour which is then in the market. His fortune is greater or less, precisely in proportion to the extent of this power; or to the quantity either of other men's labour, or, what is the same thing, of the produce of other men's labour, which it enables him to purchase or command. The exchangeable value of every thing must always be precisely equal to the extent of this power which it conveys to its owner.

But though labour be the real measure of the exchangeable value of all commodities, it is not that by which their value is commonly estimated. It is often difficult to ascertain the proportion between two different quantities of labour. The time spent in two different sorts of work will not always alone determine this proportion. The different degrees of hardship endured, and of ingenuity exercised, must likewise be taken into account. There may be more labour in an hour's hard work than in two hours easy business; or in an hour's application to a trade which it cost ten years labour to learn, than in a month's industry at an ordinary and obvious employment. But it is not easy to find any accurate measure either of hardship or ingenuity. In exchanging indeed the different productions of different sorts of labour for one another, some allowance is commonly made for both. It is adjusted, however, not by any accurate measure, but by the higgling and bargaining of the market, according to that sort of rough equality which, though not exact, is sufficient for carrying on the business of common life.

(c) 'In disputes with their workmen, masters must generally have the advantage.'

It sometimes happens, indeed, that a single independent workman has stock sufficient both to purchase the materials of his work, and to maintain himself till it be compleated. He is both master and workman, and enjoys the whole produce of his own labour, or the whole value which it adds to the materials upon which it is bestowed. It includes what are usually two distinct revenues, belonging to two distinct persons, the profits of stock, and the wages of labour.

Such cases, however, are not very frequent, and in every part of Europe, twenty workmen serve under a master for one that is independent; and the wages of labour are every where understood to be, what they usually are, when the labourer is one person, and the owner of the stock which employs him another.

What are the common wages of labour, depends every where upon the contract usually made between those two parties, whose interests are by no means the same. The workmen desire to get as much, the masters to give as little as possible. The former are disposed to combine in order to raise, the latter in order to lower the wages of labour.

It is not, however, difficult to foresee which of the two parties must, upon all ordinary occasions, have the advantage in the dispute, and force the other into a compliance with their terms. The masters, being fewer in number, can combine much more easily; and the law, besides, authorises, or at least does not prohibit their combinations, while it prohibits those of the workmen. We have no acts of parliament against combining to lower the price of work; but many against combining to raise it. In all such disputes the masters can hold out much longer. A landlord, a farmer, a master manufacturer, or merchant, though they did not employ a single workman, could generally live a year or two upon the stocks which they have already acquired. Many workmen could not subsist a week, few could subsist a month, and scarce any a year without employment. In the long-run the workman may be as necessary to his master as his master is to him; but the necessity is not so immediate.

We rarely hear, it has been said, of the combinations of masters; though frequently of those of workmen. But whoever imagines, upon this account, that masters rarely combine, is as ignorant of the world as of the subject. Masters are always and every where in a sort of tacit, but constant and uniform combination, not to raise the wages of labour above their actual rate. To violate this combination is every where a most unpopular action, and a sort of reproach to a master among his neighbours and equals. We seldom, indeed, hear of this combination, because it is the usual, and one may say, the natural state of things which nobody ever hears of. Masters too sometimes enter into particular combinations to sink the wages of labour even below this rate. These are always conducted with the utmost silence and secrecy, till the moment of execution, and when the workmen yield, as they sometimes do, without resistance, though severely felt by them, they are never heard of by other people. Such combinations, however, are frequently resisted by a contrary defensive combination of the workmen; who sometimes too, without any provocation of this kind, combine of their own accord to raise the price of their labour. Their usual pretences are, sometimes the high price of provisions; sometimes the great profit which their masters make by their work. But whether their combinations be offensive or defensive, they are always abundantly heard of. In order to bring the point to a speedy decision, they have always recourse to the loudest clamour, and sometimes to the most shocking violence and outrage. They are desperate, and act with the folly and extravagance of desperate men, who must either starve, or frighten their masters into an immediate compliance with their demands. The masters upon these occasions are just as clamorous upon the other side, and never cease to call aloud for the assistance of the civil magistrate, and the rigorous execution of those laws which have been enacted with so much severity against the combinations of servants, labourers, and journeymen. The workmen, accordingly, very seldom derive any advantage from the violence of those tumultuous combinations, which, partly from the interposition of the civil magistrate, partly from the superior steadiness of the masters, partly from the necessity which the greater part of the workmen are under of submitting for the sake of present subsistence, generally end in nothing, but the punishment or ruin of the ringleaders.

But though in disputes with their workmen, masters must generally have the advantage, there is however a certain rate below which it seems impossible to reduce, for any considerable time, the ordinary wages even of the lowest species of labour.

A man must always live by his work, and his wages must at least be sufficient to maintain him. They must even upon most occasions be somewhat more; otherwise it would be impossible for him to bring up a family, and the race of such workmen could not last beyond the first generation. Mr. Cantillon seems, upon this account, to suppose that the lowest species of common labourers must every where earn at least double their own maintenance, in order that one with another they may be enabled to bring up two children; the labour of the wife, on account of her necessary attendance on the children, being supposed no more than sufficient to provide for herself.

(d) 'It is not in the richest countries, but in those which are growing rich the fastest, that the wages of labour are highest.'

It is not the actual greatness of national wealth, but its continual increase, which occasions a rise in the wages of labour. It is not, accordingly, in the richest countries, but in the most thriving, or in those which are growing rich the fastest, that the wages of labour are highest. England is certainly, in the present times, a much richer country than any part of North America. The wages of labour, however, are much higher in North America than in any part of England. . . .

Though the wealth of a country should be very great, yet if it has been long stationary, we must not expect to find the wages of labour very high in it. . . . If in such a country the wages of labour had ever been more than sufficient to maintain the labourer, and to enable him to bring up a family, the competition of the labourers and the interest of the masters would soon reduce them to this lowest rate which is consistent with common humanity. China has been long one of the richest, that is, one of the most fertile, best cultivated, most industrious, and most populous countries in the world. It seems, however, to have been long stationary. The accounts of all travellers, inconsistent in many other respects, agree in the low wages of labour, and in the difficulty which a labourer finds in bringing up a family in China. If by digging the ground a whole day he can get what will purchase a small quantity of rice in the evening, he is contented. The condition of artificers is, if possible, still worse. Instead of waiting indolently in their work-houses, for the calls of their customers, as in Europe, they are continually running about the streets with the tools of their respective trades, offering their service, and as it were begging employment. The poverty of the lower ranks of people in China far surpasses that of the most beggarly nations in Europe. In the neighbourhood of Canton many hundred, it is commonly said, many thousand families have no habitation on the land, but live constantly in little fishing boats upon the rivers and canals. The subsistence which they find there is so scanty that they are eager to fish up the nastiest garbage thrown overboard from any European ship. Any carrion, the carcase of a dead dog or cat, for example, though half putrid and stinking, is as welcome to them as the most wholesome food to the people of other countries. Marriage is encouraged in China, not by the profitableness of children, but by the liberty of destroying them. In all great towns several are every night exposed in the street, or drowned like puppies in the water. The performance of this horrid office is even said to be the avowed business by which some people earn their subsistence.

China, however, though it may perhaps stand still, does not seem to go backwards. . . . But it would be otherwise in a country where the funds destined for the maintenance of labour were sensibly decaying. . . . This perhaps is nearly the present state of Bengal, and of some other of the English settlements in the East Indies. In a fertile country which had before been much depopulated, where subsistence, consequently, should not be very difficult, and where, notwithstanding, three or four hundred thousand people die of hunger in one year, we may be assured that the funds destined for the maintenance of the labouring poor are fast decaying. The difference between the genius of the British constitution which protects and governs North America, and that of the mercantile company which oppresses and domineers in the East Indies, cannot perhaps be better illustrated than by the different state of those countries.

The liberal reward of labour, therefore, as it is the necessary effect, so it is the natural symptom of increasing national wealth. The scanty maintenance of the labouring poor, on the other hand, is the natural symptom that things are at a stand, and their starving condition that they are going fast backwards.

In Great Britain the wages of labour seem, in the present times, to

189

be evidently more than what is precisely necessary to enable the labourer to bring up a family. . . . The common complaint that luxury extends itself even to the lowest ranks of the people, and that the labouring poor will not now be contented with the same food, cloathing and lodging which satisfied them in former times, may convince us that it is not the money price of labour only, but its real recompence, which has augmented.

Is this improvement in the circumstances of the lower ranks of the people to be regarded as an advantage or as an inconveniency to the society? The answer seems at first sight abundantly plain. Servants, labourers and workmen of different kinds, make up the far greater part of every great political society. But what improves the circumstances of the greater part can never be regarded as an inconveniency to the whole. No society can surely be flourishing and happy, of which the far greater part of the members are poor and miserable. It is but equity, besides, that they who feed, cloath and lodge the whole body of the people, should have such a share of the produce of their own labour as to be themselves tolerably well fed, cloathed and lodged.

Poverty, though it no doubt discourages, does not always prevent marriage. It seems even to be favourable to generation. A half-starved Highland woman frequently bears more than twenty children, while a pampered fine lady is often incapable of bearing any, and is generally exhausted by two or three. Barrenness, so frequent among women of fashion, is very rare among those of inferior station. Luxury in the fair sex, while it inflames perhaps the passion for enjoyment, seems always to weaken, and frequently to destroy altogether, the powers of generation.

But poverty, though it does not prevent the generation, is extremely unfavourable to the rearing of children. The tender plant is produced, but in so cold a soil, and so severe a climate, soon withers and dies. . . .

Every species of animals naturally multiplies in proportion to the means of their subsistence, and no species can ever multiply beyond it. But in civilized society it is only among the inferior ranks of people that the scantiness of subsistence can set limits to the further multiplication of the human species; and it can do so in no other way than by destroying a great part of the children which their fruitful marriages produce.

The liberal reward of labour, by enabling them to provide better for their children, and consequently to bring up a greater number, naturally tends to widen and extend those limits. It deserves to be remarked too, that it necessarily does this as nearly as possible in the proportion which the demand for labour requires. . . .

The liberal reward of labour, therefore, as it is the effect of increasing wealth, so it is the cause of increasing population. To complain of

190

it, is to lament over the necessary effect and cause of the greatest public prosperity.

It deserves to be remarked, perhaps, that it is in the progressive state, while the society is advancing to the further acquisition, rather than when it has acquired its full complement of riches, that the condition of the labouring poor, of the great body of the people, seems to be the happiest and the most comfortable. It is hard in the stationary, and miserable in the declining state. The progressive state is in reality the cheerful and the hearty state to all the different orders of the society. The stationary is dull; the declining melancholy.

The liberal reward of labour, as it encourages the propagation, so it increases the industry of the common people. The wages of labour are the encouragement of industry, which, like every other human quality, improves in proportion to the encouragement it receives. A plentiful subsistence increases the bodily strength of the labourer, and the comfortable hope of bettering his condition, and of ending his days perhaps in ease and plenty, animates him to exert that strength to the utmost. Where wages are high, accordingly, we shall always find the workmen more active, diligent, and expeditious, than where they are low; in England, for example, than in Scotland; in the neighbourhood of great towns, than in remote country places. Some workmen, indeed, when they can earn in four days what will maintain them through the week, will be idle the other three. This, however, is by no means the case with the greater part. Workmen, on the contrary, when they are liberally paid by the piece, are very apt to over-work themselves, and to ruin their health and constitution in a few years. A carpenter in London, and in some other places, is not supposed to last in his utmost vigour above eight years. Something of the same kind happens in many other trades, in which the workmen are paid by the piece; as they generally are in manufactures, and even in country labour, wherever wages are higher than ordinary. Almost every class of artificers is subject to some peculiar infirmity occasioned by excessive application to their peculiar species of work. . . . We do not reckon our soldiers the most industrious set of people among us. Yet when soldiers have been employed in some particular sorts of work, and liberally paid by the piece, their officers have frequently been obliged to stipulate with the undertaker, that they should not be allowed to earn above a certain sum every day, according to the rate at which they were paid. Till this stipulation was made, mutual emulation and the desire of greater gain, frequently prompted them to over-work themselves, and to hurt their health by excessive labour. Excessive application during four days of the week, is frequently the real cause of the idleness of the other three, so much and so loudly complained of. Great labour, either of mind or body, continued for several days together, is in most men naturally followed by a great desire of relaxation, which, if not restrained by force or by some strong necessity, is almost irresistible. It is the call of nature, which requires to be relieved by some indulgence, sometimes of ease only, but sometimes too of dissipation and diversion. If it is not complied with, the consequences are often dangerous, and sometimes fatal, and such as almost always, sooner or later, bring on the peculiar infirmity of the trade. If masters would always listen to the dictates of reason and humanity, they have frequently occasion rather to moderate, than to animate the application of many of their workmen. It will be found, I believe, in every sort of trade, that the man who works so moderately, as to be able to work constantly, not only preserves his health the longest, but, in the course of the year, executes the greatest quantity of work.

(e) 'Inequalities (in pay) arising from the Nature of the Employments themselves.'

The five following are the principal circumstances which, so far as I have been able to observe, make up for a small pecuniary gain in some employments, and counter-balance a great one in others: first, the agreeableness or disagreeableness of the employments themselves; secondly, the easiness and cheapness, or the difficulty and expence of learning them; thirdly, the constancy or inconstancy of employment in them; fourthly, the small or great trust which must be reposed in those who exercise them; and fifthly, the probability or improbability of success in them.

(f) 'The art of the farmer . . . require(s) much more skill and experience than the greater part of mechanic trades.'

Not only the art of the farmer, the general direction of the operations of husbandry, but many inferior branches of country labour, require much more skill and experience than the greater part of mechanic trades. The man who works upon brass and iron, works with instruments and upon materials of which the temper is always the same, or very nearly the same. But the man who ploughs the ground with a team of horses or oxen, works with instruments of which the health, strength, and temper, are very different upon different occasions. The condition of the materials which he works upon too is as variable as that of the instruments which he works with, and both require to be managed with much judgment and discretion. The common ploughman, though generally regarded as the pattern of stupidity and ignorance, is seldom defective in this judgment and discretion. He is less accustomed, indeed, to social intercourse than the mechanic who lives in a town. His voice and language are more uncouth and more difficult to be understood by those who are not used to them. His understanding, however, being accustomed to consider a greater variety of objects, is generally much

192

superior to that of the other, whose whole attention from morning till night is commonly occupied in performing one or two very simple operations. How much the lower ranks of people in the country are really superior to those of the town, is well known to every man whom either business or curiosity has led to converse much with both. In China and Indostan accordingly both the rank and the wages of country labourers are said to be superior to those of the greater part of artificers and manufacturers. They would probably be so every-where, if corporation laws and the corporation spirit did not prevent it.

(g) 'People of the same trade.'

People of the same trade seldom meet together, even for merriment and diversion, but the conversation ends in a conspiracy against the public, or in some contrivance to raise prices. . . .

Merchants and master manufacturers are, in this order, the two classes of people who commonly employ the largest capitals, and who by their wealth draw to themselves the greatest share of the public consideration. As during their whole lives they are engaged in plans and projects, they have frequently more acuteness of understanding than the greater part of country gentlemen. As their thoughts, however, are commonly exercised rather about the interest of their own particular branch of business, than about that of the society, their judgment, even when given with the greatest candour (which it has not been upon every occasion), is much more to be depended upon with regard to the former of those two objects, than with regard to the latter. Their superiority over the country gentleman is, not so much in their knowledge of the public interest, as in their having a better knowledge of their own interest than he has of his. It is by this superior knowledge of their own interest that they have frequently imposed upon his generosity, and persuaded him to give up both his own interest and that of the public, from a very simple but honest conviction, that their interest, and not his, was the interest of the public. The interest of the dealers, however, in any particular branch of trade or manufactures, is always in some respects different from, and even opposite to, that of the public. To widen the market and to narrow the competition, is always the interest of the dealers. To widen the market may frequently be agreeable enough to the interest of the public; but to narrow the competition must always be against it, and can serve only to enable the dealers, by raising their profits above what they naturally would be, to levy, for their own benefit, an absurd tax upon the rest of their fellow-citizens. The proposal of any new law or regulation of commerce which comes from this order, ought always to be listened to with great precaution, and ought never to be adopted till after having been long and carefully examined, not only with the most scrupulous, but with the most suspicious attention.

It comes from an order of men, whose interest is never exactly the same with that of the public, who have generally an interest to deceive and even to oppress the public, and who accordingly have, upon many occasions, both deceived and oppressed it.

(h) 'Private accumulation and public extravagance.'

. . . The principle which prompts to expence, is the passion for present enjoyment; which, though sometimes violent and very difficult to be restrained, is in general only momentary and occasional. But the principle which prompts to save, is the desire of bettering our condition, a desire which, though generally calm and dispassionate, comes with us from the womb, and never leaves us till we go into the grave. In the whole interval which separates those two moments, there is scarce perhaps a single instant in which any man is so perfectly and completely satisfied with his situation, as to be without any wish of alteration or improvement of any kind. An augmentation of fortune is the means by which the greater part of men propose and wish to better their condition. It is the means the most vulgar and the most obvious; and the most likely way of augmenting their fortune, is to save and accumulate some part of what they acquire, either regularly and annually, or upon some extraordinary occasions. Though the principle of expence, therefore, prevails in almost all men upon some occasions, and in some men upon almost all occasions, yet in the greater part of men, taking the whole course of their life at an average, the principle of frugality seems not only to predominate, but to predominate very greatly. . . .

In the midst of all the exactions of government, . . . capital has been silently and gradually accumulated by the private frugality and good conduct of individuals, by their universal, continual, and uninterrupted effort to better their own condition. It is this effort, protected by law and allowed by liberty to exert itself in the manner that is most advantageous, which has maintained the progress of England towards opulence and improvement in almost all former times, and which, it is to be hoped, will do so in all future times. England, however, as it has never been blessed with a very parsimonious government, so parsimony has at no time been the characteristical virtue of its inhabitants. It is the highest impertinence and presumption, therefore, in kings and ministers, to pretend to watch over the œconomy of private people, and to restrain their expence, either by sumptuary laws, or by prohibiting the importation of foreign luxuries. They are themselves always, and without any exception, the greatest spendthrifts in the society. Let them look well after their own expence, and they may safely trust private people with theirs. If their own extravagance does not ruin the state, that of their subjects never will.

(i) 'The beauty of the country.'

That order of things which necessity imposes in general, though not in every particular country, is, in every particular country, promoted by the natural inclinations of man. If human institutions had never thwarted those natural inclinations, the towns could no-where have increased beyond what the improvement and cultivation of the territory in which they were situated could support; till such time, at least, as the whole of that territory was completely cultivated and improved. Upon equal, or nearly equal profits, most men will chuse to employ their capitals rather in the improvement and cultivation of land, than either in manufactures or in foreign trade. The man who employs his capital in land, has it more under his view and command, and his fortune is much less liable to accidents, than that of the trader, who is obliged frequently to commit it, not only to the winds and the waves, but to the more uncertain elements of human folly and injustice, by giving great credits in distant countries to men, with whose character and situation he can seldom be thoroughly acquainted. The capital of the landlord, on the contrary, which is fixed in the improvement of his land, seems to be as well secured as the nature of human affairs can admit of. The beauty of the country besides, the pleasures of a country life, the tranquillity of mind which it promises, and wherever the injustice of human laws does not disturb it, the independency which it really affords, have charms that more or less attract every body; and as to cultivate the ground was the original destination of man, so in every stage of his existence he seems to retain a predilection for this primitive employment.

(j) 'A great bridge . . . where nobody passes.'

When high roads, bridges, canals, &c. are . . . made and supported by the commerce which is carried on by means of them, they can be made only where that commerce requires them, and consequently where it is proper to make them. Their expence too, their grandeur and magnificence, must be suited to what that commerce can afford to pay. They must be made consequently as it is proper to make them. A magnificent high road cannot be made through a desart country where there is little or no commerce, or merely because it happens to lead to the country villa of the intendant of the province, or to that of some great lord to whom the intendant finds it convenient to make his court. A great bridge cannot be thrown over a river at a place where nobody passes, or merely to embellish the view from the windows of a neighbouring palace: things which sometimes happen, in countries where works of this kind are carried on by any other revenue than that which they themselves are capable of affording.

(k) 'That drowsy stupidity, which, in a civilized society, seems to

195

benumb the understanding of almost all the inferior ranks of people.'

Ought the public . . . to give no attention, it may be asked, to the education of the people? Or if it ought to give any, what are the different parts of education which it ought to attend to in the different orders of the people? and in what manner ought it to attend to them?

In some cases the state of the society necessarily places the greater part of individuals in such situations as naturally form in them, without any attention of government, almost all the abilities and virtues which that state requires, or perhaps can admit of. In other cases the state of the society does not place the greater part of individuals in such situations, and some attention of government is necessary in order to prevent the almost entire corruption and degeneracy of the great body of the people.

In the progress of the division of labour, the employment of the far greater part of those who live by labour, that is, of the great body of the people, comes to be confined to a few very simple operations; frequently to one or two. But the understandings of the greater part of men are necessarily formed by their ordinary employments. The man whose whole life is spent in performing a few simple operations, of which the effects too are, perhaps, always the same, or very nearly the same, has no occasion to exert his understanding, or to exercise his invention in finding out expedients for removing difficulties which never occur. He naturally loses, therefore, the habit of such exertion, and generally becomes as stupid and ignorant as it is possible for a human creature to become. The torpor of his mind renders him, not only incapable of relishing or bearing a part in any rational conversation, but of conceiving any generous, noble, or tender sentiment, and consequently of forming any just judgment concerning many even of the ordinary duties of private life. Of the great and extensive interests of his country he is altogether incapable of judging; and unless very particular pains have been taken to render him otherwise, he is equally incapable of defending his country in war. The uniformity of his stationary life naturally corrupts the courage of his mind, and makes him regard with abhorrence the irregular, uncertain, and adventurous life of a soldier. It corrupts even the activity of his body, and renders him incapable of exerting his strength with vigour and perseverance, in any other employment than that to which he has been bred. His dexterity at his own particular trade seems, in this manner, to be acquired at the expence of his intellectual, social, and martial virtues. But in every improved and civilized society this is the state into which the labouring poor, that is, the great body of the people, must necessarily fall, unless government takes some pains to prevent it.

It is otherwise in the barbarous societies, as they are commonly called, of hunters, of shepherds, and even of husbandmen in that rude state of husbandry which precedes the improvement of manufactures, and the extension of forcign commerce. In such societies the varied occupations of every man oblige every man to exert his capacity, and to invent expedients for removing difficulties which are continually occurring. Invention is kept alive, and the mind is not suffered to fall into that drowsy stupidity, which, in a civilized society, seems to benumb the understanding of almost all the inferior ranks of people. . . .

The education of the common people requires, perhaps, in a civilized and commercial society, the attention of the public more than that of people of some rank and fortune. . . .

The common people . . . have little time to spare for education. Their parents can scarce afford to maintain them even in infancy. As soon as they are able to work, they must apply to some trade by which they can earn their subsistence. That trade too is generally so simple and uni- form as to give little exercise to the understanding; while, at the same time, their labour is both so constant and so severe, that it leaves them little leisure and less inclination to apply to, or even to think of any thing else.

But though the common people cannot, in any civilized society, be so well instructed as people of some rank and fortune, the most essen- tial parts of education, however, to read, write, and account, can be acquired at so early a period of life, that the greater part even of those who are to be bred to the lowest occupations, have time to acquire them before they can be employed in those occupations. For a very small expence the public can facilitate, can encourage, and can even impose upon almost the whole body of the people, the necessity of acquiring those most essential parts of education.

The public can facilitate this acquisition by establishing in every parish or district a little school, where children may be taught for a reward so moderate, that even a common labourer may afford it; the master being partly, but not wholly paid by the public; because, if he was wholly, or even principally paid by it, he would soon learn to neglect his business. In Scotland the establishment of such parish schools has taught almost the whole common people to read, and a very great proportion of them to write and account. In England the estab- lishment of charity schools has had an effect of the same kind, though not so universally, because the establishment is not so universal. If in those little schools the books, by which the children are taught to read, were a litte more instructive than they commonly are; and if, instead of a little smattering of Latin, which the children of the common people are sometimes taught there, and which can scarce ever be of any use to them; they were instructed in the elementary parts of geo- metry and mechanics, the literary education of this rank of people would perhaps be as complete as it can be. There is scarce a common

197

trade which does not afford some opportunities of applying to it the principles of geometry and mechanics, and which would not therefore gradually exercise and improve the common people in those principles, the necessary introduction to the most sublime as well as to the most useful sciences.

# THOMAS ROBERT MALTHUS          XII.3
## Malthus's Law

from *An Essay on the Principles of Population*, 1798

It is observed by Dr. Franklin, that there is no bound to the prolific nature of plants or animals but what is made by their crowding and interfering with each other's means of subsistence. Were the face of the earth, he says, vacant of other plants, it might be gradually sowed and overspread with one kind only, as, for instance, with fennel: and were it empty of other inhabitants, it might in a few ages be replenished from one nation only, as, for instance, with Englishmen. . . .

That population has this constant tendency to increase beyond the means of subsistence, and that it is kept to its necessary level by these causes, will sufficiently appear from a review of the different states of society in which man has existed. . . .

It may safely be pronounced . . . that population, when unchecked, goes on doubling itself every twenty-five years, or increases in a geometrical ratio.

It may be fairly pronounced . . . that, considering the present average state of the earth, the means of subsistence, under circumstances the most favourable to human industry, could not possibly be made to increase faster than in an arithmetical ratio.

The necessary effects of these two different rates of increase, when brought together, will be very striking. . . .

The ultimate check to population appears then to be a want of food, arising necessarily from the different ratios according to which population and food increase. But this ultimate check is never the immediate check, except in cases of actual famine.

The immediate check may be stated to consist in all those customs, and all those diseases, which seem to be generated by a scarcity of the means of subsistence; and all those causes, independent of this scarcity, whether of a moral or physical nature, which tend prematurely to weaken and destroy the human frame.

These checks to population, which are constantly operating with more or less force in every society, and keep down the number to the level of the means of subsistence, may be classed under two general heads—the preventive and the positive checks. . . .

On examining these obstacles to the increase of population which are classed under the heads of preventive and positive checks, it will appear that they are all resolvable into moral restraint, vice, and misery.

Of the preventive checks, the restraint from marriage which is not followed by irregular gratifications may properly be termed moral restraint.

Promiscuous intercourse, unnatural passions, violations of the marriage bed, and improper arts to conceal the consequences of irregular connections, are preventive checks that clearly come under the head of vice.

Of the positive checks, those which appear to arise unavoidably from the laws of nature, may be called exclusively misery; and those which we obviously bring upon ourselves, such as wars, excesses, and many others which it would be in our power to avoid, are of a mixed nature. They are brought upon us by vice, and their consequences are misery.

The sum of all these preventive and positive checks, together, forms the immediate check to population; and it is evident that, in every country where the whole of the procreative power cannot be called into action, the preventive and the positive checks must vary inversely as each other; that is, in countries either naturally unhealthy, or subject to a great mortality, from whatever cause it may arise, the preventive check will prevail very little. In those countries, on the contrary, which are naturally healthy, and where the preventive check is found to prevail with considerable force, the positive check will prevail very little, or the mortality be very small.

In every country some of these checks are, with more or less force, in constant operation; yet, notwithstanding their general prevalence, there are few states in which there is not a constant effort in the population to increase beyond the means of subsistence. This constant effort as constantly tends to subject the lower classes of society to distress, and to prevent any great permanent melioration of their condition.

These effects, in the present state of society, seem to be produced in the following manner. We will suppose the means of subsistence in any country just equal to the easy support of its inhabitants. The constant effort towards population, which is found to act even in the most vicious societies, increases the number of people before the means of subsistence are increased. The food, therefore, which before supported eleven millions, must now be divided among eleven millions and a half. The poor consequently must live much worse, and many of them be reduced to severe distress. The number of labourers also being above the proportion of work in the market, the price of labour must tend to fall, while the price of provisions would at the same time tend to rise. The labourer therefore must do more work to earn the same as he did before. During this season of distress, the discouragements to marriage and the difficulty of rearing a family are so great, that the progress of population is retarded. In the meantime, the cheapness of labour, the plenty of labourers, and the necessity of an increased industry among them, encourage cultivators to employ more labour upon their land, to turn up fresh soil, and to manure and improve more completely what is already in tillage, till ultimately the means of subsistence may become in the same proportion to the population as at the period from which we set out. The situation of the labourer being then again tolerably comfortable, the restraints to population are in some degree loosened; and, after a short period, the same retrograde and progressive movements with respect to happiness are repeated. . . .

But without attempting to establish . . . progressive and retrograde movements in different countries, which would evidently require more minute histories than we possess, and which the progress of civilisation naturally tends to counteract, the following propositions are intended to be proved:—

1. Population is necessarily limited by the means of subsistence.

2. Population invariable increases where the means of subsistence increase, unless prevented by some very powerful and obvious checks.

3. These checks, and the checks which repress the superior power of population, and keep its effects on a level with the means of subsistence, are all resolvable into moral restraint, vice, and misery.

The first of these propositions scarcely needs illustration. The second and third will be sufficiently established by a review of the immediate checks to population in the past and present state of society.

# JEREMY BENTHAM XII.4
## Labour and Repose

*from A Table of the Springs of Action, etc., 1817–43*

(a) *Labour* being necessary to the acquisition of *wealth*, and at the same time equally necessary to the preservation of *existence*, thus it is that, disguised under the name of *desire of labour*, the *desire of wealth* has been, in some measure, preserved from the reproach which, with so much profusion, has been wont to be cast upon it, when viewed in a direct point of view, and under its own name.

Meantime, as to *labour*, although the desire of it—of labour *simply* —desire of labour *for the sake of labour*,—of labour considered in the character of an *end*, without any view to any thing else, is a sort of desire that seems scarcely to have place in the human breast; yet if considered in the character of a *means*, scarce a desire can be found, to the gratification of which *labour*, and therein *the desire of labour*, is not continually rendered subservient: hence again it is, that, when abstraction is made of the consideration of the *end*, there scarcely exists a desire, the name of which has been so apt to be employed for *eulogistic purposes*, and thence to contract an *eulogistic signification*, as the appellative that has been employed in bringing to view this *desire of labour*. *Industry* is this appellative: and thus it is, that, under *another* name, the *desire of wealth* has been furnished with a sort of *letter of recommendation*, which, under its *own* name, could not have been given to it.

*Aversion*—not *desire*—is the emotion—the only emotion—which *labour*, taken by itself, is qualified to produce: of any such emotion as *love* or *desire, ease*, which is the *negative* or *absence* of labour—*ease*, not *labour*—is the object. In so far as *labour* is taken in its proper sense, *love of labour* is a contradiction in terms. . . .


(b) . . . To the individual in question, an evil is reparable, and exactly repaired, when, after having sustained the evil and received the compensation, it would be a matter of indifference whether to receive the like evil, coupled with the like compensation, or not.

What is manifest is—that to no person, other than the individual himself, can it be known whether, in his instance, between an evil sustained, and a benefit received on account of it, any compensation have place or not.


(c) For argument's sake, suppose even mutilation employed,—mutilation even in parts or organs more than one. Not altogether unsusceptible of reparation would even this punishment be: for, for suffering in this shape, reparation, and to a very wide extent, is almost everywhere actually in use: witness this, in the pensions granted in the sea or military service; and it is a matter generally understood, that by the individuals by whom on this account reparation in this shape and degree is received, it is not unusually regarded as adequate; insomuch that if asked, whether for the same reparation they would originally have been content, or would now, if it were to do over again, be content to be subjected to the same suffering, the answer would be in the affirmative. . . .


(d) The principal enjoyments of which human nature is susceptible, constancy of repetition being considered as well as magnitude, are—those produced by the operations by which the individual is preserved; those produced by the operations by which the species is preserved; that cessation from labour which is termed repose; and that pleasure of sympathy which is produced by the observation of others partaking in the same enjoyments. These four, with the exception of repose, are so many positive enjoyments upon the face of them.

Cessation from labour presents, it is true, upon the face of it no more than a negative idea; but when the condition of him by whom repose after corporeal labour is experienced, is considered, the enjoyment will be seen to be a positive quantity; for, in this case, not merely a cessation from discomfort, but a pleasurable feeling of a peculiar kind, is experienced, such as, without the antecedent labour, never can be experienced. In the case of the labourer, it may indeed be said, that before the time of repose, with its enjoyment, arrives, the labour is pushed to a degree of intensity of which pain (in those degrees, at least, in which it is denoted by the word discomfort) has been produced. But the greater the degree of the pain of suffrance, the greater the degree of the pleasure of expectation—the expectation of the pleasure of repose— with which it has been accompanied. And this pleasure of expectation has had for its accompaniment, the pleasures of expectation respectively appertaining to the other pleasures of enjoyment above-mentioned; sensibility with regard to each being increased by that very labour, to the intensity of which that of the pleasure of repose is proportioned.

Pursue the investigation throughout the several other enjoyments of which human nature is susceptible, the ultimate result will not be materially different.


(e) Considered in itself, an occupation may be either painful, pleasurable, or indifferent; but continued beyond a certain time, and without interruption (such is the constitution of man's nature,) every occupation whatsoever becomes disagreeable: not only so, but such as were in the beginning pleasurable become, by their continuance, more disagreeable than such as were originally indifferent.

To eat grapes, for instance, is what, at certain times at least, will probably be to most men rather an agreeable occupation: to pick them an indifferent one. But in two or three hours, for example, the eating them will become intolerable, while the picking them may still remain, perhaps, in itself nearly a matter of indifference.

## (a) ANON

### 'The Miller of the Dee'

Ballad, traditional

There was a jolly miller once
Lived on the river Dee;
He worked and sang from morn till night,
No lark more blithe than he.
And this the burden of his song
Forever used to be —
I care for nobody, no, not I,
If nobody cares for me.

The reason why he was so blithe,
He once did this unfold —
The bread I eat my hands have earned;
I covet no man's gold;
I do not fear next quarter-day;
In debt to none I be.
I care for nobody, no, not I,
If nobody cares for me.

A coin or two I've in my purse,
To help a needy friend;
A little I can give the poor,
And still have some to spend.
Though I may fail, yet I rejoice,
Another's good hap to see,
I care for nobody, no not I,
If nobody cares for me.

So let us his example take,
And be from malice free;
Let every one his neighbour serve,
As served he'd like to be.
And merrily push the can about,
And drink and sing with glee;
If nobody cares a doit for us,
Why not a doit care we.

*(b)* ANON

'The Jolly Grinder'

Ballad, *c*.1835

> There was a jolly Grinder once,
>     Lived by the river Don,
> He work'd and sang from morn to night,
>     And sometimes he'd work none;
> But still the burden of his song
>     For ever used to be—
> ' 'Tis never worth while to work too long,
>     For it doesn't agree with me!'
>
> He seldom on a Monday work'd,
>     Except near Christmas Day;
> It was not the labour that he'd shun,
>     For it was easier far than play;
> But still the burden of his song
>     For ever used to be—
> ' 'Tis never worth while to work too long,
>     For it doesn't agree with me!'

# XIII Poets on Poetry and the Imagination

WILLIAM BLAKE XIII.1

"Jerusalem in every man"

from *Jerusalem*, 1804–20

In Great Eternity every particular Form gives forth or Emanates
Its own peculiar Light, & the Form is the Divine Vision
And the Light is his Garment. This is Jerusalem in every Man,
A Tent & Tabernacle of Mutual Forgiveness, Male & Female Clothings.
And Jerusalem is called Liberty among the Children of Albion.

But Albion fell down, a Rocky fragment from Eternity hurl'd
By his own Spectre, who is the Reasoning Power in every Man,
Into his own Chaos, which is the Memory between Man & Man.

The silent broodings of deadly revenge springing from the
All powerful parental affection, fills Albion from head to foot.
Seeing his Sons assimilate with Luvah, bound in the bonds
Of spiritual Hate, from which springs Sexual Love as iron chains,
He tosses like a cloud outstretch'd among Jerusalem's Ruins
Which overspread all the Earth; he groans among his ruin'd porches.

But the Spectre, like a hoar frost & a Mildew, rose over Albion,
Saying, 'I am God, O Sons of Men! I am your Rational Power!
'Am I not Bacon & Newton & Locke who teach Humility to Man,
'Who teach Doubt & Experiment? & my two Wings, Voltaire, Rousseau?
'Where is that Friend of Sinners? that Rebel against my Laws
'Who teaches Belief to the Nations & an unknown Eternal Life?
'Come hither into the Desart & turn these stones to bread.
'Vain foolish Man! wilt thou believe without Experiment
'And build a World of Phantasy upon my Great Abyss,
'A World of Shapes in craving lust & devouring appetite?'

So spoke the hard cold constrictive Spectre: he is named Arthur,
Constricting into Druid Rocks round Canaan, Agag & Aram & Pharoh.
Then Albion drew England into his bosom in groans & tears,
But she stretch'd out her starry Night in Spaces against him like

A long Serpent in the Abyss of the Spectre, which augmented
The Night with Dragon wings cover'd with stars, & in the Wings
Jerusalem & Vala appear'd; & above, between the Wings magnificent,
The Divine Vision dimly appear'd in clouds of blood weeping.

## WILLIAM WORDSWORTH                                    XIII.2
"Relationship and Love"

from Preface to Third Edition of the *Lyrical
Ballads*, 1802

. . . Aristotle, I have been told, has said, that Poetry is the most philosophic of all writing: it is so: its object is truth, not individual and local,
but general, and operative; not standing upon external testimony, but
carried alive into the heart by passion; truth which is its own testimony,
which gives competence and confidence to the tribunal to which it
appeals, and receives them from the same tribunal. Poetry is the image
of man and nature. The obstacles which stand in the way of the fidelity
of the Biographer and Historian, and of their consequent utility, are
incalculably greater than those which are to be encountered by the Poet
who comprehends the dignity of his art. The Poet writes under one
restriction only, namely, the necessity of giving immediate pleasure to a
human Being possessed of that information which may be expected
from him, not as a lawyer, a physician, a mariner, an astronomer, or a
natural philosopher, but as a Man. Except this one restriction, there is
no object standing between the Poet and the image of things; between
this, and the Biographer and Historian, there are a thousand.
     Nor let this necessity of producing immediate pleasure be considered
as a degradation of the Poet's art. It is far otherwise. It is an acknowledgement of the beauty of the universe, an acknowledgement the
more sincere, because not formal, but indirect; it is a task light and easy
to him who looks at the world in the spirit of love:further, it is a
homage paid to the native and naked dignity of man, to the grand elementary principle of pleasure, by which he knows, and feels, and lives,
and moves. We have no sympathy but what is propagated by pleasure:
I would not be misunderstood; but wherever we sympathise with pain,
it will be found that the sympathy is produced and carried on by subtle
combinations with pleasure. We have no knowledge, that is, no general
principles drawn from the contemplation of particular facts, but what
has been built up by pleasure, and exists in us by pleasure alone. The
Man of science, the Chemist and Mathematician, whatever difficulties
and disgusts they may have had to struggle with, know and feel this.
However painful may be the objects with which the Anatomist's

knowledge is connected, he feels that his knowledge is pleasure; and where he has no pleasure he has no knowledge. What then does the Poet? He considers man and the objects that surround him as acting and re-acting upon each other, so as to produce an infinite complexity of pain and pleasure; he considers man in his own nature and in his ordinary life as contemplating this with a certain quantity of immediate knowledge, with certain convictions, intuitions, and deductions, which from habit acquire the quality of intuitions; he considers him as looking upon this complex scene of ideas and sensations, and finding everywhere objects that immediately excite in him sympathies which, from the necessities of his nature, are accompanied by an overbalance of enjoyment.

To this knowledge which all men carry about with them, and to these sympathies in which, without any other discipline than that of our daily life, we are fitted to take delight, the Poet principally directs his attention. He considers man and nature as essentially adapted to each other, and the mind of man as naturally the mirror of the fairest and most interesting properties of nature. And thus the Poet, prompted by this feeling of pleasure, which accompanies him through the whole course of his studies, converses with general nature, with affections akin to those, which, through labour and length of time, the Man of science has raised up in himself, by conversing with those particular parts of nature which are the objects of his studies. The knowledge both of the Poet and the Man of science is pleasure; but the knowledge of the one cleaves to us as a necessary part of our existence, our natural and unalienable inheritance; the other is a personal and individual acquisition, slow to come to us, and by no habitual and direct sympathy connecting-us with our fellow-beings. The Man of science seeks truth as a remote and unknown benefactor; he cherishes and loves it in his solitude: the Poet, singing a song in which all human beings join with him, rejoices in the presence of truth as our visible friend and hourly companion. Poetry is the breath and finer spirit of all knowledge; it is the impassioned expression which is in the countenance of all Science. Emphatically may it be said of the Poet, as Shakspeare hath said of man, 'that he looks before and after.' He is the rock of defence for human nature; an upholder and preserver, carrying everywhere with him relationship and love. In spite of difference of soil and climate, of language and manners, of laws and customs: in spite of things silently gone out of mind, and things violently destroyed; the Poet binds together by passion and knowledge the vast empire of human society, as it is spread over the whole earth, and over all time. The objects of the Poet's thoughts are everywhere; though the eyes and senses of man are, it is true, his favourite guides, yet he will follow wheresoever he can find an atmosphere of sensation in which to move his wings. Poetry is the

207

first and last of all knowledge—it is as immortal as the heart of man. If the labours of Men of science should ever create any material revolution, direct or indirect, in our condition, and in the impressions which we habitually receive, the Poet will sleep then no more than at present; he will be ready to follow the steps of the Man of science, not only in those general indirect effects, but he will be at his side, carrying sensation into the midst of the objects of the science itself. . . .

. . . The remotest discoveries of the Chemist, the Botanist, or Mineralogist, will be as proper objects of the Poet's art as any upon which it can be employed, if the time should ever come when these things shall be familiar to us, and the relations under which they are contemplated by the followers of these respective Sciences shall be manifestly and palpably material to us as enjoying and suffering beings. If the time should ever come when what is now called Science, thus familiarized to men, shall be ready to put on, as it were, a form of flesh and blood, the Poet will lend his divine spirit to aid the transfiguration, and will welcome the Being thus produced, as a dear and genuine inmate of the household of man. —It is not, then, to be supposed that any one, who holds that sublime notion of Poetry which I have attempted to convey, will break in upon the sanctity and truth of his pictures by transitory and accidental ornaments, and endeavour to excite admiration of himself by arts, the necessity of which must manifestly depend upon the assumed meanness of his subject.


## JOHN KEATS                                                    XIII.3
"The truth of Imagination"

Letter, 1817


My dear Bailey,
   . . . I wish you knew all that I think about Genius and the Heart—and yet I think you are thoroughly acquainted with my innermost breast in that respect or you could not have known me even thus long and still hold me worthy to be your dear friend. In passing however I must say of one thing that has pressed upon me lately and encreased my Humility and capability of submission and that is this truth—Men of Genius are great as certain ethereal Chemicals operating on the Mass of neutral intellect—by [but] they have not any individuality, any determined Character. I would call the top and head of those who have a proper self Men of Power—
   But I am running my head into a Subject which I am certain I could not do justice to under five years s[t]udy and 3 vols octavo—and moreover long to be talking about the Imagination—so my dear Bailey do

not think of this unpleasant affair if possible—do not—I defy any ha[r]m to come of it—I defy—I'll shall write to Crips this Week and reque[s]t him to tell me all his goings on from time to time by Letter wherever I may be—it will all go on well—so dont because you have suddenly discover'd a Coldness in Haydon suffer yourself to be teased. Do not my dear fellow. O I wish I was as certain of the end of all your troubles as that of your momentary start about the authenticity of the Imagination. I am certain of nothing but of the holiness of the Heart's affections and the truth of Imagination—What the imagination seizes as Beauty must be truth—whether it existed before or not—for I have the same Idea of all our Passions as of Love they are all in their sublime, creative of essential Beauty—In a Word, you may know my favorite Speculation by my first Book and the little song I sent in my last— which is a representation from the fancy of the probable mode of operating in these Matters—The Imagination may be compared to Adam's dream—he awoke and found it truth. I am the more zealous in this affair, because I have never yet been able to perceive how any thing can be known for truth by consequitive reasoning—and yet it must be— Can it be that even the greatest Philosopher ever (when) arrived at his goal without putting aside numerous objections—However it may be, O for a Life of Sensations rather than of Thoughts! It is 'a Vision in the form of Youth' a Shadow of reality to come—and this consideration has further conv[i]nced me for it has come as auxiliary to another favorite Speculation of mine, that we shall enjoy ourselves here after by having what we called happiness on Earth repeated in a finer tone and so repeated—And yet such a fate can only befall those who delight in sensation rather than hunger as you do after Truth—Adam's dream will do here and seems to be a conviction that Imagination and its empyreal reflection is the same as human Life and its spiritual repetition. But as I was saying—the simple imaginative Mind may have its rewards in the repeti[ti]on of its own silent Working coming continually on the spirit with a fine suddenness—to compare great things with small—have you never by being surprised with an old Melody—in a delicious place—by a delicious voice, fe[l]t over again your very speculations and surmises at the time it first operated on your soul—do you not remember forming to yourself the singer's face more beautiful that [than] it was possible and yet with the elevation of the Moment you did not think so—even then you were mounted on the Wings of Imagination so high—that the Prototype must be here after—that delicious face you will see—What a time! I am continually running away from the subject—sure this cannot be exactly the case with a complex Mind—one that is imaginative and at the same time careful of its fruits—who would exist partly on sensation partly on thought—to whom it is necessary that years should bring the philosophic Mind—such an one I consider your's and therefore it is

209

drink

necessary to your eternal Happiness that you not only (have) this old Wine of Heaven which I shall call the redigestion of our most ethereal Musings on Earth; but also increase in knowledge and know all things. I am glad to hear you are in a fair Way for Easter—you will soon get through your unpleasant reading and then!—but the world is full of troubles and I have not much reason to think myself pesterd with many —I think Jane or Marianne has a better opinion of me than I deserve— for really and truly I do not think my Brothers illness connected with mine—you know more of the real Cause than they do—nor have I any chance of being rack'd as you have been—you perhaps at one time thought there was such a thing as Worldly Happiness to be arrived at, at certain periods of time marked out—you have of necessity from your disposition been thus led away—I scarcely remember counting upon any Happiness—I look not for it if it be not in the present hour—nothing startles me beyond the Moment. The setting sun will always set me to rights—or if a Sparrow come before my Window I take part in its exist-ince and pick about the Gravel. The first thing that strikes me on hea[r]ing a Misfortune having befalled another is this. 'Well it cannot be helped.—he will have the pleasure of trying the resources of his spirit, and I beg now my dear Bailey that hereafter should you observe any thing cold in me not to but [put] it to the account of heartlessness but abstraction—for I assure you I sometimes feel not the influence of a Passion or Affection during a whole week—and so long this sometimes continues I begin to suspect myself and the genuiness of my feelings at other times—thinking them a few barren Tragedy-tears—My Brother Tom is much improved—he is going to Devonshire—whither I shall follow him—at present I am just arrived at Dorking to change the Scene —change the Air and give me a spur to wind up my Poem, of which there are wanting 500 Lines. I should have been here a day sooner but the Reynoldses persuaded me to spop [stop] in Town to meet your friend Christie—There were Rice and Martin—we talked about Ghosts—I will have some talk with Taylor and let you know—when please God I come down a[t] Christmas—I will find that Examiner if possible. My best regards to Gleig—My Brothers to you and Mrs. Bentley

Your affectionate friend
JOHN KEATS—

# P. B. SHELLEY

Poets and mechanists

from *The Defence of Poetry*, 1821

. . . Poets have been challenged to resign the civic crown to reasoners and mechanists. . . . It is admitted that the exercise of the imagination is most delightful, but it is alleged that that of reason is more useful. Let us examine, as the grounds of this distinction, what is here meant by utility. Pleasure or good, in a general sense, is that which the consciousness of a sensitive and intelligent being seeks, and in which, when found, it acquiesces. There are two kinds of pleasure, one durable, universal and permanent; the other transitory and particular. Utility may either express the means of producing the former or the latter. In the former sense, whatever strengthens and purifies the affections, enlarges the imagination, and adds spirit to sense, is useful. But a narrower meaning may be assigned to the word utility, confining it to express that which banishes the importunity of the wants of our animal nature, the surrounding men with security of life, the dispersing the grosser delusions of supersitition, and the conciliating such a degree of mutual forbearance among men as may consist with the motives of personal advantage.

Undoubtedly the promoters of utility, in this limited sense, have their appointed office in society. They follow the footsteps of poets, and copy the sketches of their creations into the book of common life. They make space, and give time. Their exertions are of the highest value, so long as they confine their administration of the concerns of the inferior powers of our nature within the limits due to the superior ones. But while the sceptic destroys gross superstitions, let him spare to deface, as some of the French writers have defaced, the eternal truths charactered upon the imaginations of men. Whilst the mechanist abridges, and the political economist combines, labour, let them beware that their speculations, for want of correspondence with those first principles which belong to the imagination, do not tend, as they have in modern England, to exasperate at once the extremes of luxury and want. They have exemplified the saying, 'To him that hath, more shall be given; and from him that hath not, the little that he hath shall be taken away.' The rich have become richer, and the poor have become poorer; and the vessel of the state is driven between the Scylla and Charybdis of anarchy and despotism. Such are the effects which must ever flow from an unmitigated exercise of the calculating faculty.

It is difficult to define pleasure in its highest sense; the definition involving a number of apparent paradoxes. For, from an inexplicable defect of harmony in the constitution of human nature, the pain of the inferior is frequently connected with the pleasures of the superior portions of our being. Sorrow, terror, anguish, despair itself, are often the chosen expressions of an approximation to the highest good. Our sympathy in tragic fiction depends on this principle; tragedy delights by affording a shadow of that pleasure which exists in pain. This is the source also of the melancholy which is inseparable from the sweetest melody. The pleasure that is in sorrow is sweeter than the pleasure of pleasure itself. And hence the saying, 'It is better to go to the house of mourning than to the house of mirth.' Not that this highest species of pleasure is necessarily linked with pain. The delight of love and friendship, the ecstacy of the admiration of nature, the joy of the perception and still more of the creation of poetry, is often wholly unalloyed.

The production and assurance of pleasure in this highest sense is true utility. Those who produce and preserve this pleasure are poets or poetical philosophers.

The exertions of Locke, Hume, Gibbon, Voltaire, Rousseau,* and their disciples, in favour of oppressed and deluded humanity, are entitled to the gratitude of mankind. Yet it is easy to calculate the degree of moral and intellectual improvement which the world would have exhibited, had they never lived. A little more nonsense would have been talked for a century or two; and perhaps a few more men, women, and children, burnt as heretics, We might not at this moment have been congratulating each other on the abolition of the Inquisition in Spain. But it exceeds all imagination to conceive what would have been the moral condition of the world if neither Dante, Petrarch, Boccaccio, Chaucer, Shakspeare, Calderon, Lord Bacon, nor Milton, had ever existed; if Raphael and Michael Angelo had never been born; if the Hebrew poetry had never been translated; if a revival of the study of Greek literature had never taken place; if no monuments of ancient sculpture had been handed down to us; and if the poetry of the religion of the ancient world had been extinguished together with its belief. The human mind could never, except by the intervention of these excitements, have been awakened to the invention of the grosser sciences, and that application of analytical reasoning to the aberrations of society, which it is now attempted to exalt over the direct expression of the inventive and creative faculty itself.

We have more moral, political, and historical wisdom, than we know how to reduce into practice; we have more scientific and economical knowledge than can be accommodated to the just distribution of the produce which it multiplies. The poetry, in these systems of thought, is concealed by the accumulation of facts and calculating processes. There is no want of knowledge respecting what is wisest and best in morals,

*Although Rousseau has been thus classed, he was essentially a poet. The others, even Voltaire, were mere reasoners.

212

government, and political economy, or at least what is wiser and better than what men now practise and endure. But we let 'I dare not wait upon I would, like the poor cat in the adage.' We want the creative faculty to imagine that which we know; we want the generous impulse to act that which we imagine; we want the poetry of life: our calculations have outrun conception; we have eaten more than we can digest. The cultivation of those sciences which have enlarged the limits of the empire of man over the external world, has, for want of the poetical faculty, proportionally circumscribed those of the internal world; and man, having enslaved the elements, remains himself a slave. To what but a cultivation of the mechanical arts in a degree disproportioned to the presence of the creative faculty, which is the basis of all knowledge, is to be attributed the abuse of all invention for abridging and combining labour, to the exasperation of the inequality of mankind? From what other cause has it arisen that the discoveries which should have lightened, have added a weight to the curse imposed on Adam? Poetry, and the principle of Self, of which money is the visible incarnation, are the God and Mammon of the world.

The functions of the poetical faculty are twofold; by one it creates new materials of knowledge, and power, and pleasure; by the other it engenders in the mind a desire to reproduce and arrange them according to a certain rhythm and order, which may be called the beautiful and the good. The cultivation of poetry is never more to be desired than at periods when, from an excess of the selfish and calculating principle, the accumulation of the materials of external life exceed the quantity of the power of assimilating them to the internal laws of human nature. The body has then become too unwieldy for that which animates it.

Poetry is indeed something divine. It is at once the centre and circumference of knowledge; it is that which comprehends all science, and that to which all science must be referred. It is at the same time the root and blossom of all other systems of thought; it is that from which all spring, and that which adorns all; and that which, if blighted, denies the fruit and the seed, and withholds from the barren world the nourishment and the succession of the scions of the tree of life. It is the perfect and consummate surface and bloom of all things; it is as the odour and the colour of the rose to the texture of the elements which compose it, as the form and splendour of unfaded beauty to the secrets of anatomy and corruption. What were virtue, love, patriotism, friendship,—what were the scenery of this beautiful universe which we inhabit; what were our consolations on this side of the grave—and what were our aspirations beyond it, if poetry did not ascend to bring light and fire from those eternal regions where the owl-winged faculty of calculation dare not ever soar? Poetry is not like reasoning, a power to be exerted according to the determination of the will. A man cannot say, 'I will compose poetry.' The greatest poet even cannot say it; for the mind in creation is as a fading coal, which some invisible influence, like an inconstant wind, awakens to transitory brightness; this power arises from within, like the colour of a flower which fades and changes as it is developed, and the conscious portions of our nature are unprophetic either of its approach or its departure. Could this influence be durable in its original purity and force, it is impossible to predict the greatness of the results; but when composition begins, inspiration is already on the decline, and the most glorious poetry that has ever been communicated to the world is probably a feeble shadow of the original conceptions of the poet. I appeal to the greatest poets of the present day, whether it is not an error to assert that the finest passages of poetry are produced by labour and study. The toil and the delay recommended by critics, can be justly interpreted to mean no more than a careful observation of the inspired moments, and an artificial connection of the spaces between their suggestions, by the intertexture of conventional expressions; a necessity only imposed by the limitedness of the poetical faculty itself: for Milton conceived the Paradise Lost as a whole before he executed it in portions. We have his own authority also for the muse having 'dictated' to him the 'unpremeditated song.' And let this be an answer to those who would allege the fifty-six various readings of the first line of the Orlando Furioso. Compositions so produced are to poetry what mosaic is to painting. The instinct and intuition of the poetical faculty is still more observable in the plastic and pictorial arts: a great statue or picture grows under the power of the artist as a child in the mother's womb; and the very mind which directs the hands in formation, is incapable of accounting to itself for the origin, the gradations, or the media of the process.

Poetry is the record of the best and happiest moments of the happiest and best minds. We are aware of evanescent visitations of thought and feeling, sometimes associated with place or person, sometimes regarding our own mind alone, and always arising unforeseen and departing unbidden, but elevating and delightful beyond all expression: so that even in the desire and the regret they leave, there cannot but be pleasure, participating as it does in the nature of its object. It is as it were the interpenetration of a diviner nature through our own; but its footsteps are like those of a wind over the sea, which the coming calm erases, and whose traces remain only, as on the wrinkled sand which paves it. These and corresponding conditions of being are experienced principally by those of the most delicate sensibility and the most enlarged imagination; and the state of mind produced by them is at war with every base desire. The enthusiasm of virtue, love, patriotism, and friendship, is essentially linked with such emotions; and whilst they last, self appears as what it is, an atom to a universe. Poets are not only subject to these experiences as spirits of the most refined organisation, but they can colour all that they combine with the evanescent hues of this ethereal world; a word, a trait in the representation of a scene or a passion, will touch the enchanted chord, and reanimate, in those who have ever experienced those emotions, the sleeping, the cold, the buried image of the past. Poetry thus makes immortal all that is best and most beautiful in the world; it arrests the vanishing apparitions which haunt the interlunations of life, and veiling them, or in language or in form, sends them forth among mankind, bearing sweet news of kindred joy to those with whom their sisters abide—abide, because there is no portal of expression from the caverns of the spirit which they inhabit into the universe of things. Poetry redeems from decay the visitations of the divinity in man.

Poetry turns all things to loveliness; it exalts the beauty of that which is most beautiful, and it adds beauty to that which is most deformed; it marries exultation and horror, grief and pleasure, eternity and change; it subdues to union, under its light yoke, all irreconcilable things. It transmutes all that it touches, and every form moving within the radiance of its presence is changed by wondrous sympathy to an incarnation of the spirit which it breathes: its secret alchemy turns to potable gold the poisonous waters which flow from death through life; it strips the veil of familiarity from the world, and lays bare the naked and sleeping beauty, which is the spirit of its forms.

All things exist as they are perceived; at least in relation to the percipient. 'The mind is its own place, and of itself can make a heaven of hell, a hell of heaven.' But poetry defeats the curse which binds us to be subjected to the accident of surrounding impressions. And whether it spreads its own figured curtain, or withdraws life's dark veil from before the scene of things, it equally creates for us a being within our being. It makes us the inhabitant of a world to which the familiar world is a chaos. It reproduces the common universe of which we are portions and percipients, and it purges from our inward sight the film of familiarity which obscures from us the wonder of our being. It compels us to feel that which we perceive, and to imagine that which we know. It creates anew the universe, after it has been annihilated in our minds by the recurrence of impressions blunted by reiteration. It justifies the bold and true word of Tasso: *Non merita nome di creatore, se non Iddio ed il Poeta.*

A poet, as he is the author to others of the highest wisdom, pleasure, virtue and glory, so he ought personally to be the happiest, the best, the wisest, and the most illustrious of men. As to his glory, let time be challenged to declare whether the fame of any other institutor of human life be comparable to that of a poet. That he is the wisest, the happiest, and the best, inasmuch as he is a poet, is equally incontrovertible: the greatest poets have been men of the most spotless virtue, of the most consummate prudence, and, if we would look into the interior of their lives, the most fortunate of men: and the exceptions, as they regard those who possessed the poetic faculty in a high yet inferior degree, will be found on consideration to confine rather than destroy the rule. Let us for a moment stoop to the arbitration of popular breath, and usurping and uniting in our own persons the incompatible characters of accuser, witness, judge and executioner, let us decide without trial, testimony, or form, that certain motives of those who are 'there sitting where we dare not soar,' are reprehensible. Let us assume that Homer was a drunkard, that Virgil was a flatterer, that Horace was a coward, that Tasso was a madman, that Lord Bacon was a peculator, that Raphael was a libertine, that Spenser was a poet laureate. It is inconsistent with this division of our subject to cite living poets, but posterity has done ample justice to the great names now referred to. Their errors have been weighed and found to have been dust in the balance; if their sins 'were as scarlet, they are now white as snow:' they have been washed in the blood of the mediator and redeemer, time. Observe in what a ludicrous chaos the imputations of real or fictitious crime have been confused in the contemporary calumnies against poetry and poets; consider how little is, as it appears—or appears, as it is; look to your own motives, and judge not, lest ye be judged.

Poetry, as has been said, differs in this respect from logic, that it is not subject to the control of the active powers of the mind, and that its birth and recurrence have no necessary connexion with the consciousness or will. It is presumptuous to determine that these are the necessary conditions of all mental causation, when mental effects are experienced insusceptible of being referred to them. The frequent recurrence of the poetical power, it is obvious to suppose, may produce in the mind a habit of order and harmony correlative with its own nature and with its effects upon other minds. But in the intervals of inspiration, and they may be frequent without being durable, a poet becomes a man, and is abandoned to the sudden reflux of the influences under which others habitually live. But as he is more delicately organised than other men, and sensible to pain and pleasure, both his own and that of others, in a degree unknown to them, he will avoid the one and pursue the other with an ardour proportioned to this difference. And he renders himself obnoxious to calumny, when he neglects to observe the circumstances under which these objects of universal pursuit and flight have disguised themselves in one another's garments.

But there is nothing necessarily evil in this error, and thus cruelty, envy, revenge, avarice, and the passions purely evil, have never formed any portion of the popular imputations on the lives of poets.

# SAMUEL TAYLOR COLERIDGE                    XIII.5
## Mechanic philosophy and vital philosophy
from *The Statesman's Manual*, 1816

Of the discursive understanding, which forms for itself general notions and terms of classification for the purpose of comparing and arranging phenomena, the characteristic is clearness without depth. It contemplates the unity of things in their limits only, and is consequently a knowledge of superficies without substance. So much so indeed, that it entangles itself in contradictions, in the very effort of comprehending the idea of substance. The completing power which unites clearness with depth, the plenitude of the sense with the comprehensibility of the understanding, is the imagination, impregnated with which the understanding itself becomes intuitive, and a living power. . . .

O! if as the plant to the orient beam, we would but open out our minds to that holier light, which 'being compared with light is found before it, more beautiful than the sun, and above all the orders of stars' (Wisdom of Solomon vii. 29), ungenial, alien, and adverse to our very nature would appear the boastful wisdom which, beginning in France, gradually tampered with the taste and literature of all the most civilized nations of Christendom, seducing the understanding from its natural allegiance, and therewith from all its own lawful claims, titles, and privileges. It was placed as a ward of honour in the courts of faith and reason; but it chose to dwell alone, and became a harlot by the wayside. The commercial spirit, and the ascendancy of the experimental philosophy which took place at the close of the seventeenth century, though both good and beneficial in their own kinds, combined to foster its corruption. Flattered and dazzled by the real or supposed discoveries which it had made, the more the understanding was enriched, the more did it become debased; till science itself put on a selfish and sensual character, and immediate utility, in exclusive reference to the gratification of the wants and appetites of the animal, the vanities and caprices of the social, and the ambition of the political, man was imposed as the test of all intellectual powers and pursuits. Worth was degraded into a lazy synonym of value; and value was exclusively attached to the interest of the senses. But though the growing alienation and self-sufficiency of the understanding was perceptible at an earlier period, yet it seems to have been about the middle of the last century, under the influence of Voltaire, D'Alembert, (and) Diderot . . . that the human understanding, and this too in its narrowest form, was tempted to throw off all show of reverence to the spiritual and even to the moral powers and impulses of the soul; and, usurping the name of reason, openly joined the banners of Antichrist, at once the pander and the prostitute of sensuality; and whether in the cabinet, laboratory, the dissecting-room, or the brothel, alike busy in the schemes of vice and irreligion. . . .

Prurient, bustling, and revolutionary, this French wisdom has never more than grazed the surfaces of knowledge. As political economy, in its zeal for the increase of food, it habitually overlooked the qualities and even the sensations of those that were to feed on it. As ethical philosophy, it recognized no duties which it could not reduce into debtor and creditor accounts on the ledgers of self-love, where no coin was sterling which could not be rendered into agreeable sensations. And even in its height of self-complacency as chemical art, greatly am I deceived if it has not from the very beginning mistaken the products of destruction, *cadavera rerum*, for the elements of composition: and most assuredly it has dearly purchased a few brilliant inventions at the loss of all communion with life and the spirit of nature. As the process, such the result!—a heartless frivolity alternating with a sentimentality as heartless—an ignorant contempt of antiquity—a neglect of moral self-discipline—a deadening of the religious sense, even in the less reflecting forms of natural piety—a scornful reprobation of all consolations and secret refreshings from above—and as the *caput mortuum* of human nature evaporated, a French nature of rapacity, levity, ferocity and presumption.

Man of understanding, canst thou command the stone to lie, canst thou bid the flower bloom, where thou has placed it in thy classification? Canst thou persuade the living or the inanimate to stand separate even as thou has separated them? And do not far rather all things spread out before thee in glad confusion and heedless intermixture, even as a lightsome chaos on which the Spirit of God is moving? Do not all press and swell under one attraction, and live together in promiscuous harmony, each joyous in its own kind, and in the immediate neighbourhood of myriad others that in the system of thy understanding are distant as the poles? If to mint and to remember names delight thee, still arrange and classify and pore and pull to pieces, and peep into death to look for life, as monkeys put their hands behind a looking-glass! Yet consider, in the first sabbath which thou imposest on the busy discursion of thought, that all this is at best little more than a technical memory: that like can only be known by like: that as truth is the correlative of being, so is the act of being the great organ of truth: that in natural no less than in moral science, *quantum sumus, scimus.* . . .

The leading differences between mechanic and vital philosophy may all be drawn from one point; namely, that the former demanding for every mode and act of existence real or possible visibility, knows only of distance and nearness, composition (or rather juxta-position) and decomposition, in short the relations of unproductive particles to each

218

other; so that in every instance the result is the exact sum of the component quantities, as in arithmetical addition. This is the philosophy of death, and only of a dead nature can it hold good. In life, much more in spirit, and in a living and spiritual philosophy, the two component counterpowers actually interpenetrate each other, and generate a higher third, including both the former, *ita tamen ut sit alia et major*.

To apply this to the subject of the present essay. The elements (the factors, as it were) of religion are reason and understanding. If the composition stopped in itself, an understanding thus rationalized would lead to the admission of the general doctrines of natural religion, the belief of a God, and of immortality; and probably to an acquiescence in the history and ethics of the Gospel. But still it would be a speculative faith, and in the nature of a theory; as if the main object of religion were to solve difficulties for the satisfaction of the intellect. Now this state of mind, which alas! is the state of too many among our self-entitled rational religionists, is a mere balance or compromise of the two powers, not that living and generative interpenetration of both which would give being to essential religion—to the religion, at the birth of which 'we receive the spirit of adoption, whereby we cry, Abba, Father; the spirit itself bearing witness with our spirit, that we are the children of God' (Rom. viii. 15, 16). In religion there is no abstraction. To the unity and infinity of the Divine Nature, of which it is the partaker, it adds the fulness, and to the fulness the grace and the creative overflowing. That which intuitively it at once beholds and adores, praying always, and rejoicing always—that doth it tend to become. In all things, and in each thing—for the Almighty goodness does not create generalities or abide in abstractions—in each, the meanest, object it bears witness to a mystery of infinite solution. Thus 'beholding as in a glass the glory of the Lord, it is changed into the same image from glory to glory' (2 Cor. iii. 18). . . .

# XIV  Irreverent Interpolations

GEORGE GORDON, LORD BYRON

## Understanding Wordsworth and Coleridge

from *Don Juan*, 1818–20

Young Juan wander'd by the glassy brooks,
Thinking unutterable things; he threw
Himself at length within the leafy nooks
    Where the wild branch of the cork forest grew;
There poets find materials for their books,
    And every now and then we read them through,
So that their plan and prosody are eligible,
Unless, like Wordsworth, they prove unintelligible.

    He, Juan (and not Wordsworth), so pursued
  His self-communion with his own high soul,
Until his mighty heart, in its great mood,
    Had mitigated part though not the whole
Of its disease; he did the best he could
    With things not very subject to control,
And turn'd, without perceiving his condition,
Like Coleridge, into a metaphysician.

    He thought about himself, and the whole earth,
  Of man the wonderful, and of the stars,
And how the deuce they ever could have birth:
    And then he thought of earthquakes, and of wars,
How many miles the moon might have in girth;
    Of air-balloons, and of the many bars
To perfect knowledge of the boundless skies;
And then he thought of Donna Julia's eyes.

    In thoughts like these true wisdom may discern
  Longings sublime, and aspirations high,
Which some are born with, but the most part learn
    To plague themselves withal, they know not why:
'Twas strange that one so young should thus concern

His brain about the action of the sky;
If *you* think 'twas philosophy that this did,
I can't help thinking puberty assisted.


# THOMAS LOVE PEACOCK                                    XIV.2
## "Romantic metaphysics"

from *Nightmare Abbey*, 1818


. . . Scythrop was left alone at Nightmare Abbey. He was a burnt child, and dreaded the fire of female eyes. He wandered about the ample pile, or along the garden-terrace, with 'his cogitative faculties immersed in cogibundity of cogitation.' The terrace terminated at the south-western tower, which, as we have said, was ruinous and full of owls. Here would Scythrop take his evening seat, on a fallen fragment of mossy stone, with his back resting against the ruined wall,—a thick canopy of ivy, with an owl in it, over his head,—and the Sorrows of Werter in his hand. He had some taste for romance reading before he went to the university, where, we must confess, in justice to his college, he was cured of the love of reading in all its shapes; and the cure would have been radical, if disappointment in love, and total solitude, had not conspired to bring on a relapse. He began to devour romances and German tragedies, and, by the recommendation of Mr. Flosky, to pore over ponderous tomes of transcendental philosophy, which reconciled him to the labour of studying them by their mystical jargon and necromantic imagery. In the congenial solitude of Nightmare Abbey, the distempered ideas of metaphysical romance and romantic metaphysics had ample time and space to germinate into a fertile crop of chimeras, which rapidly shot up into vigorous and abundant vegetation.

He now became troubled with the *passion for reforming the world*. He built many castles in the air, and peopled them with secret tribunals, and bands of illuminati, who were always the imaginary instruments of his projected regeneration of the human species. As he intended to institute a perfect republic, he invested himself with absolute sovereignty over these mystical dispensers of liberty. He slept with Horrid Mysteries under his pillow, and dreamed of venerable eleutherarchs and ghastly confederates holding midnight conventions in subterranean caves. He passed whole mornings in his nightcap, which he pulled over his eyes like a cowl, and folding his striped calico dressing-gown about him like the mantle of a conspirator.

'Action,' thus he soliloquised, 'is the result of opinion, and to new-model opinion would be to new-model society. Knowledge is power; it is in the hands of a few, who employ it to mislead the many, for their own selfish purposes of aggrandisement and appropriation. What if it were in the hands of a few who should employ it to lead the many? What if it were universal, and the multitude were enlightened? No. The many must be always in leading-strings; but let them have wise and honest conductors. A few to think, and many to act; that is the only basis of perfect society. So thought the ancient philosophers: they had their esoterical and exoterical doctrines. So thinks the sublime Kant, who delivers his oracles in language which none but the initiated can comprehend. Such were the views of those secret associations of illuminati, which were the terror of superstition and tyranny, and which, carefully selecting wisdom and genius from the great wilderness of society, as the bee selects honey from the flowers of the thorn and the nettle, bound all human excellence in a chain, which, if it had not been prematurely broken, would have commanded opinion, and regenerated the world.'

Scythrop proceeded to meditate on the practicability of reviving a confederation of regenerators. To get a clear view of his own ideas, and to feel the pulse of the wisdom and genius of the age, he wrote and published a treatise, in which his meanings were carefully wrapt up in the monk's hood of transcendental technology, but filled with hints of matter deep and dangerous, which he thought would set the whole nation in a ferment; and he awaited the result in awful expectation, as a miner who has fired a train awaits the explosion of a rock. However, he listened and heard nothing; for the explosion, if any ensued, was not sufficiently loud to shake a single leaf of the ivy on the towers of Nightmare Abbey; and some months afterwards he received a letter from his bookseller, informing him that only seven copies had been sold, and concluding with a polite request for the balance.

Scythrop did not despair. 'Seven copies,' he thought, 'have been sold. Seven is a mystical number, and the omen is good. Let me find the seven purchasers of my seven copies, and they shall be the seven golden candle-sticks with which I will illuminate the world.'

Scythrop had a certain portion of mechanical genius, which his romantic projects tended to develop. He constructed models of cells and recesses, sliding panels and secret passages, that would have baffled the skill of the Parisian police. He took the opportunity of his father's absence to smuggle a dumb carpenter into the Abbey, and between them they gave reality to one of these models in Scythrop's tower. Scythrop foresaw that a great leader of human regeneration would be involved in fearful dilemmas, and determined, for the benefit of mankind in general, to adopt all possible precautions for the preservation of himself.

The servants, even the women, had been tutored into silence. Profound stillness reigned throughout and around the Abbey, except when the occasional shutting of a door would peal in long reverberations through the galleries, or the heavy tread of the pensive butler would wake the hollow echoes of the hall. Scythrop stalked about like the grand inquisitor, and the servants flitted past him like familiars. In his evening meditations on the terrace, under the ivy of the ruined tower, the only sounds that came to his ear were the rustling of the wind in the ivy, the plaintive voices of the feathered choristers, the owls, the occasional striking of the Abbey clock, and the monotonous dash of the sea on its low and level shore. In the mean time, he drank Madeira, and laid deep schemes for a thorough repair of the crazy fabric of human nature.

# XV Satires

## P. B. SHELLEY                                                XV.1
### 'Similes for Two Political Characters'
1819

As from an ancestral oak
    Two empty ravens sound their clarion
Yell by yell, and croak by croak
When they scent the noonday smoke
    Of fresh human carrion:—

As two gibbering night-birds flit
    From their bowers of deadly yew
Through the night to frighten it
When the moon is in a fit,
    And the stars are none, or few.

As a shark and dog-fish wait
    Under an Atlantic isle,
For the negro-ship, whose freight
Is the theme of their debate,
    Wrinkling their red gills the while

Are ye, two vultures sick for battle
    Two scorpions under one wet stone
Two bloodless wolves whose dry throats rattle
Two crows perched on the murrained cattle
    Two vipers tangled into one.

## ARTHUR HUGH CLOUGH                                           XV.2
### 'The Latest Decalogue'
written 1848–52

Thou shalt have one God only; who
Would be at the expense of two?
No graven images may be

Worshipped, except the currency:
Swear not at all; for for thy curse
Thine enemy is none the worse:
At church on Sunday to attend
Will serve to keep the world thy friend:
Honour thy parents; that is, all
From whom advancement may befall:
Thou shalt not kill; but needst not strive
Officiously to keep alive:
Do not adultery commit;
Advantage rarely comes of it:
Thou shalt not steal; an empty feat,
When it's so lucrative to cheat:
Bear not false witness; let the lie
Have time on its own wings to fly:
Thou shalt not covet; but tradition
Approves all forms of competition.

The sum of all is, thou shalt love,
If any body, God above:
At any rate shall never labour
*More* than thyself to love thy neighbour.

# CHARLES DICKENS                                      XV.3
## M' Choakumchild's Model School
from *Hard Times*, 1854

Mr. Gradgrind walked homeward from the school, in a state of considerable satisfaction. It was his school, and he intended it to be a model. He intended every child in it to be a model—just as the young Gradgrinds were all models.

There were five young Gradgrinds, and they were models every one. They had been lectured at, from their tenderest years; coursed, like little hares. Almost as soon as they could run alone, they had been made to run to the lecture-room. The first object with which they had an association, or of which they had a remembrance, was a large black board with a dry Ogre chalking ghastly white figures on it.

Not that they knew, by name or nature, anything about an Ogre. Fact forbid! I only use the word to express a monster in a lecturing castle, with Heaven knows how many heads manipulated into one, taking childhood captive, and dragging it into gloomy statistical dens by the hair.

No little Gradgrind had ever seen a face in the moon; it was up in the moon before it could speak distinctly. No little Gradgrind had ever learnt the silly jingle, Twinkle, twinkle, little star; how I wonder what you are! No little Gradgrind had ever known wonder on the subject, each little Gradgrind having at five years old dissected the Great Bear like a Professor Owen, and driven Charles's Wain like a locomotive engine-driver. No little Gradgrind had ever associated a cow in a field with that famous cow with the crumpled horn who tossed the dog who worried the cat who killed the rat who ate the malt, or with that yet more famous cow who swallowed Tom Thumb: it had never heard of those celebrities, and had only been introduced to a cow as a graminivorous ruminating quadruped with several stomachs.

To his matter-of-fact home, which was called Stone Lodge, Mr. Gradgrind directed his steps. He had virtually retired from the wholesale hardware trade before he built Stone Lodge, and was now looking about for a suitable opportunity of making an arithmetical figure in Parliament. Stone Lodge was situated on a moor within a mile or two of a great town—called Coketown in the present faithful guide-book.

A very regular feature on the face of the country, Stone Lodge was. Not the least disguise toned down or shaded off that uncompromising fact in the landscape. A great square house, with a heavy portico darkening the principal windows, as its master's heavy brows overshadowed his eyes. A calculated, cast up, balanced, and proved house. Six windows on this side of the door, six on that side; a total of twelve in this wing, a total of twelve in the other wing; four-and-twenty carried over to the back wings. A lawn and garden and an infant avenue, all ruled straight like a botanical account-book. Gas and ventilation, drainage and water-service, all of the primest quality. Iron clamps and girders, fireproof from top to bottom; mechanical lifts for the housemaids, with all their brushes and brooms; everything that heart could desire.

Everything? Well, I suppose so. The little Gradgrinds had cabinets in various departments of science too. They had a little conchological cabinet, and a little metallurgical cabinet, and a little mineralogical cabinet; and the specimens were all arranged and labelled, and the bits of stone and ore looked as though they might have been broken from the parent substances by those tremendously hard instruments their own names; and, to paraphrase the idle legend of Peter Piper, who had never found his way into their nursery, If the greedy little Gradgrinds grasped at more than this, what was it for good gracious goodness' sake, that the greedy little Gradgrinds grasped at?

# XVI The Condition of England

THOMAS CARLYLE                                                      XVI.1

"The Mechanical Age"

from 'Signs of the Times', 1829

Were we required to characterise this age of ours by any single epithet, we should be tempted to call it, not an Heroical, Devotional, Philosophical, or Moral Age, but, above all others, the Mechanical Age. It is the Age of Machinery, in every outward and inward sense of that word; the age which, with its whole undivided might, forwards, teaches and practises the great art of adapting means to ends. Nothing is now done directly, or by hand; all is by rule and calculated contrivance. For the simplest operation, some helps and accompaniments, some cunning abbreviating process is in readiness. Our old modes of exertion are all discredited, and thrown aside. On every hand, the living artisan is driven from his workshop, to make room for a speedier, inanimate one. The shuttle drops from the fingers of the weaver, and falls into iron fingers that ply it faster. The sailor furls his sail, and lays down his oar; and bids a strong, unwearied servant, on vaporous wings, bear him through the waters. Men have crossed oceans by steam; the Birmingham Fire-king has visited the fabulous East; and the genius of the Cape, were there any Camoens now to sing it, has again been alarmed, and with far stranger thunders than Gamas. There is no end to machinery. Even the horse is stripped of his harness, and finds a fleet fire-horse yoked in his stead. Nay, we have an artist that hatches chickens by steam; the very brood-hen is to be superseded! For all earthly, and for some unearthly purposes, we have machines and mechanic furtherances; for mincing our cabbages; for casting us into magnetic sleep. We remove mountains, and make seas our smooth highway; nothing can resist us. We war with rude Nature; and, by our resistless engines, come off always victorious, and loaded with spoils.

What wonderful accessions have thus been made, and are still making, to the physical power of mankind; how much better fed, clothed, lodged and, in all outward respects, accommodated men now are, or might be, by a given quantity of labour, is a grateful reflection which forces itself on every one. What changes, too, this addition of power is introducing into the Social System; how wealth has more and more increased, and at the same time gathered itself more and more into masses, strangely altering the old relations, and increasing the distance between the rich and the poor, will be a question for Political Economists, and a much more complex and important one than any they have yet engaged with.

But leaving these matters for the present, let us observe how the mechanical genius of our time has diffused itself into quite other provinces. Not the external and physical alone is now managed by machinery, but the internal and spiritual also. Here too nothing follows its spontaneous course, nothing is left to be accomplished by old natural methods. Everything has its cunningly devised implements, its prëestablished apparatus; it is not done by hand, but by machinery. Thus we have machines for Education: Lancastrian machines; Hamiltonian machines; monitors, maps and emblems. Instruction, that mysterious communing of Wisdom with Ignorance, is no longer an indefinable tentative process, requiring a study of individual aptitudes, and a perpetual variation of means and methods, to attain the same end; but a secure, universal, straightforward business, to be conducted in the gross, by proper mechanism, with such intellect as comes to hand. Then, we have Religious machines, of all imaginable varieties; the Bible-Society, professing a far higher and heavenly structure, is found, on inquiry, to be altogether an earthly contrivance: supported by collection of moneys, by fomenting of vanities, by puffing, intrigue and chicane; a machine for converting the Heathen. It is the same in all other departments. Has any man, or any society of men, a truth to speak, a piece of spiritual work to do; they can nowise proceed at once and with the mere natural organs, but must first call a public meeting, appoint committees, issue prospectuses, eat a public dinner; in a word, construct or borrow machinery, wherewith to speak it and do it. Without machinery they were hopeless, helpless; a colony of Hindoo weavers squatting in the heart of Lancashire. Mark, too, how every machine must have its moving power, in some of the great currents of society; every little sect among us, Unitarians, Utilitarians, Anabaptists, Phrenologists, must have its Periodical, its monthly or quarterly Magazine;— hanging out, like its windmill, into the *popularis aura*, to grind meal for the society.

With individuals, in like manner, natural strength avails little. No individual now hopes to accomplish the poorest enterprise single-handed and without mechanical aids; he must make interest with some existing corporation, and till his field with their oxen. In these days, more emphatically than ever, 'to live, signifies to unite with a party, or to make one.' Philosophy, Science, Art, Literature, all depend on machinery. No Newton, by silent meditation, now discovers the system of the world from the falling of an apple; but some quite other than

230

Newton stands in his Museum, his Scientific Institution, and behind whole batteries of retorts, digesters, and galvanic piles imperatively 'interrogates Nature,'—who, however, shows no haste to answer. In defect of Raphaels, and Angelos, and Mozarts, we have Royal Academies of Painting, Sculpture, Music; whereby the languishing spirit of Art may be strengthened, as by the more generous diet of a Public Kitchen. Literature, too, has its Paternoster-row mechanism, its Trade-dinners, its Editorial conclaves, and huge subterranean, puffing bellows; so that books are not only printed, but, in a great measure, written and sold, by machinery.

National culture, spiritual benefit of all sorts, is under the same management. No Queen Christina, in these times, needs to send for her Descartes; no King Frederick for his Voltaire, and painfully nourish him with pensions and flattery: any sovereign of taste, who wishes to enlighten his people, has only to impose a new tax, and with the proceeds establish Philosophic Institutes. Hence the Royal and Imperial Societies, the Bibliothèques, Glypothèques, Technothèques, which front us in all capital cities; like so many well-finished hives, to which it is expected the stray agencies of Wisdom will swarm of their own accord, and hive and make honey. In like manner, among ourselves, when it is thought that religion is declining, we have only to vote half-a-million's worth of bricks and mortar, and build new churches. In Ireland it seems they have gone still farther, having actually established a 'Penny-a-week Purgatory-Society'! Thus does the Genius of Mechanism stand by to help us in all difficulties and emergencies, and with his iron back bears all our burdens.

These things, which we state lightly enough here, are yet of deep import, and indicate a mighty change in our whole manner of existence. For the same habit regulates not our modes of action alone, but our modes of thought and feeling. Men are grown mechanical in head and in heart, as well as in hand. They have lost faith in individual endeavour, and in natural force, of any kind. Not for internal perfection, but for external combinations and arrangements, for institutions, constitutions, —for Mechanism of one sort or other, do they hope and struggle. Their whole efforts, attachments, opinions, turn on mechanism, and are of a mechanical character.

We may trace this tendency in all the great manifestations of our time; in its intellectual aspect, the studies it most favours and its manner of conducting them; in its practical aspects, its politics, arts, religion, morals; in the whole sources, and throughout the whole currents, of its spiritual, no less than its material activity. . . .

Nowhere, for example, is the deep, almost exclusive faith we have in Mechanism more visible than in the Politics of this time. Civil government does by its nature include much that is mechanical, and must be treated accordingly. We term it indeed, in ordinary language, the Machine of Society, and talk of it as the grand working wheel from which all private machines must derive, or to which they must adapt, their movements. Considered merely as a metaphor, all this is well enough; but here, as in so many other cases, the 'foam hardens itself into a shell,' and the shadow we have wantonly evoked stands terrible before us and will not depart at our bidding. Government includes much also that is not mechanical, and cannot be treated mechanically; of which latter truth, as appears to us, the political speculations and exertions of our time are taking less and less cognisance.

Nay, in the very outset, we might note the mighty interest taken in *mere political arrangements*, as itself the sign of a mechanical age. The whole discontent of Europe takes this direction. The deep, strong cry of all civilised nations,—a cry which, every one now sees, must and will be answered, is: Give us a reform of Government! A good structure of legislation, a proper check upon the executive, a wise arrangement of the judiciary, is *all* that is wanting for human happiness. The Philosopher of this age is not a Socrates, a Plato, a Hooker, or Taylor, who inculcates on men the necessity and infinite worth of moral goodness, the great truth that our happiness depends on the mind which is within us, and not on the circumstances which are without us; but a Smith, a De Lolme, a Bentham, who chiefly inculcates the reverse of this,—that our happiness depends entirely on external circumstances; nay, that the strength and dignity of the mind within us is itself the creature and consequence of these. Were the laws, the government, in good order, all were well with us; the rest would care for itself! Dissentients from this opinion, expressed or implied, are now rarely to be met with; widely and angrily as men differ in its application, the principle is admitted by all.

Equally mechanical, and of equal simplicity, are the methods proposed by both parties for completing or securing this all-sufficient perfection of arrangement. It is no longer the moral, religious, spiritual condition of the people that is our concern, but their physical, practical, economical condition, as regulated by public laws. Thus is the Body-politic more than ever worshipped and tendered; but the Soul-politic less than ever. Love of country, in any high or generous sense, in any other than an almost animal sense, or mere habit, has little importance attached to it in such reforms, or in the opposition shown them. Men are to be guided only by their self-interests. Good government is a good balancing of these; and, except a keen eye and appetite for self-interest, requires no virtue in any quarter. To both parties it is emphatically a machine: to the discontented, a 'taxing-machine'; to the contented, a 'machine for securing property.' Its duties and its faults are not those of a father, but of an active parish-constable.

Thus it is by the mere condition of the machine, by preserving it untouched, or else by reconstructing it, and oiling it anew, that man's salvation as a social being is to be ensured and indefinitely promoted. Contrive the fabric of law aright, and without farther effort on your part, that divine spirit of Freedom, which all hearts venerate and long for, will of herself come to inhabit it; and under her healing wings every noxious influence will wither, every good and salutary one more and more expand. Nay, so devoted are we to this principle, and at the same time so curiously mechanical, that a new trade, specially grounded on it, has arisen among us, under the name of 'Codification,' or code-making in the abstract; whereby any people, for a reasonable consideration, may be accommodated with a patent code;—more easily than curious individuals with patent breeches, for the people does *not* need to be measured first.

To us who live in the midst of all this, and see continually the faith, hope and practice of every one founded on Mechanism of one kind or other, it is apt to seem quite natural, and as if it could never have been otherwise. Nevertheless, if we recollect or reflect a little, we shall find both that it has been, and might again be otherwise. The domain of Mechanism,—meaning thereby political, ecclesiastical or other outward establishments,—was once considered as embracing, and we are persuaded can at any time embrace, but a limited portion of man's interests, and by no means the highest portion.

To speak a little pedantically, there is a science of *Dynamics* in man's fortunes and nature, as well as of *Mechanics*. There is a science which treats of, and practically addresses, the primary, unmodified forces and energies of man, the mysterious springs of Love, and Fear, and Wonder, of Enthusiasm, Poetry, Religion, all which have a truly vital and *infinite* character; as well as a science which practically addresses the finite, modified developments of these, when they take the shape of immediate 'motives,' as hope of reward, or as fear of punishment.

Now it is certain, that in former times the wise men, the enlightened lovers of their kind, who appeared generally as Moralists, Poets or Priests, did, without neglecting the Mechanical province, deal chiefly with the Dynamical; applying themselves chiefly to regulate, increase and purify the inward primary powers of man; and fancying that herein lay the main difficulty, and the best service they could undertake. But a wide difference is manifest in our age. For the wise men, who now appear as Political Philosophers, deal exclusively with the Mechanical province; and occupying themselves in counting-up and estimating men's motives, strive by curious checking and balancing, and other adjustments of Profit and Loss, to guide them to their true advantage: while, unfortunately, those same 'motives' are so innumerable, and so variable in every individual, that no really useful conclusion can ever be drawn from their enumeration. But though Mechanism, wisely contrived, has done much for man in a social and moral point of view, we cannot be persuaded that it has ever been the chief source of his worth or happiness. Consider the great elements of human enjoyment, the attainments and possessions that exalt man's life to its present height, and see what part of these he owes to institutions, to Mechanism of any kind; and what to the instinctive, unbounded force, which Nature herself lent him, and still continues to him. Shall we say, for example, that Science and Art are indebted principally to the founders of Schools and Universities? Did not Science originate rather, and gain advancement, in the obscure closets of the Roger Bacons, Keplers, Newtons; in the workshops of the Fausts and the Watts; wherever, and in what guise soever Nature, from the first times downwards, had sent a gifted spirit upon the earth? Again, were Homer and Shakspeare members of any beneficed guild, or made Poets by means of it? Were Painting and Sculpture created by forethought, brought into the world by institutions for that end? No; Science and Art have, from first to last, been the free gift of Nature; an unsolicited, unexpected gift; often even a fatal one. These things rose up, as it were, by spontaneous growth, in the free soil and sunshine of Nature. They were not planted or grafted, nor even greatly multiplied or improved by the culture or manuring of institutions. Generally speaking, they have derived only partial help from these; often enough have suffered damage. They made constitutions for themselves. They originated in the Dynamical nature of man, not in his Mechanical nature.

## THOMAS BABINGTON MACAULAY            XVI.2
### Speech on the Reform Bill
House of Commons, 1831

All history is full of revolutions, produced by causes similar to those which are now operating in England. A portion of the community which had been of no account expands and becomes strong. It demands a place in the system, suited, not to its former weakness, but to its present power. If this is granted, all is well. If this is refused, then comes the struggle between the young energy of one class and the ancient privileges of another. Such was the struggle between the Plebeians and the Patricians of Rome. Such was the struggle of the Italian allies for admission to the full rights of Roman citizens. Such was the struggle of our North American colonies against the mother country. Such was the struggle which the Third Estate of France maintained against the aristocracy of birth. Such was the struggle which the Roman

Catholics of Ireland maintained against the aristocracy of creed. Such is the struggle which the free people of color in Jamaica are now maintaining against the aristocracy of skin. Such, finally, is the struggle which the middle classes in England are maintaining against an aristocracy of mere locality, against an aristocracy the principle of which is to invest a hundred drunken pot-wallopers in one place, or the owner of a ruined hovel in another, with powers which are withheld from cities renowned to the furthest ends of the earth for the marvels of their wealth and of their industry.

The question of Parliamentary Reform is still behind. But signs, of which it is impossible to misconceive the import, do most clearly indicate that, unless that question also be speedily settled, property, and order, and all the institutions of this great monarchy, will be exposed to fearful peril. Is it possible that gentlemen long versed in high political affairs cannot read these signs? Is it possible that they can really believe that the representative system of England, such as it now is, will last till the year 1860? If not, for what would they have us wait? Would they have us wait merely that we may show to all the world how little we have profited by our own recent experience? Would they have us wait, that we may once again hit the exact point where we can neither refuse with authority, nor concede with grace? Would they have us wait, that the numbers of the discontented party may become larger, its demands higher, its feelings more acrimonious, its organization more complete? Would they have us wait till the whole tragi-comedy of 1827 has been acted over again; till they have been brought into office by a cry of 'No Reform,' to be reformers, as they were once before brought into office by a cry of 'No Popery,' to be emancipators? Have they obliterated from their minds—gladly, perhaps, would some among them obliterate from their minds—the transactions of that year? And have they forgotten all the transactions of the succeeding year? Have they forgotten how the spirit of liberty in Ireland, debarred from its natural outlet, found a vent by forbidden passages? Have they forgotten how we were forced to indulge the Catholics in all the license of rebels, merely because we chose to withhold from them the liberties of subjects? Do they wait for associations more formidable than that of the Corn Exchange, for contributions larger than the Rent, for agitators more violent than those who, three years ago, divided with the King and the Parliament the sovereignty of Ireland? Do they wait for that last and most dreadful paroxysm of popular rage, for that last and most cruel test of military fidelity? Let them wait, if their past experience shall induce them to think that any high honor or any exquisite pleasure is to be obtained by a policy like this. Let them wait, if this strange and fearful infatuation be indeed upon them, that they should not see with their eyes, or hear with their ears, or understand with their heart. But let us know our interest and our duty better. Turn where we may, within, around, the voice of great events is proclaiming to us, Reform, that you may preserve. Now therefore while everything at home and abroad forebodes ruin to those who persist in a hopeless struggle against the spirit of the age, now, while the crash of the proudest throne of the Continent is still resounding in our ears, now, while the roof of a British palace affords an ignominious shelter to the exiled heir of forty kings, now, while we see on every side ancient institutions subverted, and great societies dissolved, now, while the heart of England is still sound, now, while old feelings and old associations retain a power and a charm which may too soon pass away, now, in this your accepted time, now, in this your day of salvation, take counsel, not of prejudice, not of party spirit, not of the ignominious pride of a fatal consistency, but of history, of reason, of the ages which are past, of the signs of this most portentous time. Pronounce in a manner worthy of the expectation with which this great debate has been anticipated, and of the long remembrance which it will leave behind. Renew the youth of the state. Save property, divided against itself. Save the multitude, endangered by its own ungovernable passions. Save the aristocracy, endangered by its own unpopular power. Save the greatest, and fairest, and most highly civilized community that ever existed, from calamities which may in a few days sweep away all the rich heritage of so many ages of wisdom and glory. The danger is terrible. The time is short. If this bill should be rejected, I pray to God that none of those who concur in rejecting it may ever remember their votes with unavailing remorse, amidst the wreck of laws, the confusion of ranks, the spoliation of property, and the dissolution of social order.

## THOMAS CARLYLE                                    XVI.3
'Midas'

from *Past and Present*, 1843

The condition of England, on which many pamphlets are now in the course of publication, and many thoughts unpublished are going on in every reflective head, is justly regarded as one of the most ominous, and withal one of the strangest, ever seen in this world. England is full of wealth, of multifarious produce, supply for human want in every kind; yet England is dying of inanition. With unabated bounty the land of England blooms and grows; waving with yellow harvests; thick-studded with workshops, industrial implements, with fifteen millions of workers, understood to be the strongest, the cunningest and the willingest our Earth ever had; these men are here; the work they have done, the fruit they have realised is here, abundant, exuberant on every hand of us: and behold, some baleful fiat as of Enchantment has gone forth, saying, 'Touch it not, ye workers, ye master-workers, ye master-idlers; none of you can touch it, no man of you shall be the better for it; this is enchanted fruit!' On the poor workers such fiat falls first, in its rudest shape; but on the rich master-workers too it falls; neither can the rich master-idlers, nor any richest or highest man escape, but all are like to be brought low with it, and made 'poor' enough, in the money sense or a far fataler one.

Of these successful skilful workers some two millions, it is now counted, sit in Workhouses, Poor-law Prisons; or have 'out-door relief' flung over the wall to them,—the workhouse Bastille being filled to bursting, and the strong Poor-law broken asunder by a stronger. They sit there, these many months now; their hope of deliverance as yet small. In workhouses, pleasantly so-named, because work cannot be done in them. Twelve-hundred-thousand workers in England alone; their cunning right-hand lamed, lying idle in their sorrowful bosom; their hopes, outlooks, share of this fair world, shut-in by narrow walls. They sit there, pent up, as in a kind of horrid enchantment; glad to be imprisoned and enchanted, that they may not perish starved. The picturesque Tourist, in a sunny autumn day, through this bounteous realm of England, descries the Union Workhouse on his path. 'Passing by the Workhouse of St. Ives in Huntingdonshire, on a bright day last autumn,' says the picturesque Tourist, 'I saw sitting on wooden benches, in front of their Bastille and within their ringwall and its railings, some half-hundred or more of these men. Tall robust figures, young mostly or of middle age; of honest countenance, many of them thoughtful and even intelligent-looking men. They sat there, near by one another; but in a kind of torpor, especially in a silence, which was very striking. In silence: for, alas, what word was to be said? An Earth all lying round, crying, Come and till me, come and reap me;—yet we here sit enchanted! In the eyes and brows of these men hung the gloomiest expression, not of anger, but of grief and shame and manifold inarticulate distress and weariness; they returned my glance with a glance that seemed to say, "Do not look at us. We sit enchanted here, we know not why. The Sun shines and the Earth calls; and, by the governing Powers and Impotences of this England, we are forbidden to obey. It is impossible, they tell us!" There was something that reminded me of Dante's Hell in the look of all this; and I rode swiftly away.'

So many hundred thousands sit in workhouses: and other hundred thousands have not yet got even workhouses; and in thrifty Scotland itself, in Glasgow or Edinburgh City, in their dark lanes, hidden from all but the eye of God, and of rare Benevolence the minister of God, there are scenes of woe and destitution and desolation, such as, one

237

may hope, the Sun never saw before in the most barbarous regions where men dwelt. Competent witnesses, the brave and humane Dr. Alison, who speaks what he knows, whose noble Healing Art in his charitable hands becomes once more a truly sacred one, report these things for us: these things are not of this year, or of last year, have no reference to our present state of commercial stagnation, but only to the common state. Not in sharp fever-fits, but in chronic gangrene of this kind is Scotland suffering. A Poor-law, any and every Poor-law, it may be observed, is but a temporary measure; an anodyne, not a remedy: Rich and Poor, when once the naked facts of their condition have come into collision, cannot long subsist together on a mere Poor-law. True enough:—and yet, human beings cannot be left to die! Scotland too, till something better come, must have a Poor-law, if Scotland is not to be a byword among the nations. O, what a waste is there; of noble and thrice-noble national virtues; peasant Stoicisms, Heroisms; valiant manful habits, soul of a Nation's worth,—which all the metal of Potosi cannot purchase back; to which the metal of Potosi, and all you can buy with *it*, is dross and dust!

Why dwell on this aspect of the matter? It is too indisputable, not doubtful now to any one. Descend where you will into the lower class, in Town or Country, by what avenue you will, by Factory Inquiries, Agricultural Inquiries, by Revenue Returns, by Mining-Labourer Committees, by opening your own eyes and looking, the same sorrowful result discloses itself: you have to admit that the working body of this rich English Nation has sunk or is fast sinking into a state, to which, all sides of it considered, there was literally never any parallel. At Stockport Assizes,—and this too has no reference to the present state of trade, being of date prior to that,—a Mother and a Father are arraigned and found guilty of poisoning three of their children, to defraud a 'burial-society' of some £3 8s. due on the death of each child: they are arraigned, found guilty; and the official authorities, it is whispered, hint that perhaps the case is not solitary, that perhaps you had better not probe farther into that department of things. This is in the autumn of 1841; the crime itself is of the previous year or season. 'Brutal savages, degraded Irish,' mutters the idle reader of Newspapers; hardly lingering on this incident. Yet it is an incident worth lingering on; the depravity, savagery and degraded Irishism being never so well admitted. In the British land, a human Mother and Father, of white skin and professing the Christian religion, had done this thing; they, with their Irishism and necessity and savagery, had been driven to do it. Such instances are like the highest mountain apex emerged into view; under which lies a whole mountain region and land, not yet emerged. A human Mother and Father had said to themselves, What shall we do to escape starvation? We are deep sunk here, in our dark cellar; and help is far.—Yes, in

238

the Ugolino Hunger-tower stern things happen; best-loved little Gaddo fallen dead on his Father's knees!—The Stockport Mother and Father think and hint: Our poor little starveling Tom, who cries all day for victuals, who will see only evil and not good in this world: if he were out of misery at once; he well dead, and the rest of us perhaps kept alive? It is thought, and hinted; at last it is done. And now Tom being killed, and all spent and eaten, Is it poor little starveling Jack that must go, or poor little starveling Will?—What a committee of ways and means!

In starved sieged cities, in the uttermost doomed ruin of old Jerusalem fallen under the wrath of God, it was prophesied and said, 'The hands of the pitiful women have sodden their own children.' The stern Hebrew imagination could conceive no blacker gulf of wretchedness; that was the ultimatum of degraded god-punished man. And we here, in modern England, exuberant with supply of all kinds, besieged by nothing if it be not by invisible Enchantments, are we reaching that?—How come these things? Wherefore are they, wherefore should they be?

Nor are they of the St. Ives workhouses, of the Glasgow lanes, and Stockport cellars, the only unblessed among us. This successful industry of England, with its plethoric wealth, has as yet made nobody rich; it is an enchanted wealth, and belongs yet to nobody. We might ask, Which of us has it enriched? We can spend thousands where we once spent hundreds; but can purchase nothing good with them. In Poor and Rich, instead of noble thrift and plenty, there is idle luxury alternating with mean scarcity and inability. We have sumptuous garnitures for our Life, but have forgotten to *live* in the middle of them. It is an enchanted wealth; no man of us can yet touch it. The class of men who feel that they are truly better off by means of it, let them give us their name!

Many men eat finer cookery, drink dearer liquors,—with what advantage they can report, and their Doctors can: but in the heart of them, if we go out of the dyspeptic stomach, what increase of blessedness is there? Are they better, beautifuler, stronger, braver? Are they even what they call 'happier'? Do they look with satisfaction on more things and human faces in this God's-Earth; do more things and human faces look with satisfaction on them? No so. Human faces gloom discordantly, disloyally on one another. Things, if it be not mere cotton and iron things, are growing disobedient to man. The Master Worker is enchanted, for the present, like his Workhouse Workman; clamours, in vain hitherto, for a very simple sort of 'Liberty:' the liberty 'to buy where he finds it cheapest, to sell where he finds it dearest.' With guineas jingling in every pocket, he was no whit richer; but now, the very guineas threatening to vanish, he feels that he is poor indeed. Poor Master Worker! And the Master Unworker, is not he in a still fataler situation? Pausing amid his game-preserves, with awful eye,—as he well

239

may! Coercing fifty-pound tenants; coercing, bribing, cajoling; 'doing what he likes with his own.' His mouth full of loud futilities, and arguments to prove the excellence of his Corn-law; and in his heart the blackest misgiving, a desperate half-consciousness that his excellent Corn-law is *in*defensible, that his loud arguments for it are of a kind to strike men too literally *dumb*.

To whom, then, is this wealth of England wealth? Who is it that it blesses; makes happier, wiser, beautifuler, in any way better? Who has got hold of it, to make it fetch and carry for him, like a true servant, not like a false mock-servant; to do him any real service whatsoever? As yet no one. We have more riches than any Nation ever had before; we have less good of them than any Nation ever had before. Our successful industry is hitherto unsuccessful; a strange success, if we stop here! In the midst of plethoric plenty, the people perish; with gold walls, and full barns, no man feels himself safe or satisfied. Workers, Master Workers, Unworkers, all men, come to a pause; stand fixed, and cannot farther. Fatal paralysis spreading inwards, from the extremities, in St. Ives workhouses, in Stockport cellars, through all limbs, as if towards the heart itself. Have we actually got enchanted, then; accursed by some God?—

Midas longed for gold, and insulted the Olympians. He got gold, so that whatsoever he touched became gold,—and he, with his long ears, was little the better for it. Midas had misjudged the celestial music-tones; Midas had insulted Apollo and the gods: the gods gave him his wish, and a pair of long ears, which also were a good appendage to it. What a truth in these old Fables!

# XVII Later Ideas of Work

THOMAS CARLYLE XVII.1

The "nobleness, even sacredness, in Work"

from *Past and Present*, 1843

There is a perennial nobleness, and even sacredness, in Work. Were he never so benighted, forgetful of his high calling, there is always hope in a man that actually and earnestly works: in Idleness alone is there perpetual despair. Work, never so Mammonish, mean, *is* in communication with Nature; the real desire to get Work done will itself lead one more and more to truth, to Nature's appointments and regulations which are truth.

The latest Gospel in this world is, Know thy work and do it. 'Know thyself': long enough has that poor 'self' of thine tormented thee; thou wilt never get to 'know' it, I believe! Think it not thy business, this of knowing thyself; thou art an unknowable individual: know what thou canst work at; and work at it, like a Hercules! That will be thy better plan.

It has been written, 'an endless significance lies in Work'; a man perfects himself by working. Foul jungles are cleared away, fair seed-fields rise instead, and stately cities; and withal the man himself first ceases to be a jungle and foul unwholesome desert thereby. Consider how, even in the meanest sorts of Labour, the whole soul of a man is composed into a kind of real harmony, the instant he sets himself to work! Doubt, Desire, Sorrow, Remorse, Indignation, Despair itself, all these like helldogs lie beleaguering the soul of the poor dayworker, as of every man: but he bends himself with free valour against his task, and all these are stilled, all these shrink murmuring far off into their caves. The man is now a man. The blessed glow of Labour in him, is it not as purifying fire, wherein all poison is burnt up, and of sour smoke itself there is made bright blessed flame!

Destiny, on the whole, has no other way of cultivating us. A formless Chaos, once set it *revolving*, grows round and ever rounder; ranges itself, by mere force of gravity, into strata, spherical courses; is no longer a Chaos, but a round compacted World. What would become of the Earth, did she cease to revolve? In the poor old Earth, so long as she revolves, all inequalities, irregularities disperse themselves; all irregularities are incessantly becoming regular. Hast thou looked on the Potter's wheel,—one of the venerablest objects; old as the Prophet Ezekiel and far older? Rude lumps of clay, how they spin themselves up, by mere quick whirling, into beautiful circular dishes. And fancy the most assiduous Potter, but without his wheel; reduced to make dishes, or rather amorphous botches, by mere kneading and baking! Even such a Potter were Destiny, with a human soul that would rest and lie at ease, that would not work and spin! Of an idle unrevolving man the kindest Destiny, like the most assiduous Potter without wheel, can bake and knead nothing other than a botch; let her spend on him what expensive colouring, what gilding and enamelling she will, he is but a botch. Not a dish; no, a bulging, kneaded, crooked, shambling, squint-cornered, amorphous botch,—a mere enamelled vessel of dishonour! Let the idle think of this.

Blessed is he who has found his work; let him ask no other blessedness. He has a work, a life-purpose; he has found it, and will follow it! How, as a free-flowing channel, dug and torn by noble force through the sour mud-swamp of one's existence, like an ever-deepening river there, it runs and flows;—draining off the sour festering water, gradually from the root of the remotest grass-blade; making, instead of pestilential swamp, a green fruitful meadow with its clear-flowing stream. How blessed for the meadow itself, let the stream and *its* value be great or small! Labour is Life: from the inmost heart of the Worker rises his god-given Force, the sacred celestial Life-essence breathed into him by Almighty God; from his inmost heart awakens him to all nobleness,— to all knowledge, 'self-knowledge' and much else, so soon as Work fitly begins. Knowledge? The knowledge that will hold good in working, cleave thou to that; for Nature herself accredits that, says Yea to that. Properly thou hast no other knowledge but what thou hast got by working: the rest is yet all a hypothesis of knowledge; a thing to be argued of in schools, a thing floating in the clouds, in endless logic-vortices, till we try it and fix it. 'Doubt, of whatever kind, can be ended by Action alone.'

And again, hast thou valued Patience, Courage, Perseverance, Openness to light; readiness to own thyself mistaken, to do better next time? All these, all virtues, in wrestling with the dim brute Powers of Fact, in ordering of thy fellows in such wrestle, there and elsewhere not at all, thou wilt continually learn. Set down a brave Sir Christopher in the middle of black ruined Stone-heaps, of foolish unarchitectural Bishops, redtape Officials, idle Nell-Gwyn Defenders of the Faith; and see whether he will ever raise a Paul's Cathedral out of all that, yea or no! Rough, rude, contradictory are all things and persons, from the mutinous masons and Irish hodmen, up to the idle Nell-Gwynn Defenders, to blustering redtape Officials, foolish unarchitectural Bishops. All

242

these things and persons are there not for Christopher's sake and his Cathedral's; they are there for their own sake mainly! Christopher will have to conquer and constrain all these,—if he be able. All these are against him. Equitable Nature herself, who carries her mathematics and architectonics not on the face of her, but deep in the hidden heart of her,—Nature herself is but partially for him; will be wholly against him, if he constrain her not! His very money, where is it to come from? The pious munificence of England lies far-scattered, distant, unable to speak, and say, 'I am here';—must be spoken to before it can speak. Pious munificence, and all help, is so silent, invisible like the gods; impediment, contradictions manifold are so loud and near! O brave Sir Christopher, trust thou in those, notwithstanding, and front all these; understand all these; by valiant patience, noble effort, insight, by man's-strength, vanquish and compel all these,—and, on the whole, strike down victoriously the last topstone of that Paul's Edifice; thy monument for certain centuries, the stamp 'Great Man' impressed very legibly on Portland stone there!—

Yes, all manner of help, and pious response from Men or Nature, is always what we call silent; cannot speak or come to light, till it be seen, till it be spoken to. Every noble work is at first 'impossible'. In very truth, for every noble work the possibilities will lie diffused through Immensity; inarticulate, undiscoverable except to faith. Like Gideon thou shalt spread out thy fleece at the door of thy tent; see whether under the wide arch of Heaven there be any bounteous moisture, or none. Thy heart and life-purpose shall be as a miraculous Gideon's fleece, spread out in silent appeal to Heaven; and from the kind Immensities, what from the poor unkind Localities and town and country Parishes there never could, blessed dew-moisture to suffice thee shall have fallen!

Work is of a religious nature:—work is of a *brave* nature; which it is the aim of all religion to be. All work of man is as the swimmer's: a waste ocean threatens to devour him; if he front it not bravely, it will keep its word. By incessant wise defiance of it, lusty rebuke and buffet of it, behold how it loyally supports him, bears him as its conqueror long. 'It is so', says Goethe, 'with all things that man undertakes in this world.'

Brave Sea-captain, Norse Sea-king,—Columbus, my hero, royallest Sea-king of all! it is no friendly environment this of thine, in the waste deep waters; around thee mutinous discouraged souls, behind thee disgrace and ruin, before thee the unpenetrated veil of Night. Brother, these wild water-mountains, bounding from their deep bases (ten miles deep, I am told), are not entirely there on thy behalf! Meseems *they* have other work than floating thee forward:—and the huge Winds, that sweep from Ursa Major to the Tropics and Equators, dancing their giant-waltz through the kingdoms of Chaos and Immensity, they care little about filling rightly or filling wrongly the small shoulder-of-mutton sails in this cockle-skiff of thine! Thou art not among articulate-speaking friends, my brother; thou art among immeasurable dumb monsters, tumbling, howling wide as the world here. Secret, far off, invisible to all hearts but thine, there lies a help in them: see how thou wilt get at that. Patiently thou wilt wait till the mad South-wester spend itself, saving thyself by dexterous science of defence, the while: valiantly, with swift decision, wilt thou strike in, when the favouring East, the Possible, springs up. Mutiny of men thou wilt sternly repress; weakness, despondency, thou wilt cheerily encourage: thou wilt swallow down complaint, unreason, weariness, weakness of others and thyself;—how much wilt thou swallow down! There shall be a depth of Silence in thee, deeper than this Sea, which is but ten miles deep: a Silence unsoundable; known to God only. Thou shalt be a Great Man. Yes, my World-Soldier, thou of the World Marine-service,—thou wilt have to be *greater* than this tumultuous unmeasured World here round thee is: thou, in thy strong soul, as with wrestler's arms, shalt embrace it, harness it down; and make it bear thee on,—to new Americas, or whither God wills!

# FRIEDRICH ENGELS                                    XVII.2
## "Not Work, but tedium"

from *The Condition of the Working Class in England*, 1844–5

. . . The supervision of machinery, the joining of broken threads, is no activity which claims the operative's thinking powers, yet it is of a sort which prevents him from occupying his mind with other things. We have seen . . . that this work affords the muscles no opportunity for physical activity. Thus it is, properly speaking, not work, but tedium, the most deadening, wearing process conceivable. The operative is condemned to let his physical and mental powers decay in this utter monotony, it is his mission to be bored every day and all day long from his eighth year. Moreover, he must not take a moment's rest; the engine moves unceasingly; the wheels, the straps, the spindles hum and rattle in his ears without a pause, and if he tried to snatch one instant, there is the overlooker at his back with the book of fines. This condemnation to be buried alive in the mill, to give constant attention to the tireless machine is felt as the keenest torture by the operatives, and its action upon mind and body is in the long run stunting in the highest degree. There is no better means of inducing stupefaction than a period of factory-work, and if the operatives have, nevertheless, not only rescued their intelligence, but cultivated and sharpened it more than other working-men, they have found this possible only in rebellion against their fate and against the bourgeoisie, the sole subject on which under all circumstances they can think and feel while at work. Or, if this indignation against the bourgeoisie does not become the supreme passion of the working-man, the inevitable consequence is drunkenness and all that is generally called demoralization. The physical enervation and the sickness, universal in consequence of the factory system, were enough to induce Commissioner Hawkins to attribute this demoralization thereto as inevitable; how much more when mental lassitude is added to them, and when the influences already mentioned which tempt every working-man to demoralization, make themselves felt here too! There is no cause for surprise, therefore, that in the manufacturing towns especially, drunkenness and sexual excesses have reached the pitch which I have already described.

# KARL MARX                                                XVII.3

## "Alienated Labour"

from *Economic-Philosophical Manuscripts*, written 1844

Political economy begins with the fact of private property; it does not explain it. It conceives the *material* process of private property, as this occurs in reality, in general and abstract formulas which then serve it as laws. It does not *comprehend* these laws; that is, it does not show how they arise out of the nature of private property. Political economy provides no explanation of the basis for the distinction of labour from capital, of capital from land. When, for example, the relation of wages to profits is defined, this is explained in terms of the interests of capitalists; in other words, what should be explained is assumed. Similarly, competition is referred to at every point and is explained in terms of external conditions. Political economy tells us nothing about the extent to which these external and apparently accidental conditions are simply the expression of a necessary development. We have seen how exchange itself seems an accidental fact. The only motive forces which political economy recognizes are *avarice* and the *war between the avaricious, competition*. . . .

. . . We have now to grasp the real connexion between this whole system of alienation—private property, acquisitiveness, the separation of labour, capital and land, exchange and competition, value and the devaluation of man, monopoly and competition—and the system of *money*.

Let us not begin our explanation, as does the economist, from a legendary primordial condition. Such a primordial condition does not explain anything; it merely removes the question into a grey and nebulous distance. It asserts as a fact or event what it should deduce, namely, the necessary relation between two things; for example, between the division of labour and exchange. In the same way theology explains the origin of evil by the fall of man; that is, it asserts as a historical fact what it should explain.

We shall begin from a *contemporary* economic fact. The worker becomes poorer the more wealth he produces and the more his production increases in power and extent. The worker becomes an ever cheaper commodity the more goods he creates. The *devaluation* of the human world increases in direct relation to the *increase in value* of the world of things. Labour does not only create goods; it also produces itself and the worker as a *commodity*, and indeed in the same proportion as it produces goods.

This fact simply implies that the object produced by labour, its product, now stands opposed to it as an *alien being*, as a *power independent* of the producer. The product of labour is labour which has been embodied in an object and turned into a physical thing; this product is an *objectification* of labour. The performance of work is at the same time its objectification. The performance of work appears in the sphere of political economy as a *vitiation* of the worker, objectification as a *loss* and as *servitude to the object*, and appropriation as *alienation*.

So much does the performance of work appear as vitiation that the worker is vitiated to the point of starvation. So much does objectification appear as loss of the object that the worker is deprived of the most essential things not only of life but also of work. Labour itself becomes an object which he can acquire only by the greatest effort and with unpredictable interruptions. So much does the appropriation of the object appear as alienation that the more objects the worker produces the fewer he can possess and the more he falls under the domination of his product, of capital.

All these consequences follow from the fact that the worker is related to the *product of his labour* as to an *alien* object. For it is clear on this presupposition that the more the worker expends himself in work the more powerful becomes the world of objects which he creates in face of himself, the poorer he becomes in his inner life, and the less he belongs to himself. . . .

(The alienation of the worker in his object is expressed as follows in the laws of political economy: the more the worker produces the less he has to consume; the more value he creates the more worthless he becomes; the more refined his product the more crude and misshapen the worker; the more civilized the product the more barbarous the worker; the more powerful the work the more feeble the worker; the more the work manifests intelligence the more the worker declines in intelligence and becomes a slave of nature.)

*Political economy conceals the alienation in the nature of labour in so far as it does not examine the direct relationship between the worker (work) and production.* Labour certainly produces marvels for the rich but it produces privation for the worker. It produces palaces, but hovels for the worker. It produces beauty, but deformity for the worker. It replaces labour by machinery, but it casts some of the workers back into a barbarous kind of work and turns the others into machines. It produces intelligence, but also stupidity and cretinism for the workers. . . .

So far we have considered the alienation of the worker only from one aspect; namely, *his relationship to the products of his labour.* However, alienation appears not merely in the result but also in the *process of production*, within *productive activity* itself. . . .

What constitutes the alienation of labour? First, that the work is *external* to the worker, that it is not part of his nature; and that, consequently, he does not fulfil himself in his work but denies himself, has a feeling of misery rather than well-being, does not develop freely his mental and physical energies but is physically exhausted and mentally debased. The worker, therefore, feels himself at home only during his leisure time, whereas at work he feels homeless. His work is not voluntary but imposed, *forced labour.* It is not the satisfaction of a need, but only a *means* for satisfying other needs. Its alien character is clearly shown by the fact that as soon as there is no physical or other compulsion it is avoided like the plague. External labour, labour in which man alienates himself, is a labour of self-sacrifice, or mortification. Finally, the external character of work for the worker is shown by the fact that it is not his own work but work for someone else, that in work he does not belong to himself but to another person.

Just as in religion the spontaneous activity of human fantasy, of the human brain and heart, reacts independently as an alien activity of gods or devils upon the individual, so the activity of the worker is not his own spontaneous activity. It is another's activity and a loss of his own spontaneity.

We arrive at the result that man (the worker) feels himself to be freely active only in his animal functions—eating, drinking and procreating, or at most also in his dwelling and in personal adornment—while in his human functions he is reduced to an animal. The animal becomes human and the human becomes animal.

Eating, drinking and procreating are of course also genuine human functions. But abstractly considered, apart from the environment of human activities, and turned into final and sole ends, they are animal functions. . . .

247

We have now to infer a third characteristic of *alienated labour* from the two we have considered.

Man is a species-being not only in the sense that he makes the community (his own as well as those of other things) his object both practically and theoretically, but also (and this is simply another expression for the same thing) in the sense that he treats himself as the present, living species, as a *universal* and consequently free being. . . .

Since alienated labour: (1) alienates nature from man; and (2) alienates man from himself, from his own active function, his life activity; so it alienates him from the species. It makes *species-life* into a means of individual life. In the first place it alienates species-life and individual life, and secondly, it turns the latter, as an abstraction, into the purpose of the former, also in its abstract and alienated form.

For labour, *life activity, productive life*, now appear to man only as *means* for the satisfaction of a need, the need to maintain his physical existence. Productive life is, however, species-life. It is life creating life. In the type of life activity resides the whole character of a species, its species-character; and free, conscious activity is the species-character of human beings. Life itself appears only as a *means of life*.

The animal is one with its life activity. It does not distinguish the activity from itself. It is *its activity*. But man makes his life activity itself an object of his will and consciousness. He has a conscious life activity. It is not a determination with which he is completely identified. Conscious life activity distinguishes man from the life activity of animals. . . . Of course, animals also produce. They construct nests, dwellings, as in the case of bees, beavers, ants, etc. But they only produce what is strictly necessary for themselves or their young. They produce only in a single direction, while man produces universally. They produce only under the compulsion of direct physical needs, while man produces when he is free from physical need and only truly produces in freedom from such need. Animals produce only themselves, while man reproduces the whole of nature. The products of animal production belong directly to their physical bodies, while man is free in face of his product. Animals construct only in accordance with the standards and needs of the species to which they belong, while man knows how to produce in accordance with the standards of every species and knows how to apply the appropriate standard to the object. Thus man constructs also in accordance with the laws of beauty.

It is just in his work upon the objective world that man really proves himself as a *species-being*. This production is his active species-life. By means of it nature appears as *his* work and his reality. . . .

Just as alienated labour transforms free and self-directed activity into a means, so it transforms the species-life of man into a means of physical existence.

248

Consciousness, which man has from his species, is transformed through alienation so that species-life becomes only a means for him. (3) Thus alienated labour turns the *species-life of man*, and also nature as his mental species-property, into an *alien* being and into a *means* for his *individual existence*. It alienates from man his own body, external nature, his mental life and his human life. (4) A direct consequence of the alienation of man from the product of his labour, from his life activity and from his species-life, is that *man is alienated* from other *men*. When man confronts himself he also confronts *other* men. What is true of man's relationship to his work, to the product of his work and to himself, is also true of his relationship to other men, to their labour and to the objects of their labour. . . .

Let us now examine further how this concept of alienated labour must express and reveal itself in reality. If the product of labour is alien to me and confronts me as an alien power, to whom does it belong? If my own activity does not belong to me but is an alien, forced activity, to whom does it belong? To a being *other* than myself. And who is this being? The *gods*? It is apparent in the earliest stages of advanced production, e.g., temple building, etc. in Egypt, India, Mexico, and in the service rendered to gods, that the product belonged to the gods. But the gods alone were never the lords of labour. And no more was *nature*. What a contradiction it would be if the more man subjugates nature by his labour, and the more the marvels of the gods are rendered superfluous by the marvels of industry, the more he should abstain from his joy in producing and his enjoyment of the product for love of these powers.

The *alien* being to whom labour and the product of labour belong, to whose service labour is devoted, and to whose enjoyment the product of labour goes, can only be *man* himself. If the product of labour does not belong to the worker, but confronts him as an alien power, this can only be because it belongs to *a man other than the worker*. If his activity is a torment to him it must be a source of *enjoyment* and pleasure to another. Not the gods, nor nature, but only man himself can be this alien power over men. . . .

Thus, through alienated labour the worker creates the relation of another man, who does not work and is outside the work process, to this labour. The relation of the worker to work also produces the relation of the capitalist (or whatever one likes to call the lord of labour) to work. *Private property* is, therefore, the product, the necessary result, of *alienated labour*, of the external relation of the worker to nature and to himself.

*Private property* is thus derived from the analysis of the concept of *alienated labour*; that is, alienated man, alienated labour, alienated life, and estranged man.

We have, of course, derived the concept of *alienated labour* (*alienated life*) from political economy, from an analysis of the *movement of private property*. But the analysis of this concept shows that although private property appears to be the basis and cause of alienated labour, it is rather a consequence of the latter, just as the gods are *fundamentally* not the cause but the product of confusions of human reason. At a later stage, however, there is a reciprocal influence.

Only in the final stage of the development of private property is its secret revealed, namely, that it is on one hand the *product* of alienated labour, and on the other hand the *means* by which labour is alienated, *the realization of this alienation*.

## KARL MARX                                            XVII.4

Adam Smith's view of work, and 'true' work

from *Outline of the Critique of Political Economy*
(*Grundrisse*), written 1857–9

A. Smith's view, [is] that *labour never changes its value*, in the sense that a *definite amount of labour* is always a definite *amount of labour for the worker*, i.e., with A. Smith, a sacrifice of the *same quantitative magnitude*. Whether I obtain much or little for an hour of work—which depends on its productivity and other circumstances—I have *worked* one hour. What I have had to pay for the result of my work, my wages, is always the same *hour of work*, let the result vary as it may. 'Equal quantities of labour must at all times and in all places have the same value for the worker. In his normal state of health, strength and activity, and with the common degree of skill and facility which he may possess, he must always give up the *identical portion of his tranquillity, his freedom*, and his *happiness*. Whatever may be the quantity or composition of the commodities he obtains in reward of his work, the *price he pays* is always the same. Of course, this price may buy sometimes a lesser, sometimes a greater quantity of these commodities, but only because their value changes, not the value of the labour which buys them. Labour alone, therefore, never changes its own value. It is therefore the *real price* of commodities, money is only their nominal value.'. . . In the sweat of thy brow shalt thou labour! was Jehovah's curse on Adam. And this is labour for Smith, a curse. 'Tranquillity' appears as the adequate state, as identical with 'freedom' and 'happiness'. It seems quite far from Smith's mind that the individual, 'in his normal state of health, strength, activity, skill, facility', also needs a normal portion of work, and of the suspension of tranquillity. Certainly, labour obtains its measure from the outside, through the aim to be attained and the obstacles to be overcome in attaining it. But Smith has no inkling whatever that this overcoming of obstacles is in itself a liberating activity—and that, further, the external aims become stripped of the semblance of merely external natural urgencies, and become posited as aims which the individual himself posits—hence as self-realization, objectification of the subject, hence real freedom, whose action is, precisely, labour. He is right, of course, that, in its historical forms as slave-labour, serf-labour, and wage-labour, labour always appears as repulsive, always as *external forced labour*; and not-labour, by contrast, as 'freedom, and happiness'. This holds doubly: for this contradictory labour; and, relatedly, for labour which has not yet created the subjective and objective conditions for itself (or also, in contrast to the pastoral etc. state, which it has lost), in which labour becomes attractive work, the individual's self-realization, which in no way means that it becomes mere fun, mere amusement, as Fourier, with *grisette*-like naïveté, conceives it. Really free working, e.g. composing, is at the same time precisely the most damned seriousness, the most intense exertion. The work of material production can achieve this character only (1) when its social character is posited, (2) when it is of a scientific and at the same time general character, not merely human exertion as a specifically harnessed natural force, but exertion as subject, which appears in the production process not in a merely natural, spontaneous form, but as an activity regulating all the forces of nature. A. Smith, by the way, has only the slaves of capital in mind. For example, even the semi-artistic worker of the Middle Ages does not fit into his definition. *But* what *we* want *here initially* is not to go into his view on labour, his philosophical view, but into the economic moment. Labour regarded merely as a *sacrifice*, and hence value-positing, as a *price* paid for things and hence giving them price depending on whether they cost more or less labour, is a purely *negative* characterization. . . . Only because products ARE labour can they be measured by the measure of labour, by labour time, the amount of labour consumed in them. The negation of tranquillity, as mere negation, ascetic sacrifice, creates nothing. *Someone may castigate and flagellate himself all day long like the monks etc., and this quantity of sacrifice he contributes will remain totally worthless.* The *natural price* of things is not the sacrifice made for them. This recalls, rather, the pre-industrial view which wants to achieve wealth by sacrificing to the gods. There has to be something besides sacrifice. The sacrifice of tranquillity can also be called the sacrifice of laziness, unfreedom, unhappiness, i.e. negation of a negative state. A. Smith considers labour psychologically, as to the fun or displeasure it holds for the individual. But it is something else, too, in addition to this *emotional* relation with his activity—firstly, for others, since A's mere sacrifice would be of no use for B; secondly, a

251

definite relation by his own self to the thing he works on, and to his own working capabilities. It is a *positive, creative activity*.

## JOHN STUART MILL XVII.5
'Of the Stationary State'

from *The Principles of Political Economy*, 1848

There is room in the world, no doubt, and even in old countries, for a great increase of population, supposing the arts of life to go on improving, and capital to increase. But even if innocuous, I confess to see very little reason for desiring it. The density of population necessary to enable mankind to obtain, in the greatest degree, all the advantages both of co-operation and of social intercourse, has, in all the most populous countries, been attained. A population may be too crowded, though all be amply supplied with food and raiment. It is not good for man to be kept perforce at all times in the presence of his species. A world from which solitude is extirpated, is a very poor ideal. Solitude, in the sense of being often alone, is essential to any depth of meditation or of character; and solitude in the presence of natural beauty and grandeur, is the cradle of thoughts and aspirations which are not only good for the individual, but which society could ill do without. Nor is there much satisfaction in contemplating the world with nothing left to the spontaneous activity of nature; with every rood of land brought into cultivation, which is capable of growing food for human beings; every flowery waste or natural pasture ploughed up, all quadrupeds or birds which are not domesticated for man's use exterminated as his rivals for food, every hedgerow or superfluous tree rooted out, and scarcely a place left where a wild shrub or flower could grow without being eradicated as a weed in the name of improved agriculture. If the earth must lose that great portion of its pleasantness which it owes to things that the unlimited increase of wealth and population would extirpate from it, for the mere purpose of enabling it to support a larger, but not a better or a happier population, I sincerely hope, for the sake of posterity, that they will be content to be stationary, long before necessity compels them to it.

It is scarcely necessary to remark that a stationary condition of capital and population implies no stationary state of human improvement. There would be as much scope as ever for all kinds of mental culture, and moral and social progress; as much room for improving the Art of Living, and much more likelihood of its being improved, when minds ceased to be engrossed by the art of getting on. Even the industrial arts might be as earnestly and as successfully cultivated, with this sole

252

difference, that instead of serving no purpose but the increase of wealth, industrial improvements would produce their legitimate effect, that of abridging labour. Hitherto it is questionable if all the mechanical inventions yet made have lightened the day's toil of any human being. They have enabled a greater population to live the same life of drudgery and imprisonment, and an increased number of manufacturers and others to make fortunes. They have increased the comforts of the middle classes. But they have not yet begun to effect those great changes in human destiny, which it is in their nature and in their futurity to accomplish. Only when, in addition to just institutions, the increase of mankind shall be under the deliberate guidance of judicious foresight, can the conquests made from the powers of nature by the intellect and energy of scientific discoverers, become the common property of the species, and the means of improving and elevating the universal lot.

# SAMUEL SMILES                                                    XVII.6
## "Self-Help"
from *Self-Help*, 1859

'Heaven helps those who help themselves' is a well-tried maxim, embodying in a small compass the results of vast human experience. The spirit of self-help is the root of all genuine growth in the individual; and, exhibited in the lives of many, it constitutes the true source of national vigour and strength. Help from without is often enfeebling in its effects, but help from within invariably invigorates. Whatever is done *for* men or classes, to a certain extent takes away the stimulus and necessity of doing for themselves; and where men are subjected to over-guidance and over-government, the inevitable tendency is to render them comparatively helpless.

Even the best institutions can give a man no active aid. Perhaps the utmost they can do is, to leave him *free* to develop himself and improve his individual condition. But in all times men have been prone to believe that their happiness and well-being were to be secured by means of institutions rather than by their own conduct. Hence the value of legislation as an agent in human advancement has always been greatly over-estimated. To constitute the millionth part of a Legislature, by voting for one or two men once in three or five years, however conscientiously this duty may be performed, can exercise but little active influence upon any man's life and character. Moreover, it is every day becoming more clearly understood, that the function of Government is negative and restrictive, rather than positive and active; being resolvable principally into protection—protection of life, liberty, and property.

Hence the chief 'reforms' of the last fifty years have consisted mainly in abolitions and disenactments. But there is no power of law that can make the idle man industrious, the thriftless provident, or the drunken sober; though every individual can be each and all of these if he will, by the exercise of his own free powers of action and self-denial. Indeed all experience serves to prove that the worth and strength of a State depend far less upon the form of its institutions than upon the character of its men. For the nation is only the aggregate of individual conditions, and civilization itself is but a question of personal improvement.

National progress is the sum of individual industry, energy, and uprightness, as national decay is of individual idleness, selfishness, and vice. What we are accustomed to decry as great social evils, will, for the most part, be found to be only the outgrowth of our own perverted life; and though we may endeavour to cut them down and extirpate them by means of Law, they will only spring up again with fresh luxuriance in some other form, unless the conditions of human life and character are radically improved. If this view be correct, then it follows that the highest patriotism and philanthropy consist, not so much in altering laws and modifying institutions, as in helping and stimulating men to elevate and improve themselves by their own free and independent action. . . .

There is no reason why the condition of the average workman in this country should not be a useful, honourable, respectable, and happy one. The whole body of the working classes might (with few exceptions) be as frugal, virtuous, well-informed, and well-conditioned as many individuals of the same class have already made themselves. What some men are, all without difficulty might be. Employ the same means, and the same results will follow. That there should be a class of men who live by their daily labour in every state is the ordinance of God, and doubtless is a wise and righteous one; but that this class should be otherwise than frugal, contented, intelligent, and happy, is not the design of Providence, but springs solely from the weakness, self-indulgence, and perverseness of man himself. The healthy spirit of self-help created amongst working people would more than any other measure serve to raise them as a class, and this, not by pulling down others, but by levelling them up to a higher and still advancing standard of religion, intelligence, and virtue.

# JOHN RUSKIN XVII.7
## 'The Nature of Gothic'
from *The Stones of Venice*, 1851–3

I shall endeavour therefore to give the reader in this chapter an idea, at once broad and definite, of the true nature of *Gothic* architecture, properly so called; not of that of Venice only, but of universal Gothic. . . . Its elements are certain mental tendencies of the builders, legibly expressed in it; as fancifulness, love of variety, love of richness, and such others. Its external forms are pointed arches, vaulted roofs, etc. . . .

I believe . . . that the characteristic or moral elements of Gothic are the following, placed in the order of their importance:

> 1. Savageness.  4. Grotesqueness.
> 2. Changefulness.  5. Rigidity.
> 3. Naturalism.  6. Redundance.

These characters are here expressed as belonging to the buildings; as belonging to the builder, they would be expressed thus:—1. Savageness or Rudeness. 2. Love of Change. 3. Love of Nature. 4. Disturbed Imagination. 5. Obstinacy. 6. Generosity. . . . The withdrawal of any one, or any two, will not at once destroy the Gothic character of a building, but the removal of a majority of them will. . . .

I am not sure when the word 'Gothic' was first generically applied to the architecture of the North; but I presume that, whatever the date of its original usage, it was intended to imply reproach, and express the barbaric character of the nations among whom that architecture arose. It never implied that they were literally of Gothic lineage, far less that their architecture had been originally invented by the Goths themselves; but it did imply that they and their buildings together exhibited a degree of sternness and rudeness, which, in contradistinction to the character of Southern and Eastern nations, appeared like a perpetual reflection of the contrast between the Goth and the Roman in their first encounter. And when that fallen Roman, in the utmost impotence of his luxury, and insolence of his guilt, became the model for the imitation of civilized Europe, at the close of the so-called Dark ages, the word Gothic became a term of unmitigated contempt, not unmixed with aversion. From that contempt, by the exertion of the antiquaries and architects of this century, Gothic architecture has been sufficiently vindicated; and perhaps some among us, in our admiration of the magnificent science of its structure, and sacredness of its expression, might desire that the term of ancient reproach should be withdrawn, and some other, of more apparent honourableness, adopted in its place. There is no chance, as there is no need, of such a substitution. As far as the epithet was used scornfully, it was used falsely; but there is no reproach in the word, rightly understood; on the contrary, there is a profound truth, which the instinct of mankind almost unconsciously recognizes. It is true, greatly and deeply true, that the architecture of the North is rude and wild; but it is not true, that, for this reason, we are to condemn it, or despise. Far otherwise: I believe it is in this very character that it deserves our profoundest reverence.

The charts of the world which have been drawn up by modern science have thrown into a narrow space the expression of a vast amount of knowledge, but I have never yet seen any one pictorial enough to enable the spectator to imagine the kind of contrast in physical character which exists between Northern and Southern countries. We know the differences in detail, but we have not that broad glance and grasp which would enable us to feel them in their fulness. We know that gentians grow on the Alps, and olives on the Apennines; but we do not enough conceive for ourselves that variegated mosaic of the world's surface which a bird sees in its migration, that difference between the district of the gentian and of the olive which the stork and the swallow see far off, as they lean upon the sirocco wind. Let us, for a moment, try to raise ourselves even above the level of their flight, and imagine the Mediterranean lying beneath us like an irregular lake, and all its ancient promontories sleeping in the sun: here and there an angry spot of thunder, a grey stain of storm, moving upon the burning field; and here and there a fixed wreath of white volcano smoke, surrounded by its circle of ashes; but for the most part a great peacefulness of light, Syria and Greece, Italy and Spain, laid like pieces of a golden pavement into the sea-blue, chased, as we stoop nearer to them, with bossy beaten work of mountain chains, and glowing softly with terraced gardens, and flowers heavy with frankincense, mixed among masses of laurel, and orange, and plumy palm, that abate with their grey-green shadows the burning of the marble rocks, and of the ledges of porphyry sloping under lucent sand. Then let us pass father towards the north, until we see the orient colours change gradually into a vast belt of rainy green, where the pastures of Switzerland, and poplar valleys of France, and dark forests of the Danube and Carpathians stretch from the mouths of the Loire to those of the Volga, seen through clefts in grey swirls of rain-cloud and flaky veils of the mist of the brooks, spreading low along the pasture lands: and then, farther north still, to see the earth heave into mighty masses of leaden rock and heathy moor, bordering with a broad waste of gloomy purple that belt of field and wood, and splintering into irregular and grisly islands amidst the northern seas, beaten by storm, and chilled by ice-drift, and tormented by furious pulses of contending tide, until the roots of the last forests fail from among the hill ravines, and the hunger of the north wind bites their peaks into barrenness; and, at last, the wall of ice, durable like iron, sets, deathlike, its white teeth against us out of the polar twilight. And, having once traversed in thought this gradation of the zoned iris of the earth in all its material vastness, let us go down nearer to it, and watch the parallel change in the belt of animal life; the multitudes of swift and brilliant creatures that glance in the air and sea, or tread the sands of the southern zone; striped zebras and spotted leopards, glistening serpents, and birds arrayed in purple and scarlet. Let us contrast their delicacy and brilliancy of colour, and swiftness of motion, with the frost-cramped strength, and shaggy covering, and dusky plumage of the northern tribes; contrast the Arabian horse with the Shetland, the tiger and leopard with the wolf and bear, the antelope with the elk, the bird of paradise with the osprey; and then, submissively acknowledging the great laws by which the earth and all that it bears are ruled throughout their being, let us not condemn, but rejoice in the expression by man of his own rest in the statutes of the lands that gave him birth. Let us watch him with reverence as he sets side by side the burning gems, and smooths with soft sculpture the jasper pillars, that are to reflect a ceaseless sunshine, and rise into a cloudless sky: but not with less reverence let us stand by him, when, with rough strength and hurried stroke, he smites an uncouth animation out of the rocks which he has torn from among the moss of the moorland, and heaves into the darkened air the pile of iron buttress and rugged wall, instinct with work of an imagination as wild and wayward as the northern sea; creatures of ungainly shape and rigid limb, but full of wolfish life; fierce as the wind that beat, and changeful as the clouds that shade them.

There is, I repeat, no degradation, no reproach in this, but all dignity and honourableness: and we should err grievously in refusing either to recognize as an essential character of the existing architecture of the North, or to admit as a desirable character in that which it yet may be, this wildness of thought, and roughness of work; this look of mountain brotherhood between the cathedral and the Alp; this magnificence of sturdy power, put forth only the more energetically because the fine finger-touch was chilled away by the frosty wind, and the eye dimmed by the moor-mist, or blinded by the hail; this out-speaking of the strong spirit of men who may not gather redundant fruitage from the earth, nor bask in dreamy benignity of sunshine, but must break the rock for bread, and cleave the forest for fire, and show, even in what they did for their delight, some of the hard habits of the arm and heart that grew on them as they swung the axe or pressed the plough.

If, however, the savageness of Gothic architecture, merely as an expression of its origin among Northern nations, may be considered, in some sort, a noble character, it possesses a higher nobility still, when

257

considered as an index, not of climate, but of religious principle. . . .

The Greek gave to the lower workman no subject which he could not perfectly execute. . . . The workman was . . . a slave.

But in the mediaeval, or especially Christian, system of ornament, this slavery is done away with altogether; Christianity having recognized, in small things as well as great, the individual value of every soul. But it not only recognizes its value; it confesses its imperfection, in only bestowing dignity upon the acknowledgment of unworthiness. . . . To every spirit which Christianity summons to her service, her exhortation is: Do what you can, and confess frankly what you are unable to do; neither let your effort be shortened for fear of failure, nor your confession silenced for fear of shame. And it is, perhaps, the principal admirableness of the Gothic schools of architecture, that they thus receive the results of the labour of inferior minds; and out of fragments full of imperfection, and betraying that imperfection in every touch, indulgently raise up a stately and unaccusable whole.

But the modern English mind has this much in common with that of the Greek, that it intensely desires, in all things, the utmost completion or perfection compatible with their nature. This is a noble character in the abstract, but becomes ignoble when it causes us to forget the relative dignities of that nature itself, and to prefer the perfectness of the lower nature to the imperfection of the higher. . . . While in all things that we see or do, we are to desire perfection, and strive for it, we are nevertheless not to set the meaner thing, in its narrow accomplishment, above the nobler thing, in its mighty progress; not to esteem smooth minuteness above shattered majesty; not to prefer mean victory to honourable defeat; not to lower the level of our aim, that we may the more surely enjoy the complacency of success. . . .

Observe, you are put to stern choice in this matter. You must either make a tool of the creature, or a man of him. You cannot make both. Men were not intended to work with the accuracy of tools, to be precise and perfect in all their actions. If you will have that precision out of them, and make their fingers measure degrees like cog-wheels, and their arms strike curves like compasses, you must unhumanize them. All the energy of their spirits must be given to make cogs and compasses of themselves. All their attention and strength must go to the accomplishment of the mean act. The eye of the soul must be bent upon the finger-point, and the soul's force must fill all the invisible nerves that guide it, ten hours a day, that it may not err from its steely precision, and so soul and sight be worn away, and the whole human being be lost at last—a heap of sawdust, so far as its intellectual work in this world is concerned: saved only by its Heart, which cannot go into the form of cogs and compasses, but expands, after the ten hours are over, into fireside humanity. On the other hand, if you will make a man of the working creature, you cannot make a tool. Let him but begin to imagine, to think, to try to do anything worth doing; and the engine-turned precision is lost at once. Out come all his roughness, all his dulness all his incapability; shame upon shame, failure upon failure, pause after pause: but out comes the whole majesty of him also; and we know the height of it only when we see the clouds settling upon him. And, whether the clouds be bright or dark, there will be transfiguration behind and within them.

And now, reader, look round this English room of yours, about which you have been proud so often, because the work of it was so good and strong, and the ornaments of it so finished. Examine again all those accurate mouldings, and perfect polishings, and unerring adjustments of the seasoned wood and tempered steel. Many a time you have exulted over them, and thought how great England was, because her slightest work was done so thoroughly. Alas! if read rightly, these perfectnesses are signs of a slavery in our England a thousand times more bitter and more degrading than that of the scourged African, or helot Greek. Men may be beaten, chained, tormented, yoked like cattle, slaughtered like summer flies, and yet remain in one sense, and the best sense, free. But to smother their souls with them, to blight and hew into rotting pollards the suckling branches of their human intelligence, to make the flesh and skin which, after the worm's work on it, is to see God, into leathern thongs to yoke machinery with,—this is to be slave-masters indeed; and there might be more freedom in England, though her feudal lords' lightest words were worth men's lives, and though the blood of the vexed husbandman dropped in the furrows of her fields, than there is while the animation of her multitudes is sent like fuel to feed the factory smoke, and the strength of them is given daily to be wasted into the fineness of a web, or racked into the exactness of a line.

And, on the other hand, go forth again to gaze upon the old cathedral front, where you have smiled so often at the fantastic ignorance of the old sculptors: examine once more those ugly goblins, and formless monsters, and stern statues, anatomiless and rigid; but do not mock at them, for they are signs of the life and liberty of every workman who struck the stone; a freedom of thought, and rank in scale of being, such as no laws, no charters, no charities can secure; but which it must be the first aim of all Europe at this day to regain for her children.

Let me not be thought to speak wildly or extravagantly. It is verily this degradation of the operative into a machine, which, more than any other evil of the times, is leading the mass of the nations everywhere into vain, incoherent, destructive struggling for a freedom of which they cannot explain the nature to themselves. Their universal outcry against wealth, and against nobility, is not forced from them either by the pressure of famine, or the sting of mortified pride. These do much, and have done much in all ages; but the foundations of society were never yet shaken as they are at this day. It is not that men are ill fed, but that they have no pleasure in the work by which they make their bread, and therefore look to wealth as the only means of pleasure. It is not that men are pained by the scorn of the upper classes, but they cannot endure their own; for they feel that the kind of labour to which they are condemned is verily a degrading one, and makes them less than men. Never had the upper classes so much sympathy with the lower, or charity for them, as they have at this day, and yet never were they so much hated by them: for, of old, the separation between the noble and the poor was merely a wall built by law; now it is a veritable difference in level of standing, a precipice between upper and lower grounds in the field of humanity. . . .

We have much studied and much perfected, of late, the great civilized invention of the division of labour; only we give it a false name. It is not, truly speaking, the labour that is divided; but the men:—Divided into mere segments of men—broken into small fragments and crumbs of life; so that all the little piece of intelligence that is left in a man is not enough to make a pin, or a nail, but exhausts itself in making the point of a pin or the head of a nail. Now it is a good and desirable thing, truly, to make many pins in a day; but if we could only see with what crystal sand their points were polished,—sand of human soul, much to be magnified before it can be discerned for what it is—we should think there might be some loss in it also. And the great cry that rises from all our manufacturing cities, louder than their furnace blast, is all in very deed for this,—that we manufacture everything there except men; we blanch cotton, and strengthen steel, and refine sugar, and shape pottery; but to brighten, to strengthen, to refine, or to form a single living spirit, never enters into our estimate of advantages. And all the evil to which that cry is urging our myriads can be met only in one way: not by teaching nor preaching, for to teach them is but to show them their misery, and to preach to them, if we do nothing more than preach, is to mock at it. It can be met only by a right understanding, on the part of all classes, of what kinds of labour are good for men, raising them, and making them happy; by a determined sacrifice of such convenience, or beauty, or cheapness as is to be got only by the degradation of the workman; and by equally determined demand for the products and results of healthy and ennobling labour.

And how, it will be asked, are these products to be recognized, and this demand to be regulated? Easily: by the observance of three broad and simple rules:

1. Never encourage the manufacture of any article not absolutely necessary, in the production of which *Invention* has no share.

2. Never demand an exact finish for its own sake, but only for some practical or noble end.

3. Never encourage imitation or copying of any kind, except for the sake of preserving records of great works. . . .

On a large scale, and in work determinable by line and rule, it is indeed both possible and necessary that the thoughts of one man should be carried out by the labour of others; in this sense I have already defined the best architecture to be the expression of the mind of manhood by the hands of childhood. But on a smaller scale, and in a design which cannot be mathematically defined, one man's thoughts can never be expressed by another: and the difference between the spirit of touch of the man who is inventing, and of the man who is obeying directions, is often all the difference between a great and a common work of art. How wide the separation is between original and second-hand execution, I shall endeavour to show elsewhere; it is not so much to our purpose here as to mark the other and more fatal error of despising manual labour when governed by intellect; for it is no less fatal an error to despise it when thus regulated by intellect, than to value it for its own sake. We are always in these days endeavouring to separate the two, we want one man to be always thinking, and another to be always working, and we call one a gentleman, and the other an operative; whereas the workman ought often to be thinking, and the thinker often to be working, and both should be gentlemen, in the best sense. As it is, we make both ungentle, the one envying, the other despising, his brother; and the mass of society is made up of morbid thinkers, and miserable workers. Now it is only by labour that thought can be made healthy, and only by thought that labour can be made happy, and the two cannot be separated with impunity. . . .

Accurately speaking, no good work whatever can be perfect, and *the demand for perfection is always a sign of a misunderstanding of the ends of art.*

This for two reasons, both based on everlasting laws. The first, that no great man ever stops working till he has reached his point of failure: that is to say, his mind is always far in advance of his powers of execution, and the latter will now and then give way in trying to follow it; besides that he will always give to the inferior portions of his work only such inferior attention as they require; and according to his greatness he becomes so accustomed to the feeling of dissatisfaction with the best he can do, that in moments of lassitude or anger with himself he will not care though the beholder be dissatisfied also. I believe there has only been one man who would not acknowledge this necessity, and strove always to reach perfection, Leonardo; the end of his vain effort being merely that he would take ten years to a picture and leave it unfinished. And therefore, if we are to have great men working at all, or less men doing their best, the work will be imperfect, however beautiful. Of human work none but what is bad can be perfect, in its own bad way.*

The second reason is, that imperfection is in some sort essential to all that we know of life. It is the sign of life in a mortal body, that is to say, of a state of progress and change. Nothing that lives is, or can be, rigidly perfect; part of it is decaying, part nascent. The foxglove blossom,—a third part bud, a third part past, a third part in full bloom,—is a type of the life of this world. And in all things that live there are certain irregularities and deficiencies which are not only signs of life, but sources of beauty. No human face is exactly the same in its lines on each side, no leaf perfect in its lobes, no branch in its symmetry. All admit irregularity as they imply change; and to banish imperfection is to destroy expression, to check exertion, to paralyze vitality. All things are literally better, lovelier, and more beloved for the imperfections which have been divinely appointed, that the law of human life may be Effort, and the law of human judgment, Mercy.

Accept this then for a universal law, that neither architecture nor any other noble work of man can be good unless it be imperfect; and let us be prepared for the otherwise strange fact, which we shall discern clearly as we approach the period of the Renaissance, that the first cause of the fall of the arts of Europe was a relentless requirement of perfection, incapable alike either of being silenced by veneration for greatness, or softened into forgiveness of simplicity.

Thus far then of the Rudeness or Savageness, which is the first mental element of Gothic architecture.


JOHN RUSKIN                                                    XVII.8

"There is no wealth but life"

from 'The Veins of Wealth', 1862

The answer which would be made by any ordinary political economist to (my) statements . . . is . . . as follows:—

'It is indeed true that certain advantages of a general nature may be obtained by the development of social affections. But political economists never professed, nor profess, to take advantages of a general nature into consideration. Our science is simply the science of getting rich. So far from being a fallacious or visionary one, it is found by experience to be practically effective. Persons who follow its precepts do

*The Elgin marbles are supposed by many persons to be 'perfect.' In the most important portions they indeed approach perfection, but only there. The draperies are unfinished, the hair and wool of the animals are unfinished, and the entire bas-reliefs of the frieze are roughly cut.

actually become rich, and persons who disobey them become poor. Every capitalist of Europe has acquired his fortune by following the known laws of our science, and increases his capital daily by an adherence to them. It is vain to bring forward tricks of logic, against the force of accomplished facts. Every man of business knows by experience how money is made, and how it is lost.'

Pardon me. Men of business do indeed know how they themselves made their money, or how, on occasion, they lost it. Playing a long-practised game, they are familiar with the chances of its cards, and can rightly explain their losses and gains. But they neither know who keeps the bank of the gambling-house, nor what other games may be played with the same cards, nor what other losses and gains, far away among the dark streets, are essentially, though invisibly, dependent on theirs in the lighted rooms. They have learned a few, and only a few, of the laws of mercantile economy; but not one of those of political economy.

Primarily, which is very notable and curious, I observe that men of business rarely know the meaning of the word 'rich.' At least if they know, they do not in their reasonings allow for the fact, that it is a relative word, implying its opposite 'poor' as positively as the word 'north' implies its opposite 'south.' Men nearly always speak and write as if riches were absolute, and it were possible, by following certain scientific precepts, for everybody to be rich. Whereas riches are a power like that of electricity, acting only through inequalities or negations of itself. The force of the guinea you have in your pocket depends wholly on the default of a guinea in your neighbour's pocket. If he did not want it, it would be of no use to you; the degree of power it possesses depends accurately upon the need or desire he has for it,—and the art of making yourself rich, in the ordinary mercantile economist's sense, is therefore equally and necessarily the art of keeping your neighbour poor.

I would not contend in this matter (and rarely in any matter), for the acceptance of terms. But I wish the reader clearly and deeply to understand the difference between the two economies, to which the terms 'Political' and 'Mercantile' might not unadvisably be attached.

Political economy (the economy of a State, or of citizens) consists simply in the production, preservation, and distribution, at fittest time and place, of useful or pleasurable things. The farmer who cuts his hay at the right time; the shipwright who drives his bolts well home in sound wood; the builder who lays good bricks in well-tempered mortar; the housewife who takes care of her furniture in the parlour, and guards against all waste in her kitchen; and the singer who rightly disciplines, and never overstrains her voice: are all political economists in the true and final sense; adding continually to the riches and well-being of the nation to which they belong.

But mercantile economy, the economy of 'merces' or of 'pay', signifies the accumulation, in the hands of individuals, of legal or moral claim upon, or power over, the labour of others; every such claim implying precisely as much poverty or debt on one side, as it implies riches or right on the other.

It does not, therefore, necessarily involve an addition to the actual property, or well-being, of the State in which it exists. But since this commercial wealth, or power over labour, is nearly always convertible at once into real property, while real property is not always convertible at once into power over labour, the idea of riches among active men in civilized nations, generally refers to commercial wealth; and in estimating their possessions, they rather calculate the value of their horses and fields by the number of guineas they could get for them, than the value of their guineas by the number of horses and fields they could buy with them.

There is, however, another reason for this habit of mind; namely, that an accumulation of real property is of little use to its owner, unless, together with it, he has commercial power over labour. Thus, suppose any person to be put in possession of a large estate of fruitful land, with rich beds of gold in its gravel, countless herds of cattle in its pastures; houses, and gardens, and storehouses full of useful stores; but suppose, after all, that he could get no servants? In order that he may be able to have servants, some one in his neighbourhood must be poor, and in want of his gold—or his corn. Assume that no one is in want of either, and that no servants are to be had. He must, therefore, bake his own bread, make his own clothes, plough his own ground, and shepherd his own flocks. His gold will be as useful to him as any other yellow pebbles on his estate. His stores must rot, for he cannot consume them. He can eat no more than another man could eat, and wear no more than another man could wear. He must lead a life of severe and common labour to procure even ordinary comforts; he will be ultimately unable to keep either houses in repair, or fields in cultivation; and forced to content himself with a poor man's portion of cottage and garden, in the midsts of a desert of waste land, trampled by wild cattle, and encumbered by ruins of palaces, which he will hardly mock at himself by calling 'his own.'

The most covetous of mankind would, with small exultation, I presume, accept riches of this kind on these terms. What is really desired, under the name of riches, is, essentially, power over men; in its simplest sense, the power of obtaining for our own advantage the labour of servant, tradesman, and artist; in wider sense, authority of directing large masses of the nation to various ends (good, trivial or hurtful, according to the mind of the rich person). . . . So that, as above stated, the art of becoming 'rich,' in the common sense, is not absolutely nor finally the art of accumulating much money for ourselves, but also of contriving that our neighbours shall have less. In accurate terms, it is 'the art of establishing the maximum inequality in our own favour.'. . . .

. . . Inequalities of wealth justly established, benefit the nation in the course of their establishment; and, nobly used, aid it yet more by their existence. . . . But . . . the circulation of wealth in a nation resembles that of the blood in the natural body. There is one quickness of the current which comes of cheerful emotion or wholesome exercise; and another which comes of shame or of fever. . . .

As diseased local determination of the blood involves depression of the general health of the system, all morbid local action of riches will be found to involve a weakening of the resources of the body politic.

The mode in which this is produced may be at once understood by examining one or two instances of the development of wealth in the simplest possible circumstances.

Suppose two sailors cast away on an uninhabited coast, and obliged to maintain themselves there by their own labour for a series of years.

If they both kept their health, and worked steadily, and in amity with each other, they might build themselves a convenient house, and in time come to possess a certain quantity of cultivated land, together with various stores laid up for future use. All these things would be real riches or property; and, supposing the men both to have worked equally hard, they would each have right to equal share or use of it. Their political economy would consist merely in careful preservation and just division of these possessions. Perhaps, however, after some time one or other might be dissatisfied with the results of their common farming; and they might in consequence agree to divide the land they had brought under the spade into equal shares, so that each might thenceforward work in his own field and live by it. Suppose that after this arrangement had been made, one of them were to fall ill, and be unable to work on his land at a critical time—say of sowing or harvest.

He would naturally ask the other to sow or reap for him.

Then his companion might say, with perfect justice, 'I will do this additional work for you; but if I do it, you must promise to do as much for me at another time. I will count how many hours I spend on your ground, and you shall give me a written promise to work for the same number of hours on mine, whenever I need your help, and you are able to give it.'

Suppose the disabled man's sickness to continue, and that under various circumstances, for several years, requiring the help of the other, he on each occasion gave a written pledge to work, as soon as he was able, at his companion's orders, for the same number of hours which the other had given up to him. What will the positions of the two men be when the invalid is able to resume work?

Considered as a 'Polis,' or state, they will be poorer than they would have been otherwise: poorer by the withdrawal of what the sick man's labour would have produced in the interval. His friend may perhaps have toiled with an energy quickened by the enlarged need, but in the end his own land and property must have suffered by the withdrawal of so much of his time and thought from them; and the united property of the two men will be certainly less than it would have been if both had remained in health and activity.

But the relations in which they stand to each other are also widely altered. The sick man has not only pledged his labour for some years, but will probably have exhausted his own share of the accumulated stores, and will be in consequence for some time dependent on the other for food, which he can only 'pay' or reward him for by yet more deeply pledging his own labour.

Supposing the written promises to be held entirely valid (among civilized nations their validity is secured by legal measures), the person who had hitherto worked for both might now, if he chose, rest altogether, and pass his time in idleness, not only forcing his companion to redeem all the engagements he had already entered into, but exacting from him pledges for further labour, to an arbitrary amount, for what food he had to advance to him.

There might not, from first to last, be the least illegality (in the ordinary sense of the word) in the arrangement; but if a stranger arrived on the coast at this advanced epoch of their political economy, he would find one man commercially Rich; the other commercially Poor. He would see, perhaps with no small surprise, one passing his days in idleness; the other labouring for both, and living sparely, in the hope of recovering his independence, at some distant period. . . .

Take another example, more consistent with the ordinary course of affairs of trade. Suppose that three men, instead of two, formed the little isolated republic, and found themselves obliged to separate in order to farm different pieces of land at some distance from each other along the coast; each estate furnishing a distinct kind of produce, and each more or less in need of the material raised on the other. Suppose that the third man, in order to save the time of all three, undertakes simply to superintend the transference of commodities from one farm to the other; on condition of receiving some sufficiently remunerative share of every parcel of goods conveyed, or of some other parcel received in exchange for it.

If this carrier or messenger always brings to each estate, from the other, what is chiefly wanted, at the right time, the operations of the two farmers will go on prosperously, and the largest possible result in produce, or wealth, will be attained by the little community. But suppose no intercourse between the landowners is possible, except through the travelling agent; and that, after a time, this agent, watching the course of each man's agriculture, keeps back the articles with which he has been entrusted until there comes a period of extreme necessity for them, on one side or other, and then exacts in exchange for them all that the distressed farmer can spare of other kinds of produce; it is easy to see that by ingeniously watching his opportunities, he might possess himself regularly of the greater part of the superfluous produce of the two estates, and at last, in some year of severest trial or scarcity, purchase both for himself, and maintain the former proprietors thenceforward as his labourers or servants.

This would be a case of commercial wealth acquired on the exactest principles of modern political economy. But more distinctly even than in the former instance, it is manifest in this that the wealth of the State, or of the three men considered as a society, is collectively less than it would have been had the merchant been content with juster profit. The operations of the two agriculturists have been cramped to the utmost; and the continual limitations of the supply of things they wanted at critical times, together with the failure of courage consequent on the prolongation of a struggle for mere existence, without any sense of permanent gain, must have seriously diminished the effective results of their labour; and the stores finally accumulated in the merchant's hands will not in anywise be of equivalent value to those which, had his dealings been honest, would have filled at once the granaries of the farmers and his own. . . .

The idea that directions can be given for the gaining of wealth, irrespectively of the consideration of its moral sources, or that any general and technical law of purchase and gain can be set down for national practice, is perhaps the most insolently futile of all that ever beguiled men through their vices. So far as I know, there is not in history record of anything so disgraceful to the human intellect as the modern idea that the commercial text, 'Buy in the cheapest market and sell in the dearest,' represents, or under any circumstances could represent, an available principle of national economy. Buy in the cheapest market?—yes; but what made your market cheap? Charcoal may be cheap among your roof timbers after a fire, and bricks may be cheap in your streets after an earthquake; but fire and earthquake may not therefore be national benefits. Sell in the dearest?—yes, truly; but what made your market dear? You sold your bread well to-day; was it to a dying man who gave his last coin for it, and will never need bread more, or to a rich man who to-morrow will buy your farm over your head; or to a soldier on his way to pillage the bank in which you have put your fortune?

None of these things you can know. One thing only you can know, namely, whether this dealing of yours is a just and faithful one, which is all you need concern yourself about respecting it; sure thus to have done your own part in bringing about ultimately in the world a state of things which will not issue in pillage or in death. And thus every question concerning these things merges itself ultimately in the great question of justice. . . .

It has been shown that the chief value and virtue of money consists in its having power over human beings. . . . But power over human beings is attainable by other means than by money. . . . The money power is always imperfect and doubtful; there are many things which cannot be reached with it, others which cannot be retained by it. Many joys may be given to men which cannot be bought for gold, and many fidelities found in them which cannot be rewarded with it. . . .

This invisible gold, also, does not necessarily diminish in spending. Political economists will do well some day to take heed of it, though they cannot take measure.

But farther. Since the essence of wealth consists in its authority over men, if the apparent or nominal wealth fail in this power, it fails in essence; in fact, ceases to be wealth at all. It does not appear lately in England, that our authority over men is absolute. The servants show some disposition to rush riotously upstairs, under an impression that their wages are not regularly paid. We should augur ill of any gentleman's property to whom this happened every other day in his drawing-room.

So also, the power of our wealth seems limited as respects the comfort of the servants, no less than their quietude. The persons in the kitchen appear to be ill-dressed, squalid, half-starved. One cannot help imagining that the riches of the establishment must be of a very theoretical and documentary character.

Finally. Since the essence of wealth consists in power over men, will it not follow that the nobler and the more in number the persons are over whom it has power, the greater the wealth? Perhaps it may even appear after some consideration, that the persons themselves *are* the wealth—that these pieces of gold with which we are in the habit of guiding them, are, in fact, nothing more than a kind of Byzantine harness or trappings, very glittering and beautiful in barbaric sight, wherewith we bridle the creatures; but that if these same living creatures could be guided without the fretting and jingling of the Byzants in their mouths and ears, they might themselves be more valuable than their bridles. In fact, it may be discovered that the true veins of wealth are purple—and not in Rock, but in Flesh—perhaps even that the final outcome and consummation of all wealth is in the producing as many as possible full-breathed, bright-eyed, and happy-hearted human creatures. . . .

# XVIII Ideas of Reform and Revolution

ADAM SMITH

## The man of "humanity and benevolence" and the man of "system"

from *The Theory of Moral Sentiments*, 1759

The man whose public spirit is promoted altogether by humanity and benevolence, will respect the established powers and privileges even of individuals, and still more those of the great orders and societies into which the state is divided. Though he should consider some of them as in some measure abusive, he will content himself with moderating, what he often cannot annihilate without great violence. When he cannot conquer the rooted prejudices of the people by reason and persuasion, he will not attempt to subdue them by force, but will religiously observe what by Cicero is justly called the divine maxim of Plato, never to use violence to his country, no more than to his parents. He will accommodate, as well as he can, his public arrangements to the confirmed habits and prejudices of the people, and will remedy, as well as he can, the inconveniencies which may flow from the want of those regulations which the people are averse to submit to. When he cannot establish the right, he will not disdain to ameliorate the wrong; but, like Solon, when he cannot establish the best system of laws, he will endeavour to establish the best that the people can bear.

The man of system, on the contrary, is apt to be very wise in his own conceit, and is often so enamoured with the supposed beauty of his own ideal plan of government, that he cannot suffer the smallest deviation from any part of it. He goes on to establish it completely and in all its parts, without any regard either to the great interests or to the strong prejudices which may oppose it: he seems to imagine that he can arrange the different members of a great society with as much ease as the hand arranges the different pieces upon a chess-board; he does not consider that the pieces upon the chess-board have no other principle of motion besides that which the hand impresses upon them; but that, in the great chess-board of human society, every single piece has a principle of motion of its own, altogether different from that which the legislature might choose to impress upon it. If those two principles coincide and act in the same direction, the game of human society will go on easily and harmoniously, and is very likely to be happy and successful. If they are opposite or different, the game will go on miserably, and the society must be at all times in the highest degree of disorder.

Some general, and even systematical, idea of the perfection of policy and law, may no doubt be necessary for directing the views of the statesman. But to insist upon establishing, and upon establishing all at once, and in spite of all opposition, every thing which that idea may seem to require, must often be the highest degree of arrogance. It is to erect his own judgment into the supreme standard of right and wrong. It is to fancy himself the only wise and worthy man in the commonwealth, and that his fellow-citizens should accommodate themselves to him, and not he to them.

# KARL MARX and FRIEDRICH ENGELS          XVIII.2
## Communism

from *Manifesto of the Communist Party*, 1847

A spectre is haunting Europe—the spectre of communism. All the powers of old Europe have entered into a holy alliance to exorcise this spectre: Pope and Tsar, Metternich and Guizot, French Radicals and German police-spies.

Where is the party in opposition that has not been decried as communistic by its opponents in power? Where is the opposition that has not hurled back the branding reproach of communism, against the more advanced opposition parties, as well as against its reactionary adversaries?

Two things result from this fact:

I. Communism is already acknowledged by all European powers to be itself a power.

II. It is high time that Communists should openly, in the face of the whole world, publish their views, their aims, their tendencies, and meet this nursery tale of the spectre of communism with a manifesto of the party itself.

To this end, Communists of various nationalities have assembled in London and sketched the following manifesto, to be published in the English, French, German, Italian, Flemish and Danish languages.

BOURGEOIS AND PROLETARIANS

The history of all hitherto existing society is the history of class struggles. . . .

Our epoch, the epoch of the bourgeoisie, possesses, however, this distinctive feature: It has simplified the class antagonisms. Society as a whole is more and more splitting up into two great hostile camps, into two great classes directly facing each other—bourgeoisie and proletariat

From the serfs of the Middle Ages sprang the chartered burghers of the earliest towns. From these burgesses the first elements of the bourgeoisie were developed.

The discovery of America, the rounding of the Cape, opened up fresh ground for the rising bourgeoisie. The East-Indian and Chinese markets, the colonization of America, trade with the colonies, the increase in the means of exchange and in commodities generally, gave to commerce, to navigation, to industry, an impulse never before known, and thereby, to the revolutionary element in the tottering feudal society, a rapid development. . . .

The bourgeoisie, historically, has played a most revolutionary part.

The bourgeoisie, wherever it has got the upper hand, has put an end to all feudal, patriarchal, idyllic relations. It has pitilessly torn asunder the motley feudal ties that bound man to his 'natural superiors', and has left no other nexus between man and man than naked self-interest, than callous 'cash payment'. It has drowned the most heavenly ecstasies of religious fervour, of chivalrous enthusiasm, of philistine sentimentalism, in the icy water of egotistical calculation. It has resolved personal worth into exchange value, and in place of the numberless indefeasible chartered freedoms, has set up that single, unconscionable freedom—Free Trade. In one word, for exploitation, veiled by religious and political illusions, it has substituted naked, shameless, direct, brutal exploitation.

The bourgeoisie has stripped of its halo every occupation hitherto honoured and looked up to with reverent awe. It has converted the physician, the lawyer, the priest, the poet, the man of science, into its paid wage labourers.

The bourgeoisie has torn away from the family its sentimental veil, and has reduced the family relation to a mere money relation.

The bourgeoisie has disclosed how it came to pass that the brutal display of vigour in the Middle Ages, which reactionaries so much admire, found its fitting complement in the most slothful indolence. It has been the first to show what man's activity can bring about. It has accomplished wonders far surpassing Egyptian pyramids, Roman aqueducts, and Gothic cathedrals; it has conducted expeditions that put in the shade all former exoduses of nations and crusades.

The bourgeoisie cannot exist without constantly revolutionizing the instruments of production, and thereby the relations of production, and with them the whole relations of society. Conservation of the old modes of production in unaltered form, was, on the contrary, the first condition of existence for all earlier industrial classes. Constant revolutionizing of production, uninterrupted disturbance of all social

271

conditions, everlasting uncertainty and agitation distinguish the bourgeois epoch from all earlier ones. All fixed, fast frozen relations, with their train of ancient and removable prejudices and opinions, are swept away, all new-formed ones become antiquated before they can ossify. All that is solid melts into air, all that is holy is profaned, and man is at last compelled to face with sober senses his real conditions of life and his relations with his kind. . . .

The bourgeoisie, by the rapid improvement of all instruments of production, by the immensely facilitated means of communication, draws all, even the most barbarian, nations into civilization. The cheap prices of its commodities are the heavy artillery with which it batters down all Chinese walls, with which it forces the barbarians' intensely obstinate hatred of foreigners to capitulate. It compels all nations, on pain of extinction, to adopt the bourgeois mode of production; it compels them to introduce what it calls civilization into their midst, i.e. to become bourgeois themselves. In one word, it creates a world after its own image. . . .

Modern bourgeois society with its relations of production, of exchange and of property, a society that has conjured up such gigantic means of production and of exchange, is like the sorcerer who is no longer able to control the powers of the nether world whom he has called up by his spells. For many a decade past the history of industry and commerce is but the history of the revolt of modern productive forces against modern conditions of production, against the property relations that are the conditions for the existence of the bourgeoisie and of its rule. It is enough to mention the commercial crises that by their periodical return put the existence of the entire bourgeois society on its trial, each time more threateningly. In these crises a great part not only of the existing products, but also of the previously created productive forces, are periodically destroyed. In these crises there breaks out an epidemic that, in all earlier epochs, would have seemed an absurdity—the epidemic of over-production. Society suddenly finds itself put back into a state of momentary barbarism; it appears as if a famine, a universal war of devastation had cut off the supply of every means of subsistence; industry and commerce seem to be destroyed. And why? Because there is too much civilization, too much means of subsistence, too much industry, too much commerce. The productive forces at the disposal of society no longer tend to further the development of the conditions of bourgeois property; on the contrary, they have become too powerful for these conditions, by which they are fettered, and so soon as they overcome these fetters, they bring disorder into the whole of bourgeois society, endanger the existence of bourgeois property. The conditions of bourgeois society are too narrow to comprise the wealth created by them. And how does the bourgeoisie get over these crises? On the one hand, by enforced destruction of a mass of productive forces; on the other, by the conquest of new markets, and by the more thorough exploitation of the old ones. That is to say, by paving the way for more extensive and more destructive crises, and by diminishing the means whereby crises are prevented.

The weapons with which the bourgeoisie felled feudalism to the ground are now turned against the bourgeoisie itself.

But not only has the bourgeoisie forged the weapons that bring death to itself; it has also called into existence the men who are to wield those weapons—the modern working class—the proletarians.

In proportion as the bourgeoisie, i.e. capital, is developed, in the same proportion is the proletariat, the modern working class, developed —a class of labourers, who live only so long as they find work, and who find work only so long as their labour increases capital. These labourers, who must sell themselves piecemeal, are a commodity, like every other article of commerce, and are consequently exposed to all the vicissitudes of competition, to all the fluctuations of the market.

Owing to the extensive use of machinery and to division of labour, the work of the proletarians has lost all individual character, and, consequently, all charm for the workman. He becomes an appendage of the machine, and it is only the most simple, most monotonous, and most easily acquired knack, that is required of him. Hence, the cost of production of a workman is restricted, almost entirely, to the means of subsistence that he requires for his maintenance, and for the propagation of his race. But the price of a commodity, and therefore also of labour, is equal to its cost of production. In proportion, therefore, as the repulsiveness of the work increases, the wage decreases. Nay more, in proportion as the use of machinery and division of labour increases, in the same proportion the burden of toil also increases, whether by prolongation of the working hours, by increase of the work exacted in a given time, or by increased speed of the machinery, etc.

Modern industry has converted the little workshop of the patriarchal master into the great factory of the industrial capitalist. Masses of labourers, crowded into the factory, are organized like soldiers. As privates of the industrial army they are placed under the command of a perfect hierarchy of officers and sergeants. Not only are they slaves of the bourgeois class, and of the bourgeois state, they are daily and hourly enslaved by the machine, by the overlooker, and, above all, by the individual bourgeois manufacturer himself. The more openly this despotism proclaims gain to be its end and aim, the more petty, the more hateful and the more embittering it is.

The less the skill and exertion of strength implied in manual labour, in other words, the more modern industry becomes developed, the more is the labour of men superseded by that of women. Differences of

273

age and sex have no longer any distinctive social validity for the working class. All are instruments of labour, more or less expensive to use, according to their age and sex.

No sooner is the exploitation of the labourer by the manufacturer, so far at an end, that he receives his wages in cash, than he is set upon by the other portions of the bourgeoisie, the landlord, the shopkeeper, the pawnbroker, etc.

The lower strata of the middle class—the small tradespeople, shopkeepers, and retired tradesmen generally, the handicraftsmen and peasants—all these sink gradually into the proletariat, partly because their diminutive capital does not suffice for the scale on which modern industry is carried on, and is swamped in the competition with the large capitalists, partly because their specialized skill is rendered worthless by new methods of production. Thus the proletariat is recruited from all classes of the population.

The proletariat goes through various stages of development. With its birth begins its struggle with the bourgeoisie. At first the contest is carried on by individual labourers, then by the work people of a factory, then by the operatives of one trade, in one locality, against the individual bourgeois who directly exploits them. They direct their attacks not against the bourgeois conditions of production, but against the instruments of production themselves; they destroy imported wares that compete with their labour, they smash to pieces machinery, they set factories ablaze, they seek to restore by force the vanished status of the workman of the Middle Ages.

At this stage the labourers still form an incoherent mass scattered over the whole country, and broken up by their mutual competition. If anywhere they unite to form more compact bodies, this is not yet the consequence of their own active union, but of the union of the bourgeoisie, which class, in order to attain its own political ends, is compelled to set the whole proletariat in motion, and is moreover yet, for a time, able to do so. At this stage, therefore, the proletarians do not fight their enemies, but the enemies of their enemies, the remnants of absolute monarchy, the land-owners, the non-industrial bourgeois, the petty bourgeoisie. Thus the whole historical movement is concentrated in the hands of the bourgeoisie; every victory so obtained is a victory for the bourgeoisie.

But with the development of industry the proletariat not only increases in number; it becomes concentrated in greater masses, its strength grows, and it feels that strength more. The various interests and conditions of life within the ranks of the proletariat are more and more equalized, in proportion as machinery obliterates all distinctions of labour, and nearly everywhere reduces wages to the same low level. The growing competition among the bourgeois, and the resulting commercial crises, make the wages of the workers ever more fluctuating. The unceasing improvement of machinery, ever more rapidly developing, makes their livelihood more and more precarious; the collisions between individual workmen and individual bourgeois take more and more the character of collisions between two classes. Thereupon the workers begin to form combinations (trade unions) against the bourgeois; they club together in order to keep up the rate of wages; they found permanent associations in order to make provision beforehand for these occasional revolts. Here and there the contest breaks out into riots.

Now and then the workers are victorious, but only for a time. The real fruit of their battles lies, not in the immediate result, but in the ever expanding union of the workers. This union is helped on by the improved means of communication that are created by modern industry, and that place the workers of different localities in contact with another. . . .

This organization of the proletarians into a class, and consequently into a political party, is continually being upset again by the competition between the workers themselves. But it ever rises up again, stronger, firmer, mightier. It compels legislative recognition of particular interests of the workers, by taking advantage of the divisions among the bourgeoisie itself. Thus the Ten-Hours Bill in England was carried.

Altogether, collisions between the classes of the old society further in many ways the course of development of the proletariat. The bourgeoisie finds itself involved in a constant battle. At first with the aristocracy; later on, with those portions of the bourgeoisie itself, whose interests have become antagonistic to the progress of industry; at all times with the bourgeoisie of foreign countries. In all these battles it sees itself compelled to appeal to the proletariat, to ask for its help, and thus, to drag it into the political arena. The bourgeoisie itself, therefore, supplies the proletariat with its own elements of political and general education, in other words, it furnishes the proletariat with weapons for fighting the bourgeoisie.

Further, as we have already seen, entire sections of the ruling classes are, by the advance of industry, precipitated into the proletariat, or are at least threatened in their conditions of existence. These also supply the proletariat with fresh elements of enlightenment and progress.

Finally, in times when the class struggle nears the decisive hour, the process of dissolution going on within the ruling class, in fact within the whole range of old society, assumes such a violent, glaring character, that a small section of the ruling class cuts itself adrift, and joins the revolutionary class, the class that holds the future in its hands. Just as, therefore, at an earlier period, a section of the nobility went over to the bourgeoisie, so now a portion of the bourgeoisie goes over to the proletariat, and in particular, a portion of the bourgeois ideologists, who have raised themselves to the level of comprehending theoretically the historical movement as a whole.

Of all the classes that stand face to face with the bourgeoisie today, the proletariat alone is a really revolutionary class. The other classes decay and finally disappear in the face of modern industry; the proletariat is its special and essential product.

The lower middle class, the small manufacturer, the shopkeeper, the artisan, the peasant, all these fight against the bourgeoisie, to save from extinction their existence as fractions of the middle class. They are therefore not revolutionary, but conservative. Nay, more, they are reactionary, for they try to roll back the wheel of history. If by chance they are revolutionary, they are so only in view of their impending transfer into the proletariat; they thus defend not their present, but their future interests; they desert their own standpoint to place themselves at that of the proletariat.

The 'dangerous class', the social scum, that passively rotting mass thrown off by the lowest layers of old society, may, here and there, be swept into the movement by a proletarian revolution; its conditions of life, however, prepare it far more for the part of a bribed tool of reactionary intrigue.

In the conditions of the proletariat, those of old society at large are already virtually swamped. The proletarian is without property; his relation to his wife and children has no longer anything in common with the bourgeois family relations; modern industrial labour, modern subjection to capital, the same in England as in France, in America as in Germany, has stripped him of every trace of national character. Law, morality, religion, are to him so many bourgeois prejudices, behind which lurk in ambush just as many bourgeois interests.

All the preceding classes that got the upper hand, sought to fortify their already acquired status by subjecting society at large to their conditions of appropriation. The proletarians cannot become masters of the productive forces of society, except by abolishing their own previous mode of appropriation, and thereby also every other previous mode of appropriation. They have nothing of their own to secure and to fortify; their mission is to destroy all previous securities for, and insurances of, individual property.

All previous historical movements were movements of minorities, or in the interest of minorities. The proletarian movement is the self-conscious, independent movement of the immense majority, in the interest of the immense majority. The proletariat, the lowest stratum of our present society, cannot stir, cannot raise itself up, without the whole superincumbent strata of official society being sprung into the air.

Though not in substance, yet in form, the struggle of the proletariat with the bourgeoisie is at first a national struggle. The proletariat of each country must, of course, first of all settle matters with its own bourgeoisie.

In depicting the most general phases of the development of the proletariat, we traced the more or less veiled civil war, raging within existing society, up to the point where that war breaks out into open revolution, and where the violent overthrow of the bourgeoisie lays the foundation for the sway of the proletariat.

Hitherto, every form of society has been based, as we have already seen, on the antagonism of oppressing and oppressed classes. But in order to oppress a class, certain conditions must be assured to it under which it can, at least, continue its slavish existence. The serf, in the period of serfdom, raised himself to membership in the commune, just as the petty bourgeois, under the yoke of feudal absolutism, managed to develop into a bourgeois. The modern labourer, on the contrary, instead of rising with the progress of industry, sinks deeper and deeper below the conditions of existence of his own class. He becomes a pauper, and pauperism develops more rapidly than population and wealth. And here it becomes evident that the bourgeoisie is unfit any longer to be the ruling class in society, and to impose its conditions of existence upon society as an overriding law. It is unfit to rule because it is incompetent to assure an existence to its slave within his slavery, because it cannot help letting him sink into such a state, that it has to feed him, instead of being fed by him. Society can no longer live under this bourgeoisie, in other words, its existence is no longer compatible with society.

The essential condition for the existence and for the sway of the bourgeois class is the formation and augmentation of capital; the condition for capital is wage labour. Wage labour rests exclusively on competition between the labourers. The advance of industry, whose involuntary promoter is the bourgeoisie, replaces the isolation of the labourers, due to competition, by their revolutionary combination, due to association. The development of modern industry, therefore, cuts from under its feet the very foundation on which the bourgeoisie produces and appropriates products. What the bourgeoisie therefore produces, above all, are its own grave-diggers. Its fall and the victory of the proletariat are equally inevitable.

# JOHN STUART MILL  XVIII.3

## 'The Probable Futurity of the Labouring Classes'

from *The Principles of Political Economy*, added
to 3rd edn., 1852

When I speak, either in this place or elsewhere, of 'the labouring classes', or of labourers as a 'class', I use those phrases in compliance with custom, and as descriptive of an existing, but by no means a necessary or permanent state of social relations. I do not recognise as either just or salutary, a state of society in which there is any 'class' which is not labouring; any human beings exempt from bearing their share of the necessary labours of human life, except those unable to labour, or who have fairly earned rest by previous toil. So long, however, as the great social evil exists of a non-labouring class, labourers also constitute a class, and may be spoken of, though only provisionally, in that character.

Considered in its moral and social aspect, the state of the labouring people has latterly been a subject of much more speculation and discussion than formerly; and the opinion, that it is not now what it ought to be, has become very general. The suggestions which have been promulgated, and the controversies which have been excited, on detached points rather than on the foundations of the subject, have put in evidence the existence of two conflicting theories, respecting the social position desirable for manual labourers. The one may be called the theory of dependence and protection, the other that of self-dependence.

According to the former theory, the lot of the poor, in all things which affect them collectively, should be regulated *for* them, not *by* them. They should not be required or encouraged to think for themselves, or give to their own reflection or forecast an influential voice in the determination of their destiny. It is supposed to be the duty of the higher classes to think for them, and to take the responsibility of their lot, as the commander and officers of an army take that of the soldiers composing it. This function, it is contended, the higher classes should prepare themselves to perform conscientiously, and their whole demeanour should impress the poor with a reliance on it, in order that, while yielding passive and active obedience to the rules prescribed for them, they may resign themselves in all other respects to a trustful *insouciance*, and repose under the shadow of their protectors. The relation between rich and poor, according to this theory (a theory also applied to the relation between men and women), should be only partly authoritative: it should be amiable, moral, and sentimental: affectionate tutelage on the one side, respectful and grateful deference on the other. The rich should be *in loco parentis* to the poor, guiding and restraining them like children. Of spontaneous action on their part there should be no need. They should be called on for nothing but to do their day's work, and to be moral and religious. Their morality and religion should be provided for them by their superiors, who should do all that is necessary to ensure their being, in return for labour and attachment, properly fed, clothed, housed, spiritually edified, and innocently amused.

This is the ideal of the future, in the minds of those whose dissatisfaction with the Present assumes the form of affection and regret towards the Past. Like other ideals, it exercises an unconscious influence on the opinions and sentiments of numbers who never consciously guide themselves by any ideal. It has also this in common with other ideals, that it has never been historically realised. It makes its appeal to our imaginative sympathies in the character of a restoration of the good times of our forefathers. But no times can be pointed out in which the higher classes of this or any other country performed a part even distantly resembling the one assigned to them in this theory. It is an idealisation, grounded on the conduct and character of here and there an individual. All privileged and powerful classes, as such, have used their power in the interest of their own selfishness, and have indulged their self importance in despising, and not in lovingly caring for, those who were, in their estimation, degraded, by being under the necessity of working for their benefit. I do not affirm that what has always been must always be, or that human improvement has no tendency to correct the intensely selfish feelings engendered by power; but though the evil may be lessened, it cannot be eradicated, until the power itself is withdrawn. This, at least, seems to me undeniable, that long before the superior classes could be sufficiently improved to govern in the tutelary manner supposed, the inferior classes would be too much improved to be so governed.

I am quite sensible of all that is seductive in the picture of society which this theory presents. Though the facts of it have no prototype in the past, the feelings have. In them lies all that there is of reality in the conception. As the idea is essentially repulsive of a society only held together by the relations and feelings arising out of pecuniary interests, so there is something naturally attractive in a form of society abounding in strong personal attachments and disinterested self-devotion. Of such feelings it must be admitted that the relation of protector and protected has hitherto been the richest source. The strongest attachments of human beings in general, are towards the things or the persons that stand between them and some dreaded evil. Hence, in an age of lawless violence and insecurity, and general hardness and roughness of manners, in which life is beset with dangers and sufferings at every step, to those who have neither a commanding position of their own, nor a claim on the protection of some one who has—a generous giving of protection, and a grateful receiving of it, are the strongest ties which connect human beings; the feelings arising from that relation are their warmest feelings; all the enthusiasm and tenderness of the most sensitive natures gather round it; loyalty on the one part and chivalry on the other are principles exalted into passions. I do not desire to depreciate these qualities. The error lies in not perceiving, that these virtues and sentiments, like the clanship and the hospitality of the wandering Arab, belong emphatically to a rude and imperfect state of the social union, and that the feelings between protector and protected, whether between kings and subjects, rich and poor, or men and women, can no longer have this beautiful and endearing character, where there are no longer any serious dangers from which to protect. What is there in the present state of society to make it natural that human beings, of ordinary strength and courage, should glow with the warmest gratitude and devotion in return for protection? The laws protect them; wherever the laws do not criminally fail in their duty. To be under the power of some one, instead of being as formerly the sole condition of safety, is now, speaking generally, the only situation which exposes to grievous wrong. The so-called protectors are now the only persons against whom, in ordinary circumstances, protection is needed. The brutality and tyranny with which every police report is filled, are those of husbands to wives, of parents to children. That the law does not prevent these atrocities, that it is only now making a first timid attempt to repress and punish them, is no matter of necessity, but the deep disgrace of those by whom the laws are made and administered. No man or woman who either possesses or is able to earn an independent livelihood, requires any other protection than that which the law could and ought to give. This being the case, it argues great ignorance of human nature to continue taking for granted that relations founded on protection must always subsist, and not to see that the assumption of the part of protector, and of the power which belongs to it, without any of the necessities which justify it, must engender feelings opposite to loyalty.

Of the working men, at least in the more advanced countries of Europe, it may be pronounced certain, that the patriarchal or paternal system of government is one to which they will not again be subject. That question was decided, when they were taught to read, and allowed access to newspapers and political tracts; when dissenting preachers were suffered to go among them, and appeal to their faculties and feelings in opposition to the creeds professed and countenanced by their superiors; when they were brought together in numbers, to work socially under the same roof; when railways enabled them to shift from place to place, and change their patrons and employers as easily as their coats; when they were encouraged to seek a share in the government, by means of the electoral franchise. The working classes have taken their interests into their own hands, and are perpetually showing that they think the interests of their employers not identical with their own, but opposite to them. Some among the higher classes flatter themselves that these tendencies may be counteracted by moral and religious education; but they have let the time go by for giving an education which can serve their purpose. The principles of the Reformation have reached as low down in society as reading and writing, and the poor will not much longer accept morals and religion of other people's prescribing. I speak more particularly of this country, especially the town population, and the districts of the most scientific agriculture or the highest wages, Scotland and the north of England. Among the more inert and less modernised agricultural population of the southern counties, it might be possible for the gentry to retain, for some time longer, something of the ancient deference and submission of the poor, by bribing them with high wages and constant employment; by ensuring them support, and never requiring them to do anything which they do not like. But these are two conditions which never have been combined, and never can be, for long together. A guarantee of subsistence can only be practically kept up, when work is enforced, and superfluous multiplication restrained, by at least a moral compulsion. It is then that the would-be revivers of old times which they do not understand, would feel practically in how hopeless a task they were engaged. The whole fabric of patriarchal or seignorial influence, attempted to be raised on the foundation of caressing the poor, would be shattered against the necessity of enforcing a stringent Poor-law.

It is on a far other basis that the well-being and well-doing of the labouring people must henceforth rest. The poor have come out of leading-strings, and cannot any longer be governed or treated like children. To their own qualities must now be commended the care of their destiny. Modern nations will have to learn the lesson, that the well-being of a people must exist by means of the justice and self-government, the δικαιοσύνη and σωφροσύνη, of the individual citizens. The theory of dependence attempts to dispense with the necessity of these qualities in the independent classes. But now, when even in position they are becoming less and less dependent, their minds less and less acquiescent in the degree of dependence which remains, the virtues of independence are those which they stand in need of. Whatever advice, exhortation, or guidance is held out to the labouring classes, must henceforth be tendered to them as equals, and accepted by them with their eyes open. The prospect of the future depends on the degree in which they can be made rational beings.

There is no reason to believe that prospect other than hopeful. The progress indeed has hitherto been, and still is, slow. But there is a spontaneous education going on in the minds of the multitude, which may be greatly accelerated and improved by artificial aids. The instruction obtained from newspapers and political tracts may not be the most solid kind of instruction, but it is an immense improvement upon none at all. What it does for a people, has been admirably exemplified during the cotton crisis, in the case of the Lancashire spinners and weavers; who have acted with the consistent good sense and forbearance so justly applauded, simply because, being readers of newspapers, they understood the causes of the calamity which had befallen them, and knew that it was in no way imputable either to their employers or to the Government. It is not certain that their conduct would have been as rational and exemplary, if the distress had preceded the salutary measure of fiscal emancipation which gave existence to the penny press. The institutions for lectures and discussion, the collective deliberations on questions of common interest, the trades unions, the political agitation, all serve to awaken public spirit, to diffuse variety of ideas among the mass, and to excite thought and reflection in the more intelligent. Although the too early attainment of political franchise by the least educated class might retard, instead of promoting, their improvement, there can be little doubt that it has been greatly stimulated by the attempt to acquire them. In the meantime, the working classes are now part of the public; in all discussions on matters of general interest they, or a portion of them, are now partakers; all who use the press as an instrument may, if it so happens, have them for an audience; the avenues of instruction through which the middle classes acquire such ideas as they have, are accessible to, at least, the operatives in the towns. With these resources, it cannot be doubted that they will increase in intelligence, even by their own unaided efforts; while there is reason to hope that great improvements both in the quality and quantity of school education will be effected by the exertions either of Government or of individuals, and that the progress of the mass of the people in mental cultivation, and in the virtues which are dependent on it, will take place more rapidly, and with fewer intermittences and aberrations, than if left to itself.

From this increase of intelligence, several effects may be confidently anticipated. First: that they will become even less willing than at present to be led and governed, and direct into the way they should go, by the mere authority and *prestige* of superiors. If they have not now, still less will they have hereafter, any deferential awe, or religious principle of obedience, holding them in mental subjection to a class above them. The theory of dependence and protection will be more and more intolerable to them, and they will require that their conduct and condition shall be essentially self-governed. It is, at the same time, quite possible that they may demand, in many cases, the intervention of the legislature in their affairs, and the regulation by law of various things which concern them, often under very mistaken ideas of their interest. Still, it is their own will, their own ideas and suggestions, to which they will demand that effect should be given, and not rules laid down for them by other people. It is quite consistent with this, that they should feel respect for superiority of intellect and knowledge, and defer much to the opinions, on any subject, of those whom they think well acquainted with it. Such deference is deeply grounded in human nature; but they will judge for themselves of the persons who are and are not entitled to it.

It appears to me impossible but that the increase of intelligence, of education, and of the love of independence among the working classes, must be attended with a corresponding growth of the good sense which manifests itself in provident habits of conduct, and that population, therefore, will bear a gradually diminishing ratio to capital and employment. This most desirable result would be much accelerated by another change, which lies in the direct line of the best tendencies of the time; the opening of industrial occupations freely to both sexes. The same reasons which make it no longer necessary that the poor should depend on the rich, make it equally unnecessary that women should depend on men, and the least which justice requires is that law and custom should not enforce dependence (when the correlative protection has become superfluous) by ordaining that a woman, who does not happen to have a provision by inheritance, shall have scarcely any means open to her of gaining a livelihood, except as a wife and mother. Let women who prefer that occupation, adopt it; but that there should be no option, no other career possible for the great majority of women, except in the humbler departments of life, is a flagrant social injustice. The ideas and institutions by which the accident of sex is made the groundwork of an inequality of legal rights and a forced dissimilarity of social functions, must ere long be recognised as the greatest hindrance to moral, social, and even intellectual improvement. On the present occasion I shall only indicate, among the probable consequences of the industrial and social independence of women, a great diminution of the evil of over-population. It is by devoting one-half of the human species to that exclusive function, by making it fill the entire life of one sex, and interweave itself with almost all the objects of the other, that the animal instinct in question is nursed into the disproportionate preponderance which it has hitherto exercised in human life.

The political consequences of the increasing power and importance of the operative classes, and of the growing ascendancy of numbers, which even in England and under the present institutions, is rapidly giving to the will of the majority at least a negative voice in the acts of government, are too wide a subject to be discussed in this place. But, confining ourselves to economical considerations, and notwithstanding the effect which improved intelligence in the working classes, together with just laws, may have in altering the distribution of the produce to their advantage, I cannot think that they will be permanently contented with the condition of labouring for wages as their ultimate state. They may be willing to pass through the class of servants in their way to that of employers; but not to remain in it all their lives. To begin as hired labourers, then after a few years to work on their own account, and finally employ others, is the normal condition of labourers in a new country, rapidly increasing in wealth and population, like America or Australia. But in an old and fully peopled country, those who begin life as labourers for hire, as a general rule, continue such to the end, unless they sink into the still lower grade of recipients of public charity. In the present stage of human progress, when ideas of equality are daily spreading more widely among the poorer classes, and can no longer be checked by anything short of the entire suppression of printed discussion and even of freedom of speech, it is not to be expected that the division of the human race into two hereditary classes, employers and employed, can be permanently maintained. The relation is nearly as unsatisfactory to the payer of wages as to the receiver. If the rich regard the poor as, by a kind of natural law, their servants and dependents, the rich in their turn are regarded as a mere prey and pasture for the poor; the subject of demands and expectations wholly indefinite, increasing in extent with every concession made to them. The total absence of regard for justice or fairness in the relations between the two, is as marked on the side of the employed as on that of the employers. We look in vain among the working classes in general for the just pride which will choose to give good work for good wages: for the most part, their sole endeavour is to receive as much, and return as little in the shape of service, as possible. It will sooner or later become insupportable to the employing classes to live in close and hourly contact with persons whose interests and feelings are in hostility to them. Capitalists are almost as much interested as labourers, in placing the operations of industry on such a footing, that those who labour for them may feel the same interest in the work, which is felt by those who labour on their own account.

# JOHN STUART MILL                                    XVIII.4

## Socialism, Communism and Private Property

from *The Principles of Political Economy*, added
to 2nd edn., 1849

Private property, as an institution, did not owe its origin to any of
those considerations of utility, which plead for the maintenance of it
when established. Enough is known of rude ages, both from history and
from analogous states of society in our own time, to show that tribunals
(which always precede laws) were originally established, not to determine rights, but to repress violence and terminate quarrels. With this
object chiefly in view, they naturally enough gave legal effect to first
occupancy, by treating as the aggressor the person who first commenced
violence, by turning, or attempting to turn, another out of possession.
The preservation of the peace, which was the original object of civil
government, was thus attained; while by confirming, to those who
already possessed it, even what was not the fruit of personal exertion,
a guarantee was incidentally given to them and others that they would
be protected in what was so.

In considering the institution of property as a question in social
philosophy, we must leave out of consideration its actual origin in any
of the existing nations of Europe. We may suppose a community un-
hampered by any previous possession; a body of colonists, occupying
for the first time an uninhabited country; bringing nothing with them
but what belonged to them in common, and having a clear field for the
adoption of the institutions and polity which they judged most expedient; required, therefore, to choose whether they would conduct the
work of production on the principle of individual property, or on some
system of common ownership and collective agency.

If private property were adopted, we must presume that it would be
accompanied by none of the initial inequalities and injustices which
obstruct the beneficial operation of the principle in old societies. Every
full-grown man or woman, we must suppose, would be secured in the
unfettered use and disposal of his or her bodily and mental faculties;
and the instruments of production, the land and tools, would be divided fairly among them, so that all might start, in respect to outward
appliances, on equal terms. It is possible also to conceive that in this
original apportionment, compensation might be made for the injuries
of nature, and the balance redressed by assigning to the less robust
members of the community advantages in the distribution, sufficient to
put them on a par with the rest. But the division, once made, would not
again be interfered with; individuals would be left to their own exertions and to the ordinary chances, for making an advantageous use of

what was assigned to them. If individual property, on the contrary, were excluded, the plan which must be adopted would be to hold the land and all instruments of production as the joint property of the community, and to carry on the operations of industry on the common account. The direction of the labour of the community would devolve upon a magistrate or magistrates, whom we may suppose elected by the suffrages of the community, and whom we must assume to be voluntarily obeyed by them. The division of the produce would in like manner be a public act. The principle might either be that of complete equality, or of apportionment to the necessities or deserts of individuals, in whatever manner might be conformable to the ideas of justice or policy prevailing in the community.

Examples of such associations, on a small scale, are the monastic orders, the Moravians and others: and from the hopes which they hold out of relief from the miseries and iniquities of a state of much inequality of wealth, schemes for a larger application of the same idea have reappeared and become popular at all periods of active speculation on the first principles of society. In an age like the present, when a general reconsideration of all first principles is felt to be inevitable, and when more than at any former period of history the suffering portions of the community have a voice in the discussion, it was impossible but that ideas of this nature should spread far and wide. The late revolutions in Europe have thrown up a great amount of speculation of this character, and an unusual share of attention has consequently been drawn to the various forms which these ideas have assumed: nor is this attention likely to diminish, but on the contrary, to increase more and more.

The assailants of the principle of individual property may be divided into two classes: those whose scheme implies absolute equality in the distribution of the physical means of life and enjoyment, and those who admit inequality, but grounded on some principle, or supposed principle, of justice or general expediency, and not, like so many of the existing social inequalities, dependent on accident alone. At the head of the first class, as the earliest of those belonging to the present generation, must be placed Mr Owen and his followers. M. Louis Blanc and M. Cabet have more recently become conspicuous as apostles of similar doctrines (though the former advocates equality of distribution only as a transition to a still higher standard of justice, that all should work according to their capacity, and receive according to their wants). The characteristic name for this economical system is Communism, a word of continental origin, only of late introduced into this country. The word Socialism, which originated among the English Communists, and was assumed by them as a name to designate their own doctrine, is now, on the Continent, employed in a larger sense; not necessarily

9. J. Pye: View of Mr. Owen's village of Union Orbiton, near Glasgow (1823)

10. G. Arnold: Pont-y-Cysylltau Aqueduct (1826)

11. George Cruikshank: London going out of Town or The March of Bricks and Mortar (1829)

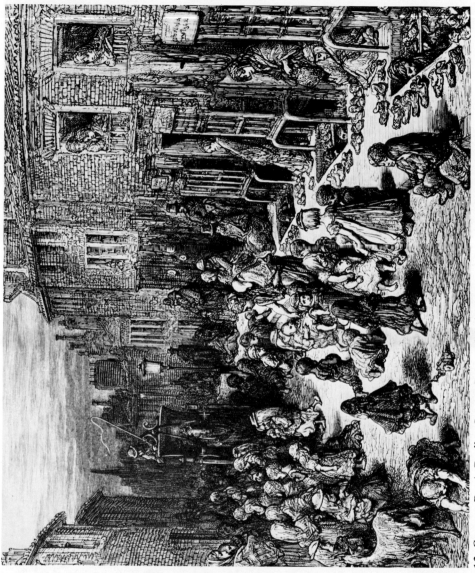

12. Gustave Doré: Dudley Street, Seven Dials (1872)

13. J. B. Pyne: The Bristol Riots—prisoners escorted by torchlight (1832). *Detail*

14. Ford Madox Brown: John Kay, Inventor of the Fly Shuttle 1753 (1879–93)

implying Communism, or the entire abolition of private property, but applied to any system which requires that the land and the instruments of production should be the property, not of individuals, but of communities or associations, or of the government. Among such systems the two of highest intellectual pretension are those which, from the names of their real or reputed authors, have been called St Simonism and Fourierism; the former, defunct as a system, but which during the few years of its public promulgation, sowed the seeds of nearly all the Socialist tendencies which have since spread so widely in France: the second, still flourishing in the number, talent, and zeal of its adherents.

Whatever may be the merits or defects of these various schemes, they cannot be truly said to be impracticable. No reasonable person can doubt that a village community, composed of a few thousand inhabitants cultivating in joint ownership the same extent of land which at present feeds that number of people, and producing by combined labour and the most improved processes the manufactured articles which they required, could raise an amount of productions sufficient to maintain them in comfort; and would find the means of obtaining, and if need be, exacting, the quantity of labour necessary for this purpose, from every member of the association who was capable of work.

The objection ordinarily made to a system of community of property and equal distribution of the produce, that each person would be incessantly occupied in evading his fair share of the work, points, undoubtedly, to a real difficulty. But those who urge this objection, forget how great an extent the same difficulty exists under the system on which nine-tenths of the business of society is now conducted. The objection supposes, that honest and efficient labour is only to be had from those who are themselves individually to reap the benefit of their own exertions. But how small a part of all the labour performed in England, from the lowest paid to the highest, is done by persons working for their own benefit? From the Irish reaper or hodman to the chief justice or the minister of state, nearly all the work of society is remunerated by day wages or fixed salaries. A factory operative has less personal interest in his work than a member of a Communist association, since he is not, like him, working for a partnership of which he is himself a member. It will no doubt be said, that though the labourers themselves have not, in most cases, a personal interest in their work, they are watched and superintended, and their labour directed, and the mental part of the labour performed, by persons who have. Even this, however, is far from being universally the fact. In all public, and many of the largest and most successful private undertakings, not only the labours of detail, but the control and superintendence are entrusted to salaried officers. And though the 'master's eye', when the master is

287

vigilant and intelligent, is of proverbial value, it must be remembered that in a Socialist farm or manufactory, each labourer would be under the eye not of one master, but of the whole community. In the extreme case of obstinate perseverance in not performing the due share of work, the community would have the same resources which society now has for compelling conformity to the necessary conditions of the association. Dismissal, the only remedy at present, is no remedy when any other labourer who may be engaged does no better than his predecessor: the power of dismissal only enables an employer to obtain from his workmen the customary amount of labour, but that customary labour may be of any degree of inefficiency. Even the labourer who loses his employment by idleness or negligence, has nothing worse to suffer, in the most unfavourable case, than the discipline of a workhouse, and if the desire to avoid this be a sufficient motive in the one system, it would be sufficient in the other. I am not undervaluing the strength of the incitement given to labour when the whole or a large share of the benefit of extra exertion belongs to the labourer. But under the present system of industry this incitement, in the great majority of cases, does not exist. If Communistic labour might be less vigorous than that of a peasant proprietor, or a workman labouring on his own account, it would probably be more energetic than that of a labourer for hire, who has no personal interest in the matter at all. The neglect by the uneducated classes of labourers for hire, of the duties which they engage to perform, is in the present state of society most flagrant. Now it is an admitted condition of the Communist scheme that all shall be educated: and this being supposed, the duties of the members of the association would doubtless be as diligently performed as those of the generality of salaried officers in the middle or higher classes; who are not supposed to be necessarily unfaithful to their trust, because so long as they are not dismissed, their pay is the same in however lax a manner their duty is fulfilled. Undoubtedly, as a general rule, remuneration by fixed salaries does not in any class of functionaries produce the maximum of zeal; and this is as much as can be reasonably alleged against Communistic labour.

That even this inferiority would necessarily exist, is by no means so certain as is assumed by those who are little used to carry their minds beyond the state of things with which they are familiar. Mankind are capable of a far greater amount of public spirit than the present age is accustomed to suppose possible. History bears witness to the success with which large bodies of human beings may be trained to feel the public interest their own. And no soil could be more favourable to the growth of such a feeling, than a Communist association, since all the ambition, and the bodily and mental activity, which are now exerted in the pursuit of separate and self-regarding interests, would require another sphere of employment, and would naturally find it in the pursuit of the general benefit of the community. The same cause, so often assigned in explanation of the devotion of the Catholic priest or monk to the interest of his order—that he has no interest apart from it—would, under Communism, attach the citizen to the community. And independently of the public motive, every member of the association would be amenable to the most universal, and one of the strongest of personal motives, that of public opinion. The force of this motive in deterring from any act or omission positively reproved by the community, no one is likely to deny; but the power also of emulation, in exciting to the most strenuous exertions for the sake of the approbation and admiration of others, is borne witness to by experience in every situation in which human beings publicly compete with one another, even if it be in things frivolous, or from which the public derive no benefit. A contest, who can do most for the common good, is not the kind of competition which Socialists repudiate. To what extent, therefore, the energy of labour would be diminished by Communism, or whether in the long run it would be diminished at all, must be considered for the present an undecided question.

Another of the objections to Communism is similar to that, so often urged against poor-laws: that if every member of the community were assured of subsistence for himself and any number of children, on the sole condition of willingness to work, prudential restraint on the multiplication of mankind would be at an end, and population would start forward at a rate which would reduce the community through successive stages of increasing discomfort to actual starvation. There would certainly be much ground for this apprehension if Communism provided no motives to restraint, equivalent to those which it would take away. But Communism is precisely the state of things in which opinion might be expected to declare itself with greatest intensity against this kind of selfish intemperance. Any augmentation of numbers which diminished the comfort or increased the toil of the mass, would then cause (which now it does not) immediate and unmistakable inconvenience to every individual in the association; inconvenience which could not then be imputed to the avarice of employers, or the unjust privileges of the rich. In such altered circumstances opinion could not fail to reprobate, and if reprobation did not suffice, to repress by penalties of some description, this or any other culpable self-indulgence at the expense of the community. The Communistic scheme, instead of being peculiarly open to the objection drawn from danger of over-population, has the recommendation of tending in an especial degree to the prevention of that evil.

A more real difficulty is that of fairly apportioning the labour of the community among its members. There are many kinds of work, and by what standard are they to be measured one against another? Who is to judge how much cotton spinning, or distributing goods from the stores, or bricklaying, or chimney sweeping, is equivalent to so much ploughing? The difficulty of making the adjustment between different qualities of labour is so strongly felt by Communist writers, that they have usually thought it necessary to provide that all should work by turns at every description of useful labour: an arrangement which by putting an end to the division of employments, would sacrifice so much of the advantage of co-operative production as greatly to diminish the productiveness of labour. Besides, even in the same kind of work, nominal equality of labour would be so great a real inequality, that the feeling of justice would revolt against its being enforced. All persons are not equally fit for all labour; and the same quantity of labour is an unequal burthen on the weak and the strong, the hardy and the delicate, the quick and the slow, the dull and the intelligent.

But these difficulties, though real, are not necessarily insuperable. The apportionment of work to the strength and capacities of individuals, the mitigation of a general rule to provide for cases in which it would operate harshly, are not problems to which human intelligence, guided by a sense of justice, would be inadequate. And the worst and most unjust arrangement which could be made of these points, under a system aiming at equality, would be so far short of the inequality and injustice with which labour (not to speak of remuneration) is now apportioned, as to be scarcely worth counting in the comparison. We must remember too that Communism, as a system of society, exists only in idea; that its difficulties, at present, are much better understood than its resources; and that the intellect of mankind is only beginning to contrive the means of organising it in detail, so as to overcome the one and derive the greatest advantage from the other.

If, therefore, the choice were to be made between Communism with all its chances, and the present state of society with all its sufferings and injustices; if the institution of private property necessarily carried with it as a consequence, that the produce of labour should be apportioned as we now see it, almost in an inverse ratio to the labour—the largest portions to those who have never worked at all, the next largest to those whose work is almost nominal, and so in a descending scale, the remuneration dwindling as the work grows harder and more disagreeable, until the most fatiguing and exhausting bodily labour cannot count with certainty on being able to earn even the necessaries of life; if this, or Communism, were the alternative, all the difficulties, great or small, of Communism would be but as dust in the balance. But to make the comparison applicable, we must compare Communism at its best, with the régime of individual property, not as it is, but as it might be made. The principle of private property has never yet had a fair trial in any country; and less so, perhaps, in this country than in some others. The social arrangements of modern Europe commenced from a distribution of property which was the result, not of just partition, or acquisition by industry, but of conquest and violence: notwithstanding what industry has been doing for many centuries to modify the work of force, the system still retains many and large traces of its origin. The laws of property have never yet conformed to the principles on which the justification of private property rests. They have made property of things which never ought to be property, and absolute property where only a qualified property ought to exist. They have not held the balance fairly between human beings, but have heaped impediments upon some, to give advantage to others; they have purposely fostered inequalities and prevented all from starting fair in the race. That all should indeed start on perfectly equal terms, is inconsistent with any law of private property: but if as much pains as has been taken to aggravate the inequality of chances arising from the natural working of the principle, had been taken to temper that inequality by every means not subversive of the principle itself; if the tendency of legislation had been to favour the diffusion, instead of the concentration of wealth—to encourage the subdivision of the large masses, instead of striving to keep them together; the principle of individual property would have been found to have no necessary connexion with the physical and social evils which almost all Socialist writers assume to be inseparable from it.

Private property, in every defence made of it, is supposed to mean, the guarantee to individuals, of the fruits of their own labour and abstinence. The guarantee to them of the fruits of the labour and abstinence of others, translated to them without any merit or exertion of their own, is not of the essence of the institution, but a mere incidental consequence, which when it reaches a certain height, does not promote, but conflicts with the ends which render private property legitimate. To judge of the final destination of the institution of property, we must suppose everything rectified, which causes the institution to work in a manner opposed to that equitable principle, of proportion between remuneration and exertion, on which in every vindication of it that will bear the light, it is assumed to be grounded. We must also suppose two conditions realised, without which neither Communism nor any other laws or institutions could make the condition of the mass of mankind other than degraded and miserable. One of these conditions is, universal education; the other, a due limitation of the numbers of the community. With these, there could be no poverty even under the present social institutions: and these being supposed, the question of Socialism is not, as generally stated by Socialists, a question of flying to the sole refuge against the evils which now bear down humanity; but a mere question of comparative advantages, which futurity must determine. We are too ignorant either of what individual agency in its best form, or Socialism in its best form, can accomplish, to be qualified to decide which of the two will be the ultimate form of human society.

If a conjecture may be hazarded, the decision will probably depend mainly on one consideration, viz. which of the two systems is consistent with the greatest amount of human liberty and spontaneity. After the means of subsistence are assured, the next in strength of the personal wants of human beings is liberty; and (unlike the physical wants, which as civilisation advances become more moderate and more amenable to control) it increases instead of diminishing in intensity, as the intelligence and the moral faculties are more developed. The perfection both of social arrangements and of practical morality would be, to secure to all persons complete independence and freedom of action, subject to no restriction but that of not doing injury to others: and the education which taught, or the social institutions which required them to exchange the control of their own actions for any amount of comfort or affluence, or to renounce liberty for the sake of equality, would deprive them of one of the most elevated characteristics of human nature. It remains to be discovered how far the preservation of this characteristic would be found compatible with the communistic organisation of society. No doubt, this, like all the other objections to the Socialist schemes, is vastly exaggerated. The members of the association need not be required to live together more than they do now, nor need they be controlled in the disposal of their individual share of the produce, and of the probably large amount of leisure which, if they limited their production to things really worth producing, they would possess. Individuals need not be chained to an occupation, or to a particular locality. The restraints of Communism would be freedom in comparison with the present condition of the majority of the human race. The generality of labourers in this and most other countries, have as little choice of occupation or freedom of locomotion, are practically as dependent on fixed rules and on the will of others, as they could be on any system short of actual slavery; to say nothing of the entire domestic subjection of one half the species, to which it is the signal honour of Owenism and most other forms of Socialism that they assign equal rights, in all respects, with those of the hitherto dominant sex. But it is not by comparison with the present bad state of society that the claims of Communism can be estimated; nor is it sufficient that it should promise greater personal and mental freedom than is now enjoyed by those who have not enough of either to deserve the name. The question is whether there would be any asylum left for individuality of character; whether public opinion would not be a tyrannical yoke; whether the absolute dependence of each on all, and surveillance of each by all, would not grind all down into a tame uniformity of thoughts, feelings, and actions. This is already one of the glaring evils of the existing state of society, notwithstanding a much greater diversity of education and pursuits, and a much less absolute dependence of the individual on the mass, than would exist in the Communistic régime. No society in which eccentricity is a matter of reproach, can be in a wholesome state. It is yet to be ascertained whether the Communistic scheme would be consistent with that multiform development of human nature, those manifold unlikenesses, that diversity of tastes and talents, and variety of intellectual points of view, which not only form a great part of the interest of human life, but by bringing intellects into a stimulating collision, and by presenting to each innumerable notions that he would not have conceived of himself, are the mainspring of mental and moral progression.

# XIX Moral Philosophy: Concepts of Nature and Utility

ADAM SMITH                                                                XIX.1

Philosophic calm

from 'The Principles which lead and direct
Philosophical Enquiries, illustrated by the History
of Astronomy', written 1750s

Philosophy is the science of the connecting principles of nature. Nature, after the largest experience that common observation can acquire, seems to abound with events which appear solitary and incoherent with all that go before them, which therefore disturb the easy movement of the imagination; which make its ideas succeed each other, if one may say so, by irregular starts and sallies; and which thus tend, in some measure, to introduce . . . confusions and distractions. . . . Philosophy, by representing the invisible chains which bind together all these disjointed objects, endeavours to introduce order into this chaos of jarring and discordant appearances, to allay this tumult of the imagination, and to restore it, when it surveys the great revolutions of the universe, to that tone of tranquillity and composure, which is both most agreeable in itself, and most suitable to its nature. Philosophy, therefore, may be regarded as one of those arts which address themselves to the imagination. . . . It is the most sublime of all the agreeable arts, and its revolutions have been the greatest, the most frequent, and the most distinguished of all those that have happened in the literary world.

ADAM SMITH                                                                XIX.2

'Of the Beauty which the Appearance of Utility
bestows upon all the Productions of Art, and of
the extensive Influence of this Species of Beauty'

from *The Theory of Moral Sentiments*, 1759

That utility is one of the principal sources of beauty, has been observed by every body who has considered with any attention what constitutes the nature of beauty. The conveniency of a house gives pleasure to the spectator as well as its regularity; and he is as much hurt when he observes the contrary defect, as when he sees the correspondent windows of different forms, or the door not placed exactly in the middle of the building. That the fitness of any system or machine to produce the end for which it was intended, bestows a certain propriety and beauty upon the whole, and renders the very thought and contemplation of it agreeable, is so very obvious, that nobody has overlooked it. . . .

But that this fitness, this happy contrivance of any production of art, should often be more valued than the very end for which it was intended; and that the exact adjustment of the means for attaining any conveniency or pleasure should frequently be more regarded than that very conveniency or pleasure, in the attainment of which their whole merit would seem to consist, has not, so far as I know, been yet taken notice of by any body. That this, however, is very frequently the case, may be observed in a thousand instances, both in the most frivolous and in the most important concerns of human life.

When a person comes into his chamber and finds the chairs all standing in the middle of the room, he is angry with his servant, and rather than see them continue in that disorder, perhaps takes the trouble himself to set them all in their places with their backs to the wall. The whole propriety of this new situation arises from its superior conveniency in leaving the floor free and disengaged. To attain this conveniency he voluntarily puts himself to more trouble than all he could have suffered from the want of it; since nothing was more easy than to have set himself down upon one of them, which is probably what he does when his labour is over. What he wanted therefore, it seems, was not so much this conveniency, as that arrangement of things which promotes it. Yet it is this conveniency which ultimately recommends that arrangement, and bestows upon it the whole of its propriety and beauty.

A watch, in the same manner, that falls behind above two minutes in a day, is despised by one curious in watches. He sells it perhaps for a couple of guineas, and purchases another at fifty, which will not lose above a minute in a fortnight. The sole use of watches, however, is to tell us what o'clock it is, and to hinder us from breaking any engagement, or suffering any other inconveniency by our ignorance in that particular point. But the person so nice with regard to this machine will not always be found either more scrupulously punctual than other men, or more anxiously concerned upon any other account to know precisely what time of day it is. What interests him is not so much the attainment of this piece of knowledge, as the perfection of the machine which serves to attain it.

How many people ruin themselves by laying out money on trinkets of frivolous utility? What pleases these lovers of toys, is not so much the utility as the aptness of the machines which are fitted to promote it. All their pockets are stuffed with little conveniencies. They contrive new pockets, unknown in the clothes of other people, in order to carry a greater number. They walk about loaded with a multitude of baubles, in weight, and sometimes in value, not inferior to an ordinary Jew's-box, some of which may sometimes be of some little use, but all of which might at all times be very well spared, and of which the whole utility is certainly not worth the fatigue of bearing the burden.

Nor is it only with regard to such frivolous objects that our conduct is influenced by this principle; it is often the secret motive of the most serious and important pursuits of both private and public life.

The poor man's son, whom heaven in its anger has visited with ambition, when he begins to look around him, admires the condition of the rich. He finds the cottage of his father too small for his accommodation, and fancies he should be lodged more at his ease in a palace. He is displeased with being obliged to walk afoot, or to endure the fatigue of riding on horseback. He sees his superiors carried about in machines, and imagines that in one of these he could travel with less inconveniency. He feels himself naturally indolent, and willing to serve himself with his own hands as little as possible; and judges that a numerous retinue of servants would save him from a great deal of trouble. He thinks if he had attained all these, he would sit still contentedly, and be quiet, enjoying himself in the thought of the happiness and tranquillity of his situation. He is enchanted with the distant idea of this felicity. It appears in his fancy like the life of some superior rank of beings, and, in order to arrive at it, he devotes himself for ever to the pursuit of wealth and greatness. To obtain the conveniencies which these afford, he submits in the first year, nay, in the first month of his application, to more fatigue of body and more uneasiness of mind, than he could have suffered through the whole of his life from the want of them. He studies to distinguish himself in some laborious profession. With the most unrelenting industry he labours night and day to acquire talents superior to all his competitors. He endeavours next to bring those talents into public view, and with equal assiduity solicits every opportunity of employment. For this purpose he makes his court to all mankind; he serves those whom he hates, and is obsequious to those whom he despises. Through the whole of his life he pursues the idea of a certain artificial and elegant repose which he may never arrive at, for which he sacrifices a real tranquillity that is at all times in his power, and which, if in the extremity of old age he should at last attain to it, he will find to be in no respect preferable to that humble security and contentment which he had abandoned for it. It is then, in the last dregs of life, his body wasted with toil and diseases, his mind galled and ruffled by the memory of a thousand injuries and disappointments which he imagines he has met with from the injustice of his enemies, or from the perfidy and ingratitude of his friends, that he begins at last to find that wealth and greatness are mere trinkets of frivolous utility, no more adapted for procuring ease of body or tranquillity of mind, than the tweezer-cases of the lover of toys; and like them, too, more troublesome to the person who carries them about with him than all the advantages they can afford him are commodious. There is no other real difference between them, except that the conveniencies of the one are somewhat more observable than those of the other. . . . But in the langour of disease and the weariness of old age, the pleasures of the vain and empty distinctions of greatness disappear. To one in this situation they are no longer capable of recommending those toilsome pursuits in which they had formerly engaged him. In his heart he curses ambition, and vainly regrets the ease and the indolence of youth, pleasures which are fled for ever, and which he has foolishly sacrificed for what, when he has got it, can afford him no real satisfaction. In this miserable aspect does greatness appear to every man when reduced, either by spleen or disease, to observe with attention his own situation, and to consider what it is that is really wanting to his happiness. Power and riches appear then to be, what they are, enormous and operose machines contrived to produce a few trifling conveniencies to the body, consisting of springs the most nice and delicate, which must be kept in order with the most anxious attention, and which, in spite of all our care, are ready every moment to burst into pieces, and to crush in their ruins their unfortunate possessor. They are immense fabrics which it requires the labour of a life to raise, which threaten every moment to overwhelm the person that dwells in them, and which, while they stand, though they may save him from some smaller inconveniencies, can protect him from none of the severer inclemencies of the season. They keep off the summer shower, not the winter storm, but leave him always as much, and sometimes more, exposed than before to anxiety, to fear, and to sorrow; to diseases, to danger, and to death.

But though this splenetic philosophy, which in time of sickness or low spirits is familiar to every man, thus entirely depreciates those great objects of human desire, when in better health and in better humour, we never fail to regard them under a more agreeable aspect. Our imagination, which in pain and sorrow seems to be confined and cooped up within our own persons, in times of ease and prosperity expands itself to every thing around us. We are then charmed with the beauty of that accommodation which reins in the palaces and economy of the great; and admire how every thing is adapted to promote their ease, to prevent their wants, to gratify their wishes, and to amuse and entertain their most frivolous desires. If we consider the real satisfaction which all these things are capable of affording, by itself and separated from the beauty of that arrangement which is fitted to promote it, it will always appear in the highest degree contemptible and trifling. But we rarely view it in this abstract and philosophical light. We naturally confound it in our imagination with the order, the regular and harmonious movement of the system, the machine or economy by means of which it is produced. The pleasures of wealth and greatness, when considered in this complex view, strike the imagination as something grand, and beautiful, and noble, of which the attainment is well worth all the toil and anxiety which we are so apt to bestow upon it.

And it is well that nature imposes upon us in this manner. It is this deception which rouses and keeps in continual motion the industry of mankind. It is this which first prompted them to cultivate the ground, to build houses, to found cities and commonwealths, and to invent and improve all the sciences and arts, which ennoble and embellish human life; which have entirely changed the whole face of the globe, have turned the rude forests of nature into agreeable and fertile plains, and made the trackless and barren ocean a new fund of subsistence, and the great high road of communication to the different nations of the earth. The earth, by these labours of mankind, has been obliged to redouble her natural fertility, and to maintain a greater multitude of inhabitants.

It is to no purpose that the proud and unfeeling landlord views his extensive fields, and without a thought for the wants of his brethren, in imagination consumes himself the whole harvest that grows upon them. The homely and vulgar proverb, that the eye is larger than the belly, never was more fully verified than with regard to him. The capacity of his stomach bears no proportion to the immensity of his desires, and will receive no more than that of the meanest peasant. The rest he is obliged to distribute among those who prepare, in the nicest manner, that little which he himself makes use of, among those who fit up the palace in which this little is to be consumed, among those who provide and keep in order all the different baubles and trinkets which are employed in the economy of greatness; all of whom thus derive from his luxury and caprice that share of the necessaries of life which they would in vain have expected from his humanity or his justice. The produce of the soil maintains at all times nearly that number of inhabitants which it is capable of maintaining. The rich only select from the heap what is most precious and agreeable. They consume little more than the poor; and in spite of their natural selfishness and rapacity, though they mean only their own conveniency, though the sole end which they propose from the labours of all the thousands whom they employ be the gratification of their own vain and insatiable desires, they divide with the poor the produce of all their improvements. They are led by an invisible hand to make nearly the same distribution of the necessaries of life which would have been made had the earth been divided into equal portions among all its inhabitants; and thus, without intending it, without knowing it, advance the interest of the society, and afford means to the multiplication of the species. When providence divided the earth among a few lordly masters, it neither forgot nor abandoned those who seemed to have been left out in the partition. These last, too, enjoy their share of all that it produces. In what constitutes the real happiness of human life, they are in no respect inferior to those who would seem so much above them. In ease of body and peace of mind, all the different ranks of life are nearly upon a level, and the beggar, who suns himself by the side of the highway, possesses that security which kings are fighting for.

The same principle, the same love of system, the same regard to the beauty of order, of art and contrivance, frequently serves to recommend those institutions which tend to promote the public welfare. When a patriot exerts himself for the improvement of any part of the public police, his conduct does not always arise from pure sympathy with the happiness of those who are to reap the benefit of it. It is not commonly from a fellow-feeling with carriers and waggoners that a public-spirited man encourages the mending of high roads. When the Legislature establishes premiums and other encouragements to advance the linen or woollen manufactures, its conduct seldom proceeds from pure sympathy with the wearer of cheap or fine cloth, and much less from that with the manufacturer or merchant. The perfection of police, the extension of trade and manufactures, are noble and magnificent objects. The contemplation of them pleases us, and we are interested in whatever can tend to advance them. They make part of the great system of government, and the wheels of the political machine seem to move with more harmony and ease by means of them. We take pleasure in beholding the perfection of so beautiful and so grand a system, and we are uneasy till we remove any obstruction that can in the least disturb or encumber the regularity of its motions. All constitutions of government, however, are valued only in proportion as they tend to promote the happiness of those who live under them. This is their sole use and end. From a certain spirit of system, however, from a certain love of art and contrivance, we sometimes seem to value the means more than the end, and to be eager to promote the happiness of our fellow-creatures, rather from a view to perfect and improve a certain beautiful and orderly system than from any immediate sense or feeling of what they either suffer or enjoy. There have been men of the greatest public spirit, who have shewn themselves in other respects not very sensible to the feelings of humanity. And, on the contrary, there have been men of the greatest humanity, who seem to have been entirely devoid of public spirit. Every man may find in the circle of his acquaintance instances both of the one kind and the other.

# JEREMY BENTHAM                                    XIX.3
## Of the Principle of Utility

from *An Introduction to the Principles of Morals and Legislation*, written 1780

I. Nature has placed mankind under the governance of two sovereign masters, *pain* and *pleasure*. It is for them alone to point out what we ought to do, as well as to determine what we shall do. On the one hand the standard of right and wrong, on the other the chain of causes and effects, are fastened to their throne. They govern us in all we do, in all we say, in all we think: every effort we can make to throw off our subjection, will serve but to demonstrate and confirm it. In words a man may pretend to abjure their empire: but in reality he will remain subject to it all the while. The *principle of utility* recognizes this subjection, and assumes it for the foundation of that system, the object of which is to rear the fabric of felicity by the hands of reason and of law. Systems which attempt to question it, deal in sounds instead of sense, in caprice instead of reason, in darkness instead of light

But enough of metaphor and declamation: it is not by such means that moral science is to be improved.

II. The principle of utility is the foundation of the present work: it will be proper therefore at the outset to give an explicit and determinate account of what is meant by it. By the principle of utility is meant that principle which approves or disapproves of every action whatsoever, according to the tendency which it appears to have to augment or diminish the happiness of the party whose interest is in question: or, what is the same thing in other words, to promote or to oppose that happiness. I say of every action whatsoever; and therefore not only of every action of a private individual, but of every measure of government.

III. By utility is meant that property in any object, whereby it tends to produce benefit, advantage, pleasure, good, or happiness, (all this in the present case comes to the same thing) or (what comes again to the same thing) to prevent the happening of mischief, pain, evil, or unhappiness to the party whose interest is considered: if that party be the community in general, then the happiness of the community: if a particular individual, then the happiness of that individual.

IV. The interest of the community is one of the most general expressions that can occur in the phraseology of morals: no wonder that the meaning of it is often lost. When it has a meaning, it is this. The community is a fictitious *body*, composed of the individual persons who are considered as constituting as it were its *members*. The interest of the community then is, what?—the sum of the interests of the several members who compose it.

V. It is in vain to talk of the interest of the community, without understanding what is the interest of the individual. A thing is said to promote the interest, or to be *for* the interest, of an individual, when it tends to add to the sum total of his pleasures: or, what comes to the same thing, to diminish the sum total of his pains.

VI. An action then may be said to be conformable to the principle of utility, or, for shortness sake, to utility, (meaning with respect to the community at large) when the tendency it has to augment the happiness of the community is greater than any it has to diminish it.

VII. A measure of government (which is but a particular kind of action, performed by a particular person or persons) may be said to be conformable to or dictated by the principle of unity, when in like manner the tendency which it has to augment the happiness of the community is greater than any which it has to diminish it.

VIII. When an action, or in particular a measure of government, is supposed by a man to be conformable to the principle of utility, it may be convenient, for the purposes of discourse, to imagine a kind of law or dictate, called a law or dictate of utility: and to speak of the action in question, as being conformable to such law or dictate.

IX. A man may be said to be a partizan of the principle of utility, when the approbation or disapprobation he annexes to any action, or to any measure, is determined by, and proportioned to the tendency which he conceives it to have to augment or to diminish the happiness of the community: or in other words, to its conformity or unconformity to the laws or dictates of utility.

X. Of an action that is conformable to the principle of utility, one may always say either that it is one that ought to be done, or at least that it is not one that ought not to be done. One may say also, that it is right it should be done; at least that it is not wrong it should be done: that it is a right action; at least that it is not a wrong action. When thus interpreted, the words *ought*, and *right* and *wrong*, and others of that stamp, have a meaning: when otherwise, they have none.

# JEREMY BENTHAM                                                    XIX.4

## Self interest

from *The Book of Fallacies*, 1824

In every human breast, rare and short-lived ebullitions, the result of some extraordinary strong stimulus or incitement excepted, self-regarding interest is predominant over social interest: each person's own individual interest, over the interests of all other persons taken together.

In the few instances, if any, in which, throughout the whole tenour or the general tenour of his life, a person sacrifices his own individual interest to that of any other person or persons, such person or persons will be a person or persons with whom he is connected by some domestic or other private and narrow tie of sympathy; not the whole number, or the majority of the whole number, of the individuals of which the political community to which he belongs is composed.

If in any political community there be any individuals by whom, for a constancy, the interests of all the other members put together are preferred to the interest composed of their own individual interest, and that of the few persons particularly connected with them, these public-spirited individuals will be so few, and at the same time so impossible to distinguish from the rest, that to every practical purpose they may, without any practical error, be laid out of the account.

# JOHN STUART MILL                                              XIX.5
## 'Nature'

from *Nature, the Utility of Religion, and Theism,*
written 1850–8

Nature, natural, and the group of words derived from them, or allied to them in etymology, have at all times filled a great place in the thoughts and taken a strong hold on the feelings of mankind. That they should have done so is not surprising, when we consider what the words, in their primitive and most obvious signification, represent; but it is unfortunate that a set of terms which play so great a part in moral and metaphysical speculation, should have acquired many meanings different from the primary one, yet sufficiently allied to it to admit of confusion. The words have thus become entangled in so many foreign associations, mostly of a very powerful and tenacious character, that they have come to excite, and to be the symbols of, feelings which their original meaning will by no means justify; and which have made them one of the most copious sources of false taste, false philosophy, false morality, and even bad law.

The most important application of the Socratic Elenchus, as exhibited and improved by Plato, consists in dissecting large abstractions of this description; fixing down to a precise definition the meaning which as popularly used they merely shadow forth, and questioning and testing the common maxims and opinions in which they bear a part. It is to be regretted that among the instructive specimens of this kind of investigation which Plato has left, and to which subsequent times have been so much indebted for whatever intellectual clearness they have attained, he has not enriched posterity with a dialogue περὶ φύσεως.

303

If the idea denoted by the word had been subjected to his searching analysis, and the popular commonplaces in which it figures had been submitted to the ordeal of his powerful dialectics, his successors probably would not have rushed, as they speedily did, into modes of thinking and reasoning of which the fallacious use of that word formed the corner stone; a kind of fallacy from which he was himself singularly free.

According to the Platonic method which is still the best type of such investigations, the first thing to be done with so vague a term is to ascertain precisely what it means. It is also a rule of the same method, that the meaning of an abstraction is best sought for in the concrete—of an universal in the particular. Adopting this course with the word Nature, the first question must be, what is meant by the 'nature' of a particular object? as of fire, of water, or of some individual plant or animal? Evidently the *ensemble* or aggregate of its powers or properties: the modes in which it acts on other things (counting among those things the senses of the observer) and the modes in which other things act upon it; to which, in the case of a sentient being, must be added, its own capacities of feeling, or being conscious. The Nature of the thing means all this; means its entire capacity of exhibiting phenomena. And since the phenomena which a thing exhibits, however much they vary in different circumstances, are always the same in the same circumstances, they admit of being described in general forms of words, which are called the *laws* of the thing's nature. Thus it is a law of the nature of water that under the mean pressure of the atmosphere at the level of the sea, it boils at 212° Fahrenheit.

As the nature of any given thing is the aggregate of its powers and properties, so Nature in the abstract is the aggregate of the powers and properties of all things. Nature means the sum of all phenomena, together with the causes which produce them; including not only all that happens, but all that is capable of happening; the unused capabilities of causes being as much a part of the idea of Nature, as those which take effect. Since all phenomena which have been sufficiently examined are found to take place with regularity, each having certain fixed conditions, positive and negative, on the occurrence of which it invariably happens; mankind have been able to ascertain, either by direct observation or by reasoning processes grounded on it, the conditions of the occurrence of many phenomena; and the progress of science mainly consists in ascertaining those conditions. When discovered they can be expressed in general propositions, which are called laws of the particular phenomenon, and also, more generally, Laws of Nature. Thus, the truth that all material objects tend towards one another with a force directly as their masses and inversely as the square of their distance, is a law of Nature. The proposition that air and food are necessary to to animal life, if it be as we have good reason to believe, true without exception, is also a law of nature, though the phenomenon of which it is the law is special, and not, like gravitation, universal.

Nature, then, in this its simplest acceptation, is a collective name for all facts, actual and possible: or (to speak more accurately) a name for the mode, partly known to us and partly unknown, in which all things take place. For the word suggests, not so much the multitudinous detail of the phenomena, as the conception which might be formed in their manner of existence as a mental whole, by a mind possessing a complete knowledge of them: to which conception it is the aim of science to raise itself, by successive steps of generalization from experience.

Such, then, is a correct definition of the word Nature. But this definition corresponds only to one of the senses of that ambiguous term. It is evidently inapplicable to some of the modes in which the word is familiarly employed. For example, it entirely conflicts with the common form of speech by which Nature is opposed to Art, and natural to artificial. For in the sense of the word Nature which has just been defined, and which is the true scientific sense, Art is as much Nature as anything else; and everything which is artificial is natural— Art has no independent powers of its own: Art is but the employment of the powers of Nature for an end. Phenomena produced by human agency, no less than those which as far as we are concerned are spontaneous, depend on the properties of the elementary forces, or of the elementary substances and their compounds. The united powers of the whole human race could not create a new property of matter in general, or of any one of its species. We can only take advantage for our purposes of the properties which we find. A ship floats by the same laws of specific gravity and equilibrium, as a tree uprooted by the wind and blown into the water. The corn which men raise for food, grows and produces its grain by the same laws of vegetation by which the wild rose and the mountain strawberry bring forth their flowers and fruit. A house stands and holds together by the natural properties, the weight and cohesion of the materials which compose it: a steam engine works by the natural expansive force of steam, exerting a pressure upon one part of a system of arrangements, which pressure, by the mechanical properties of the lever, is transferred from that to another part where it raises the weight or removes the obstacle brought into connexion with it. In these and all other artificial operations the office of man is, as has often been remarked, a very limited one; it consists in moving things into certain places. We move objects, and by doing this, bring some things into contact which were separate, or separate others which were in contact: and by this simple change of place, natural forces previously dormant are called into action, and produce the desired effect. Even the volition which designs, the intelligence which contrives, and the muscular

305

force which executes these movements, are themselves powers of Nature.

It thus appears that we must recognize at least two principal meanings in the word Nature. In one sense, it means all the powers existing in either the outer or the inner world and everything which takes place by means of those powers. In another sense, it means, not everything which happens, but only what takes place without the agency, or without the voluntary and intentional agency, of man. This distinction is far from exhausting the ambiguities of the word; but it is the key to most of those on which important consequences depend.

Such, then, being the two principal senses of the word Nature; in which of these is it taken, or is it taken in either, when the word and its derivatives are used to convey ideas of commendation, approval, and even moral obligation? . . . .

When it is asserted, or implied, that Nature, or the laws of Nature, should be conformed to, is the Nature which is meant, Nature in the first sense of the term, meaning all which is—the powers and properties of all things? But in this signification, there is no need of a recommendation to act according to nature, since it is what nobody can possibly help doing, and equally whether he acts well or ill. There is no mode of acting which is not conformable to Nature in this sense of the term, and all modes of acting are so in exactly the same degree. Every action is the exertion of some natural power, and its effects of all sorts are so many phenomena of nature, produced by the powers and properties of some of the objects of nature, in exact obedience to some law or laws of nature. When I voluntarily use my organs to take in food, the act, and its consequences, take place according to laws of nature: if instead of food I swallow poison, the case is exactly the same. To bid people conform to the laws of nature when they have no power but what the laws of nature give them—when it is a physical impossibility for them to do the smallest thing otherwise than through some law of nature, is an absurdity. . . .

Let us then consider whether we can attach any meaning to the supposed practical maxim of following Nature, in this second sense of the word, in which Nature stands for that which takes place without human intervention. In Nature as thus understood, is the spontaneous course of things when left to themselves, the rule to be followed in endeavouring to adapt things to our use? But it is evident at once that the maxim, taken in this sense, is not merely, as it is in the other sense, superfluous and unmeaning, but palpably absurd and self-contradictory. For while human action cannot help conforming to Nature in the one meaning of the term, the very aim and object of action is to alter and improve Nature in the other meaning. If the natural course of things were perfectly right and satisfactory, to act at all would be a gratuitous

306

meddling, which as it could not make things better, must make them worse. Or if action at all could be justified, it would only be when in direct obedience to instincts, since these might perhaps be accounted part of the spontaneous order of Nature; but to do anything with fore-thought and purpose, would be a violation of that perfect order. If the artificial is not better than the natural, to what end are all the arts of life? To dig, to plough, to build, to wear clothes, are direct infringe-ments of the injunction to follow nature.

Accordingly it would be said by every one, even of those most under the influence of the feelings which prompt the injunction, that to apply it to such cases as those just spoken of, would be to push it too far. Everybody professes to approve and admire many great triumphs of Art over Nature: the junction by bridges of shores which Nature had made separate, the draining of Nature's marshes, the excavation of her wells, the dragging to light of what she has buried at immense depths in the earth; the turning away of her thunderbolts by lightning rods, of her inundations by embankments, of her ocean by breakwaters. But to commend these and similar feats, is to acknowledge that the ways of Nature are to be conquered, not obeyed: that her powers are often towards man in the position of enemies, from whom he must wrest, by force and ingenuity, what little he can for his own use, and deserves to be applauded when that little is rather more than might be expected from his physical weakness in comparison to those gigantic powers. All praise of Civilization, or Art, or Contrivance, is so much dispraise of Nature; an admission of imperfection, which it is man's business, and merit, to be always endeavouring to correct or mitigate. . . .

With regard to [the] hypothesis, that all natural impulses, all propen-sities sufficiently universal and sufficiently spontaneous to be capable of passing for instincts, must exist for good ends, and ought to be only regulated, not repressed; this is of course true of the majority of them, for the species could not have continued to exist unless most of its inclinations had been directed to things needful or useful for its preser-vation. But unless the instincts can be reduced to a very small number indeed, it must be allowed that we have also bad instincts which it should be the aim of education not simply to regulate but to extirpate, or rather (what can be done even to an instinct) to starve them by dis-use. Those who are inclined to multiply the number of instincts, usually include among them one which they call destructiveness: an instinct to destroy for destruction's sake. I can conceive no good reason for pre-serving this, no more than another propensity which if not an instinct is very like one, what has been called the instinct of domination; a delight in exercising despotism, in holding other beings in subjection to our will. The man who takes pleasure in the mere exertion of authority, apart from the purpose for which it is to be employed, is the last person

307

in whose hands one would willingly entrust it. Again, there are persons who are cruel by character, or, as the phrase is, naturally cruel; who have a real pleasure in inflicting, or seeing the infliction of pain. This kind of cruelty is not mere hardheartedness, absence of pity or remorse; it is a positive thing; a particular kind of voluptuous excitement. The East, and Southern Europe, have afforded, and probably still afford, abundant examples of this hateful propensity. I suppose it will be granted that this is not one of the natural inclinations which it would be wrong to suppress. The only question would be whether it is not a duty to suppress the man himself along with it.

But even if it were true that every one of the elementary impulses of human nature has its good side, and may by a sufficient amount of artificial training be made more useful than hurtful; how little would this amount to, when it must in any case be admitted that without such training all of them, even those which are necessary to our preservation, would fill the world with misery, making human life an exaggerated likeness of the odious scene of violence and tyranny which is exhibited by the rest of the animal kingdom, except in so far as tamed and disciplined by man. There, indeed, those who flatter themselves with the notion of reading the purposes of the Creator in his works, ought in consistency to have seen grounds for inferences from which they have shrunk. If there are any marks at all of special design in creation, one of the things most evidently designed is that a large proportion of all animals should pass their existence in tormenting and devouring other animals. They have been lavishly fitted out with the instruments necessary for that purpose; their strongest instincts impel them to it, and many of them seem to have been constructed incapable of supporting themselves by any other food. If a tenth part of the pains which have been expended in finding benevolent adaptations in all nature, had been employed in collecting evidence to blacken the character of the Creator, what scope for comment would not have been found in the entire existence of the lower animals, divided, with scarcely an exception, into devourers and devoured, and a prey to a thousand ills from which they are denied the faculties necessary for protecting themselves! If we are not obliged to believe the animal creation to be the work of a demon, it is because we need not suppose it to have been made by a Being of infinite power. But if imitation of the Creator's will as revealed in nature, were applied as a rule of action in this case, the most atrocious enormities of the worst men would be more than justified by the apparent intention of Providence that throughout all animated nature the strong should prey upon the weak.

The preceding observations are far from having exhausted the almost infinite variety of modes and occasions in which the idea of conformity to nature is introduced as an element into the ethical appreciation of actions and dispositions. The same favourable prejudgment follows the word nature through the numerous acceptations, in which it is employed as a distinctive term for certain parts of the constitution of humanity as contrasted with other parts. We have hitherto confined ourselves to one of these acceptations, in which it stands as a general designation for those parts of our mental and moral constitution which are supposed to be innate, in contradistinction to those which are acquired; as when nature is contrasted with education; or when a savage state, without laws, arts, or knowledge, is called a state of nature; or when the question is asked whether benevolence, or the moral sentiment, is natural or acquired; or whether some persons are poets or orators by nature and others not. But in another and a more lax sense, any manifestations by human beings are often termed natural, when it is merely intended to say that they are not studied or designedly assumed in the particular case; as when a person is said to move or speak with natural grace; or when it is said that a person's natural manner or character is so and so; meaning that it is so when he does not attempt to control or disguise it. In a still looser acceptation, a person is said to be naturally, that which he was until some special cause had acted upon him, or which it is supposed he would be if some such cause were withdrawn. Thus a person is said to be naturally dull, but to have made himself intelligent by study and perseverance; to be naturally cheerful, but soured by misfortune; naturally ambitious, but kept down by want of opportunity. Finally, the word natural, applied to feelings or conduct, often seems to mean no more than that they are such as are ordinarily found in human beings; as when it is said that a person acted, on some particular occasion, as it was natural to do; or that to be affected in a particular way by some sight, or sound, or thought, or incident in life, is perfectly natural.

In all these senses of the term, the quality called natural is very often confessedly a worse quality than the one contrasted with it; but whenever its being so is not too obvious to be questioned, the idea seems to be entertained that by describing it as natural, something has been said amounting to a considerable presumption in its favour. For my part I can perceive only one sense in which nature, or naturalness, in a human being, are really terms of praise; and then the praise is only negative: namely when used to denote the absence of affectation. Affectation may be defined, the effort to appear what one is not, when the motive or the occasion is not such as either to excuse the attempt, or to stamp it with the more odious name of hypocrisy. It must be added that the deception is often attempted to be practised on the deceiver himself as well as on others; he imitates the external signs of qualities which he would like to have, in hopes to persuade himself that he has them. Whether in the form of deception or of self-deception, or of something

309

hovering between the two, affectation is very rightly accounted a reproach, and naturalness, understood as the reverse of affectation, a merit. But a more proper term by which to express this estimable quality would be sincerity; a term which has fallen from its original elevated meaning, and popularly denotes only a subordinate branch of the cardinal virtue it once designated as a whole.

Sometimes also, in cases where the term affectation would be inappropriate, since the conduct or demeanour spoken of is really praiseworthy, people say in disparagement of the person concerned, that such conduct or demeanour is not natural to him; and make uncomplimentary comparisons between him and some other person, to whom it is natural: meaning that what in the one seemed excellent was the effect of temporary excitement, or of a great victory over himself, while in the other it is the result to be expected from the habitual character. This mode of speech is not open to censure, since nature is here simply a term for the person's ordinary disposition, and if he is praised it is not for being natural, but for being naturally good.

Conformity to nature, has no connection whatever with right and wrong. The idea can never be fitly introduced into ethical discussions at all, except, occasionally and partially, into the question of degrees of culpability. To illustrate this point, let us consider the phrase by which the greatest intensity of condemnatory feeling is conveyed in connection with the idea of nature—the word unnatural. That a thing is unnatural, in any precise meaning which can be attached to the word, is no argument for its being blamable; since the most criminal actions are to a being like man, not more unnatural than most of the virtues. The acquisition of virtue has in all ages been accounted a work of labour and difficulty, while the *descensus Averni* on the contrary is of proverbial facility: and it assuredly requires in most persons a greater conquest over a greater number of natural inclinations to become eminently virtuous than transcendently vicious. But if an action, or an inclination, has been decided on other grounds to be blamable, it may be a circumstance in aggravation that it is unnatural, that is, repugnant to some strong feeling usually found in human beings; since the bad propensity, whatever it be, has afforded evidence of being both strong and deeply rooted, by having overcome that repugnance. This presumption of course fails if the individual never had the repugnance: and the argument, therefore, is not fit to be urged unless the feeling which is violated by the act, is not only justifiable and reasonable, but is one which it is blamable to be without.

The corresponding plea in extenuation of a culpable act because it was natural, or because it was prompted by a natural feeling, never, I think, ought to be admitted. There is hardly a bad action ever perpetrated which is not perfectly natural, and the motives to which are not perfectly natural feelings. In the eye of reason, therefore, this is no excuse, but it is quite 'natural' that it should be so in the eyes of the multitude; because the meaning of the expression is, that they have a fellow feeling with the offender. When they say that something which they cannot help admitting to be blamable, is nevertheless natural, they mean that they can imagine the possibility of their being themselves tempted to commit it. Most people have a considerable amount of indulgence towards all acts of which they feel a possible source within themselves, reserving their rigour for those which, though perhaps really less bad, they cannot in any way understand how it is possible to commit. If an action convinces them (which it often does on very inadequate grounds) that the person who does it must be a being totally unlike themselves, they are seldom particular in examining the precise degree of blame due to it, or even if blame is properly due to it at all. They measure the degree of guilt by the strength of their antipathy; and hence differences of opinion, and even differences of taste, have been objects of as intense moral abhorrence as the most atrocious crimes.

It will be useful to sum up in a few words the leading conclusions of this Essay.

The word Nature has two principal meanings: it either denotes the entire system of things, with the aggregate of all their properties, or it denotes things as they would be, apart from human intervention.

In the first of these senses, the doctrine that man ought to follow nature is unmeaning; since man has no power to do anything else than follow nature; all his actions are done through, and in obedience to, some one or many of nature's physical or mental laws.

In the other sense of the term, the doctrine that man ought to follow nature, or in other words, ought to make the spontaneous course of things the model of his voluntary actions, is equally irrational and immoral.

Irrational, because all human action whatever, consists in altering, and all useful action in improving, the spontaneous course of nature:

Immoral, because the course of natural phenomena being replete with everything which when committed by human beings is most worthy of abhorrence, any one who endeavoured in his actions to imitate the natural course of things would be universally seen and acknowledged to be the wickedest of men.

The scheme of Nature regarded in its whole extent, cannot have had, for its sole or even principal object, the good of human or other sentient beings. What good it brings to them, is mostly the result of their own exertions. Whatsoever, in nature, gives indication of beneficent design, proves this beneficience to be armed only with limited power; and the duty of man is to co-operate with the beneficent powers,

311

not by imitating but by perpetually striving to amend the course of nature—and bringing that part of it over which we can exercise control, more nearly into conformity with a high standard of justice and goodness.

# XX  Later Painting

JOHN RUSKIN                                                    XX.1

'Millais and Turner'

from 'Pre-Raphaelitism', 1851

Suppose, for instance, two men, equally honest, equally industrious, equally impressed with a humble desire to render some part of what they saw in nature faithfully; and, otherwise, trained in convictions such as I have above endeavoured to induce. But one of them is quiet in temperament, has a feeble memory, no invention and excessively keen sight. The other is impatient in temperament, has a memory which nothing escapes, an invention which never rests, and is comparatively near-sighted.

Set them both free in the same field in a mountain valley. One sees everything, small and large, with almost the same clearness; mountains and grasshoppers alike; the leaves on the branches, the veins in the pebbles, the bubbles in the stream; but he can remember nothing and invent nothing. Patiently he sets himself to his mighty task; abandoning at once all thoughts of seizing transient effects, or giving general impressions of that which his eyes present to him in microscopical dissection, he chooses some small portion out of the infinite scene, and calculates with courage the number of weeks which must elapse before he can do justice to the intensity of his perceptions, or the fulness of matter in his subject.

Meantime, the other has been watching the change of the clouds, and the march of the light along the mountain sides; he beholds the entire scene in broad, soft masses of true gradation, and the very feebleness of his sight is in some sort an advantage to him, in making him more sensible of the aerial mystery of distance, and hiding from him the multitudes of circumstances which it would have been impossible for him to represent. But there is not one change in the casting of the jagged shadows along the hollows of the hills, but it is fixed on his mind for ever; not a flake of spray has broken from the sea of cloud about their bases, but he has watched it as it melts away, and could recall it to its lost place in heaven by the slightest effort of his thoughts. Not only so, but thousands and thousands of such images, of older scenes, remain congregated in his mind, each mingling in new associations with those now visibly passing before him, and these again confused with other images of his own ceaseless, sleepless imagination, flashing by in sudden troops. Fancy how his paper will be covered with stray symbols and blots, and undecipherable shorthand:—as for his sitting down to 'draw from Nature', there was not one of the things which he wished to represent, that stayed for so much as five seconds together: but none of them escaped for all that: they are sealed up in that strange storehouse of his; he may take one of them out perhaps, this day twenty years, and paint it in his dark room, far away. Now observe, you may tell both of these men, when they are young, that they are to be honest, that they have an important function, and that they are not to care what Raphael did. This you may wholesomely impress on them both. But fancy the exquisite absurdity of expecting either of them to possess any of the qualities of the other.

I have supposed the feebleness of sight in the last, and of invention in the first painter, that the contrast between them might be more striking; but, with very slight modification, both the characters are real. Grant to the first considerable inventive power, with exquisite sense of colour; and give to the second, in addition to all his other faculties, the eye of an eagle; and the first is John Everett Millais, the second Joseph Mallord William Turner.


## H. C. MARILLIER                                        XX.2
### The Pre-Raphaelite Brotherhood
from *Dante Gabriel Rossetti*, 1899

In the inauguration of the 'Brotherhood' Rossetti took a specially active part, and the title itself was invented by him. One would not be far wrong in saying that the whole idea was his, and that the two companions who share the honour of its conception were dragged, enthusiastically enough without doubt, not for the first or last time at the glowing wheels of his fervid chariot. 'Rossetti,' says one of them—Mr. Hunt, of course, for Millais was remarkably reticent about those early days—'Rossetti, with his spirit alike subtle and fiery, was essentially a proselytiser, sometimes to an almost absurd degree, but possessed, alike in his poetry and painting, with an appreciation of beauty of the most intense quality.' Millais is credited in the same sentence with a rare combination of artistic faculty and British common sense. 'He was,' says Mr. Hunt, 'beyond almost anyone with whom I have been acquainted, full of a generous quick enthusiasm; a spirit on fire with eagerness to seize whatever he saw was good, which shone in every line of his face, and made it, as Rossetti once said, look sometimes like the face of an angel.' His whole after-career shows how completely this 'Brother' was fascinated and dominated at the time by the imaginative natures round him, and with what wonderful results for art. Though younger than his companions in age, in painting he was already their superior, and his brilliant reputation as a student was invaluable in the hour of strife; but in imaginative and poetic qualities he was, compared with Rossetti, deficient, and such poetic charm as breathes from his early pictures, and from an occasional later one like *The Vale of Rest*, is unquestionably owing in part to the influences under which he fell, and to that 'spirit on fire with eagerness to seize whatever he saw was good.' Of the third member of the trio, the writer of the foregoing appreciations, a fair impression can be got from the autobiographical sketch which he contributed to the 'Contemporary Review' (April, May, June, 1886), in which with almost anatomical minuteness he lays bare the secrets of his early struggle to win a way betwixt art and commerce, and his heroic sacrifices for the former. At the time of the formation of the 'Brotherhood' he was twenty-one years old, and practically out of his studenthood, his style being already formed on the almost painfully laborious lines from which it has never deviated. In the sense in which the 'Brotherhood' professed to be pre-Raphaelite, i.e., in adherence to nature and in choice of great subjects, Holman Hunt was, if the phrase may be permitted, the most eminently pre-Raphaelite of them all. And he has remained so. The long series of journeys undertaken in the East for the purpose of acquiring the proper setting and the true local colour for his scriptural subjects prove that to him at least the profession of 'seeking nature' in its extreme sense was a real one, and not a passing whim begotten of youthful enthusiasm. Mr. Hunt says, nevertheless, that the title of 'Pre-Raphaelite' was adopted partly in a spirit of fun, and, like other names which have acquired honour, was originally a term of reproach invented by their enemies. On this account they prudently decided to keep it secret, and to let no outward symbol of their union appear beyond the mystic initials P.R.B., which were to be used on all their pictures and in private intercourse. . . .

Two men who were much in sympathy with the movement, one of them its more than putative father—Madox Brown and William Bell Scott—might well have joined it; but the former disapproved of anything resembling an artistic clique, and the latter had somewhat similar reasons for not being personally associated with the organization. . . .

The weekly attendances of the Brethren, at first a constant source of pleasure and mutual help, had become very irregular by December, 1850. . . . An attempt was made to revive them in January, 1851, but without effect, and . . . Millais's election to the Academy in 1853 gave a final quietus to the organization, which for some time previously had ceased to exist save in name.

# FORD MADOX HUEFFER

'Work', 1863

from *The Life of Ford Madox Brown*, 1896

August of 1863 saw the completion of the large *Work*.

With regard to the great picture itself I here transcribe Madox Brown's own descriptive comment. It would be a difficult, if not an absolutely impossible, matter to procure a better one—a more characteristic would be out of the question:—

This picture was begun in 1852 at Hampstead. The background, which represents the main street of that suburb not far from the Heath, was painted on the spot.

At that time extensive excavations were going on in the neighbourhood, and, seeing and studying daily as I did the British excavator, or *navvy*, as he designates himself, in the full swing of his activity (with his manly and picturesque costume, and with the rich glow of colour which exercise under a hot sun will impart), it appeared to me that he was at least as worthy of the powers of an English painter as the fisherman of the Adriatic, the peasant of the Campagna, or the Neapolitan lazzarone. Gradually this idea developed itself into that of *Work* as it now exists, with the British excavator for a central group, as the outward and visible type of *Work*. Here are presented the young navvy in the pride of manly health and beauty; the strong fully-developed navvy who does his work and loves his beer; the selfish old bachelor navvy, stout of limb, and perhaps a trifle tough in those regions where compassion is said to reside; the navvy of strong animal nature, who, but that he was when young *taught* to work at useful work, might even now be working at the *useless crank*. Then Paddy with his larry and his pipe in his mouth. The young navvy who occupies the place of hero in this group, and in the picture, stands on what is termed a landing-stage, a platform placed half-way down the trench; two men from beneath shovel the earth up to him as he shovels it on to the pile outside. Next in value of significance to these is the ragged wretch who has never been *taught* to *work*; with his restless, gleaming eyes he doubts and despairs of every one. But for a certain effeminate gentleness of disposition and a love of nature he might have been a burglar! He lives in Flower and Dean Street, where the policemen walk two and two, and the worst cut-throats surround him, but he is harmless; and before the dawn you may see him miles out in the country, collecting his wild weeds and singular plants to awaken interest, and perhaps find a purchaser in some sprouting botanist. When exhausted he will return to his den, his creel of flowers then rests in an open court-yard, the thoroughfare for the crowded inmates of this haunt of vice, and played in by mischievous boys, yet the basket rarely gets interfered with, unless through the unconscious lurch of some drunkard. The breadwinning implements are sacred with the very poor. In the very opposite scale from the man who can't work, at the further corner of the picture, are two men who appear as having nothing to do. These are the brain-workers, who, seeming to be idle, work, and are the cause of well-ordained work and happiness in others—sages, such as in ancient Greece published their opinions in the market square.

16. W. Holman Hunt: The Hireling Shepherd (1351)

15. Henry P. Barker: Miners at Play (1830)

you are about to pass. I would, if permitted, observe that, though at first they may appear just such a group of ragged dirty brats as anywhere get in the way and make a noise, yet, being considered attentively, they, like insects, molluscs, miniature plants, &c., develop qualities to form a most interesting study, and occupy the mind at times when all else might fail to attract. That they are motherless, the baby's black ribbons and their extreme dilapidation indicate, making them all the more worthy of consideration; a mother, however destitute, would scarcely leave the eldest one in such a plight. As to the father, I have no doubt he drinks, and will be sentenced in the police-court for neglecting them. The eldest girl, not more than ten, poor child! is very worn-looking and thin; her frock, evidently the compassionate gift of some grown-up person, she has neither the art nor the means to adapt to her own diminutive proportions—she is fearfully untidy, therefore, and her way of wrenching her brother's hair looks vixenish and against her. But then a germ or rudiment of good housewifery seems to pierce through her disordered envelope, for the younger ones are taken care of, and nestle to her as to a mother; the sunburnt baby, which looks wonderfully solemn and intellectual, as all babies do, as I have no doubt your own little cherub looks at this moment asleep in its charming bassinet, is fat and well-to-do, it has even been put into poor mourning for its mother. The other little one, though it sucks a piece of carrot in lieu of a sugar-plum, and is shoeless, seems healthy and happy, watching the workmen. The care of the two little ones is an anxious charge for the elder girl, and she has become a premature scold all through having to manage that *boy*—that boy, though a merry, good-natured-looking young Bohemian, is evidently the plague of her life, as boys always are. Even now he *will* not leave that workman's barrow alone, and gets his hair well pulled, as is natural. The dog which accompanies them is evidently of the same outcast sort as themselves. The having to do battle for his existence in a hard world has soured his temper, and he frequently fights, as by his torn ear you may know; but the poor children may do as they like with him; rugged democrat as he is, he is gentle to them, only he hates minions of aristocracy in red jackets. The old bachelor navvy's small valuable bull-pup also instinctively distrusts outlandish-looking dogs in jackets.

The couple on horseback in the middle distance consists of a gentleman, still young, and his daughter. (The rich and the poor both marry early, only those of moderate incomes procrastinate.) This gentleman is evidently very rich, probably a colonel in the army, with a seat in Parliament, and fifteen thousand a year and a pack of hounds. He is not an over-dressed man of the tailor's dummy sort—he does not put his fortune on his back, he is too rich for that; moreover, he looks to me an honest, true hearted gentleman (he was painted from one I know), and could he only be got to hear what the two sages in the corner have to say, I have no doubt he would be easily won over. But the road is blocked, and the daughter says we must go back, papa, round the other way.

The man with the beer-tray, calling 'Beer ho!' so lustily, is a specimen of town pluck and energy contrasted with country thews and sinews. He is hump-backed, stunted in his growth, and in all matters of taste vulgar as Birmingham can make him look in the 19th century. As a child he was probably starved, stunted with gin, and suffered to get run over. But energy has brought him through to be a prosperous beer-man, and 'very much respected,' and in his way he also is a sort of hero; that black eye was got probably doing the police of his master's establishment, and

Perhaps one of these may already, before he or others know it, have moulded a nation to his pattern, converted a hitherto combative race to obstinate passivity; with a word may have centupled the tide of emigration, with another, have quenched the political passions of both factions—may have reversed men's notions upon criminals, upon slavery, upon many things, and still be walking about little known to some. The other, in friendly communion with the philosopher, smiling perhaps at some of his wild sallies and cynical thrusts (for Socrates at times strangely disturbs the seriousness of his auditory by the mercilessness of his jokes—against vice and foolishness), is intended for a kindred and yet very dissimilar spirit. A clergyman, such as the Church of England offers examples of—a priest without guile—a gentleman without pride, much in communion with the working classes, 'honouring all men,' 'never weary in well-doing.' Scholar, author, philsopher, and teacher, too, in his way, but not above practical efforts, if even for a small resulting good. Deeply penetrated as he is with the axiom that each unit of humanity feels as much as all the rest combined, and impulsive and hopeful in nature, so that the remedy suggests itself to him concurrently with the evil.

Next to these, on the shaded bank, are different characters out of work: haymakers in quest of employment; a Stoic from the Emerald Island, with hay stuffed in his hat to keep the draught out, and need for Stoicism just at present, being short of baccy; a young shoeless Irishman, with his wife, feeding their first-born with cold pap; an old sailor turned haymaker; and two young peasants in search of harvest work, reduced in strength, perhaps by fever—possibly by famine. Behind the Pariah, who never has learned to work, appears a group of a very different class, who, from an opposite cause, have not been sufficiently used to work either. These are the *rich*, who 'have no need to work'—not at least for bread—*the 'bread of life'* is neither here nor there. The pastrycook's tray, the symbol of superfluity, accompanies these. It is peculiarly English; I never saw it abroad that I remember, though something of the kind must be used. For some years after returning to England I could never quite get over a certain socialistic twinge on seeing it pass, unreasonable as the feeling may have been. Past the pastrycook's tray come two married ladies. The elder and more serious of the two devotes her energies to tract distributing, and has just flung one entitled, 'The Hodman's Haven; or, Drink for Thirsty Souls,' to the somewhat uncompromising specimen of navvy humanity descending the ladder: he scorns it, but with good-nature. This well-intentioned lady has, perhaps, never reflected that excavators may have notions to the effect that ladies might be benefited by receiving tracts containing navvies' ideas! nor yet that excavators are skilled workmen, shrewd thinkers chiefly, and, in general, men of great experience in life, as life presents itself to them.

In front of her is the lady whose only business in life as yet is to dress and look beautiful for our benefit. She probably possesses everything that can give enjoyment to life; how then can she but enjoy the passing moment, and, like a flower, feed on the light of the sun? Would anyone wish it otherwise? Certainly not I, dear lady. Only in your own interest, seeing that certain blessings cannot be insured for ever—as, for instance, health may fail, beauty fade, pleasures through repetition pall —I will not hint at the greater calamities to which flesh is heir—seeing all this, were you less engaged watching that exceedingly beautiful tiny greyhound in a red jacket that *will* run through that lime, I would beg to call your attention to my group of small, exceedingly ragged, dirty children in the foreground of my picture, where

17. Ford Madox Brown: Work (1860)

18. Eyre Crowe: The Dinner Hour, Wigan (1874)

In an encounter with some huge ruffian whom he has conquered in fight, and hurled out through the swing-doors of the palace of gin prone on to the pavement. On the wall are posters and bills, one of the 'Boys' Home, 41 Euston Road,' which the lady who is giving tracts will no doubt subscribe to presently and place the urchin playing with the barrow in; one of 'The Working Men's College, Great Ormond Street,' or if you object to these, then a police bill offering 50*l*. reward in a matter of highway robbery. Back in the distance we see the Assembly-room of the 'Flamstead Institute of Arts,' where Professor Snoöx is about to repeat his interesting lecture on the habits of the domestic cat. Indignant pussies up on the roof are denying his theory *in toto*.

The less important characters in the background require little comment. Bobus, our old friend, 'the sausage-maker of Houndsditch,' from 'Past and Present,' having secured a colossal fortune (he boasts of it *now*) by anticipating the French Hippophage Society in the introduction of horseflesh as a *cheap* article of human food, is at present going in for the county of Middlesex, and, true to his old tactics, has hired all the idlers in the neighbourhood to carry his boards. These being one too many for the bearers, an old woman has volunteered to carry the one in excess.

The episode of the policeman who has caught an orange-girl in the heinous offence of resting her basket on a post, and who himself administers justice in the shape of a push that sends her fruit all over the road, is one of common occurrence, or used to be—perhaps the police now 'never do such things.'

I am sorry to say that most of my friends, on examining this part of my picture, have laughed over it as a good joke. Only two men saw the circumstance in a different light; one of them was the young Irishman who feeds his infant with pap. Pointing to it with his thumb, his mouth quivering at the reminiscence, he said, 'That, Sir, *I* know to be true.' The other was a clergyman; his testimony would perhaps have more weight. I dedicate this portion of the work to the Commissioners of Police.

Through this picture I have gained some experience of the navvy class, and I have usually found, that if you can break through the upper crust of *mauvaise honte* which surrounds them in common with most Englishmen, and which, in the case of the navvies, I believe to be the cause of much of their bad language, you will find them serious, intelligent men, and with much to interest in their conversation, which, moreover, contains about the same amount of morality and sentiment that is commonly found among men in the active and hazardous walks of life, for that their career is one of hazard and danger none should doubt. Many stories might be told of navvies' daring and endurance, were this the place for them. One incident peculiarly connected with this picture is the melancholy fact that one of the very men who sat for it lost his life by a scaffold accident before I had yet quite done with him. I remember the poor fellow telling me, among other things, how he never but once felt nervous with his work, and this was having to trundle barrows of earth over a plank-line crossing a rapid river at a height of *eighty feet* above the water. But it was not the height he complained of, it was the *gliding motion of the water underneath*.

I have only to observe, in conclusion, that the effect of hot July sunlight, attempted in this picture, has been introduced because it seems peculiarly fitted to display *work* in all its severity, and not from any predilection for this kind of light over any other.

N.B.—In several cases I have had the advantage of sittings from personages of note, who, at a loss of time to themselves, have kindly contributed towards the greater truthfulness of some of the characters. As my object, however, in all cases, is to delineate types and not individuals, and as, moreover, I never contemplated employing their renown to benefit my own reputation, I refrain from publishing ther names.

The most noted of the sitters for *Work* are, of course, Thomas Carlyle and Frederick Denison Maurice. The Carlylean *motif* of the picture is indeed so obvious that it is scarcely necessary to mention it.

I am not quite able to say whether the subject was suggested by 'Past and Present' itself, or whether it was entirely self-evolved. I happen to possess the artist's copy of that work. It is of the American edition of 1840, and was therefore most probably acquired from a second-hand bookstall. The date of its acquisition is not indicated, but it bears signs of frequent perusal, whilst passages relating to the great Mr. Bobus and many enunciating the gospel of *Work* are pencil-marked.

# XXI Later Descriptive Writing

ALFRED TENNYSON                                             XXI.1
'Mariana'
from *Poems Chiefly Lyrical*, 1830

> 'Mariana in the moated grange.'
> *Measure for Measure*

With blackest moss the flower-plots
   Were thickly crusted, one and all:
The rusted nails fell from the knots
   That held the pear to the gable-wall.
The broken sheds look'd sad and strange:
   Unlifted was the clinking latch;
   Weeded and worn the ancient thatch
Upon the lonely moated grange.
      She only said, 'My life is dreary,
        He cometh not,' she said;
      She said, 'I am aweary, aweary,
        I would that I were dead!'

Her tears fell with the dews at even;
   Her tears fell ere the dews were dried;
She could not look on the sweet heaven,
   Either at morn or eventide.
After the flitting of the bats,
   When thickest dark did trance the sky,
   She drew her casement-curtain by,
And glanced athwart the glooming flats.
      She only said, 'The night is dreary,
        He cometh not,' she said;
      She said, 'I am aweary, aweary,
        I would that I were dead!'

Upon the middle of the night,
   Waking she heard the night-fowl crow:
The cock sung out an hour ere light:
   From the dark fen the oxen's low

Came to her: without hope of change,
  In sleep she seem'd to walk forlorn,
  Till cold winds woke the gray-eyed morn
About the lonely moated grange.
    She only said, 'The day is dreary.
    He cometh not,' she said;
    She said, 'I am aweary, aweary,
    I would that I were dead!'

About a stone-cast from the wall
  A sluice with blacken'd waters slept,
And o'er it many, round and small,
  The cluster'd marish-mosses crept.
Hard by a poplar shook alway,
  All silver-green with gnarled bark:
  For leagues no other tree did mark
The level waste, the rounding gray.
    She only said, 'My life is dreary,
    He cometh not,' she said;
    She said, 'I am aweary, aweary,
    I would that I were dead!'

And ever when the moon was low,
  And the shrill winds were up and away,
In the white curtain, to and fro,
  She saw the gusty shadow sway.
But when the moon was very low,
  And wild winds bound within their cell,
  The shadow of the poplar fell
Upon her bed, across her brow.
    She only said, 'The night is dreary,
    He cometh not,' she said;
    She said, 'I am aweary, aweary,
    I would that I were dead!'

All day within the dreamy house,
  The doors upon their hinges creak'd;
The blue fly sung in the pane; the mouse
  Behind the mouldering wainscot shriek'd,
Or from the crevice peer'd about.
    Old faces glimmer'd thro' the doors,
    Old footsteps trod the upper floors,
Old voices called her from without.
    She only said, 'My life is dreary,

He cometh not,' she said;
She said, 'I am aweary, aweary,
I would that I were dead!'

The sparrow's chirrup on the roof,
The slow clock ticking, and the sound
Which to the wooing wind aloof
The poplar made, did all confound
Her sense; but most she loathed the hour
When the thick-moted sunbeam lay
Athwart the chambers, and the day
Was sloping toward his western bower.
Then, said she, 'I am very dreary,
He will not come,' she said;
She wept, 'I am aweary, aweary,
Oh God, that I were dead!'

# HARTLEY COLERIDGE                    XXI.2
'November'

from *Poems*, 1833

The mellow year is hasting to its close;
The little birds have almost sung their last,
Their small notes twitter in the dreary blast—
That shrill-piped harbinger of early snows;
The patient beauty of the scentless rose,
Oft with the Morn's hoar crystal quaintly glass'd,
Hangs, a pale mourner for the summer past,
And makes a little summer where it grows:
In the chill sunbeam of the faint brief day
The dusky waters shudder as they shine,
The russet leaves obstruct the struggling way
Of oozy brooks, which no deep banks define,
And the gaunt woods, in ragged, scant array,
Wrap their old limbs with sombre ivy twine.

# MATTHEW ARNOLD                                          XXI.3

## A summer's day

from 'The Scholar Gipsy', 1853

Go, for they call you, Shepherd, from the hill;
Go, Shepherd, and untie the wattled cotes:
No longer leave thy wistful flock unfed,
Nor let thy bawling fellows rack their throats,
Nor the cropp'd grasses shoot another head.
But when the fields are still,
And the tired men and dogs all gone to rest,
And only the white sheep are sometimes seen
Cross and recross the strips of moon-blanch'd green;
Come, Shepherd, and again begin the quest.

Here, where the reaper was at work of late,
In this high field's dark corner, where he leaves
His coat, his basket, and his earthen cruise,
And in the sun all morning binds the sheaves,
Then here, at noon, comes back his stores to use;
Here will I sit and wait,
While to my ear from uplands far away
The bleating of the folded flocks is borne,
With distant cries of reapers in the corn—
All the live murmur of a summer's day.

Screen'd is this nook o'er the high, half-reap'd field,
And here till sundown, Shepherd, will I be.
Through the thick corn the scarlet poppies peep,
And round green roots and yellowing stalks I see
Pale pink convolvulus in tendrils creep:
And air-swept lindens yield
Their scent, and rustle down their perfumed showers
Of bloom on the bent grass where I am laid,
And bower me from the August sun with shade;
And the eye travels down to Oxford's towers:

# ALFRED TENNYSON XXI.4

## Camelot and the Lady of the Lake

from 'Gareth and Lynette', 1859

> . . . Southward they set their faces. The birds made
> Melody on branch and melody in mid air
> The damp hill-slopes were quicken'd into green,
> And the live green had kindled into flowers,
> For it was past the time of Easter-day.
>
> So, when their feet were planted on the plain
> That broaden'd toward the base of Camelot,
> Far off they saw the silver-misty morn
> Rolling her smoke about the royal mount,
> That rose between the forest and the field.
> At times the summit of the high city flash'd;
> At times the spires and turrets halfway down
> Prick'd thro' the mist; at times the great gate shone
> Only, that open'd on the field below;
> Anon, the whole fair city had disappear'd.
>
> Then those who went with Gareth were amazed,
> One crying, 'Let us go no further, lord;
> Here is a city of enchanters, built
> By fairy kings.' The second echo'd him,
> 'Lord, we have heard from our wise man at home
> To northward, that this king is not the King,
> But only changeling out of Fairyland,
> Who drave the heathen hence by sorcery
> And Merlin's glamour.' Then the first again,
> 'Lord, there is no such city anywhere,
> But all a vision.'
>                         Gareth answer'd them
> With laughter, swearing he had glamour enow
> In his own blood, his princedom, youth, and hopes,
> To plunge old Merlin in the Arabian sea;
> So push'd them all unwilling toward the gate.
> And there was no gate like it under heaven.
> For barefoot on the keystone, which was lined
> And rippled like an ever-fleeting wave,
> The Lady of the Lake stood; all her dress
> Wept from her sides as water flowing away;
> But like the cross her great and goodly arms

325

Stretch'd under all the cornice and upheld.
And drops of water fell from either hand;
And down from one a sword was hung, from one
A censer, either worn with wind and storm;
And o'er her breast floated the sacred fish;
And in the space to left of her, and right,
Were Arthur's wars in weird devices done,
New things and old co-twisted, as if Time
Were nothing, so inveterately that men
Were giddy gazing there; and over all
High on the top were those three queens, the friends
Of Arthur, who should help him at his need.

## GERARD MANLEY HOPKINS — XXI.5
### 'Winter with the Gulf Stream'
published 1863

The boughs, the boughs are bare enough
But earth has never felt the snow.
Frost-furred our ivies are and rough

With bills of rime the brambles shew.
The hoarse leaves crawl on hissing ground
Because the sighing wind is low.

But if the rain-blasts be unbound
And from dank feathers wring the drops
The clogged brook runs with choking sound

Kneading the mounded mire that stops
His channel under clammy coats
Of foliage fallen in the copse.

A simple passage of weak notes
Is all the winter bird dare try.
The bugle moon by daylight floats

So glassy white about the sky,
So like a berg of hyaline,
And pencilled blue so daintily,

I never saw her so divine.
But through black branches, rarely drest
In scarves of silky shot and shine,

The webbed and the watery west
Where yonder crimson fireball sits
Looks laid for feasting and for rest.

I see long reefs of violets
In beryl-covered fens so dim,
A gold-water Pactolus frets

Its brindled wharves and yellow brim,
The waxen colours weep and run,
And slendering to his burning rim

Into the flat blue mist the sun
Drops out and all our day is done.

# XXII Responses to Music

ADAM SMITH XXII.1

"A well-composed concerto of instrumental Music"

from 'Of the Nature of that Imitation which takes place in what are called the Imitative Arts', written 1750s

Time and measure are to instrumental Music what order and method are to discourse; they break it into proper parts and divisions, by which we are enabled both to remember better what is gone before, and frequently to foresee somewhat of what is to come after: we frequently foresee the return of a period which we know must correspond to another which we remember to have gone before; and, according to the saying of an ancient philosopher and musician, the enjoyment of Music arises partly from memory and partly from foresight. . . .

A well-composed concerto of instrumental Music, by the number and variety of the instruments, by the variety of the parts which are performed by them, and the perfect concord or correspondence of all these different parts; by the exact harmony or coincidence of all the different sounds which are heard at the same time, and by that happy variety of measure which regulates the succession of those which are heard at different times, presents an object so agreeable, so great, so various, and so interesting, that alone, and without suggesting any other object, either by imitation or otherwise, it can occupy, and as it were fill up, completely the whole capacity of the mind, so as to leave no part of its attention vacant for thinking of any thing else. In the contemplation of that immense variety of agreeable and melodious sounds, arranged and digested, both in their coincidence and in their succession, into so complete and regular a system, the mind in reality enjoys not only a very great sensual, but a very high intellectual, pleasure, not unlike that which it derives from the contemplation of a great system in any other science. A full concerto of such instrumental Music, not only does not require, but it does not admit of any accompaniment. A song or a dance, by demanding an attention which we have not to spare, would disturb, instead of heightening, the effect of the Music; they may often very properly succeed, but they cannot accompany it. That music seldom means to tell any particular story, or to imitate any particular event, or in general to suggest any particular object, distinct from that

329

combination of sounds of which itself is composed. Its meaning, there-fore, may be said to be complete in itself, and to require no interpreters to explain it. What is called the subject of such Music is merely, as has already been said, a certain leading combination of notes, to which it frequently returns, and to which all its digressions and variations bear a certain affinity. It is altogether different from what is called the subject of a poem or a picture, which is always something which is not either in the poem or in the picture, or something quite distinct from that com-bination, either of words on the one hand, or of colours on the other, of which they are respectively composed. The subject of a composition of instrumental Music is a part of that composition: the subject of a poem or picture is no part of either.

## SAMUEL TAYLOR COLERIDGE XXII.2
### 'Lines Composed in a Concert-Room'
from *The Morning Post*, 1799

> Nor cold, nor stern, my soul! yet I detest
>     These scented Rooms, where, to a gaudy throng,
> Heaves the proud Harlot her distended breast,
>     In intricacies of laborious song.
>
> These feel not Music's genuine power, nor deign
>     To melt at Nature's passion-warbled plaint;
> But when the long-breathed singer's uptrilled strain
>     Bursts in a squall—they gape for wonderment.
>
> Hark! the deep buzz of Vanity and Hate!
>     Scornful, yet envious, with self-torturing sneer
> My lady eyes some maid of humbler state,
>     While the pert Captain, or the primmer Priest,
>     Prattles accordant scandal in her ear.
>
> O give me, from this loathsome scene released,
>     To hear our old Musician, blind and grey,
> (Whom stretching from my nurse's arms I kissed,)
>     His Scottish tunes and warlike marches play,
> By moonshine, on the balmy summer-night,
>     The while I dance amid the tedded hay
> With merry maids, whose ringlets toss in light.
> Or lies the purple evening on the bay
> Of the calm glossy lake, O let me hide

Unheard, unseen, behind the alder-trees,
Around whose roots the fisher's boat is tied,
    On whose trim seat doth Edmund stretch at ease,
And while the lazy boat sways to and fro,
    Breathes in his flute sad airs, so wild and slow,
That his own cheek is wet with quiet tears.

But O, dear Anne! when midnight wind careers,
And the gust pelting on the out-house shed
    Makes the cock shrilly in the rainstorm crow,
    To hear thee sing some ballad full of woe,
Ballad of ship-wreck's sailor floating dead,
    Whom his own true-love buried in the sands!
Thee, gentle woman, for thy voice remeasures
Whatever tones and melancholy pleasures
    The things of Nature utter; birds or trees,
Or moan of ocean-gale in weedy caves,
Or where the stiff grass mid the heath-plant waves,
    Murmur and music then of sudden breeze.

Dear Maid! whose form in solitude I seek,
    Such songs in such a mood to hear thee sing,
    It were a deep delight!—But thou shalt fling
Thy white arm round my neck, and kiss my cheek,
    And love the brightness of my gladder eye
    The while I tell thee what a holier joy

It were in proud and stately step to go,
    With trump and timbrel clang, and popular shout,
    To celebrate the shame and absolute rout
Unhealable of Freedom's latest foe,
    Whose tower'd might shall to its centre nod.
When human feelings, sudden, deep and vast,
As all good spirits of all ages past
    Were armied in the hearts of living men,
Shall purge the earth, and violently sweep
These vile and painted locusts to the deep.

# XXIII Folk Music and Gipsy Music

## FRANZ LISZT

### Gipsy Music

from *The Gipsy in Music*, 1859

If the Bohemian type, so free from all exterior restraint and arbitrary convention—and if Bohemian art, in expressing the revolt of the soul against compression of the torrential outpour of its infinite desires have so powerfully combined to engage the attention of artists and poets as to become equally admired and popular in our high European Christian society (in spite of that scared poltroon shrinking at all contact with the despised Gipsy) that fact must be accepted as proof that Bohemian sentiment, or, in other words, the tendencies governing Bohemian existence and expressed by its art are less exclusively its own than would appear at a first glance.

Do we not meet in every society, however civilised and prosaic it may be, or however occupied it may seem with positive duties and mercantile profits—exceptional individuals, strongly inclined to resist all regulation of their ardent and subversive desires?

The difference is that, there, such groups occur but rarely; because, by its silently deteriorating influence, the atmosphere of civilisation chills and weakens those children who threaten to become ungovernable, if they are not at an early age brought under conventional rule. For all that, such instances occur; and, under the form of eccentricity, are far more frequent than is generally supposed.

We regard such persons as defectives, incapable as they are of performing their share of servile regulated work in the great social factory; but they, on the contrary, glory in their inaptitude, calling the malady from which they suffer 'sacred,' and one from which they would consent on no conditions to be relieved.

Poetic pathology has by no means left this sad anomaly without admirable descriptions; they exist in every style, under various titles, by various authors, dating from every period and in divers tongues.

We possess some beautiful examples of this—some in fresco, some in water-colour—written by princes of the poetic art. We shall not quote any, because each reader will certainly find it more agreeable to recall to mind the immortal and well-known specimens he treasures from the literature of any language with which he is familiar. Moreover the identity of sentiment, the resemblance of impressions, the conformity of emotions, of sighs and languors, of joys and heart-breakings do not constitute identity.

Byron was the first to set the fashion of the hero draped in the folds of a brown mantle; and, carping at a society which he has only been able to contemplate from the angle provided by the high position in it to which he was born. The exterior resemblance of the portraits is of no avail; for the costume and language of such heroes is different altogether from that of the Bohemian: half naked, half starved, half benumbed, half on the look-out.

Such personalities may resemble the Bohemian in being half sad, half happy, half cruel, half good, half insolent, half respectful. But, however we may be struck by these points in common, they alone would not justify us in making comparisons which demand a sustained parallel.

These considerations combine therefore to make it certain that more than one of these ideal figures, absolutely differing from the Bohemian in carriage, manner, constitution, language and education, has only been admired by us because he presented us, under other forms, with the very sentiments which the Gipsy had already revealed and reawakened by his melodies and violin. . . .

### *With the Gipsy in the Open.*

It would be necessary to have often slept under the canopy of far-off skies and been awakened by the rays of the rising sun which, brightening the morning dew, fall upon the sleeper's eyelids like little fiery tongues—one must also know what it is fearlessly to allow the serpent to coil itself cold and sticky over the naked legs; and, half-awake, to feel its creeping motion over the forehead; or to have idled the long day through, lying at length amongst the high growth of fields where the scythe has never been, in order to be prepared to enter into the spirit of our present subject.

To have, time and again, studied the irregular melodies of the hurricane, richly orchestrated as they are by the fir-trees with their thousand needle-points and by the reeds with their myriads of pipes; to have learned to understand the confidential and endearing whisperings that the euphonies of the twilight whisper so low, so low, into the ear of a passionate lover of the landscape—these are but other essentials to the same end.

But it would also be necessary to have learned to recognise each tree by the aroma of its sap, to know something about the mysterious language of the birds, and to understand alike the gay finch and the chattering grasshopper. To have often gone astraddle at night-fall over the open country when the setting sun gives the atmosphere such a glow as to make it seem like going through a damp fire, because it warms the eyes whilst it cools the body, and to have done this until a pale obscurity follows in which the stars of heaven appear to frolic and blink their eyes, becoming every moment more in number, more smiling and loving, more coquettish and teasing, than before.

This, too—But, on the other hand, one must have also seen, on black nights, the moon, red as a disc of polished copper, rise over a plain where everything seemed dead; from which every animal had fled and where nothing but a thick brushwood was left to form upon the horizon its uncanny outlook, like the back of an enormous rhinocerous or the silhouette of some giant elephant asleep.

When one had done each and all of these things, in other words, when one has led the Gipsy life, and then only, does it become clear how impossible it is for the Gipsy to exist deprived of the various exhilarations with which such life is replete. He cannot sleep in a stone cage and with a low ceiling over his head. Accustomed to the free breath of the infinite, he would have to suffocate under such conditions. His eye, accustomed to the diaphanous ether of the open, would weep on encountering nothing but narrow walls; and his ear decay, if seeking in vain the wide modulations of the evening storm.

What is there which could replace the impression, to which the Gipsy is accustomed, of those moving scenes of tragedies, carried out in places from which man is usually absent?

What would there be to recall to him the sanguinary dramas which unfold themselves round about the setting sun as at a hero's death?

What is there to compare to the loving caresses of the dewy mist, or to the far-off tints which envelop in uncertainty outlines but gradually revealed by the rising sun on a bright spring morning?

What kind of well-being lies with the power of industry to supply, capable of being compared with that happy contentment, seeming to double the vital forces, which arises after a warm summer rain in the open country; at sight of the earth, all foliage bathed; and the sky, reconciled and radiant again?

Is there anything to vie with the crushing fury which roars in the thunder of a July storm, when the forest voices repeat it in a fearsome chorus?

Does a rival exist of the elegiac sadness of the scene presented by the wood, when the autumn wind strips it of its foliage, and, as if in anger, casts the recently enchanting leafy decorations, now faded, hither and thither?

And where is the power whose pomp can approach that of the cold rigours of the frost; the appearance of which seems like that of some inhuman master, as the chatter of the busy cheerful waters is at once

335

stilled, all song is at an end, the very blood-flow of the plants is now suspended, the very earth now hardened?

The pleasures invented by man can never prove other than sickly and insipid to the man accustomed to drink from the cup which Nature offers him, intending him to enjoy every drink and to relish every drop. Of what value are town-baubles to the man who enjoys braving the winter, and feeling the fire of his cheeks resisting its cold breath—who prefers being alone and unsheltered from its biting rod, in the midst of a desert of ironic splendour?

One becomes insensible to the refinements of an idle Sybaritism when one has experienced the soothing thrill and pleasant torpor of the cold; which gives less presentiment of it the nearer death approaches. How insignificant, too, must appear our illuminations by gas, and even our dazzling sumptuousness of electrical displays; to one who has witnessed a caprice of the whirlwind, when the entire bright covering of the hill-tops, the whole mass of diamond-like snow, is at once carried away and played with as the wind toys with the folds of a silken flag?

And our theatres, with their display of light! How *he* must disdain them, whose theatre is the grand work of God; and who, should he wish for any light other than that which he receives from above, prefers the joyous fantastic glare of his heap of twigs and dry leaves. . . .

Nature remains an entire dead letter for the citizen or worker who looks upon her as so much raw material for various manufacturers to exploit in their respective workshops. She scarcely murmurs more than a few incoherent words (either terrible in her anger or smiling in her goodness) to the scientific man; who, armed with fire and iron, is endeavouring to discover her secrets. . . .

### The Gipsy's idea of Liberty.

In direct opposition to the Jewish nation, with its blind obedience to absolute regulations, the Gipsy race rejects all despotism of law, its entire earthly desire being limited to that of existence; so much so that, whatever intervenes to fix or limit the means even to that one end, encounters from it a disdain—foolish but sublime. It maintains its individuality both by its constant association with Nature and by its profound indifference for all other men; with whom it only comes in contact for the purpose of procuring the means wherewith to live.

If it delights in deceiving others, that happens entirely without hatred or malice aforethought. Any spite or ill-feeling which it may nourish is ephemeral; always accidental and applying to persons only—never as illustrating any principle. If it laughs at the superiority of civilised mankind that happens only in the same sense that a fox would laugh at a farmer whose poultry yard he had despoiled.

Even if the Gipsy race is not always entirely inoffensive, yet from the moment that its wants are satisfied at all events it has never any premeditated desire to injure in the mass. It is concerned only to preserve the liberty of the wild horse; for it has never been able to understand the preference for a house-roof, however finely constructed, to the heavenly arch-roof, of the forests.

Authority, law, rule, principle, precept, obligation, duty—these are all notions and things insupportable to this strange race; not only because to admit them would necessitate an amount of reflection and mental application which would be most repugnant to it, but also because, in the alternative case, it enjoys all the chance consequences of a life without object or result—a life the idle vagabondage of which is subject only to the incitations of imagination and desire.

This search for a degree of liberty so absolute as to become savage engenders naturally an invincible dislike for work, as well as for that commerce of which the industrious Jew is so fond. The dislike thus formed arises from the inevitable restraint applying to all civilised life on account of its subjection to rule; and to all habitation which ventures to forsake the grottos and the mountains.

In order not to allow the slightest encroachment upon this frenzied liberty, or any other kind of change to occur in it, the Gipsies make no difficulty about submitting to any procedure or expedient (even those of a description impossible of acceptance by nations less uncultivated) for the purpose of avoiding any loss of freedom in the supply of their few wants.

How different are they in all this to the Israelites with whom the sense of right and wrong is so superfine, so constantly kept alive by obedience to meticulous precept, and by their faith in the Decalogue; the latter teaching them to abstain from the theft of a single crown, at the very moment when they are extorting ten thousand by usury. The reason for this is that theft is forbidden, but usurious gain from the Gentile praiseworthy.

As they possess neither Bible nor Testament, the Gipsies see no necessity to tax their intelligence with the comprehension of abstract ideas, as they find it already functions very well within the circle of *instinct*. Having a vague consciousness of their own harmlessness they are content to live in the sun, charmed by its sparkling warmth, and enlivened by its cheerful rays, to give themselves up to a small number of primordial and elementary passions, but never to permit any conventional virtue to trouble their free and easy manners. To be completely untroubled is more to them than any advantages which might accompany the repression of even the least of their desires.

They draw the need for the unlimited independence which has become the distinctive trait of their character from a practically unceasing

337

excitement, caused by incessant contact with Nature. Refusing ever to withdraw from this contact, the consequent mental stimulation becomes with them so habitual that they would be unable to exist if deprived of this unbroken continuation of lively and penetrating sensations. For them there is nothing in the wide world capable of compensating for these pleasures; which are taken in at every pore, and eagerly responded to by every sense. One might consider them as always intoxicated with the milk of Cybele, which they partake of to such mad excess that the vertigo from it disturbs their reason and disarranges all their feeling.

Nothing in Gipsy estimation equals the liberty of satisfying even the least of their desires at any moment. They will throw off every moral shackle, every social dependence, and every interior drawback, rather than cease for a moment to feel able to follow up the electric spark of a desired sensation.

To 'feel' is an expression which compactly describes the whole of their being; they must 'feel,' at any price. They have no more taste for command than for obedience; both being regarded by them as burdens of subjection. The idea of 'possession' is as foreign to them as that of 'duty'; and, as a matter of fact, the verbs to 'have' and to 'owe' do not exist in their language. Hence, cause and effect, prevision and relation of past to future, are ideas not only repugnant but impossible to entertain.

What an antithesis with the Israelites; who make the continuation of their existence depend upon the constant increase of their possessions.

### The Gipsy life and civilisation.

The permanent illegality of desire, when it is uncontrolled, collides with other equally precious faculties and rightly disgusts the moral sense. But if we recall our attention to the conduct of society (of which the Gipsies are content with the remains of banqueting and the left-off clothing) what shall we see?

That the Gipsy never hurts it in anything which causes it to flourish. He does not try to strangle it; as does that other nation which, on that very account, seems to be esteemed by it all the more. Nor does he threaten its security even (on the worst supposition) if he makes off with a parcel of its goods. But, on the other hand, we see that same society, with its arrogant sense of superior virtue, just as much entangled in the mire of its prosaic egotism, just as deprived of pity, justice, charity or conscience, as the Gipsies are with all their poetic egoism, however turbulent and furious.

In our society we have rapine, pillage, theft, burglary and murder. Add to these the refinements of either gradual or quick poisoning; lying, either bare-faced or hypocritical; and calumny, either sharp, like a dagger, or dirty and viperous. Add to these again adultery, debauchery, prostitution and promiscuity; all existing there, latent and tacit, like sleeping reptiles in a vase covered over with flowers. You cannot be sure of not being robbed on the highway, or assaulted for the same purpose in a wood. Honest folk are continually liable to have the fruit of years of labour, their honour and good name, or their dearest affections, taken from them by some brutal hand; that is, when they are not carried off by sly measures and drawn into the impenetrable dens of the tricksters.

It is in our society that fraud, from its high position, vents insolence upon truth humiliated; that violence gives a knowing smile to justice (the forms of which it finds to suit its purpose); that cupidity working with the force of duplicity, or duplicity of force, throws ironic glances upon the man who is in the right, and whom they have despoiled. It seems almost as if it were in their minds to ask—

'How much the better off are you for your gift of reason?'

In the midst of civilisation those heart fibres which culture of the intelligence tends to soften are fully exposed to the danger of being bruised and broken by the many evil expedients invented by envy, intrigue, duplicity, false witness, libertinage and vengeance. The governing power in this society is a form of egotism the most implacable in its heartlessness, the most inexorable in its ferocity, and the most dissembling in its effrontery. Its rods are none the less cruel for being provided with golden handles; and do not, for that reason, cause any less blood to flow from the just and the feeble.

In our society the inexperienced youth, the lone widow, the forsaken veteran, the naïve scholar, the dreamy poet and the man who is well-to-do but unsuspecting are not likely to meet with a fate which the Gipsy would be disposed to envy; especially if he could be made aware of all the secrets, afflictions, tribulations, humiliations and heartbreakings incidental to it. His immorality could not feel as if it had much to blush for; as compared with that of the strong and the shrewd in our civilisation.

It would hence seem justifiable to ask of the nations who look at the Gipsy from such a lofty eminence whether it is really their pure morality—whether it is their unrivalled evangelical holiness which dictates the profound contempt they have for him. The unfortunate effects of his poetic eogism fall, at all events, only on himself, whilst the canting egotism of civilisation imposes itself with audacity upon victims whom it defames at the same time that it ruins them.

The poetic egoism of the Gipsy does not disguise its giving over of the feeble to the strong. But, whereas this is done by him in a manner less tenacious, unpremeditated and without system, the prosaic egotism of society enlaces the weak-minded and unsuspecting victim with the bands of trickery; arranging that force itself shall fall into the traps laid for it by astuteness.

Between this and the method of the Gipsy (whose ignorance of well-being and intellectual idleness should be some excuse) we cannot see any distinction which justifies the Gipsy's punishment in being much the greater.

The impulse which spurs the Gipsy on to the quick possession of the objects of his desires takes its root in the noblest regions of our nature; although, in his case, it has taken an unhealthy character. This is a trait which Christians especially should not misunderstand, however disastrous its effects; particularly as they cannot fail to note that the Gipsy's sufferings, after all, are caused by his habit of too much feeling without thought—too much dreaming without calculation, and too much imagining without judgment. . . .

### Course of the Decline

Nowadays Bohemian musicians, instead of the nomads they formerly were, have become commercial travellers. Instead of moving off along with their tribe, folding their tent and lifting their cooking vessel into the dusty wagon, they go from one capital to another by railway in company; so as to carry on business in the European style. Ever since they began to sniff a new musical atmosphere, causing art to become to them less a joy than a trade; ever since they first acquired the greed for gain, that passion for lucre common to the great commercial centres and infinitely more corrupting and corrupted than the thieving habit when exercised with a sort of primitive *naïveté*; ever since all this, they have devoted themselves to speculation; and, like many others, now seek reputation merely in order to find money. Given up to that mammon-worship, which is specially hideous when artists engage in it, they now forsake art for the sake of gain.

What could the used-up and partly gangrenous populations of the immense capitals understand about an art which had gradually unfolded itself in the bosom of nature, and which had taken at least four centuries of growth to reach its present stature of a great towering tree overshadowing with its superb branches an entire country? Curiosity and the idle search for something new contested, at first, with the vulgar crowd for interest in the new comer; but as soon as they perceived that the sentiments expressed in this strange noble idiom were completely unknown to them, they wanted to return again to their usual diet—to listen again to the common run of ritornello, ariette, valse, and so forth.

By way of punishment for the fault they had committed in giving themselves up to a sordid interest the Bohemians were gradually compelled to sacrifice their art and mix up the passionate accents of their adorable melodies with romances, cavatinas and pot-pourris in order to secure and retain their listeners. Engaged in such a trade, their entire merit disappears; by degrees they even lose the very habit of their art; and in many places they never play Bohemian music at all except on request and in return for a stipulated payment.

But after all their principal object is attained. A public (which we will not call ignoble, but which, to say the least, is far from being noble) finds itself in public gardens, cafés, alcazars or exhibitions; where, for a couple of francs a head, it is admitted to see and hear certain worn-out theatrical pieces. They are invariably old acquaintances; and remind one of the ball-dresses which, after having displayed their first bloom, finally arrive as used-up finery at the shop of the second-hand dealer.

This public, on viewing the Bohemians, estimate them for what, henceforth, they really are; that is to say, workmen, money-getters, ready to perform a fire-swallowing or any other conjuring trick. This public, moreover, being fairly unscrupulous itself, judges our Bohemians to be the same; and accordingly, having read a wonderful account of their virtuosity beforehand, they think they *must* have really heard something quite exceptional.

In point of fact, however, they have been listening to the most miserable re-hash imaginable. Still, that will not prevent them from returning home quite satisfied with the performance: a performance which might equally well have been given by the first scratch orchestra.

It must be allowed, however, that not alone amongst musicians is this falling off in the national type to be observed. In allowing the outlines of their individuality to become faded they share in the fate of the greater part of schools and nations at the present day, carried away by the general impulse in favour of destroying the salient features by which the sentiments and modes of life and speech of each one of them is distinguished.

National character proceeds in the direction of effacement in everything and everywhere. To speak only of music, we see the ultra-Italian masters pretending that they are but slightly removed in style from the ultra-Germans; whilst the theatres of Paris and London are a selected composition of divers elements drawn from France, Italy and Germany.

It would be useless to deceive oneself. If nowadays, on the one hand, the human mind seems to attain a prodigious development in all branches of its activity—(science, literature, art, industry, commerce, speculation, research)—and not only in every branch but in all sub-divisions of each; on the other, it loses in the originality of individuals what it gains in extension of the mass.

In the same degree that works assume gigantic proportions they demand the co-operation of the many. Not being able to avoid lending himself to the exigencies of this giant associate, henceforth indispensable, the individual feels himself, if not crushed, at least flattened, under the colossal cylinder that this new Briareus with a hundred arms applies to his passions and peculiarities. The artist, for example, is seized from his infancy by every interior and excitable motive, as well as by interests of the liveliest and dearest kind, and then placed in the vice of social and conventional necessities; where an immense flattening mill receives all the roughnesses presented by his temperament.

After the crushing process (by which he is deprived of every speciality appertaining to his personal character) he is thrown into a final mould, that of society decorum; which has the effect of making him seem like everybody else. In this condition he sallies forth, a commonplace being; colourless and insipid. He is simply the exact copy of his predecessor, his neighbour and his successor—unless perchance he should happen to be superior to the whole of them; which, however, no one has any right to be. . . .

Nothing was so fatal to Bohemian art as the loss of the Bohemian type; which brought in its train the neglect or the silence of Bohemian sentiment. Soon, Bohemian musicians, issuing from the homogeneous world which Hungary had created for them, wanted to make themselves admired by those who were unable to enter into their ideas. The obligation of appealing to a cosmopolitan public naturally spreads the habit of collaboration. This, in its turn, more and more frequently takes the place of inspiration and individual will; just as machinery is everywhere replacing handiwork.

Our Bohemians, therefore, once having entered the universal forum, could no longer dispense with playing Meyerbeer and Donizetti; Strauss and Lanner. Soon, no doubt, we shall hear them giving some Mendelssohn, Schumann, Berlioz and Wagner at their concerts. They, the immediate children of fantasy and pure inspiration, will now dispose themselves to recite productions due to reflection and thought!

Seeing troupes organise and file off in every direction ornamented by the white panache of the locomotive, seeing them appear and disappear at international exhibitions of Paris, Vienna, London, Philadelphia and Melbourne, can only mean that the time will soon arrive when their glory will be merely a remembrance—when Bohemian art will be a thing which once was, but is no more. . . .

## BÉLA BARTÓK                                        XXIII.2

### 'Gipsy Music or Hungarian Music?'

from *Ethnographia*, 1931

To start without preliminaries, I should like to state that what people (including Hungarians) call 'gipsy music' is not gipsy music but Hungarian music; it is not old folk music but a fairly recent type of Hungarian popular art music composed, practically without exception, by Hungarians of the upper middle class. But while a Hungarian gentleman may compose music, it is traditionally unbecoming to his social status to perform it 'for money'—only gipsies are supposed to do that.

It is futile to look for logic in the use of language. The living tongue puts out the most peculiar offshoots, which we simply have to accept as the consequence of a natural growth, even though they are illogical. Thus, if we take the phrase 'gipsy music' as an example of incorrect usage we should long since have acquiesced in its acceptance were it not for the continued ill effects of this false terminology. When Franz Liszt's well known book on gipsy music appeared it created strong indignation at home. But why? Simply because Liszt dared to affirm in his book that what the Hungarians call gipsy music *is really gipsy music!* It seems that Liszt fell an innocent victim of this loose terminology. He must have reasoned that since the Hungarians themselves call this music 'gipsy' and not 'Hungarian' it cannot conceivably be Hungarian music. A century later the situation has not changed materially. When Hungarian music is mentioned in foreign lands the gipsy is mentioned in the same breath. Still, the incorrect use of the term 'gipsy music' is the lesser of the evils; the real damage is done by our official musical representatives and by the rank and file of simple music lovers who attribute to gipsy music an artistic significance to which it is not at all entitled. This official belief, extolled and disseminated both at home and abroad, is echoed by the multitude, incapable of competent judgment.

In reality the truth is simply this. The music that is nowadays played 'for money' by urban gipsy bands is nothing but popular art music of recent origin. The role of this popular art music is to furnish entertainment and to satisfy the musical needs of those whose artistic sensibilities are of a low order. This phenomenon is but a variant of the types of music that fulfill the same function in Western European countries; of the song hits, operetta airs, and other products of light music as performed by salon orchestras in restaurants and places of entertainment. That this Hungarian popular art music, incorrectly called gipsy music, has more value than the abovementioned foreign trash is perhaps a matter of pride for us, but when it is held up as something superior to so-called 'light music', when it is represented as being something more than music of a lower order destined to gratify undeveloped musical tastes, we must raise our voices in solemn protest. It is possible that in the 'good old days', say a hundred or a hundred and fifty years ago, the repertory of the urban gipsy bands was of greater worth than in our time, but unfortunately there are no documents available that would serve as evidence. But when it comes to their modern repertory there is no gainsaying that this is music of a low specific gravity. It is a matter for rejoicing that our light music is provided, for the most part, by this

Hungarian specialty that we call popular art music, and nothing is farther from our mind than to condemn gipsy musicians, the purveyors of this mass article. On the contrary, we wish them to hold fast to their position against the onslaught of the jazz and salon orchestras; we wish that they may continue to cling to their old repertory with its original coloring and physiognomy, without the admixture of waltzes, song hits, jazz elements, and whatnot. On the other hand, we cannot indulge in the desire, no matter how dear to us—for it will be of no avail—, that shallow musical taste be changed overnight, that the large public should turn its back on this popular art music and seek higher musical spheres, national or foreign. The half-educated multitude of urban and semi-rural populations wants mass products; let us be pleased that in music at least they are partial to domestic factory articles and do not let us indulge in utopian dreams for a quick improvement since they are unattainable.

## BÉLA BARTÓK                                                        XXIII.3

### 'The Liszt Problems'

from an address to the Hungarian Academy, 1936

The third question concerns Liszt's famous book on gipsy music. Today we all know that Liszt's statement—that what the gipsies in Hungary play, as well as Hungarian peasant music itself, is of gipsy origin—is quite wrong. We all know, from absolutely convincing proofs, that this music is of Hungarian origin; it would be a pity to waste another word on proving it. But what we must try to find out in this connexion is how much we should blame Liszt for this mistake. It is my conviction that we can only partly blame Liszt himself. The whole question of the so-called gipsy-music strictly belongs to the domain of folk-lore research. But in Liszt's time, folk-lore as a scientific subject did not exist at all. Nobody then had any idea that to examine such matters it was really necessary to make an exhaustive collection of the widest possible range of relevant facts; consequently Liszt himself lacked all the essential conditions under which he might have been able to see the question more clearly. All the notions of that time concerning folk-music were of the most primitive kind, and quite erroneous. For instance, nobody had any inkling that the original and basic mode of expression in folk art was collective; nor had they any conception of the social role of folk music; and they knew absolutely nothing of the nature, the possibilities, and the significance of borrowed influences in folk music. This is the reason why not even Liszt could see such questions clearly, especially such a complicated one as that of the origin of gipsy music. Of course, if he had devoted himself to ten years' work of collecting folk music, if he had gone to some of the thousands of Hungarian villages and had made an objective study of their music, the results would undoubtedly have led him to very different conclusions. But how could he have undertaken such a task? He would have had to abandon so many other more important, or at that time apparently more important, things. And in any case, from certain details in his book it is clear that such a task would not have been to his liking. One sees that the classical simplicity of the peasant melodies did not interest him (if indeed he was ever able to hear them at their most beautiful) and for this again we must blame his period, the nineteenth century. Liszt, like so many of his contemporaries, was fascinated rather by frills and decorations, show and glittering ornamentation, than by perfectly plain, unornamented simplicity. This explains why he placed the extravagant, rhapsodic gipsy music higher than the peasant performances. But apart from all this, we must blame ourselves, or more properly our grandfathers.

At the very beginning of our inquiry we come up against a mistake: the mere name of this kind of music. But who called it 'gipsy-music'? We ourselves. Any foreigner, not knowing all the complicated details of the gipsy question, would be astounded to learn with what a shock and with what opposition our fathers and grandfathers received Liszt's book, because he stated in it that what they called gipsy-music was in truth gipsy-music. What is worse, however, is that even then it did not occur to them how ridiculously inappropriate the name was, and that nobody, from that day to this, has thought that perhaps it would be a good idea to find another, less misleading name for this kind of music.

Liszt therefore, starting from the name, obviously began his examination on the assumption that what he was working on was music of gipsy origin. What other experience had he had in this connexion? He knew that the Hungarian nobility everywhere was catered for musically by gipsies, who moreover showed surprising musical ability. The things in their programmes that were of art-music origin were probably not in print, and only with the most exhaustive and exhausting research would it have been possible to collect sufficient data to dispose of these things with objective proofs. It is likely that the gipsy bands of that time performed much better musical material, and much more interestingly than today, and probable, too, that rather more in their programmes was of folk descent. Liszt could only have arrived at the truth about these folk elements if, as I said before, he had made a basic study of them in the villages among the peasants themselves. It is obvious, however, that on account of his poor knowledge of Hungarian, he could have done this only with the help of his Hungarian friends of the upper classes. And we know from experience that these country gentry are the last people to choose for such work. In the course of our work in collecting folk tunes, how many times we have heard from such people as country lawyers, teachers and squires remarks like this: 'But these peasants don't know anything; or anyway they don't understand, so it's not worth making a step.'

I may refer here to 'Ethnographia' 1933, Nos. I and II, in which a new collector complains in the following terms: 'This (*i.e.* collecting in one district of the county of Borsod) would be possible only with the help of the local administrative and upper classes. But the coldness and apathy in these official circles frustrates everything, and forces me to transfer the centre of my activities to another part of the county.' Finally, I may mention the controversy of the last few years, partly carried on in the newspaper columns, in which the devotees of the dilettantish art-music—who are unfortunately still in the majority in the upper classes—do their best to disparage the music of the peasants. I can safely say that, except in the Székely districts, I have never seen such indifference, and even contempt, shown towards the music of the peasants as in Hungarian country districts. To discover why this is, is not my task here, but we can be sure that such boundless antipathy did not arise at the beginning of the twentieth century, but obviously existed long ago. One can imagine what the result would be if an in-experienced collector had such a prejudiced, or at best indifferent, guide for his researches. Could Liszt have heard the peasants sing and make music in such circumstances? Obviously the peasants he heard were those ordered to the castle to sing what their master wanted and demanded. One can imagine no more unsuitable way of doing folk-lore research. Even in much better circumstances, when I have been collect-ing, it has often happened that in the beginning the peasants have tried to sing the 'urban' music that the upper classes like, and I have been able only with great difficulty to make them understand that I want to hear something quite different, something that they know, either from experience or by instinct, that their masters look down upon and despise. What then could Liszt have got, in the conditions in which he worked, other than the worthless things the peasants had learned, per-haps well, perhaps badly, from the higher classes?

I repeat, we can only partly blame Liszt for his erroneous inferences; from what he saw and heard he could hardly have come to any dif-ferent conclusions from the ones he puts forward in his book. More-over, the courage and conviction with which Liszt stated his opinions, wrong as they were, demands our admiration, for he must have known that by doing so he would rouse considerable opposition and enmity among his own people. We must blame ourselves for not being able to, or not wanting to, or at best for failing to guide him in the right direc-tion, though the way was open to us in our own villages.

# ZOLTÁN KODÁLY XXIII.4

## Folk Music

from *Folk Music of Hungary*, 1937

It is with pleasure that I offer this book to English readers, in the hope of supplying them with ample information about Hungarian folk music.

Interest in the subject has never been lacking. Dame Sybil Thorndike, when interviewed once about my music, instantly mentioned a song from Francis Korbay's *Hungarian Melodies*—it was undoubtedly the similarity of our names that caused the confusion. Unfortunately, Korbay's very popular volume contains hardly a single genuine folk song, and the same applies to other popular publications.

Folk music was similarly absent from the repertory of famous town gipsy bands. Only during the last few decades, stimulated by the Hungarian Radio, did they begin gradually to learn traditional peasant tunes, the accompaniment of which still consists too often of inappropriate harmonies derived from their hackneyed routine.

Bartók's book *Hungarian Folk Music* (Oxford University Press, 1931) provided thorough information to those interested. Unfortunately, Bartók's study only reached a small circle of experts, and the public hardly at all. Generally speaking, Hungarian folk music is still identified with gipsy music, and folk song is confused with popular art music. Yet in its narrower sense, Hungarian folk music has little or nothing in common with the music offered over the radio as 'Hungarian folk-tunes,' or, since Sarasate, as 'gipsy melodies.' Performed by gipsy orchestras or in other popular arrangements, such music has been the basis of all generalizations about 'Hungarian music' for nearly a hundred years. Nor is it in any way the creation of gipsies, as is still frequently asserted as a result of Franz Liszt's monumental error.

It is generally possible to identify the composers of the various tunes, which include the themes of Brahms' *Hungarian Dances* and Liszt's *Hungarian Rhapsodies*. They all lived in the nineteenth century, and the most outstanding were Hungarians of noble descent. To quote a few:

Kálmán Simonffy of Marosvásárhely [1832–1889], Elemér Szentirmay, whose real name was János Németh of Zsid and Vadasfa [1836–1908].

Béni Egressy, whose full name was Benjámin Galambos of Egressy [1814–1851].

Others came from bourgeois families which had been assimilated, such as

Béla Kéler [1820–1882] and Károly Thern [1817–1886], both from the Szepes region which, from the twelfth century onwards, was settled by Germans.

Of countless gipsy musicians very few were composers:
Miska Farkas [1829–1890] and Pál Rácz [1837–1886].

The gipsy contribution was not very distinguished, with the possible exception of Pista Dankó [1858–1903]; his compositions evidently postdate Liszt, since Liszt's *Des Bohémiens et de leur musique en Hongrie* appeared in 1859.

A number of songs, written by still unidentified composers, show by their style that they belong to this period.

Although text and melody were sometimes written by the same person, the harmonic accompaniment was generally written by another, as happened in polyphonic sixteenth-century *chansons* and the minnesingers' *töne*.

The Hungarian composers mentioned above were nearly always inexperienced amateurs. The tunes became common property soon after their appearance, and nobody inquired after their origin. Everything was freely reprinted, despite the Copyright Law of 1886, until with the beginning of the twentieth century the modern idea of author's right came into existence.

Hence in its essentials the style of Hungarian popular music, as generally known, was formed in the middle of the nineteenth century. Its rhythmical characteristics spring from language and dance. Its tunes were a later outcrop of an older type in which Western European influences are traceable. A single feature, the so-called 'gipsy scale,' points to a Southern Oriental (Arabic) origin, and may possibly have reached Hungary through the gipsies.

Gipsies falsify the folk songs they play by introducing the augmented intervals of this scale, which are never used by peasants. It should be emphasized, however, that the gipsy scale by no means predominates in gipsy style, and that modern major and minor scales are much more frequent.

Gipsy composers follow faithfully in the footsteps of other native and assimilated Hungarians. The most prolific, Pista Dankó, is even strongly under the influence of indigenous Hungarian peasant music. He wrote more than four hundred songs to contemporary Hungarian texts, whereas other gipsy composers confined themselves to the wordless and instrumentally conceived *csárdás*.

This is not to say that real gipsy music does not exist; it consists of short songs in Romany which are known and sung today mainly by nomadic 'tent-colonies' and to a lesser extent by settled village gipsies; the civilized town gipsies, and hence the musicians, do not know them at all. Still unexplored territory, these songs have essentially nothing in common with the Hungarian popular style or with true folk song. A more thoroughgoing stylistic analysis may some day make it possible to trace the origins of certain features in gipsy compositions. But gipsy

348

composers at best are never more than second-rate imitators of the regular Hungarian style.

In recent decades there has been a revival of this style, which has assumed at least quantitative importance. The chief exponents are again native Hungarians such as Lóránd Fráter of Ipp and Érkeserű [1872–1923] and Árpád Balázs [1874–1941], or assimilated Hungarians such as Ernő Lányi [1861–1923]. There is a conspicuous absence of gipsy composers.

Hence it is entirely erroneous to regard the music played by gipsies from about 1850 onwards as 'gipsy music.' It is quite clear that most of the pieces were, and still are, written not by gipsies but by Hungarians, and any gipsies concerned have taken over a style created by others. In origin and character this style belonged to the town tradition of printed art music, and had nothing to do with 'ancient tradition' and the like. True, it spread by word of mouth; gipsies performed it without written music and it was sung by large numbers of musically illiterate people. It was assimilated by the average Hungarian, and more especially by the town-dweller, although a great deal of it also found its way into the villages. Superficial observers may be forgiven for having fallen into the trap of thinking that it was typical folk song. . . .

The old folk tradition is not visible even in the musical style immediately preceding this, a style which flourished in Hungary during the first half of the nineteenth century. It too was town art music, in essence nothing but dance music; at first it was even written by foreigners and immigrants, and, like its later counterpart, was to be found in print.

The first *Danses Hongroises*—sometimes just called *Hongroises*—were composed by men with names such as Bengraf, Franz Tost, Drechsler, Mohaupt, Stocker. It is still a mystery where they got the Hungarian trimmings for their mediocre pieces, formed and harmonized in Viennese style. A few copies of anonymous dances of that period, published in Vienna, and including the source of Haydn's 'Rondo all'ongarese,' show traces of an earlier, more primitive instrumental tradition. This may have survived amongst gipsy musicians of the day, since scattered traces of it still remain in remote villages.

Later music in this style was provided by János Lavotta of Izsépfalva and Kevelháza [1763–1820], János Svastits of Bocsár [c. 1800–1874], the Vice-Paladin Kázmér of Sárközy [1799–1876], and the physician J. B. of Hunyady [1807–1865]—all Hungarians—and also by the Czech Anton Csermák [1807–1865], self-styled baronet of Dlujk and Rouhans, the gipsy János Bihari [1764–1827] and the Jewish Márk Rózsavölgyi [1789–1848], whose death inspired Petőfi's famous, deepfelt poem. Newly awakened national feeling swept aside differences of birth and background: in the service of 'national music' they all found themselves on common ground.

Most of this music seems old-fashioned and dated now. Only the compositions of Bihari still teem with life. But since he had no knowledge of musical notation, there will never be any certainty about what is his and what has been added by those who noted down and copied his music. At all events, several of his pieces are related to traditional Hungarian peasant music. He forms the only link between peasant tradition and the urban dance music which produced the *csárdás* about 1830.

# XXIV English Folk Songs and Industrial Songs

JOHN ASHTON                                                        XXIV.1

Street Ballads

from *Modern Street Ballads*, 1888

Over Street Ballads may be raised the wail of 'Ichabod, Ichabod, their glory is departed.' They held their own for many centuries, bravely and well, but have succumbed to a changed order of things, and a new generation has arisen, who will not stop in the streets to listen to these ballads being sung, but prefer to have their music served up to them 'piping hot,' with the accompaniment of warmth, light, beer, and tobacco (for which they duly have to pay) at the Music Halls; but whether the change be for the better, or not, may be a moot question.

These Street Ballads were produced within a very few hours of the publication of any event of the slightest public interest; and, failing that, the singers had always an unlimited store to fall back upon, on domestic, or humorous subjects, love, the sea, etc., etc. Of their variety we may learn something, not only from this book, but from the ballad of 'Chaunting Benny' of which the following is a portion:—

> 'My songs have had a tidy run, I've plenty in my fist, Sirs,
> And if you wish to pick one out, I'll just run through my list, Sirs.
>
> Have you seen "My daughter Fan," "She wore a wreath of roses,"
> And here you see "My son Tom," "The Sun that lights the roses,"
> "Green grow the rushes, O," "On the Banks of Allan Water,"
> "Such a getting out of bed," with "Brave Lord Ullin's daughter."
>
> "Poor Bessie was a Sailor's bride," "Sitting on a rail," Sirs,
> "Is there a heart that never loved?" "The Rose of Allandale," Sirs,
> "The Maid of Judah," "Out of Place," with "Plenty to be sad at,"
> "I say, my rum un, who are you?" with "What a shocking bad hat," '
>     etc., etc.

Rough though some of these Street Ballads may be, very few of them were coarse, and, on reading them, we must ever bear in mind the class for whom they were produced, who listened to them, and—practical proof of interest—bought them. In this collection I have introduced nothing which can offend anybody except an absolute prude; in fact, 'My bear dances only to the genteelest of tunes.'

351

There are plenty of my readers old enough to remember many of these Ballads, and they will come none the worse because they bring with them the reminiscence of their youth. *Forsan et haec olim meminisse juvabit.* They owe a great deal of their charm to the fact that they were absolutely contemporary with the events they describe, and, though sometimes rather faulty in their history, owing to the pressure under which they were composed and issued, yet those very inaccuracies prove their freshness.

The majority were illustrated—if, indeed, any can be called illustrated—for the woodcuts were generally served out with a charming impartiality, and without the slightest regard to the subject of the ballad. What previous work these blocks had served, goodness only knows; they were probably bought at trade sales, and had illustrated books that were out of date or unsaleable. They vary from the sixteenth century to Bewick, some of whose works are occasionally met with; but, taking them as a whole, we must fain confess that art as applied to these Ballads was at its very lowest. Their literary merit is not great—but what can you expect for half-a-crown? which was the price which Jemmy Catnach of Monmouth Court, Seven Dials, used to pay for their production. Catnach issued a large number from his press (in fact, his successor, Fortey, advertised that he had four thousand different sorts for sale), and his name is used as a 'household word' to designate this class of Ballad. But, in fact, he only enjoyed the largest share of the London trade, whilst the Provinces were practically independent—Liverpool, Manchester, Birmingham, Newcastle, Preston, Hull, Sheffield, Durham, etc., had their own ballad-mongers, who wrote somewhat after the manner of the author of 'The Bard of Seven Dials.'

> 'And it's my plan, that some great man
> Dies with a broken head, Sirs,
> Vith a bewail, I does detail
> His death 'afore e's dead, Sirs.
> And while his friends and foes contends,
> They all my papers buy, Sirs,
> Yes, vithout doubt, I sells 'em out,
> 'Cos there my talent lies, Sirs.'

The Ballad singers and vendors made money rapidly over any event which took the popular fancy—a good blood-curdling murder being very profitable; and the business required very little capital, even that being speedily turned over. Generally, the singers worked singlehanded, but sometimes two would join, and then the Ballad took an antiphonal form, which must have relieved them very much, and the crowd which gathered round them was the surest proof that their vocal efforts were appreciated.

They are gone—probably irrevocably—but a trace of the vendor still lingers amongst us. One or two still remain about Gray's Inn Road, Farringdon Road, and other neighbourhoods; but I venture to say, as they drop out, they will find no successors. You may know them, if ever lucky enough to meet with one, by their canvas screens, on which are pinned the ballads—identical with that immortal screen of which Mr. Silas Wegg (in Dickens's 'Our Mutual Friend') was the proud proprietor; but these modern Ballads are mostly reproductions of Music Hall songs, and have very little in common with those about which I write.

## ANON                                                                XXIV.2

'If it wasn't for the 'ouses in between'

Music Hall Song, 1894

If you saw my little backyard, 'Wot a pretty spot!' you'd cry—
    It's a picture on a summer day;
Wiv the turnip tops and cabbages wot people don't buy
    I makes it on a Sunday look all gay.
The neighbours fink I grows 'em, and you'd fancy you're in Kent,
    Or at Epsom, if you gaze into the mews;
It's a wonder as the landlord doesn't want to raise the rent,
    Because we've got such nobby distant views.

    Oh! it really is a werry pretty garden,
    And Chingford to the eastward could be seen;
      Wiv a ladder and some glasses,
      You could see to 'Ackney Marshes,
    If it wasn't for the 'ouses in between.

We're as countrified as can be wiv a clothes-prop for a tree,
    The tub-school makes a rustic little stile;
Every time the blooming clock strikes there's a cuckoo sings to me,
    And I've painted up 'To Leather Lane, a mile'.
Wiv tom-ar-toes and wiv radishes wot 'adn't any sale,
    The backyard looks a puffick mass o' bloom;
And I've made a little beehive wiv some beetles in a pail,
    And a pitchfork wiv the 'andle o' the broom.

    Oh! it really is a werry pretty garden,
    An' the Rye 'Ouse from the cockloft could be seen;
      Where the chickweed man undresses,
      To bathe amoung the watercresses,
    If it wasn't for the 'ouses in between.

There's the bunny shares 'is egg-box wiv the cross-eyed cock and
  hen
    Though they 'as got the pip, and him the morf;
In a dog's-'ouse on the line-post there was pigeons nine or ten,
    Till someone took a brick and knock'd it off.
The dust-cart though it seldom comes, is just like 'arvest 'ome
    And we mean to rig a dairy up some'ow—
Put the donkey in the wash-house wiv some imitation 'orns,
    For we're teaching 'im to moo just like a cow.

    Oh! it really is a werry pretty garden,
    And 'Endon to the westward could be seen;
      And by clinging to the chimbley,
      You could see across to Wembley,
    If it wasn't for the 'ouses in between.

Though the gas-works isn't wiolets, they improve the rural scene—
    For mountains they would werry nicely pass;
There's the mushrooms in the dust-hole, with the cowcumbers so
  green—
    It only wants a bit o' 'ot-'ouse glass.
I wears this milkman's nightshirt, and I sits outside all day,
    Like the plough-boy cove what mizzled o'er the Lea;
And when I goes indoors at night they dunno what I say,
    'Cause my language gets as yokel as can be.

    Oh! it really is a werry pretty garden,
    And the soap works from the 'ouse-tops could be seen;
      If I got a rope and pulley,
      I'd enjoy the breeze more fully,
    If it wasn't for the 'ouses in between.

# SIR HUBERT PARRY                                    XXIV.3

## Folk Song

Inaugural Address to the Folk Song Society, 1898

Ladies and Gentlemen,—I think I may premise that this Society is
engaged upon a wholesome and seasonable enterprise. For, in these
days of high pressure and commercialism, when a little smattering of
knowledge of the science of heredity impels people to think it is hopeless to contend against their bad impulses, because they are bound to
inherit the bad qualities of countless shoals of ancestors, there is a

tendency with some of us to become cynical; and the best remedy available is to revive a belief in, and love of our fellow-creatures. And this love and well-thinking of our fellow-creatures must come to those who study folk-music; for one of the strangest things about it is that there is nothing in it common or unclean. It is a question, indeed, worthy of the serious consideration of some future philosopher—How has the unregenerate public arrived at such a happy result that in true folk-songs there is no sham, no got-up glitter, and no vulgarity? Yet so it is; and the pity of it is that these treasures of humanity are getting rare, for they are written in characters the most evanescent you can imagine, upon the sensitive brain fibres of those who learn them, and have but little idea of their value. Moreover, there is an enemy at the doors of folk-music which is driving it out, namely, the common popular songs of the day; and this enemy is one of the most repulsive and most insidious. If one thinks of the outer circumference of our terribly overgrown towns, where the jerry-builder holds sway; where one sees all around the tawdriness of sham jewellery and shoddy clothes, pawnshops and flaming gin-palaces; where stale fish and the miserable piles of Covent Garden refuse which pass for vegetables are offered for food —all such things suggest to one's mind the boundless regions of sham. It is for the people who live in these unhealthy regions—people who, for the most part, have the most false ideals, or none at all—who are always struggling for existence, who think that the commonest rowdyism is the highest expression of human emotion; it is for them that the modern popular music is made, and it is made with a commercial intention out of snippets of musical slang. And this product it is which will drive out folk-music if we do not save it. For even in country districts where folk-songs linger, the people think themselves behindhand if they do not know the songs of the seething towns; and as soon as the little urchins of distant villages catch the sound of a music hall tune, away goes the hope of their troubling their heads with the old fashioned folk-songs. But the old folk-music is among the purest products of the human mind. It grew in the heart of the people before they devoted themselves so assiduously to the making of quick returns; and it grew there because it pleased them to make it, and because what they made pleased them; and that is the only way good music is ever made.

I take it that we are engaged chiefly with the folk-songs of England, and England is poorly represented in collections so far. Other nations have been far more keen about the matter. Even Russia, which not so very long ago began to emerge from a state far removed from our idea of civilisation, had more than a century ago a very fine collection of folk-music. In this country we have not, until recently, had any idea of concentrating our attention on the collecting of our folk-songs, and now that we propose to remedy the deficiency, what difficulties beset

355

us! Some people seem to think they have but to walk out along the by-ways and hedges, and pick them up; but in reality, the collection of folk-songs requires the most extraordinary faculty of accurate attention, of accurate retention, of self-criticism and practice as well, to distinguish what is genuine from what is emasculated. The attention required makes it almost impossible to take down folk-songs with certainty. To my mind, the only way to do it with absolute accuracy, would be to make use of the phonograph, and have an apparatus with resonators and self-recording instruments, to put down the actual vibration value of all the notes, and so arrive at an exact record of the songs as they are sung. But we cannot expect such perfection yet. So we must be content to do what we can with patience and devotion; and we have the better hope because we have among the members of the Folk-Song Society several enthusiasts who have already practised the art, and have developed a wonderful gift in this direction. I hope that, with their assistance we shall preserve much precious folk-music from being lost, and I trust that before long we shall find England more satisfactorily represented in folk collections than has hitherto been the case. In the neighbouring countries of Ireland and Scotland folk-music has attracted more attention; and moreover town civilisation is not so rife in them, and in out-of-the-way places, old tunes survive much longer, and the marked characteristics which they possess make it in some respects more easy to collect them. English tunes are not marked by such characteristic traits of melody and rhythm, and are rather more difficult to lay hold of. Still we have no need to be ashamed of them, for they are characteristic of the race, of the quiet reticence of our country folk, courageous and content, ready to meet what chance shall bring with a cheery heart. All the things that mark the folk-music of the race, also betoken the qualities of the race, and as a faithful reflection of ourselves, we needs must cherish it. Moreover it is worth remembering that the great composers of other countries have concentrated upon their folk-music much attention, since style is ultimately national. True style comes not from the individual but from the products of crowds of fellow-workers, who sift, and try, and try again, till they have found the thing that suits their native taste; and the purest product of such efforts is folk-song, which, when it is found outlasts the greatest works of art, and becomes an heritage to generations. And in that heritage may lie the ultimate solution of the problem of characteristic national art.

I think also we may legitimately reflect that in these late days when we are beginning to realize how little happiness money profits can bring, and how much joy there lies in the simple beauty of primitive thought, and the emotions which are common to all men alike, even to the sophisticated, it is a hopeful sign, that a society like ours should be founded:—to save something primitive and genuine from extinction; to put on record what loveable qualities there are in unsophisticated humanity; and to comfort outselves by the hope that at bottom, our puzzling friend, Democracy, has permanent qualities hidden away somewhere, which may yet bring it out of the slough which the scramble after false ideals, the strife between the heads that organize and the workmen who execute, and the sordid vulgarity of our great city-populations, seem in our pessimistic moments to indicate as its inevitable destiny.

## CECIL SHARP
XXIV.4

### 'The Decline of the Folk Song'

from *English Folk Song: Some Conclusions*, 1907

Folk songs and folk dances, in days gone by, played an important part in the social life of the English village. That life is now waning, and with it are passing away the old traditions and customs. It is, happily, still possible, here and there, and in out-of-the-way nooks and corners, to come upon peasant men and women old enough to remember the village life of sixty, seventy, or even eighty years ago; and they will sing to you the songs and explain to you the dances that, in their young days, and on summer evenings, were sung and danced on the village greens. The English peasant still exists, although the peasantry as a class is extinct. Reformers would dispel the gloom which has settled upon the countryside, and revive the social life of the villages. Do what they will, however, it will not be the old life that they will restore. That has gone past recall. It will be of a new order, and one that will bear but little resemblance to the old social life of the 'Merrie England' of history.

Already many of the old singers from whom three or four years ago I recovered songs are dead and gone; and, of the rest, few will be able to 'tune a zong' many years hence. Mr Baring-Gould tells me that, without a single exception, all his old singers have gone to their long rest. The seventy-nine songs in *Folk-Songs from Somerset* were contributed by thirty-eight singers, whose ages average over seventy years apiece. In less than a decade, therefore, English folk singing will be extinct.

I have learned that it is, as a rule, only waste of time to call upon singers under the age of sixty. Their songs are nearly all modern; if, by chance, they happen to sing an old one, it is so infected with the modern spirit that it is hardly worth the gathering. There are, of course, exceptions; but they are few. Cripples, and those whose infirmities have kept them within doors engaged in sedentary occupations, sometimes retain the old traditions with greater fidelity than their more

357

fortunate brothers and sisters. But they are not many, and their songs, moreover, are not always trustworthy.

It appears, then, that the last generation of folk singers must have been born not later than sixty or seventy years ago—say 1840. Why the chain of tradition snapped, and without warning, at that particular link, it is difficult to say. Some would attribute it to the invention of railways, to the spread of education, to the industrial revival, or even to the political unrest which followed the passing of the Reform Bill and the repeal of the corn laws. On the other hand, there are those who would ascribe the cause not to an altered environment, but to a fundamental change in the outlook of the people themselves, arising from their attainment of a particular stage of their development. Be this as it may, it is the fact of the decadence of the folk song, not the causes which have led to its decline, with which we are here concerned. And the fact is beyond dispute.

Some critics see in the rejection of the folk song by the country people of the last generation proof that its vitality is exhausted. They argue that the folk song was the product of a society, which, in the natural course of things, has come to an end; that, as the survival of a past age, it has nothing in common with the complexities of modern life. They accordingly ridicule all attempts to popularize the folk song in the town and the country villages, and would relegate the collectors' gatherings to the museums and libraries for the benefit of antiquarians and archaeologists.

This view, which on the face of it sounds reasonable enough, rests upon the assumption that the country people of the last generation rejected the folk song for the sole reason that it did not attract them nor satisfy their desires so well as the modern music of the towns. This, however, is not really so, as the following incident brought very clearly to my notice a few years ago.

I had collected a large number of songs in Hambridge—from the grandparents, of course—with the co-operation of the Vicar, the Rev. C. L. Marson. We published several of these songs, and the Vicar directed that they should be taught in the village school. The children eagerly received them, and once again the old traditional songs were heard, between school hours, from end to end of the long village street. Then, strangely enough, the fathers and mothers of the schoolchildren pricked up their ears; the old songs caught their fancy. They learned them from their children and sang them with evident pleasure. That is to say, the men and women who forty or fifty years ago had scornfully refused to accept these same songs from their parents were now learning them with avidity from their own children! Clearly, the fault was not with the songs, nor with their attractiveness. This experience does not stand alone. The experiment has since been repeated in other country villages with, in every case, identically the same result, . . .

Other nations have, long ago, recognized the value of the folk song in elementary education. Hitherto, from lack of the necessary material, we have been debarred from following the example set by our continental neighbours. Now, however, that we possess that material in abundance, we have no longer any excuse for refusing to follow in their footsteps.

If some such scheme as this which we have been considering were adopted in the State schools throughout the country, and in the preparatory schools of the upper and middle classes as well, not only would the musical taste of the nation be materially raised, but a beneficent and enduring effect would be produced upon the national character. For good music purifies, just as bad music vulgarizes; indeed, the effect of music upon the minds of children is so subtle and so far-reaching that it is impossible to exaggerate the harmful influence upon character which the singing of coarse and vulgar tunes may have. Up till now, the street song has had an open field; the music taught in the schools has been hopelessly beaten in the fight for supremacy. But the mind that has been fed upon the pure melody of the folk will instinctively detect the poverty-stricken tunes of the music-hall, and refuse to be captivated and deluded by their superficial attractiveness. Good taste is, perhaps, largely a matter of environment; but it is also the result of careful and early training. Matthew Arnold somewhere recommends retaining in the memory certain passages of poetry of undoubted and admitted excellence, to be used as touchstones with which to preserve a high standard of poetical taste. The same will be done with regard to music, if schoolteachers will but adopt a wise and intelligent scheme of musical education, and give their children nothing but the best music, and music, moreover, that they like and can understand; and these conditions can best be satisfied by giving them the folk songs of their own country.

We may look, therefore, to the introduction of folk songs in the elementary schools to effect an improvement in the musical taste of the people, and to refine and strengthen the national character. Our system of education is, at present, too cosmopolitan; it is calculated to produce citizens of the world rather than Englishmen. And it is Englishmen, English citizens, that we want. How can this be remedied? By taking care, I would suggest, that every child born of English parents is, in its earliest years, placed in possession of all those things which are the distinctive products of its race. The first and most important of these is the mother tongue. Its words, its grammatical constructions, its idioms, are all characteristic of the race which has evolved them, and whose ideas and thoughts they are thus peculiarly fitted to express. The English tongue differs from the French or German precisely as the Englishman differs from the Frenchman or the German. Irish patriots are fully alive to this, and, from their own point of view, are quite right in advocating the revival of the Irish language.

Then there are the folk tales, legends, and proverbs, which are peculiar to the English; the national sports, pastimes, and dances also. All these things belong of right to the children of our race, and it is as unwise as it is unjust to rob them of this their national inheritance.

Finally, there are the folk songs, those simple ditties which have sprung like wild flowers from the very hearts of our countrymen, and which are as redolent of the English race as its language. If every English child be placed in possession of all these products, he will know and understand his country and his countrymen far better than he does at present; and knowing and understanding them he will love them the more, realize that he is united to them by the subtle bond of blood and of kinship, and become, in the highest sense of the word, a better citizen, and a truer patriot.

There is still another and wide field to exploit. We are too apt to forget the needs of those tens of thousands of our countrymen who regard music simply from the point of view of melody, who never get beyond something which they can sing, a tune that they can whistle or tap their umbrellas to. All of these are, of course, in the elementary stage of musical education. The pity of it is that the majority of them remain there all their lives, lingering with their feet on the lowest rung of the ladder. It is only the few, the very few, who rise from the bottom and win their way to higher things. And the reason, of course, is that the tunes that attract them, and which they habitually sing, are bad tunes and, therefore, uneducative.

The important thing to remember, and one that would-be reformers too often forget, is that bad tunes are popular, not because of their badness, but because of their attractiveness. The classes who sing bad tunes sing them simply because they never hear good ones that appeal to them with equal force. They are never called upon to exercise a choice. It is a case of bad tunes or nothing. Place, however, good tunes into competition with bad ones, and the good tunes will win the day, provided that—and this is the essential condition—they are at least as 'catchy' and attractive as the bad ones.

Now one of the most remarkable qualities of the folk song is its power of appeal to the uncritical, to those who, unversed in the subtleties of musical science, yet 'know what they like'. Its value lies in its possession of this dual quality of excellence and attractiveness. Flood the streets, therefore, with folk tunes, and those who now vulgarize themselves and others by singing coarse music hall songs will soon drop them in favour of the equally attractive but far better tunes of the folk. This will make the streets a pleasanter place for those who have sensitive ears, and will do incalculable good in civilizing the masses. Not only

360

will the streets of towns and cities be purged, but those of country villages also. A few weeks ago I was hunting for songs on Exmoor, and had spent two or three hours one afternoon listening to and noting down several exquisite melodies that were sung to me by an old man, eighty-six years of age. In the evening of the same day, my peace was rudely disturbed by the raucous notes of coarse music-hall songs, shouted out, at the tops of their voices, by the young men of the village, who were spending the evening in the bar of my hotel. The contrast between the old-fashioned songs and kindly manners of my friend the old parish clerk who lived hard by and the songs and uncouth behaviour of the present occupants of the bar struck me very forcibly, and threw into strong relief the deplorable deterioration that, in the last thirty years or so, has taken place in the manners and amusements of the country villagers.

It is, however, not only to the uncritical that the folk song makes its especial appeal. There are those who have always been attracted by music and who, being cultivated people, perhaps versed in one of the sister arts, have had the good sense to perform and listen to nothing but the best music; but who, nevertheless, have never been really moved by it. This may be because they began their musical education at the wrong end, with advanced and complex harmonized compositions, instead of with simple melody. To such people, the advent of the folk song has been a revelation. Its pure and simple strains, appealing less to the intellect than to the emotions, have struck home, gone straight to their hearts, and caused many of them to realize for the first time what music really means. To cultivated people such as these the folk song will be an education, helping them to appreciate the beauties of the more advanced modern music which hitherto they have only dimly apprehended.

The views elaborated above will not, of course, be accepted without question.

# A. L. LLOYD

XXIV.5

## 'What Happened to the Work Songs?'

from *The Singing Englishman*, 1944

Some say the railways killed English folksong. Some say it was education; some say the industrial revolution. And others, this is God's truth, say the folk songs were 'not altered by environment, but by a fundamental change in the outlook of the people themselves, arising from the attainment of a particlar stage in their development' (Cecil Sharp:

*English Folksong, Some conclusions*). How, you may well ask, do people reach a stage in development, without a change in circumstances? How does their outlook alter, except as their social environment alters? The experts are dumb. Perhaps they think these changes just come over the people for no special reason like a flock of pigeons off the top of Nelson's cocked hat.

No doubt there are plenty of reasons for the regression—observe I do not say disappearance—of folksongs; and it would seem that some of these reasons are psychological and some are physical and both kinds affect each other. The chief reason, and the one from which all other reasons branch, is the change in society itself. There are no two ways about it; what we quickest recognise as folksong is the product of a social system that has come to an end. Social customs, social ideas have altered now; there is your psychological reason. Physical things have altered too, and the coming of the railways is surely one thing which has caused the old kind of song to die away; modern transport gives people access to amusements and diversions they did not have in the days when country labourers had only two or three ideas about livening a dull evening, and one of them was by making up and singing songs round the kitchen fire. Even the installation first of gaslight, later of electric light, in villages and isolated farms has done something to dry up the source of many songs, for nowadays there is no ground for the kind of economy which brought country neighbours together round the one candle, and this was a great stimulus to the making up of songs in former times. But more serious than the development of railways and the installation of gasmeters, more deadly than the invention of the phonograph and the radio and the daily delivery of newspapers, is the development of industrial technique and the alteration or disappearance of jobs which formerly were accompanied by singing. And on top of this, the growth of industrial noise is something that has done a great deal to kill the oldstyle folksong.

Most commonly people blame mechanical music, the gramophone or the radio, and that does turn many singers into listeners, true, and the news service of radio and press makes all those songs unnecessary which once used to spread information about the latest battle, murder, or who-slept-with-who. But folk-music was already on the way out before the appearance of the gramophone about 1900 or the radio about 1920; so that cannot be the whole reason or anything like it. What we know for sure is this: many folksongs were closely related to a certain stage of technical development, and as modern times changed all that, the songs no longer applied. Most jobs have been revolutionised in the last 150 years. A change in the way of living destroys a folksong quicker than anything else and a little quick progress and a little bad luck has destroyed whole categories of songs in a single decade. Girls used to sit and sing to the whir of the spinning wheel. Nowadays the rhythm and tempo of that kind of work has quite altered, and the old spinning songs do not fit any more; and if a Bradford mill hand did fancy singing then she would have her work cut out trying to hear her own voice above the clatter of machinery. In any case, any radio-amplified 'Music-while-you-Work' tune fits better into her life than songs like:

> She pressed herself against the wall,
> Line, twine, the willow and the dee,
> And there she has her two babes born
> With a tweedle, tweedle twine-O.
> She took a penknife long and sharp,
> Line, twine, the willow and the dee,
> And pressed it through their tender heart,
> With a tweedle, tweedle twine-O.
> She dug a grave by the light of the sun
> Line, twine, the willow and the dee,
> And buried them under a marble stone
> With a tweedle, tweedle twine-O.
> So when she went straightway to church,
> Line, twine, the willow and the dee,
> She seen two sweet babes in the porch
> With a tweedle, tweedle twine-O.
> So when she went to her father's hall,
> Line, twine, the willow and the dee,
> She seen two sweet babes playing at ball,
> With a tweedle, tweedle twine-O.
> Babes, ah babes, I wish you was mine,
> Line, twine, the willow and the dee,
> I'd dress you up in the silk so fine
> With a tweedle, tweedle twine-O.
> Mother, o mother, we once was thine,
> Line, twine, the willow and the dee,
> You did not dress us in the silk so fine,
> With a tweedle, tweedle twine-O.
> You dug a grave by the light of the sun,
> Line, twine, the willow and the dee,
> And buried us under a marble stone,
> With a tweedle, tweedle twine-O.

When the sails of the windmill turned to some professional purpose there were many songs about millers, and millers' daughters especially, and they are as well known as any. But now the farm worker no longer brings his wheat to the mill as grain and takes it away as flour, for his wife to bake into bread. What happens now is the farmer sells his corn to a big miller's agent, as like as not over the telephone, and buys his bread from the machine bakers in the nearest town, whose motorvan comes round the villages daily. So the miller and the miller's daughter are no longer something special in the working life and the social life of the countryside. There is quite a chance the miller is an obscure and wealthy gentleman with pinstripe trousers and a City office, and whatever his daughter may do, if he has a daughter, she is not likely to do it in the same circumstances as was once conventional for millers' daughters, if the songs are anything to go by, for many of the old mill songs are like this one from the North-east:

> The young man and the miller's lass they set out on the hill,
>     Hey, with a gay and a grinding O.
> They took a sack of corn and they went to grind the mill.
>     And the mill turns about with a grinding O.
>
> The young man barred the door and the maiden she did sigh,
>     Hey, with a gay and a grinding O.
> And then it came into her head that with him she would lie,
>     And the mill turns about with a grinding O.
>
> She has cast off her petticoat and so she has her gown,
>     Hey, with a gay and a grinding O.
> And all upon the running corn she straightway did lay down,
>     And the mill turns about with a grinding O.
>
> So up then starts the young man and run from mill to town,
>     Hey, with a gay and a grinding O.
> And there he spied the miller all a-walking up and down,
>     And the mill turns about with a grinding O.
>
> O I have served you seven long year and never sought a fee,
>     Hey, with a gay and a grinding O.
> And I will serve you seven more if you'll keep your lass from me,
>     And the mill turns about with a grinding O.

This song ran well to the rhythm of the milling; but the business has altered now, technically and socially, and to the extent that such songs are right out.

Much the same thing goes for a great deal of agricultural work. Once, reaping songs were common in England, whose rhythm fitted perfectly the movement of the sickle. Such songs do not go at all to the clatter of the modern mechanical combine harvester which will reap the crop, thresh the grain, bag the wheat, and even sew the sacks if you like, and all you need is a man to drive the tractor and another to look after the combine, and they have no special rhythm to work to; for them also, any Bing Crosby or Vera Lynn song fits their work as well as, or better than, the good old ones.

# A. L. LLOYD

## 'The Industrial Songs'

from *Folk Song in England*, 1967

No one can write truly of folklore who does not know how to recognize the spirit of the people in relation to work, and how to use its positive characteristics as illustrations. (Wilhelm Heinrich Riehl, 1861.)

Capitalism killed folk song, we are told: enclosure starved it, the steam-engine put paid to it, the miseries of nineteenth century industrialism blighted the culture of the working people. A gloomy picture: is it just?

In the novel conditions brought by the industrial revolution the old oral culture was in agony, but a new lower-class culture was developing, based mainly on book not word of mouth. As the workers' movement grew during the nineteenth century, with its choirs and brass bands, reading circles and amateur theatricals, the children and grandchildren of the folk singers and storytellers were to find new forms of culture, more educated and literary, with a new content. It was a slow dour process, hindered by long working hours and overbearing masters, but it meant that when the mainly unwritten culture of the peasantry was reduced to rubble, the field was by no means left free to 'bourgeois' culture, that is to the fine arts and popular entertainments licensed and provided by the established order. Particularly in the domain of song. As the old lyric of the countryside crumbled away, a new lyric of the industrial towns arose, frail at first but getting stronger, reflecting the life and aspirations of a raw class in the making, of men handling new-fashioned tools, thinking new thoughts, standing in novel relationship to each other and to their masters. This fresh lyric we call 'workers' song'.

If, for convenience, we consider the realm of song partitioned into three areas—peasant folk song, bourgeois social song, workers' song— we must bear in mind that the division is but rough, that each of these kinds merges with and acts upon the other (for instance there is a layer of country folk song that is bourgeois-conditioned), and that within each handy category are subdivisions it would be unhandy to ignore. So, within the broad region of workers' song we find an order best described as 'industrial folk songs' quite distinct from the non-folkloric labour anthems and 'literary' political mass-songs with their agitational content, elated feeling, and hymnlike style. We are speaking of a kind of folk song that, far from being destroyed by the industrial revolution, was actually created by its conditions. Miraculously enough, Jean Genet is not alone in being struck by that 'strangest of poetic phenomena: that the most terrible and dismal part of the whole world, the blackest, most burnt-out . . . the severe naked world of factory workers, is entwined with marvels of popular song.'

An anxious query arises: 'This so-called industrial folk song, is it *authentic*?' What is authenticity? We have seen that the old classic kind of rural song is itself no thoroughbred; for centuries it was 'contaminated' by print, and influenced in sundry ways by the usages of the towns and even by borrowings from abroad. The major scale, unitary rhythm, equal verses, all had their hybridizing effect. Many forms of folk song lie close to the world of the professional arts, and the out-and-out purist might deny the label of 'folk song proper' to a great part of the traditional repertory preferring to limit the term to a few ceremonial and functional pieces such as wassail songs and shanties—and by no means all of them! The citizenship of the home-made song of industrial workers is particularly equivocal. Some would call it stateless, and ponder whether to issue it with a passport that allows limited entry to the domain of literature but is not valid for the realm of folklore. A vain preoccupation. It is more fruitful to reflect on the aims of the creators and bearers than to fret over the pedigree of the songs themselves. The first question is: 'Who uses this song, and for what purpose?' The question: 'How was the song made?' is but secondary, though not negligible if we are to keep within reasonable bounds of definition.

By 'industrial folk song' let us understand the kind of vernacular songs made by workers themselves directly out of their own experiences, expressing their own interests and aspirations, and incidentally passed on among themselves mainly by oral means, though this is no *sine qua non*. The kind of songs created from outside by learned writers, on behalf of the working class, is not our concern here. In destination, both kinds may be similar, but in the manner of their creation and expression, as well as in dissemination and often in function too, they are distinct. In England, distinct to an unusual degree, it seems. In most European countries, although in the period of transition from handcraft to machines the workers' home-made songs hardly differed from 'classic' folk song, once industry was consolidated and large-scale workers' organizations were under way, the proletarian lyricists quickly accepted the influence of literary political hymns, and their creations came more and more to resemble fine art compositions, even if only in a half-educated way. In England, on the other hand, the folk song style persisted with peculiar stubbornness. The literary songs of Chartism and subsequent 'chants of Labour', national or international, were fairly well accepted by our organized workers, if not with the burning enthusiasm their Continental comrades showed for the anthems of revolution. But this kind of song had little influence on the sort of thing the singing miners, mill-hands and foundry-workers made for themselves. Our working class only gradually isolated itself from the peasantry to form its own culture, and if the newer tradition is generally different from the old in content, the benevolent ghosts of the fine oral culture

366

of the past are still strongly present in some corners, to surprise the explorer with their 'melodious twang'.

Not that many song-seekers have tried these corridors so far. Till now, industrial folk song has hardly been studied at all. The great collectors, we have seen, confined their attention to the rural past and shunned the industrial present. Their concern was to rescue country lore from the onslaught of modern times, partly out of a romantic preference for rustic lanes over milltown alleys and for men of the soil over their sons in the mine, but chiefly no doubt because they were looking for beauties not documents, and they mistrusted their chance of finding much radiance among the slag-heaps. Understandable enough, but their preoccupation with country folkways allowed them only a partial view of our traditional song, for even a superficial glance shows that not only has industry a folklore of its own, but also the *creation* of folk music and poetry has, within the last hundred years or so, passed almost entirely into the hands and mouths of industrial workers. The performance of country song still goes on, though rather faintly now; but the composition of new stuff in the villages had practically ceased by the 1850s. Not so in industrial areas. Miners, textile workers and others went on making their own songs. And if this do-it-yourself song creation rather dwindled in the period between the World Wars, it has lately taken a new lease of life and flourishes quite vigorously again, for example with the new *genre* of elegies on mines being closed down by the National Coal Board ('Lament for Albert', 'Farewell to 'Cotia', etc.). Early in the nineteenth century, in middle class drawing rooms and parlours, sentimental romances of the Dibdin or Haynes Bayley kind were flourishing, while in the cottages the classic folk ballads were dying and their singers falling silent before the bawling of the broadside-sellers. And at the same time starting up in the years shortly before Waterloo, we are faced with the significant appearance of the new industrial ballad, at first mainly among weavers, but rapidly spreading and growing in power among miners and other workers.

# XXV Retrospect

GERARD MANLEY HOPKINS          XXV.1
'Binsey Poplars' felled 1879
written 1879

My aspens dear, whose airy cages quelled,
Quelled or quenched in leaves the leaping sun,
All felled, felled, are all felled;
 Of a fresh and following folded rank
   Not spared, not one
   That dandled a sandalled
   Shadow that swam or sank
On meadow and river and wind-wandering weed-winding bank.

 O if we but knew what we do
   When we delve or hew—
  Hack and rack the growing green!
   Since country is so tender
  To touch, her being só slender,
  That, like this sleek and seeing ball
  But a prick will make no eye at all,
  Where we, even where we mean
   To mend her we end her,
   When we hew or delve:
After-comers cannot guess the beauty been.
 Ten or twelve, only ten or twelve
  Strokes of havoc únselve
   The sweet especial scene,
  Rural scene, a rural scene,
  Sweet especial rural scene.

# GEORGE ELIOT XXV.2

## Gwendolen "desires to be independent"

from *Daniel Deronda*, 1874–6

Gwendolen met him with unusual gravity, and holding out her hand, said, 'It is most kind of you to come, Herr Klesmer. I hope you have not thought me presumptuous.'. . .

She continued standing near the piano, and Klesmer took his stand at the other end of it, with his back to the light and his terribly omniscient eyes upon her. No affectation was of use, and she began without delay.

'I wish to consult you, Herr Klesmer. We have lost all our fortune; we have nothing. I must get my own bread, and I desire to provide for my mamma, so as to save her from any hardship. The only way I can think of—and I should like it better than anything—is to be an actress—to go on the stage. But of course I should like to take a high position, and I thought—if you thought I could,'—here Gwendolen became a little more nervous,—'it would be better for me to be a singer—to study singing also.'

Klesmer put down his hat on the piano, and folded his arms, as if to concentrate himself.

'I know,' Gwendolen resumed, turning from pale to pink and back again—'I know that my method of singing is very defective; but I have been ill taught. I could be better taught; I could study. And you will understand my wish:—to sing and act too, like Grisi, is a much higher position. Naturally, I should wish to take as high a rank as I can. And I can rely on your judgment. I am sure you will tell me the truth.'

Gwendolen somehow had the conviction that now she made this serious appeal the truth would be favourable.

Still Klesmer did not speak. He drew off his gloves quickly, tossed them into his hat, rested his hands on his hips, and walked to the other end of the room. He was filled with compassion for this girl: he wanted to put a guard on his speech. When he turned again, he looked at her with a mild frown of inquiry, and said with gentle though quick utterance, 'You have never seen anything, I think, of artists and their lives?—I mean of musicians, actors, artists of that kind?'

'Oh no,' said Gwendolen, not perturbed by a reference to this obvious fact in the history of a young lady hitherto well provided for.

'You are,—pardon me,' said Klesmer, again pausing near the piano—'in coming to a conclusion on such a matter as this, everything must be taken into consideration,—you are perhaps twenty?'

'I am twenty-one,' said Gwendolen, a slight fear rising in her. 'Do you think I am too old?'

Klesmer pouted his under lip and shook his long fingers upward in a manner totally enigmatic.

'Many persons begin later than others,' said Gwendolen. . . .

Klesmer took no notice, but said with more studied gentleness than ever, 'You have probably not thought of an artistic career until now: you did not entertain the notion, the longing—what shall I say?—you did not wish yourself an actress, or anything of that sort, till the present trouble?'

'Not exactly; but I was fond of acting. I have acted; you saw me, if you remember—you saw me here in charades, and as Hermione,' said Gwendolen, really fearing that Klesmer had forgotten.

'Yes, yes,' he answered quickly, 'I remember—I remember perfectly,' and again walked to the other end of the room. It was difficult for him to refrain from this kind of movement when he was in any argument either audible or silent.

Gwendolen felt that she was being weighed. The delay was unpleasant. But she did not yet conceive that the scale could dip on the wrong side, and it seemed to her only graceful to say, 'I shall be very much obliged to you for taking the trouble to give me your advice, whatever it may be.'

'Miss Harleth,' said Klesmer, turning towards her and speaking with a slight increase of accent, 'I will veil nothing from you in this matter. I should reckon myself guilty if I put a false visage on things—made them too black or too white. The gods have a curse for him who willingly tells another the wrong road. . . .'

Gwendolen felt a sinking of heart under this unexpected solemnity, and kept a sort of fascinated gaze on Klesmer's face, while he went on.

'You are a beautiful young lady—you have been brought up in ease— you have done what you would—you have not said to yourself, "I must know this exactly," "I must understand this exactly," "I must do this exactly"'—in uttering these three terrible *musts*, Klesmer lifted up three long fingers in succession. 'In sum, you have not been called upon to be anything but a charming young lady, whom it is an impoliteness to find fault with.'

He paused an instant; then resting his fingers on his hips again, and thrusting out his powerful chin, he said—

'Well, then, with that preparation, you wish to try the life of the artist; you wish to try a life of arduous, unceasing work, and—uncertain praise. Your praise would have to be earned, like your bread; and both would come slowly, scantily—what do I say?—they might hardly come at all.'

This tone of discouragement, which Klesmer half hoped might suffice without anything more unpleasant, roused some resistance in Gwendolen. With a slight turn of her head away from him, and an air of pique, she said—

'I thought that you, being an artist, would consider the life one of the most honourable and delightful. And if I can do nothing better?—I suppose I can put up with the same risks as other people do.'

'Do nothing better?' said Klesmer, a little fired. 'No, my dear Miss Harleth, you could do nothing better—neither man nor women could do anything better—if you could do what was best or good of its kind. I am not decrying the life of the true artist. I am exalting it. I say, it is out of the reach of any but choice organisations—natures framed to love perfection and to labour for it; . . . An honourable life? Yes. But the honour comes from the inward vocation and the hard-won achievement: there is no honour in donning the life as a livery.'. . .

[Gwendolen] said, in a tone of some insistance—

'I am quite prepared to bear hardships at first. Of course no one can become celebrated all at once. And it is not necessary that every one should be first-rate—either actresses or singers. If you would be so kind as to tell me what steps I should take, I shall have the courage to take them. I don't mind going up hill. It will be easier than the dead level of being a governess. I will take any steps you recommend.'

Klesmer was more convinced now that he must speak plainly.

'I will tell you the steps, not that I recommend, but that will be forced upon you. It is all one, so far, what your goal may be—excellence, celebrity, second, third rateness—it is all one. You must go to town under the protection of your mother. You must put yourself under training—musical, dramatic, theatrical:—whatever you desire to do you have to learn—' here Gwendolen looked as if she were going to speak, but Klesmer lifted up his hand and said decisively, 'I know. You have exercised your talents—you recite—you sing—from the drawing-room *standpunkt*. My dear Fräulein, you must unlearn all that. You have not yet conceived what excellence is: you must unlearn your mistaken admirations. You must know what you have to strive for, and then you must subdue your mind and body to unbroken discipline. Your mind, I say. For you must not be thinking of celebrity:—put that candle out of your eyes, and look only at excellence. You would of course earn nothing—you could get no engagement for a long while. You would need money for yourself and your family. But that,' here Klesmer frowned and shook his fingers as if to dismiss a triviality—'that could perhaps be found.'. . .

Gwendolen's eyes began to burn, but the dread of showing weakness urged her to added self-control. She compelled herself to say in a hard tone—

'You think I want talent, or am too old to begin.'

Klesmer made a sort of hum and then descended on an emphatic 'Yes! The desire and the training should have begun seven years ago—or a good deal earlier. A mountebank's child who helps her father to earn shillings when she is six years old—a child that inherits a singing throat from a long line of choristers and learns to sing as it learns to talk, has a likelier beginning. Any great achievement in acting or in music grows with the growth. . . . Genius at first is little more than a great capacity for receiving discipline. . . .'

'I did not pretend to genius,' said Gwendolen, still feeling that she might somehow do what Klesmer wanted to represent as impossible. 'I only supposed that I might have a little talent—enough to improve.'

'I don't deny that,' said Klesmer. 'If you had been put in the right track some years ago and had worked well, you might now have made a public singer, though I don't think your voice would have counted for much in public. For the stage your personal charms and intelligence might then have told without the present drawback of inexperience—lack of discipline—lack of instruction.'. . .

'I understand, of course, that no one can be a finished actress at once. It may be impossible to tell beforehand whether I should succeed; but that seems to me a reason why I should try. I should have thought that I might have taken an engagement at a theatre meanwhile, so as to earn money and study at the same time.'

'Can't be done, my dear Miss Harleth—I speak plainly—it can't be done. I must clear your mind of these notions, which have no more resemblance to reality than a pantomime. Ladies and gentlemen think that when they have made their toilet and drawn on their gloves they are as presentable on the stage as in a drawing-room. No manager thinks that. With all your grace and charm, if you were to present yourself as an aspirant to the stage, a manager would either require you to pay as an amateur for being allowed to perform, or he would tell you to go and be taught—trained to bear yourself on the stage, as a horse, however beautiful, must be trained for the circus; to say nothing of that study which would enable you to personate a character consistently, and animate it with the natural language of face, gesture, and tone. For you to get an engagement fit for you straight away is out of the question.'

'I really cannot understand that,' said Gwendolen, rather haughtily—then, checking herself, she added in another tone—'I shall be obliged to you if you will explain how it is that such poor actresses get engaged. I have been to the theatre several times, and I am sure there were actresses who seemed to me to act not at all well and who were quite plain.'

'Ah, my dear Miss Harleth, that is the easy criticism of the buyer. We who buy slippers toss away this pair and the other as clumsy; but there went an apprenticeship to the making of them. Excuse me: you could not at present teach one of those actresses; but there is certainly much that she could teach you. For example, she can pitch her voice so as to be heard: ten to one you could not do it till after many trials. Merely to stand and move on the stage is an art—requires practice. It is understood that we are not now talking of a *comparse* in a petty theatre who earns the wages of a needlewoman. That is out of the question for you.'

'Of course I must earn more than that,' said Gwendolen, with a sense of wincing rather than of being refuted; 'but I think I could soon learn to do tolerably well all those little things you have mentioned. I am not so very stupid. And even in Paris I am sure I saw two actresses playing important ladies' parts who were not at all ladies and quite ugly. I suppose I have no particular talent, but I *must* think it is an advantage, even on the stage, to be a lady and not a perfect fright.'. . .

'I desire to be independent,' said Gwendolen, deeply stung and confusedly apprehending some scorn for herself in Klesmer's words. 'That was my reason for asking whether I could not get an immediate engagement. Of course I cannot know how things go on about theatres. But I thought that I could have made myself independent. I have no money, and I will not accept help from any one.'

Her wounded pride could not rest without making this disclaimer.


## ARNOLD TOYNBEE                                                   XXV.3
### 'The chief features of the Revolution'
from *The Industrial Revolution*, 1884

The essence of the Industrial Revolution is the substitution of competition for the mediaeval regulations which had previously controlled the production and distribution of wealth. On this account it is not only one of the most important facts of English history, but Europe owes to it the growth of two great systems of thought—Economic Science, and its antithesis, Socialism. The development of Economic Science in England has four chief landmarks, each connected with the name of one of the four great English economists. The first is the publication of Adam Smith's *Wealth of Nations* in 1776, in which he investigated the causes of wealth and aimed at the substitution of industrial freedom for a system of restriction. The production of wealth, not the welfare of man, was what Adam Smith had primarily before his mind's eye; in his own words, 'the great object of the Political Economy of every country is to increase the riches and power of that country.' His great book appeared on the eve of the Industrial Revolution. A second stage in the growth of the science is marked by Malthus's *Essay on Population*, published in 1798, which may be considered the product of that revolution, then already in full swing. Adam Smith had concentrated all his attention on a large production; Malthus directed his inquiries, not to the causes of wealth but to the causes of poverty, and found them in his theory of population. A third stage is marked by Ricardo's *Principles of Political Economy and Taxation*, which appeared in 1817, and in which Ricardo sought to ascertain the laws of the distribution of wealth. Adam Smith had shown how wealth could be produced under a system of industrial freedom, Ricardo showed how wealth is distributed under such a system, a problem which could not have occurred to any one before his time. The fourth stage is marked by John Stuart Mill's *Principles of Political Economy*, published in 1848. Mill himself asserted that 'the chief merit of his treatise' was the distinction drawn between the laws of production and those of distribution, and the problem he tried to solve was, how wealth *ought to be* distributed. A great advance was made by Mill's attempt to show what was and what was not inevitable under a system of free competition. In it we see the influence which the rival system of Socialism was already beginning to exercise upon the economists. The whole spirit of Mill's book is quite different from that of any economic works which had up to his time been written in England. Though a re-statement of Ricardo's system, it contained the admission that the distribution of wealth is the result of 'particular social arrangements,' and it recognised that competition alone is not a satisfactory basis of society.

Competition, heralded by Adam Smith, and taken for granted by Ricardo and Mill, is still the dominant idea of our time; though since the publication of the *Origin of Species*, we hear more of it under the name of the 'struggle for existence.' I wish here to notice the fallacies involved in the current arguments on this subject. In the first place it is assumed that all competition is a competition for existence. This is not true. There is a great difference between a struggle for mere existence and a struggle for a particular kind of existence. For instance, twelve men are struggling for employment in a trade where there is only room for eight; four are driven out of that trade, but they are not trampled out of existence. A good deal of competition merely decides what kind of work a man is to do; though of course when a man can only do one kind of work, it may easily become a struggle for bare life. It is next assumed that this struggle for existence is a law of nature, and that therefore all human interference with it is wrong. To that I answer that the whole meaning of civilisation is interference with this brute struggle. We intend to modify the violence of the fight, and to prevent the weak being trampled under foot.

Competition, no doubt, has its uses. Without competition no progress would be possible, for progress comes chiefly from without; it is external pressure which forces men to exert themselves. Socialists, however, maintain that this advantage is gained at the expense of an enormous waste of human life and labour, which might be avoided by regulation. But here we must distinguish between competition in production and competition in distribution, a difference recognised in modern legislation, which has widened the sphere of contract in the one direction, while it has narrowed it in the other. For the struggle of men to outvie one another in production is beneficial to the community; their struggle over the division of the joint produce is not. The stronger side will dictate its own terms; and as a matter of fact, in the early days of competition the capitalists used all their power to oppress the labourers, and drove down wages to starvation point. This kind of competition has to be checked; there is no historical instance of its having lasted long without being modified either by combination or legislation, or both. In England both remedies are in operation, the former through Trades-Unions, the latter through factory legislation. In the past other remedies were applied. It is this desire to prevent the evils of competition that affords the true explanation of the fixing of wages by Justices of the Peace, which seemed to Ricardo a remnant of the old system of tyranny in the interests of the strong. Competition, we have now learnt, is neither good nor evil in itself; it is a force which has to be studied and controlled; it may be compared to a stream whose strength and direction have to be observed, that embankments may be thrown up within which it may do its work harmlessly and beneficially. But at the period we are considering it came to be believed in as a gospel, and, the idea of necessity being superadded, economic laws deduced from the assumption of universal unrestricted competition were converted into practical precepts, from which it was regarded as little short of immoral to depart.

Coming to the facts of the Industrial Revolution, the first thing that strikes us is the far greater rapidity which marks the growth of population. Before 1751 the largest decennial increase, so far as we can calculate from our imperfect materials, was 3 per cent. For each of the next three decennial periods the increase was 6 per cent.; then between 1781 and 1791 it was 9 per cent.; between 1791 and 1801, 11 per cent.; between 1801 and 1811, 14 per cent.; between 1811 and 1821, 18 per cent. This is the highest figure ever reached in England, for since 1815 a vast emigration has been always tending to moderate it; between 1815 and 1880 over eight millions (including Irish) have left our shores. But for this our normal rate of increase would be 16 or 18 instead of 12 per cent. in every decade.

Next we notice the relative and positive decline in the agricultural population. In 1811 it constituted 35 per cent. of the whole population of Great Britain; in 1821, 33 per cent.; in 1831, 28 per cent. And at the same time its actual numbers have decreased. In 1831 there were 1,243,057 adult males employed in agriculture in Great Britain; in 1841 there were 1,207,989. In 1851 the whole number of persons engaged in agriculture in England was 2,084,153; in 1861 it was 2,010,454, and in 1871 it was 1,657,138. Contemporaneously with this change, the centre of density of population has shifted from the Midlands to the North; there are at the present day 458 persons to the square mile in the counties north of the Trent, as against 312 south of the Trent. And we have lastly to remark the change in the relative population of England and Ireland. Of the total population of the three kingdoms, Ireland had in 1821 32 per cent., in 1881 only 14.6 per cent.

An agrarian revolution plays as large part in the great industrial change of the end of the eighteenth century as does the revolution in manufacturing industries, to which attention is more usually directed. Our next inquiry must therefore be: What were the agricultural changes which led to this noticeable decrease in the rural population? The three most effective causes were: the destruction of the common-field system of cultivation; the enclosure, on a large scale, of common and waste lands; and the consolidation of small farms into large. We have already seen that while between 1710 and 1760 some 300,000 acres were enclosed, between 1760 and 1843 nearly 7,000,000 underwent the same process. Closely connected with the enclosure system was the substitution of large for small farms. In the first half of the century Laurence, though approving of consolidation from an economic point of view, had thought that the odium attaching to an evicting landlord would operate as a strong check upon it. But these scruples had now disappeared. Eden in 1795 notices how constantly the change was effected, often accompanied by the conversion of arable to pasture; and relates how in a certain Dorsetshire village he found two farms where twenty years ago there had been thirty. The process went on uninterruptedly into the present century. Cobbett, writing in 1826, says: 'In the parish of Burghclere one single farmer holds, under Lord Carnarvon, as one farm, the lands that those now living remember to have formed fourteen farms, bringing up in a respectable way fourteen families.' The consolidation of farms reduced the number of farmers, while the enclosures drove the labourers off the land, as it became impossible for them to exist without their rights of pasturage for sheep and geese on common lands.

Severely, however, as these changes bore upon the rural population, they wrought, without doubt, distinct improvement from an agricultural point of view. They meant the substitution of scientific for unscientific culture. 'It has been found,' says Laurence, 'by long experience, that common or open fields are great hindrances to the public good, and to the honest improvement which every one might make of his own.' Enclosures brought an extension of arable cultivation and the tillage of inferior soils; and in small farms of 40 to 100 acres, where the land was exhausted by repeated corn crops, the farm buildings of clay and mud walls and three-fourths of the estate often saturated with water, consolidation into farms of 100 to 500 acres meant rotation of crops, leases of nineteen years, and good farm buildings. The period was one of great agricultural advance; the breed of cattle was improved, rotation of crops was generally introduced, the steam-plough was invented, agricultural societies were instituted. In one respect alone the change was injurious. In consequence of the high prices of corn which prevailed during the French war, some of the finest permanent pastures were broken up. Still, in spite of this, it was said in 1813 that during the previous ten years agricultural produce had increased by one-fourth, and this was an increase upon a great increase in the preceding generation.

Passing to manufactures, we find here the all-prominent fact to be the substitution of the factory for the domestic system, the consequence of the mechanical discoveries of the time. Four great inventions altered the character of the cotton manufacture; the spinning-jenny, patented by Hargreaves in 1770; the water-frame, invented by Arkwright the year before; Crompton's mule introduced in 1779, and the self-acting mule, first invented by Kelly in 1792, but not brought into use till Roberts improved it in 1825. None of these by themselves would have revolutionised the industry. But in 1769—the year in which Napoleon and Wellington were born—James Watt took out his patent for the steam-engine. Sixteen years later it was applied to the cotton manufacture. In 1785 Boulton and Watt made an engine for a cotton-mill at Papplewick in Notts, and in the same year Arkwright's patent expired. These two facts taken together mark the introduction of the factory system. But the most famous invention of all, and the most fatal to domestic industry, the power-loom, though also patented by Cartwright in 1785, did not come into use for several years, and till the power-loom was introduced the workman was hardly injured. At first, in fact, machinery raised the wages of spinners and weavers owing to the great prosperity it brought to the trade. In fifteen years the cotton trade trebled itself; from 1788 to 1803 has been called its 'golden age'; for, before the power-loom but after the introduction of the mule and other mechanical improvements by which for the first time yarn sufficiently fine for muslin and a variety of other fabrics was spun, the demand became such that 'old barns, cart-houses, out-buildings of all descriptions were repaired, windows broke through the old blank walls, and all fitted up for loom-shops; new weavers' cottages with loom-shops arose in every direction, every family bringing home weekly from 40 to 120 shillings per week.' At a later date, the condition of the workman was very different. Meanwhile, the iron industry had been equally revolutionised by the invention of smelting by pit-coal brought into use between 1740 and 1750, and by the application in 1788 of the steam-engine to blast furnaces. In the eight years which followed this later date, the amount of iron manufactured nearly doubled itself.

A further growth of the factory system took place independent of machinery, and owed its origin to the expansion of trade, an expansion which was itself due to the great advance made at this time in the means of communication. The canal system was being rapidly developed throughout the country. In 1777 the Grand Trunk canal, 96 miles in length, connecting the Trent and Mersey, was finished; Hull and Liverpool were connected by one canal while another connected them both with Bristol; and in 1792, the Grand Junction canal, 90 miles in length, made a water-way from London through Oxford to the chief midland towns. Some years afterwards, the roads were greatly improved under Telford and Macadam; between 1818 and 1829 more than a thousand additional miles of turnpike road were constructed; and the next year, 1830, saw the opening of the first railroad. These improved means of communication caused an extraordinary increase in commerce, and to secure a sufficient supply of goods it became the interest of the merchants to collect weavers around them in great numbers, to get looms together in a workshop, and to give out the warp themselves to the workpeople. To these latter this system meant a change from independence to dependence; at the beginning of the century the report of a committee asserts that the essential difference between the domestic and the factory system is, that in the latter the work is done 'by persons who have no property in the goods they manufacture.' Another direct consequence of this expansion of trade was the regular recurrence of periods of over-production and of depression, a phenomenon quite unknown under the old system, and due to this new form of production on a large scale for a distant market.

These altered conditions in the production of wealth necessarily involved an equal revolution in its distribution. In agriculture the prominent fact is an enormous rise in rents. Up to 1795, though they had risen in some places, in others they had been stationary since the Revolution. But between 1790 and 1833, according to Porter, they at least doubled. In Scotland, the rental of land, which in 1795 had amounted to £2,000,000, had risen in 1815 to £5,278,685. A farm in Essex, which before 1793 had been rented at 10s. an acre, was let in 1812 at 50s., though, six years after, this had fallen again to 35s. In Berks and Wilts, farms which in 1790 were let at 14s., were let in 1810 at 70s., and in 1820 at 50s. Much of this rise, doubtless, was due to money invested in improvements—the first Lord Leicester is said to have expended £400,000 on his property—but it was far more largely the effect of the enclosure system, of the consolidation of farms, and of the high price of corn during the French war. Whatever may have been its causes, however, it represented a great social revolution, a

379

change in the balance of political power and in the relative position of classes. The farmers shared in the prosperity of the landlords; for many of them held their farms under beneficial leases, and made large profits by them. In consequence, their character completely changed; they ceased to work and live with their labourers, and became a distinct class. The high prices of the war time thoroughly demoralised them, for their wealth then increased so fast, that they were at a loss what to do with it. Cobbett has described the change in their habits, the new food and furniture, the luxury and drinking, which were the consequences of more money coming into their hands than they knew how to spend. Meanwhile, the effect of all these agrarian changes upon the condition of the labourer was an exactly opposite and most disastrous one. He felt all the burden of high prices, while his wages were steadily falling, and he had lost his common-rights. It is from this period, viz., the beginning of the present century, that the alienation between farmer and labourer may be dated.

Exactly analogous phenomena appeared in the manufacturing world. The new class of great capitalist employers made enormous fortunes, they took little or no part personally in the work of their factories, their hundreds of workmen were individually unknown to them; and as a consequence, the old relations between masters and men disappeared, and a 'cash nexus' was substituted for the human tie. The workmen on their side resorted to combination, and Trades-Unions began a fight which looked as if it were between mortal enemies rather than joint producers.

The misery which came upon large sections of the working people at this epoch was often, though not always, due to a fall in wages, for, as I said above, in some industries they rose. But they suffered likewise from the conditions of labour under the factory system, from the rise of prices, especially from the high price of bread before the repeal of the corn-laws, and from those sudden fluctuations of trade, which, ever since production has been on a large scale, have exposed them to recurrent periods of bitter distress. The effects of the Industrial Revolution prove that free competition may produce wealth without producing well-being. We all know the horrors that ensued in England before it was restrained by legislation and combination.

# WILLIAM MORRIS                                    XXV.4

## Two kinds of work

from 'Useful work versus Useless Toil', 1884–5

Here . . . are two kinds of work—one good, the other bad; one not far removed from a blessing, a lightening of life; the other a mere curse, a burden to life.

What is the difference between them, then? This: one has hope in it, the other has not. It is manly to do the one kind of work, and manly also to refuse to do the other.

What is the nature of the hope which, when it is present in work, makes it worth doing?

It is threefold, I think—hope of rest, hope of product, hope of pleasure in the work itself; and hope of these also in some abundance and of good quality; rest enough and good enough to be worth having; product worth having by one who is neither a fool or an ascetic; pleasure enough for all for us to be conscious of it while we are at work; not a mere habit, the loss of which we shall feel as a fidgety man feels the loss of the bit of string he fidgets with.

I have put the hope of rest first because it is the simplest and most natural part of our hope. Whatever pleasure there is in some work, there is certainly some pain in all work, the beast-like pain of stirring up our slumbering energies to action, the beast-like dread of change when things are pretty well with us; and the compensation for this animal pain in animal rest. We must feel while we are working that the time will come when we shall not have to work. Also the rest, when it comes, must be long enough to allow us to enjoy it; it must be longer than is merely necessary for us to recover the strength we have expended in working, and it must be animal rest also in this, that it must not be disturbed by anxiety, else we shall not be able to enjoy it. If we have this amount and kind of rest we shall, so far, be no worse off than the beasts.

As to the hope of product, I have said that Nature compels us to work for that. It remains for *us* to look to it that we *do* really produce something, and not nothing, or at least nothing that we want or are allowed to use. If we look to this and use our wills we shall, so far, be better than machines.

The hope of pleasure in the work itself: how strange that hope must seem to some of my readers—to most of them! Yet I think that to all living things there is a pleasure in the exercise of their energies, and that even beasts rejoice in being lithe and swift and strong. But a man at work, making something which he feels will exist, because he is working at it and wills it, is exercising the energies of his mind and soul as well as of his body. Memory and imagination help him as he works. Not only his own thoughts, but the thoughts of the men of past ages guide his hands; and, as a part of the human race, he creates. If we work thus we shall be men, and our days will be happy and eventful.

Thus worthy work carries with it the hope of pleasure in rest, the hope of the pleasure in our using what it makes, and the hope of pleasure in our daily creative skill.

All other work but this is worthless; it is slaves' work—mere toiling to live, that we may live to toil.

Therefore, since we have, as it were, a pair of scales in which to weigh the work now done in the world, let us use them. Let us estimate the worthiness of the work we do, after so many thousand years of toil, so many promises of hope deferred, such boundless exultation over the progress of civilization and the gain of liberty.

Now, the first thing as to the work done in civilization and the easiest to notice is that it is portioned out very unequally amongst the different classes of society. First, there are people—not a few—who do no work, and make no pretence of doing any. Next, there are people, and very many of them, who work fairly hard, though with abundant easements and holidays, claimed and allowed; and lastly, there are people who work so hard that they may be said to do nothing else than work, and are accordingly called 'the working classes,' as distinguished from the middle classes and the rich, or aristocracy, whom I have mentioned above.


## OSCAR WILDE                                     XXV.5
### 'The Soul of Man under Socialism'
written 1891

Now as the State is not to govern, it may be asked what the State is to do. The State is to be a voluntary association that will organize labour, and be the manufacturer and distributor of necessary commodities. The State is to make what is useful. The individual is to make what is beautiful. And as I have mentioned the word labour, I cannot help saying that a great deal of nonsense is being written and talked nowadays about the dignity of manual labour. There is nothing necessarily dignified about manual labour at all, and most of it is absolutely degrading. It is mentally and morally injurious to man to do anything in which he does not find pleasure, and many forms of labour are quite pleasureless activities, and should be regarded as such. To sweep a slushy crossing for eight hours on a day when the east wind is blowing is a disgusting occupation. To sweep it with mental, moral, or physical dignity seems to me to be impossible. To sweep it with joy would be appalling. Man is made for something better than disturbing dirt. All work of that kind should be done by a machine.

And I have no doubt that it will be so. Up to the present, man has been, to a certain extent, the slave of machinery, and there is something tragic in the fact that as soon as man had invented a machine to do his work he began to starve. This, however, is, of course, the result of our property system and our system of competition. One man owns a machine which does the work of five hundred men. Five hundred men are, in consequence, thrown out of employment, and, having no work to do, become hungry and take to thieving. The one man secures the produce of the machine and keeps it, and has five hundred times as much as he should have, and probably, which is of much more import-ance, a great deal more than he really wants. Were that machine the property of all, everybody would benefit by it. It would be an immense advantage to the community. All unintellectual labour, all monotonous, dull labour, all labour that deals with dreadful things, and involves un-pleasant conditions, must be done by machinery. Machinery must work for us in coal mines, and do all sanitary services, and be the stoker of steamers, and clean the streets, and run messages on wet days, and do anything that is tedious or distressing. At present machinery competes against man. Under proper conditions machinery will serve man. There is no doubt at all that this is the future of machinery; and just as trees grow while the country gentleman is asleep, so while Humanity will be amusing itself, or enjoying cultivated leisure—which, and not labour, is the aim of man—or making beautiful things, or reading beautiful things, or simply contemplating the world with admiration and delight, machinery will be doing all the necessary and unpleasant work. The fact is, that civilization requires slaves. The Greeks were quite right there. Unless there are slaves to do the ugly, horrible, uninteresting work, cul-ture and contemplation become almost impossible. Human slavery is wrong, insecure, and demoralizing. On mechanical slavery, on the slavery of the machine, the future of the world depends. And when scientific men are no longer called upon to go down to a depressing East End and distribute bad cocoa and worse blankets to starving people, they will have delightful leisure in which to devise wonderful and marvellous things for their own joy and the joy of every one else. There will be great storages of force for every city, and for every house if required, and this force man will convert into heat, light, or motion, according to his needs. Is this Utopian? A map of the world that does not include Utopia is not worth even glancing at, for it leaves out the one country at which Humanity is always landing. And when Humanity lands there, it looks out, and, seeing a better country, sets sail. Progress is the realization of Utopias.

# THOMAS HARDY                                          XXV.6

## "The threshing-machine"

from *Tess of the d'Urbervilles*, 1891

It is the threshing of the last wheat-rick at Flintcomb-Ash Farm. The dawn of the March morning is singularly inexpressive, and there is nothing to show where the eastern horizon lies. Against the twilight rises the trapezoidal top of the stack, which has stood forlornly here through the washing and bleaching of the wintry weather.

When Izz Huett and Tess arrived at the scene of operations only a rustling denoted that others had preceded them; to which, as the light increased, there were presently added the silhouettes of two men on the summit. They were busily 'unhaling' the rick, that is, stripping off the thatch before beginning to throw down the sheaves; and while this was in progress Izz and Tess, with the other women-workers, in their whitey-brown pinners, stood waiting and shivering, Farmer Groby having insisted upon their being on the spot thus early to get the job over if possible by the end of the day. Close under the eaves of the stack, and as yet barely visible, was the red tyrant that the women had come to serve—a timber-framed construction, with straps and wheels appertaining—the threshing-machine which, whilst it was going, kept up a despotic demand upon the endurance of their muscles and nerves.

A little way off there was another indistinct figure; this one black, with a sustained hiss that spoke of strength very much in reserve. The long chimney running up beside an ash-tree, and the warmth which radiated from the spot, explained without the necessity of much daylight that here was the engine which was to act as the *primum mobile* of this little world. By the engine stood a dark motionless being, a sooty and grimy embodiment of tallness, in a sort of trance, with a heap of coals by his side: it was the engine-man. The isolation of his manner and colour lent him the appearance of a creature from Tophet, who had strayed into the pellucid smokelessness of this region of yellow grain and pale soil, with which he had nothing in common, to amaze and to discompose its aborigines.

What he looked he felt. He was in the agricultural world, but not of it. He served fire and smoke; these denizens of the fields served vegetation, weather, frost, and sun. He travelled with his engine from farm to farm, from county to county, for as yet the steam threshing-machine was itinerant in this part of Wessex. He spoke in a strange northern accent; his thoughts being turned inwards upon himself, his eye on his iron charge, hardly perceiving the scenes around him, and caring for them not at all: holding only strictly necessary intercourse with the natives, as if some ancient doom compelled him to wander here against his will in the service of his Plutonic master. The long strap which ran from the driving-wheel of his engine to the red thresher under the rick was the sole tie-line between agriculture and him.

While they uncovered the sheaves he stood apathetic beside his portable repository of force, round whose hot blackness the morning air quivered. He had nothing to do with preparatory labour. His fire was waiting incandescent, his steam was at high pressure, in a few seconds he could make the long strap move at an invisible velocity. Beyond its extent the environment might be corn, straw, or chaos; it was all the same to him. If any of the autochthonous idlers asked him what he called himself, he replied shortly, 'an engineer.'

The rick was unhaled by full daylight; the men then took their places, the women mounted, and the work began. Farmer Groby—or, as they called him, 'he'—had arrived ere this, and by his orders Tess was placed on the platform of the machine, close to the man who fed it, her business being to untie every sheaf of corn handed on to her by Izz Huett, who stood next, but on the rick; so that the feeder could seize it and spread it over the revolving drum, which whisked out every grain in one moment.

They were soon in full progress, after a preparatory hitch or two, which rejoiced the hearts of those who hated machinery. The work sped on till breakfast-time, when the thresher was stopped for half an hour, and on starting again after the meal the whole supplementary strength of the farm was thrown into the labour of constructing the straw-rick, which began to grow beside the stack of corn. A hasty lunch was eaten as they stood, without leaving their positions, and then another couple of hours brought them near to dinner-time; the inexorable wheels continuing to spin, and the penetrating hum of the thresher to thrill to the very marrow all who were near the revolving wire-cage.

The old men on the rising straw-rick talked of the past days when they had been accustomed to thresh with flails on the oaken barn-floor; when everything, even to winnowing, was effected by hand-labour, which, to their thinking, though slow, produced better results. Those, too, on the corn-rick talked a little; but the perspiring ones at the machine, including Tess, could not lighten their duties by the exchange of many words. It was the ceaselessness of the work which tried her so severely, and began to make her wish that she had never come to Flintcomb-Ash. The women on the corn-rick—Marian, who was one of them, in particular—could stop to drink ale or cold tea from the flagon now and then, or to exchange a few gossiping remarks while they wiped their faces or cleared the fragments of straw and husk from their clothing; but for Tess there was no respite; for, as the drum never stopped, the man who fed it could not stop, and she, who had to supply the man with untied sheaves, could not stop either, unless Marian changed places with her, which she sometimes did for half an hour in spite of Groby's objection that she was too slow-handed for a feeder.

For some probably economical reason it was usually a woman who was chosen for this particular duty, and Groby gave as his motive in selecting Tess that she was one of those who best combined strength with quickness in untying, and both with staying power, and this may have been true. The hum of the thresher, which prevented speech, increased to a raving whenever the supply of corn fell short of the regular quantity. . . .

Dinner-time came, and the whirling ceased; whereupon Tess left her post, her knees trembling so wretchedly with the shaking of the machine that she could scarcely walk.

'You ought to het a quart o' drink into 'ee, as I've done,' said Marian. 'You wouldn't look so white then. Why, souls above us, your face is as if you'd been hagrode!'. . .

In the afternoon the farmer made it known that the rick was to be finished at night, since there was a moon by which they could see to work, and the man with the engine was engaged for another farm on the morrow. Hence the twanging and humming and rustling proceeded with even less intermission than usual. . . .

Thus the afternoon dragged on. The wheat-rick shrank lower, and the straw-rick grew higher, and the corn-sacks were carted away. At six o'clock the wheat-rick was about shoulder-high from the ground. But the unthreshed sheaves remaining untouched seemed countless still, notwithstanding the enormous numbers that had been gulped down by the insatiable swallower, fed by the man and Tess, through whose two young hands the greater part of them had passed. And the immense stack of straw where in the morning there had been nothing, appeared as the *faeces* of the same buzzing red glutton. From the west sky a wrathful shine—all that wild March could afford in the way of sunset —had burst forth after the cloudy day, flooding the tired and sticky faces of the threshers, and dyeing them with a coppery light, as also the flapping garments of the women, which clung to them like dull flames.

A panting ache ran through the rick. The man who fed was weary, and Tess could see that the red nape of his neck was encrusted with dirt and husks. She still stood at her post, her flushed and perspiring face coated with the corn-dust, and her white bonnet embrowned by it. She was the only woman whose place was upon the machine so as to be shaken bodily by its spinning, and the decrease of the stack now separated her from Marian and Izz, and prevented their changing duties with her as they had done. The incessant quivering, in which every fibre of her frame participated, had thrown her into a stupefied reverie in which her arms worked on independently of her consciousness. She hardly knew where she was, and did not hear Izz Huett tell her from below that her hair was tumbling down.

By degrees the freshest among them began to grow cadaverous and saucer-eyed. Whenever Tess lifted her head she beheld always the great upgrown straw-stack, with the men in shirt-sleeves upon it, against the gray north sky; in front of it the long red elevator like a Jacob's ladder, on which a perpetual stream of threshed straw ascended, a yellow river running up-hill, and spouting out on the top of the rick.

# D. H. LAWRENCE

## "Ugliness"

XXV.7

from 'Nottingham and the Mining Country', 1929

Even fifty years ago the squares were unpopular. It was 'common' to live in the Square. It was a little less common to live in the Breach, which consisted of six blocks of rather more pretentious dwellings erected by the company in the valley below, two rows of three blocks, with an alley between. And it was most 'common', most degraded of all to live in Dakins Row, two rows of the old dwellings, very old, black four-roomed little places, that stood on the hill again, not far from the Square.

So the place started. Down the steep street between the squares, Scargill Street, the Wesleyans' chapel was put up, and I was born in the little corner shop just above. Across the other side of the Square the miners themselves built the big, barn-like Primitive Methodist chapel. Along the hill-top ran the Nottingham Road, with its scrappy, ugly mid-Victorian shops. The little market-place, with a superb outlook, ended the village on the Derbyshire side, and was just here left bare, with the Sun Inn on one side, the chemist across, with the gilt pestle-and-mortar, and a shop at the other corner, the corner of Alfreton Road and Nottingham Road.

In this queer jumble of the old England and the new, I came into consciousness. As I remember, little local speculators already began to straggle dwellings in rows, always in rows, across the fields: nasty red-brick, flat-faced dwellings with dark slate roofs. The bay-window period only began when I was a child. But most of the country was untouched.

There must be three or four hundred company houses in the squares and the streets that surround the squares, like a great barracks wall. There must be sixty or eighty company houses in the Breach. The old Dakins Row will have thirty to forty little holes. Then counting the old cottages and rows left with their old gardens down the lanes and along the twitchells, and even in the midst of Nottingham Road itself, there were houses enough for the population, there was no need for much building. And not much building went on when I was small.

We lived in the Breach, in a corner house. A field-path came down under a great hawthorn hedge. On the other side was the brook, with the old sheep-bridge going over into the meadows. The hawthorn hedge by the brook had grown tall as tall trees, and we used to bathe from there in the dipping-hole, where the sheep were dipped, just near the fall from the old mill-dam, where the water rushed. The mill only ceased grinding the local corn when I was a child. And my father, who always worked in Brinsley pit, and who always got up at five o'clock, if not at four, would set off in the dawn across the fields at Coney Grey, and hunt for mushrooms in the long grass, or perhaps pick up a skulking rabbit, which he would bring home at evening inside the lining of his pit-coat.

So that the life was a curious cross between industrialism and the old agricultural England of Shakespeare and Milton and Fielding and George Eliot. The dialect was broad Derbyshire, and always 'thee' and 'thou'. The people lived almost entirely by instinct, men of my father's age could not really read. And the pit did not mechanize men. On the contrary. Under the butty system, the miners worked underground as a sort of intimate community, they knew each other practically naked, and with curious close intimacy, and the darkness and the underground remoteness of the pit 'stall', and the continual presence of danger, made the physical, instinctive, and intuitional contact between men very highly developed, a contact almost as close as touch, very real and very powerful. This physical awareness and intimate *togetherness* was at its strongest down pit. When the men came up into the light, they blinked. They had, in a measure, to change their flow. Nevertheless, they brought with them above ground the curious dark intimacy of the mine, the naked sort of contact, and if I think of my childhood, it is always as if there was a lustrous sort of inner darkness, like the gloss of coal, in which we moved and had our real being. My father loved the pit. He was hurt badly, more than once, but he would never stay away. He loved the contact, the intimacy, as men in the war loved the intense male comradeship of the dark days. They did not know what they had lost till they lost it. And I think it is the same with the young colliers of to-day.

Now the colliers had also an instinct of beauty. The colliers' wives had not. The colliers were deeply alive, instinctively. But they had no daytime ambition, and no daytime intellect. They avoided, really, the rational aspect of life. They preferred to take life instinctively and intuitively. They didn't even care very profoundly about wages. It was the women, naturally, who nagged on this score. There was a big discrepancy, when I was a boy, between the collier who saw, at the best, only a brief few hours of daylight—often no daylight at all during the winter weeks—and the collier's wife, who had all the day to herself when the man was down pit.

The great fallacy is, to pity the man. He didn't dream of pitying himself, till agitators and sentimentalists taught him to. He was happy: or more than happy, he was fulfilled. Or he was fulfilled on the receptive side, not on the expressive. The collier went to the pub and drank in order to continue his intimacy with his mates. They talked endlessly, but it was rather of wonders and marvels, even in politics, than of facts. It was hard facts, in the shape of wife, money, and nagging home necessities, which they fled away from, out of the house to the pub, and out of the house to the pit.

The collier fled out of the house as soon as he could, away from the nagging materialism of the woman. With the women it was always: This is broken, now you've got to mend it! or else: We want this, that, and the other, and where is the money coming from? The collier didn't know and didn't care very deeply—his life was otherwise. So he escaped. He roved the countryside with his dog, prowling for a rabbit, for nests, for mushrooms, anything. He loved the countryside, just the indiscriminating feel of it. Or he loved just to sit on his heels and watch—anything or nothing. He was not intellectually interested. Life for him did not consist in facts, but in a flow. Very often, he loved his garden. And very often he had a genuine love of the beauty of flowers. I have known it often and often, in colliers.

Now the love of flowers is a very misleading thing. Most women love flowers as possessions, and as trimmings. They can't look at a flower, and wonder a moment, and pass on. If they see a flower that arrests their attention, they must at once pick it, pluck it. Possession! A possession! Something added on to *me*! And most of the so-called love of flowers to-day is merely this reaching out of possession and egoism: something I've *got*: something that embellishes *me*. Yet I've seen many a collier stand in his back garden looking down at a flower with that odd, remote sort of contemplation which shows a *real* awareness of the presence of beauty. It would not even be admiration, or joy, or delight, or any of those things which so often have a root in the possessive instinct. It would be a sort of contemplation: which shows the incipient artist.

The real tragedy of England, as I see it, is the tragedy of ugliness. The country is so lovely: the man-made England is so vile. I know that the ordinary collier, when I was a boy, had a peculiar sense of beauty, coming from his intuitive and instinctive consciousness, which was awakened down pit. And the fact that he met with just cold ugliness and raw materialism when he came up into daylight, and particularly when he came to the Square or the Breach, and to his own table, killed something in him, and in a sense spoiled him as a man. The woman almost invariably nagged about material things. She was taught to do it; she was encouraged to do it. It was a mother's business to see that her sons

389

'got on', and it was the man's business to provide the money. In my father's generation, with the old wild England behind them, and the lack of education, the man was not beaten down. But in my generation, the boys I went to school with, colliers now, have all been beaten down, what with the din-din-dinning of Board Schools, books, cinemas, clergymen, the whole national and human consciousness hammering on the fact of material prosperity above all things.

The men are beaten down, there is prosperity for a time, in their defeat—and then disaster looms ahead. The root of all disaster is disheartenment. And men are disheartened. The men of England, the colliers in particular, are disheartened. They have been betrayed and beaten.

Now though perhaps nobody knew it, it was ugliness which betrayed the spirit of man, in the nineteenth century. The great crime which the moneyed classes and promoters of industry committed in the palmy Victorian days was the condemning of the workers to ugliness, ugliness, ugliness: meanness and formless and ugly surroundings, ugly ideals, ugly religion, ugly hope, ugly love, ugly clothes, ugly furniture, ugly houses, ugly relationship between workers and employers. The human soul needs actual beauty even more than bread. The middle classes jeer at the colliers for buying pianos—but what is the piano, often as not, but a blind reaching out for beauty? To the woman it is a possession and a piece of furniture and something to feel superior about. But see the elderly colliers trying to learn to play, see them listening with queer alert faces to their daughter's execution of *The Maiden's Prayer*, and you will see a blind, unsatisfied craving for beauty. It is far more deep in the men than in the women. The women want show. The men want beauty, and still want it.

If the company, instead of building those sordid and hideous Squares, then, when they had that lovely site to play with, there on the hill top: if they had put a tall column in the middle of the small market-place, and run three parts of a circle of arcade round the pleasant space, where people could stroll or sit, and with the handsome houses behind! If they had made big, substantial houses, in apartments of five and six rooms, and with handsome entrances. If above all, they had encouraged song and dancing—for the miners still sang and danced—and provided handsome space for these. If only they had encouraged some form of beauty in dress, some form of beauty in interior life—furniture, decoration. If they had given prizes for the handsomest chair or table, the loveliest scarf, the most charming room that the men or women could make! If only they had done this, there would never have been an industrial problem. The industrial problem arises from the base forcing of all human energy into a competition of mere acquisition.

You may say the working man would not have accepted such a form of life: the Englishman's home is his castle, etc., etc.—'my own little home'. But if you can hear every word the next-door-people say, there's not much castle. And if you can see everybody in the square if they go to the w.c.! And if your one desire is to get out of the 'castle' and your 'own little home'!—well, there's not much to be said for it. Anyhow it's only the woman who idolizes 'her own little home'—and it's always the woman at her worst, her most greedy, most possessive, most mean. There's nothing to be said for the 'little home' any more: a great scrabble of ugly pettiness over the face of the land.

As a matter of fact, till 1800 the English people were stricly a rural people—very rural. England has had towns for centuries, but they have never been real towns, only clusters of village streets. Never the real *urbs*. The English character has failed to develop the real *urban* side of a man, the civic side. Siena is a bit of a place, but it is a real city, with citizens intimately connected with the city. Nottingham is a vast place sprawling towards a million, and it is nothing more than an amorphous agglomeration. There *is* no Nottingham, in the sense that there is Siena. The Englishman is stupidly undeveloped, as a citizen. And it is partly due to his 'little home' stunt, and partly to his acceptance of hopeless paltriness in his surrounding. The new cities of America are much more genuine cities, in the Roman sense, than is London or Manchester. Even Edinburgh used to be more of a true city than any town England ever produced.

That silly little individualism of 'the Englishman's home is his castle' and 'my own little home' is out of date. It would work almost up to 1800, when every Englishman was still a villager, and a cottager. But the industrial system has brought a great change. The Englishman still likes to think of himself as a 'cottager'—'my home, my garden'. But it is puerile. Even the farm labourer to-day is psychologically a town-bird. The English are town-birds through and through, to-day, as the inevitable result of their complete industrialization. Yet they don't know how to build a city, how to think of one, or how to live in one. They are all suburban, pseudo-cottagy, and not one of them knows how to be truly urban.

# Sources and Notes

**I.1**  Reprinted in Defoe, *A Tour Through the Whole Island of Great Britain*, 1724–6, ed. by G. D. H. Cole and D. C. Browning, London, Dent, Everyman, 1962, pp. 193–5.

**I.2**  From *The Adventurer*, No. 67, 26 June 1753.
  **artists**: artisans

**I.3**  From ninth note to *Discours sur cette question proposée par l'Académie de Dijon: Quelle est L'Origine de L'Inégalité parmi les hommes et si elle est autorisée par la loi naturelle?*, Paris, 1754, translated by the present editor. Recent French editions include *Du Contrat Social, Discours*, etc., Paris, Garnier, 1962. English translations include G. D. H. Cole, trans. and ed., Rousseau, *Social Contract, Discourses* etc., Everyman 1913, repr. 1961, pp. 222–4.

**II.1**  Ballad 1695, collected from the singing of Bob and Ron Copper of Rottingdean, Sussex, by Peter Kennedy, on 'Jack of All Trades' (Caedmon Records, Lochrae Corporation, New York 1961).

**II.2**  *Windsor Forest*, 1704–13, lines 121–34.

**II.3**  *Pastorals* 'The Fourth Pastoral or Daphne', written 1704 according to Pope, and published in 1713, lines 53–60, 77–92.
  **Philomela**: the nightingale.
  **To thee**: Daphne, whose death the shepherds are lamenting.
  **Boreas**: the north wind.

**II.4**  *Poems on Several Subjects* 1730. There is also a modern reprint: Stephen Duck, *The Thresher's Labour*, Chelsea, The Swan Press, 1930. For a comment on this poem see E. P. Thompson 'Time, Work-Discipline and Industrial Capitalism' in *Past and Present*, no. 38 (1967), pp. 62–3; and for a discussion, together with a comment on II.1 and II.5, see Alasdair Clayre, *Work and Play: Ideas and Experience of Work and Leisure* Weidenfeld 1974, Harper 1975, Ch. 8. The book also discusses some other issues raised in this anthology.

**II.5**  *The Village*, 1783, Book I, lines 7–14, 39–54, 109–18, 135–206.

**II.6**  In Margaret Llewellyn Davies, ed., *Life as We Have Known it*, London, 1931; quoted in Jennie Kitteringham, 'Country Work Girls in nineteenth-century England' in Raphael Samuel, ed., *Village Life and Labour*, Routledge & Kegan Paul, 1975.

**II.7**  *From Crow-Scaring to Westminster: An Autobiography*, National Union of Agricultural Workers, 1922, Ch. 2.

**II.8**  Letter in the *Nottinghamshire Guardian* of 20 September 1860, signed 'One of the Village' reprinted in *Notes and Queries*, 2nd series, 13 October 1860, p. 285; quoted in David H. Morgan, 'The Place of harvesters in nineteenth-century village life' in Raphael Samuel, ed., *Village Life and Labour*, Routledge & Kegan Paul, 1975.

392

**III.1**  *Three Essays*, 1792, Essay II.

    **lusus naturae**: freak of nature.
    **vox faucibus haeret**: the voice sticks in the throat.
    **deliquium**: melting away.

**III.2**  Letter to Archdeacon John Fisher in R. B. Beckett, ed., *John Constable's Correspondence*, VI, Ipswich, Suffolk Records Society, 1962–8 Vol. VI.

**III.3**  From *Modern Painters*, 1860, Vol. V, Part 9, Ch. 9, 'The Two Boyhoods'. Here Ruskin compares Turner's boyhood with that of Giorgione da Castelfranco (1477–1510), the Venetian painter.

    **Bello ovile dov'io dormii agnello**: 'Fair sheep-fold where, a little lamb, I slept'; from Dante, *Paradiso* xxv.5: Florence, the city of Dante's birth.
    **Salvator Rosa**: seventeenth-century Italian painter.
    **Albrecht Dürer**: sixteenth-century German painter.

**IV.1**  *Lyrical Ballads*, 1798.

**IV.2**  Written a few miles above Tintern Abbey, on revisiting the banks of the Wye during a tour, July 13, 1798; first published in *Lyrical Ballads*, 1798.

**IV.3**  Written 1797; first published in *Lyrical Ballads*, 1798.

**IV.4**  *The Prelude*, 1805, Book XIII, Conclusion, lines 1–65.

**IV.5**  *Childe Harold's Pilgrimage*, 1816, Canto 3, stanzas XIII–XVI.

**IV.6**  *Don Juan*, 1818–20, Canto 2, stanzas 185–8.

**IV.7**  *The Heart of Midlothian*, 1818, Ch. 50.

**IV.8**  Modern editions include Eric Robinson and Geoffrey Summerfield, eds., John Clare *The Shepherd's Calendar*, London, Oxford University Press, 1964, from whose glossary the following notes are taken:

    **icle**: icicle.
    **douse**: to drench, soak.
    **pooty**: a snail-shell.
    **a**: on the.
    **strunt**: strut.
    **stulp**: the stump of a tree.
    **burring**: droning, purring.
    **eke**: add to, enlarge.
    **croodle**: huddle, for warmth or protection.

**IV.9**  'The Nightingale's Nest' belongs with a series of rough drafts mainly about birds, written in a separate notebook, 1825–30; first published in *The Rural Muse*, 1835.

**IV.10**  Written 1819, published 1820, in *'Lamia' and other poems*.

**IV.11**  Written 1818, published 1820, in *'Lamia' and other poems*, stanzas 10–11, 14–16, 18.

    **lazar**: leper.

**V.1**  *Parliamentary Papers*, 1806, Vol. III.

**V.2**  From *The Philosophy of Manufactures*, London, 1835, pp. 6-9, 11-14, 16–21, 22-5, 29-32, 40-3, section reproduced in Eugene C. Black, *Victorian Culture and Society*, Harper & Row, 1973, Ch. 1.

    **materiam superabat opus**: the work exceeded the material.

**V.3**   *The Curse of the Factory System or A short account of the origin of factory cruelties; of the attempts to protect the children by law; of their present sufferings; our duty towards them; . . . the folly of the political economists; a warning against sending the children of the south into the factories of the north,* by John Fielden, M.P. for Oldham and manufacturer at Todmorden in Lancashire, London, A. Cobbett, 1836, first edition, pp. 31–3, 34–5, 56, 68–9.

**V.4**   From *Capital,* 1867, Vol. I, Ch. 15, selection from section 1, section 8, edited by Engels, translated by Moore and Aveling, Sonnenshein 1887.

> **Manufacture:** Marx here uses the term 'Manufacture' not in the usual present-day sense of mass-production by machinery but by contrast in the earlier and literal sense of making things by hand. 'Manufacture' here refers to those pre-industrial forms of hand-production, including production with divided labour, that large-scale industry supplanted.

**VI.1**   *Navigable Rivers and Canals,* 1831, pp. 5–18.

**VI.2**   *Railways of Great Britain and Ireland,* 1842, pp. 312–24.

**VII.1**   *Yorkshire Directory,* 1823, reprinted David and Charles, 1969.

**VII.2**   *Yorkshire Directory,* 1848, reprinted David and Charles, 1969.

**VII.3**   *The Life of Charlotte Brontë,* 1856, excerpts from the Introduction, pp. 1–3, 9, 10, 12, 13, 15, 16, 19, 20.

> **Lamartine:** French poet and political leader, like Kossuth and Dembinsky active in the revolution of 1848.
> **Kossuth:** Hungarian patriot.
> **Dembinsky:** Polish patriot, who joined the Hungarians under Kossuth.
> **John Newton:** (1725–1807) slave-ship captain turned poet and hymn-writer.
> **Cowper:** see biographical notes.

**VII.4**   *The Morning Chronicle,* 26 Nov. 1849, 'The Rural Cloth-Workers of Yorkshire: Saddleworth', Letter XIII. Reprinted in P. E. Razzell and E. W. Wainwright, eds., *The Victorian Working Class,* Cass, 1973, Section III.

*The Morning Chronicle* was a middle-class English newspaper which supported the moderate Liberalism associated with Gladstone and the 'Peelite' rebels from the Tory Party after 1846. Its 'Labour and the Poor' series was a pioneer effort in investigative journalism, most notable as Henry Mayhew's first venture into this field. The paper also covered the growing industrial towns of the North, whose society was otherwise little known to Londoners.

**VII.5**   From K. G. Pontin, ed., *Baines' Account of the Woollen Manufacture of England,* Ch. 1, reprinted David and Charles, 1970.

**VII.6**   From *The Voice of the People,* Bradford, 1858. Reprinted in archive teaching unit: 'Saltaire', Bradford Museums, 1976.

Bradford, the capital of the worsted trade, was in 1858 in course of very rapid industrial growth, observed sardonically by this dialect writer in a short-lived radical newspaper. He begins by imagining the ghost of an old weaver remembering a factory-owner of the old school, then goes on to attack the new masters, including the German businessmen who were based in large numbers in Bradford, and ends with an attack on 'Tim Pepper'—Sir Thomas Salt—the builder of the model town of Saltaire.

**VIII.1** *Journeys to England and Ireland,* 1835, trans. G. Lawrence and K. P. Mayer, ed. J. P. Mayer, London, 1958, pp. 105–8, 2 July 1835.

**VIII.2** Contained in a broadside of J. Swindells of Manchester.

Related songs include 'The Scenes of Manchester', a broadside ballad from the *London Singer's Magazine*, probably written about the same date.

**VIII.3** Printed on a broadside by Cadman of Manchester. This version is reprinted by kind permission of Roy Palmer.

**VIII.4** Ch. 2 'The Great Towns'. The book was first published in Leipzig in 1845, and first published in English as *The Condition of the Working Class in England in 1844*, New York, 1887, London, 1892. This English text from Institute of Marxism-Leninism, Moscow, verified with second German edition, Stuttgart, 1892, published with an introduction by Eric Hobsbawm, Panther, 1969, pp. 78–9, 82–4.

**VIII.5** *Hard Times*, 1854, Book I, ch. 5; Book II, ch. 1. 'Coketown' is based on Preston.

**VIII.6** *The Old Curiosity Shop*, 1841, Ch. 44.

**IX.1** *Parliamentary Papers*, 1842, Vol. XXVI, pp. 369–72.

**IX.2** From 'Modern Manufacture and Design', Lecture delivered at the Mechanics' Institute, Bradford, 1 March 1859, printed in *The Two Paths*, 1859.

**IX.3** From 'The Mystery of Life and Its Arts', Lecture delivered at the Exhibition Palace, Dublin, 13 May 1868, added to 1871 edition of *Sesame and Lilies*, 1865.

**X.1** *Lyrical Ballads*, 1798.

**X.2** Early nineteenth century. This version comes from a broadside printed by Bebbington of Manchester *c*. 1860.

**X.3** *Parliamentary Papers*, 1831–32, Vol. XV, pp. 445ff. Reprinted in E. R. Pike, ed., *Human Documents of the Industrial Revolution in Britain*, George Allen & Unwin, 1966.

**X.4** *Report of the Royal Commission on the Poor Laws* 1834. Available in a Pelican edition, eds S. G. and E. O. A. Checkland, Penguin Books, 1973, pp. 373–7.

'Out-door' relief, as opposed to 'in-door': relief which is not given in a workhouse. Such relief was given either in kind or in money. Practices varied from one district to another. Partial relief was sometimes given by exemption of poor people from payment of rates. Occasional relief might involve either providing or granting an allowance for clothes, especially shoes.

Relief 'in aid of wages': an allowance made on a regular, rather than an occasional, basis. Sometimes a scale would be set for this form of relief in a large district. A labourer in Cambridgeshire, for example, was eligible for a sum equivalent to the price of two quartern loaves of bread per week for each member of his family, if he had a wife and four or more children, according to a scale set in 1821.

**X.5** *Lyrical Ballads*, Postscript to edition of 1835–6.

**X.6** *The Morning Chronicle*, 6 December 1849, 'The "Stuff" Districts of Yorkshire: Halifax and Bradford'. Letter XV, in the series 'Labour and the Poor', reprinted in *The Yorkshire Textile Districts in 1849*, ed. C. Aspin, Helmshire Local History Society, 1974.

**X.7**   C. Aspin, ed., *The Yorkshire Textile Districts in 1849*, Helmshire Local History Society, 1974.

This letter was written to, but not published in, Feargus O'Connor's *Northern Star* newspaper, in 1847 or 1848. Its writer was probably George Rhodes, a Saddleworth weaver and farmer, who had been between 1827 and 1830 the Secretary of the weaver's trade union in Saddleworth.

**X.8**   Originally appeared in *The Morning Chronicle*. (See notes to VII.4.) Printed in Henry Mayhew, *London Labour and the London Poor* (1851–62), Vol. II, pp. 224–6.

**X.9**   *Household Words*, I, 204–7 (25 May 1850).

**X.10**   *North and South*, 1855, Ch. 17.

**Hoo**: she.
**clem**: starve.
**mappen**: perhaps.
**common on**: eat.

**X.11**   Contained in a broadside of Harkness of Preston, dating from the cotton workers' strike of 1853.

**XI.1**   'Autumn' from *The Seasons*, 1726–30, lines 23–150.

**The Virgin (Virgo) and Libra**: The signs of the zodiac for late August to late October.

**XI.2**   *The Task*, 1784, Book I, 'The Sofa'.

**XI.3**   *The Excursion*, 1814, Book VIII, lines 118–42, 151–216.

**XII.1**   *The Theory of Moral Sentiments*, 1759. From 'Of the Utility of this constitution of Nature', London, Bohn, 1861, pp. 124–6.

**XII.2**   (a) Book I, Ch. 1; edited by Edwin Cannan, 2 vols., Methuen, 1904, Vol. I, 5–14.

(b) Book I, Ch. 5; Vol. I, 32–3.

(c) Book I, Ch. 5; Vol. I, 67–70.

(d) Book I, Ch. 5; Vol. I, 70–84.

(e) Book I, Ch. 10, part i; Vol. I, 102.

(f) Book I, Ch. 10, part ii; Vol. I, 128–9.

(g) Book I, Ch. 10, part ii; Vol. I, 130. Book I, Ch. 11; Vol. I, 249–50.

(h) Book II, Ch. 3; Vol. I, 323–9.

(i) Book III, Ch. 1; Vol. I, 356–7.

(j) Book V, Ch. 1, part iii, Art. 1; Vol. II, 216.

(k) Book V, Ch. 1, part iii, Art. 2; Vol. II, 266, 270.

**XII.3**   First edition, London, J. Johnson, 1798; from 1807 edition, pp. 1–29, reprinted in J. F. C. Harrison, ed., *British Society and Politics*, Harper & Row, 1965.

**XII.4**   (a) *A Table of the Springs of Action*, 1817, p. 20, reprinted in Werner Stark, ed., *The Economic Writings of Jeremy Bentham*, London, George Allen and Unwin, 1954, iii, pp. 427–8.

(b) J. Bentham, *Works*, ed. J. Bowring, 1843, ii, p. 28; *Economic Writings*, iii, p. 438.

(c) *Works*, ii, p. 156, *Economic Writings*, iii, p. 439.

(d) *Works*, ix, p. 14–15, *Economic Writings*, iii, pp. 445–6.

(e) *The Rationale of Punishment*, 1830, p. 157 and in *Works*, ed. Bowring, i, p. 438; *Economic Writings*, iii, p. 446.

**XII.5**  (a) This version is taken from William Chappell's *Popular Music of the Olden Time*, 1859.

(b) A parody of 'The Miller of Dee', printed on a broadside by Joseph Ford of Sheffield *c*. 1835.

**XIII.1**  From *Jerusalem*, 1804–20, III, 54, in G. Keynes, ed., *Poetry and Prose of William Blake*, Nonesuch, 1927, pp. 500–1.

**XIII.2**  *Lyrical Ballads*, third edition, 1802 (addition to the Preface of 1800).

**XIII.3**  Letter to Mr B. Bailey, Magdalen Hall, Oxford, posted Leatherhead, 22 November 1817. *The Letters of John Keats*, 1814–21, Vol. I, ed. Hyder Edward Rollins, Harvard University Press, Cambridge, Mass., pp. 182–7.

**XIII.4**  First edition 1821, pp. 7ff., reprinted in R. J. White, ed., *The Political Tracts of Wordsworth, Coleridge and Shelley*, Cambridge University Press, 1953, pp. 203ff.

> Non merita nome di creatore, se non Iddio ed il Poeta: Only God and the poet deserve the name of Creator.

**XIII.5**  Appendix A to *The Statesman's Manual or The Bible the Best Guide to Political Skill and Foresight, A Lay Sermon*, first edition, London 1816, from pp. 44ff.; reprinted in R. J. White, ed., *The Political Tracts of Wordsworth, Coleridge and Shelley*, Cambridge University Press, 1953, pp. 36ff.

> cadavera rerum: the corpses of things.
> caput mortuum: skull.
> quantum sumus, scimus: we know as much as we are.
> ita tamen ut sit alia et major: so that it shall be both different and greater.

**XIV.1**  *Don Juan*, 1818–23, Canto 1, stanzas 90–3.

**XIV.2**  *Nightmare Abbey*, 1818, Ch. 2. This is in the main a skit on Shelley. Reprinted in *The Complete Novels*, ed. David Garnett, Rupert Hart-Davis, 1963, from which some of the following information is derived.

> 'his cogitative faculties . . .': from Henry Carey, *Chrononhotonthologos*, the most Tragical Tragedy that ever was tragedized by any Company of Tragedians, 1734, Act I, Sc. I.
> the Sorrows of Werter: Goethe's *Die Leiden des jungen Werthers* (*The Sufferings of Young Werther*).
> Horrid Mysteries: *Horrid Mysteries*, a translation (by P. Will 1796) from the German of the Marquis of Grosse.
> eleutherarchs: Beings who figure in Hogg's novel *The Memoirs of Prince Alexy Haimatoff*.
> Kant: the German philosopher of the Enlightenment.
> illuminati: enlightened ones.

**XV.1**  Written 1819. The 'political characters' are supposed to be Sidmouth and Castlereagh. Printed in David Wright, ed., *The Penguin Book of English Romantic Verse*.

**XV.2**  Written between 1848 and 1852. Printed incomplete in 1862, in Clough's collected *Shorter Poems*. The last four lines were not printed until 1951. A recent edition of Clough's poems is A. L. P. Norrington, ed., *Poetical Works of Arthur Hugh Clough*, Oxford University Press, 1968.

**XV.3**  *Hard Times*, 1854, from Ch. 3.

**XVI.1**   Contributed to the *Edinburgh Review*, Vol. XLIX, June 1829, pp. 441–4.

**XVI.2**   Speech in the House of Commons on 2 March 1831; reprinted in Thomas Babington Macaulay's *Miscellaneous Writings and Speeches*, 1889 edn, pp. 483–92.

**XVI.3**   *Past and Present*, 1843, Ch. I, Proem to Book I.

> **Midas:** Legendary king in Greek mythology who asked the gods that everything he touched should be turned to gold. He was punished for the impiety of his demand by the fulfilment of his wish.
>
> **Queen Christina etc.:** Seventeenth-century Queen of Sweden who invited the French philosopher Descartes to her court; in the eighteenth century King Frederick the Great of Prussia was the patron of Voltaire.

**XVII.1**   *Past and Present*, 1843, Book III, Ch. XI.

**XVII.2**   See note to VIII.4; Panther edn, 1969, pp. 204–5.

**XVII.3**   *Economic Philosophical Manuscripts*, 1844, in *Marx–Engels Gesamtausgabe*, Moscow, Marx–Engels Institute, 1927–, Vol. I/3. This translation from K. Marx, *Early Writings*, trans. and ed. T. B. Bottomore, London, C. A. Watts & Co. Ltd., 1963, pp. 120–31.

**XVII.4**   From Notebook VI, *Grundrisse der Kritik der Politischen Ökonomie (Rohentwurf) 1857-8, Anhang 1850-59*, Berlin, 1953, p. 515. This version translated by M. Nicolaus, 1973 © Martin Nicolaus 1973, pp. 610–12, 613. Reprinted by permission of Penguin Books Ltd., and Random House, Inc. See Clayre, *Work and Play*, 54–6.

**XVII.5**   *The Principles of Political Economy*, 1848, Book IV, Ch. VI, Section 2.

**XVII.6**   *Self-Help*, 1859, pp. 1–2, 232–4.

**XVII.7**   From *The Stones of Venice*, 1851-3, Vol. II, Ch. 5.

**XVII.8**   Published in *Unto this Last*, 1862.

**XVIII.1**   *The Theory of Moral Sentiments*, 1759, London, Bohn, 1861, pp. 342–4.

> **Solon:** the law-giver of Athens.

**XVIII.2**   *Manifesto of the Communist Party*, 1847, Preface and Chapter I: 'Bourgeois and Proletarians'.

**XVIII.3**   Added by Mill to the third (1852) edition of *The Principles of Political Economy*, Book IV, Ch. VII, University of Toronto Press, 1965; reprinted Routledge & Kegan Paul, 1968.

> **in loco parentis:** in place of a parent.
>
> δικαιοσύνη (**dikaiosune**), σωφροσύνη (**sophrosune**): reference to virtues ('justice', 'temperance') prized by the ancient Greeks.

**XVIII.4**   Added by Mill to the 2nd (1849) edition.

> **Moravians:** A Protestant denomination which originated among the followers of the reformer, John Huss, in the fifteenth century. A small group survived and formed a model community of Christian life in what is now Germany. Other such communities have since been formed elsewhere in Europe and the United States.
>
> **Mr Owen:** Robert Owen (1771-1858) was an industrialist and philanthropist who sought to reorganize society on the basis of co-operative communities.
>
> **St Simonism:** A system associated with the French socialist, Saint-Simon (1760-1825), in which all property is owned by the state and is enjoyed by the worker according to the quantity and quality of work done.
>
> **Fourierism:** A system associated with the French reformer, F. M. C. Fourier (1772-1837), in which economic activities would be carried out in *Phalanstères*, groups of about

1,600 people bound together by mutual love, working without machinery, mainly grow-ing flowers and vegetables, making durable objects by hand, and enjoying frequent large meals and a régime of free love. Fourier did not advocate the complete abandonment of private property.

**XIX.1**  In *Essays on Philosophical Subjects*, ed. Dugald Stewart, Dublin 1795, pp. 26-8.

**XIX.2**  *The Theory of Moral Sentiments*, 1759, from Part IV, ch. 1, London, Bohn, 1861, pp. 257-68.

**XIX.3**  *An Introduction to the Principles of Morals and Legislation*, first printed 1780, first published 1789. From Second edition 1823, with textual modifications.

**XIX.4**  *The Book of Fallacies*, 1824, pp. 352-3, and *Works*, ed. Bowring, ii, p. 482; reprinted in *Economic Writings*, ed. W. Stark, iii, pp. 432-3.

**XIX.5**  From *Nature, the Utility of Religion, and Theism*, 1850-8.

**XX.1**  From 'Pre-Raphaelitism', 1851, pp. 21-4, reprinted with *Lectures on Architecture and Painting*, Library Edition of Ruskin's Works, Vol. XII. This extract reprinted in Kenneth Clark, ed., *Ruskin Today*, Penguin, 1964, pp. 217-18.

**XX.2**  From H. C. Marillier, *Dante Gabriel Rossetti—An Illustrated Memorial of his Art and Life*, London, George Bell & Sons, 1899, pp. 18-21.

**XX.3**  From Ford Madox Hueffer, *Ford Madox Brown: A Record of his Life and Work*, London, New York, and Bombay, Longmans, Green, and Co., 1896, pp. 189-95.

**XXI.1**  *Poems Chiefly Lyrical*, 1830.

**XXI.2**  *Poems*, Leeds, 1833, Sonnet XVI, p. 16; reprinted in *Poems, edited with a Memoir of his Life by his Brother* (Derwent), London, Moxon, 1857, Vol. I, p. 20.

**XXI.3**  *Poems*, 1853.

**XXI.4**  From *Idylls of the King*, 1859, pp. 21-3.

**XXI.5**  First published 1863, revised 1871; from *The Poems of Gerard Manley Hopkins*, ed. R. Bridges, 1918, fourth edition, ed. W. H. Gardner, Oxford, 1967.

**XXII.1**  *Essays on Philosophical Subjects*, ed. Dugald Stewart, Dublin, 1795, pp. 233-6.

**XXII.2**  First published in *The Morning Post*, 24 September 1799.

**XXIII.1**  An account of the nature and importance, as Liszt saw it, of the so-called Hungarian gipsy music. First published Paris, 1859. Translated by Edwin Evans, London, William Reeves, 1926. Selection from Chapters 20, 8, and 7.

**XXIII.2**  First published in *Ethnographia* (The Journal of the Hungarian Ethno-graphic Society), XLII:2 (1931), reprinted in *Musical Quarterly*, XXXIII (1947).

**XXIII.3**  Reprinted in *Monthly Musical Record*, Oct., Nov., Dec. 1948. This ex-tract is from the December issue.

**XXIII.4**  Preface to *Folk Music of Hungary*, trans. and revised by Ronald Tempest and Cynthia Jolly, London, 1960.

**gipsy scale**: an unusual scale which uses some intervals larger than most scales (i.e. augmented intervals).

**XXIV.1**   From the Introduction to *Modern Street Ballads*, 1888.

**Thomas Bewick**: (1753-1828). Celebrated wood-engraver who worked for most of his life in Newcastle. His most famous work is his *History of British Birds*, 2 vols., 1797, 1804.

**Jemmy Catnach**: Jeremy Catnach (1792-1841), leading London printer of broadsides, active from 1813 to 1838. His firm continued after this, passing into the hands of W. S. Fortey.

**XXIV.2**   Music Hall song, 1894. probably by Edgar Bateman.

**XXIV.3**   Printed in the *Journal of the Folk Song Society*, Vol. I, 1899.

**XXIV.4**   Sharp, *English Folk Song: Some Conclusions*, 1907, Ch. 10.

**Mr Baring-Gould**: The Rev. Sabine Baring-Gould (1834-1924), a leading English folk-song collector, active about the same time as Cecil Sharp.

**Folk-Songs from Somerset**: Collections published by Sharp, 1904-9 (5 vols.).

**XXIV.5**   Lloyd, *The Singing Englishman*, Workers' Musical Association, 1944, pp. 52-4.

**XXIV.6**   Lloyd, *Folksong in England*, Lawrence and Wishart, 1967, Ch. 5.

**Jean Genet**: b. 1910. French writer.

**Dibdin**: (1745-1814). Composer of songs and stage music.

**Haynes Bayley**: Thomas Haynes Bayley (1797-1829), writer of poems and song-lyrics (including that of 'Home Sweet Home').

**XXV.1**   Dated 13 March 1879, published in *The Poems of Gerard Manley Hopkins*, edited with notes by Robert Bridges, 1918. Fourth edition edited by W. H. Gardner, Oxford, 1967.

**XXV.2**   *Daniel Deronda*, 1874-6, Book III, Ch. 23.

**XXV.3**   *The Industrial Revolution*, 1884, Ch. VIII; reprinted as a Beacon edition, 1957.

**XXV.4**   Pamphlet, 1885, issued by the *Socialist League*. First published in volume form in William Morris, *Signs of Change*, Reeves and Turner, 1888. Reprinted in William Morris, *Selected Writings*, ed. G. D. H. Cole, Nonesuch, 1948; this extract, pp. 604-5.

**XXV.5**   First published separately, London, A. L. Humphreys, 1907. Reprinted in Oscar Wilde, *Plays, Stories and Poems*, Everyman, 1961, pp. 269-70.

**XXV.6**   *Tess of the d'Urbervilles*, 1891, Chs. 67-8. By permission of the Trustees of the Hardy estate and Macmillan, London and Basingstoke.

**XXV.7**   From 'Nottingham and the Mining Countryside', *The New Adelphi*, June-August 1930; reprinted in D.H. Lawrence, *Selected Essays*, Penguin, 1950. By permission of Laurence Pollinger Ltd., the estate of the late Mrs Frieda Lawrence, and The Viking Press.

# Biographical Notes on Authors

**XXI.3    Mathew Arnold** (1822–88), poet. The son of Thomas Arnold, the famous headmaster of Rugby. In 1847 he became private secretary to Lord Lansdowne, then president of the council running Lord John Russell's liberal administration, and in 1851 accepted an appointment as inspector of schools. He was an early advocate of state education. In 1857 Arnold was elected to the Oxford Professorship of Poetry, which he held till 1867, when his *New Poems* were published. Thereafter he turned his attention mainly to criticism.

**VII.5    Sir Edward Baines** (1800–90). Son of a famous provincial newspaperman, Edward Baines of the *Leeds Mercury*, Baines was a leading Yorkshire Liberal and advocate of temperance, serving as M.P. for Leeds between 1859 and 1874, becoming a knight, and writing histories of the cotton and woollen industries.

**XXIII.2,3    Béla Bartók** (1881–1845) was a Hungarian composer, pianist, and folklorist, equally important for his own works and for his pioneering contribution to the collection, classification, and study of East European folk-music. In the early years of the century a close association with the rising tide of Hungarian nationalism, together with the influence of native folk-song, had a profound effect on his style. He left Hungary in 1940 and spent his last years in the U.S.A.

**XII.3, XIX.3,4    Jeremy Bentham** (1748–1832). Educated from very early years by his father, a London attorney, Jeremy Bentham later went to Westminster and Queen's College, Oxford. He was called to the Bar, but preferred to write about the principles of legislation and moral philosophy, and to invent new government institutions. He attacked all forms of government and law founded merely on authority and tradition. A formalizer of utilitarian ideas—which he derived from Helvétius and Hume—and of the 'greatest happiness' principle, Bentham held that acts should be judged by their consequences, and that the criterion of a right action should be that it promoted the greatest happiness of the greatest number.

**XIII.1    William Blake** (1757–1827) was born in London, the son of a hosier. He went to a drawing school at ten, and early in life collected prints of Raphael and Michelangelo; he started writing poetry about the age of twelve. At fourteen he was apprenticed to an engraver, who frequently required him to draw the monuments at Westminster Abbey; here he came to love Gothic art.

In 1778 he became a student at the Royal Academy, but soon left and made his living engraving for booksellers. He married in 1782 and his wife helped him with his engraving when he printed his own books, starting with *Songs of Innocence*.

Blake's visionary genius was not widely recognized in his own time, and he spent many years in poverty, exacerbated by a charge of sedition brought against him in the Napoleonic wars. In his last years he became the centre of a group of young painters who revered him, including Samuel Palmer (see plate 1).

**IV.5,6, XIV.1    George Gordon, Lord Byron** (1788–1824) was born in Scotland,

and succeeded to a peerage as a boy. He was educated at Harrow and Trinity College, Cambridge, and travelled in the Near East, returning to England to find himself famous, with his *Childe Harold's Pilgrimage*. Forced to leave England after many love-affairs and the breakdown of his marriage, and because he was deeply in debt, he lived for a time with the Shelley family on Lake Geneva, and wrote *Don Juan* in exile in Italy. He died in Greece where he had gone to fight for the cause of the Greeks against their Turkish rulers.

**XVI.1,3, XVII.1    Thomas Carlyle** (1795–1889), Scottish essayist and historian. Born at Ecclefechan in Annandale, Carlyle studied at Edinburgh University with a view to ordination, but became a schoolmaster. Best remembered as a social commentator, Carlyle was also a historian, biographer, satirist, and translator. Among his best-known works are 'Signs of the Times' (1829), *Sartor Resartus* (1833–4), *The French Revolution* (1837), *Chartism* (1839), *On Heroes, Hero Worship, and The Heroic in History* (1841), and *Past and Present* (1843). It was partly his reading of the medieval chronicle of Jocelin of Brakelond that inspired him to write *Past and Present*.

**IX.1    Edwin Chadwick** (1800–90). Born in Manchester, Chadwick became the disciple of Bentham, and proceeded to reform the statutory social services of the country in a logical, Benthamite manner. Starting with the Poor Law, he then pursued pauperism to its roots in disease which urban conditions allowed to spread rapidly. On a scientifically false diagnosis—the 'atmospheric impurities' he indicated were innocent, disease was borne by polluted water supplies—he and other resolute sanitary reformers were nevertheless able to abate the worst of the evils. Chadwick represented a movement within utilitarianism towards collectivist intervention in order to secure 'the greatest good to the greatest number' by direct legislation.

**IV.8,9    John Clare** (1793–1864), was the son of a thresher receiving parish relief. His father was also a ballad singer, who reputedly knew more than a hundred songs. At the age of seven, John Clare started work on a farm, and began writing verse after reading Thomson's *Seasons*. He achieved immediate popularity on the publication of his first book *Poems descriptive of Rural Life and Scenery by John Clare, a Northamptonshire peasant*. But his fame soon declined; his next three books were unsuccessful; and he lived in poverty. Unable to make a living either as a farmworker or as a poet, he was incarcerated in Northampton Asylum, where he died.

**XV.2    Arthur Hugh Clough** (1819–61), the son of a cotton merchant, was educated in the setting of *Tom Brown's Schooldays*, Rugby, and at Balliol College, Oxford; he became a Fellow of Oriel, and Principal of University Hall, London. Several of his poems followed classical Greek and Latin metres.

**XXI.2    Hartley Coleridge** (1796–1849). The eldest son of Samuel Taylor Coleridge and the subject of his father's poem *Frost at Midnight*. Like his father, he was brilliant and erratic: he tried to teach (and was dismissed from Oxford for intemperance); and he tried to write. His greatest contribution to literature was a handful of exquisite sonnets, and to scholarship his editions of the dramatic works of Ford and Massinger. He was a much-loved figure among the people of his native Lake District.

**IV.1, XIII.5, XXII.2    Samuel Taylor Coleridge** (1772–1834) was born at Ottery St. Mary, Devon, the son of a vicar, and was educated at Christ's Hospital, Westminster, and at Jesus College, Cambridge. In 1795 he met Wordsworth, and they published together the first edition of the *Lyrical Ballads*, which included 'The Ancient Mariner'. Apart from poetry, he wrote literary criticism and philosophical and political tracts. His early ideas were radical: he believed in 'Pantisocracy', a form of primitive communism. Coleridge was influenced by German 'idealist' thought in which he was well read. He proposed a new though conservative rejuvenating force for society, a class of the educated and the artists, which he called the 'clerisy'.

**III.2  John Constable** (1776–1837) was born in East Bergholt, Suffolk, the son of a prosperous local miller. He was a little slow to take up his vocation as a painter, not enrolling at the Royal Academic Schools in London until 1799, where he soon determined to devote himself exclusively to landscape painting. By 1802 he was making oil sketches in the open air and was widely recognized as an original talent, although compared to his great contemporary, Turner, he failed to achieve any very wide acclaim or success. His most prolific period was between 1817 and 1825, when he produced *The Hay Wain* and other large pictures. He was made A.R.A. in 1819. His work is valued now for the freshness of its response to nature. Constable's talent was more quickly recognized in France than in England, and he was said to have exerted an influence on the open-air Barbizon School and thereby, ultimately, on the Impressionists.

**XI.2  William Cowper** (1731–1800) was born at Great Berkhampstead, Hertfordshire, the son of a rector, was educated at Westminster School and called to the Bar in 1754. He suffered from depression, and in 1783 tried to commit suicide. He was succoured throughout his life by good friends. His poetry set a model of more 'natural' style than that of the dominant schools of his time, the imitators either of Milton or of Pope.

**II.5  George Crabbe** (1754–1832) was a doctor and practised in Aldeburgh, Suffolk. He went to London in 1780 and was there befriended by Edmund Burke. He took orders and was curate of Aldeburgh in 1781, and chaplain to the Duke of Rutland 1782–5. Crabbe was helped in the revision of *The Village* by Burke and by Dr. Johnson. In *The Village* he consciously set out to present the realities of rural life without any of the idealization of pastoral convention.

**I.1  Daniel Defoe** (1660–1731). Best remembered as the writer of *Robinson Crusoe* (1719) and *Moll Flanders* (1720), Defoe was also a businessman, journalist, and government agent. He had been closely involved in the negotiations for the Anglo-Scottish Union, about 1707, and his *Tour Through the Whole Island of Great Britain*, which was published between 1724 and 1727, drew partly on his memories of travels at that time.

**VIII.5,6, X.9, XV.3  Charles Dickens** (1812–70) was born into a poor family in London, the son of a government clerk whose fortunes were in steady decline throughout Dickens's childhood and who was in prison for debt for several years. After very little formal education Dickens worked for a short time in a factory. He learnt shorthand and became first a parliamentary reporter, then a reporter on *The Morning Chronicle* and began to write sketches of London life (*Sketches by Boz*). His novels were published in serial form. The first of these, *The Pickwick Papers* (1836–7) made him famous at once. His popularity has never since suffered a decline.

**II.4  Stephen Duck** (1705–56), the Thresher Poet, was born of poor parents at Charlton, Wiltshire. He had some education till the age of fourteen, then became a farm labourer. He read Shakespeare, Milton, and Dryden, and in 1730, at the suggestion of a neighbouring parson, Arthur Stanley, he wrote *The Thresher's Labour*. It achieved immediate fame and went through ten editions in 1730, though it also aroused some mocking opposition from other poets of the day. Pope did not think much of Stephen Duck's verse, but nevertheless promoted his cause with the court, and Duck became a librarian to the Queen and married a royal housekeeper. In 1746 he was ordained. He died by drowning himself in a fit of melancholy.

**II.7  George Edwards (1850–1933).** An agricultural labourer and Primitive Methodist lay preacher, Sir George Edwards took a leading role in the re-establishment of agricultural trade unionism in the 1890s and the creation of the Labour Party in East Anglia, which he served as M.P. for South Norfolk between 1922 and 1924.

**XXV.2  George Eliot (Mary Ann Evans) (1819–80)** was born in the Midlands. Her first important work was a translation from the German of Strauss's *Life of Jesus*. She moved to London and became a contributor to *The Westminster Review*. From 1854 till his death she lived with George Henry Lewes, who encouraged her gifts for fiction. Among her other novels, besides *Daniel Deronda*, are *Adam Bede* (1859), *The Mill on the Floss* (1860), and *Middlemarch* (1871–2).

**VIII.4, XVII.2, XVIII.2  Friedrich Engels (1820–95)** was the son of a wealthy German textile manufacturer and worked in his father's factory in Manchester. In *The Condition of the Working Class in England*, although he had only just met Marx when it was written, Engels had reached practical conclusions similar to Marx's philosophical ones. Financed by his own parents, he financed Marx, and remained his friend throughout his life, even owning to the fatherhood of Marx's illegitimate child in order to protect Marx's family. After Marx's death, Engels edited the second and third volumes of *Das Kapital* from his unpublished writings and remained a leader of the revolutionary movement in Britain and Europe.

**V.3  John Fielden (1784–1847)** was the son of a Quaker yeoman farmer who founded a mill in Todmorden, Lancashire. He and his brothers inherited the family cotton-spinning business, but unlike many mill-owners, he supported factory reform and shorter hours. He entered Parliament after the passing of the first Reform Bill in 1832, and became the main Lancashire spokesman in the movement to limit the working day. He became a Chartist, and sponsored the successful Ten Hours Bill in 1847.

**VII.3, X.10  Mrs. Gaskell (1810–65).** Mrs. Elizabeth Gaskell was the wife of a Unitarian minister whose church was in Manchester. She married in 1832, and had an unrivalled opportunity for direct observation of the hardships of the working people during the formative years of industrial Manchester. *Mary Barton* (1848) and *North and South* (1855) are her two best-known novels. She published a life of her friend Charlotte Brontë in 1856.

**III.1  William Gilpin (1724–1804)** was born near Carlisle and was educated at Oxford, though he said that the teaching there was no more than 'solemn trifling'. He was ordained in 1746 and spent much of his life teaching at a school in Cheam, Surrey, which gave him the opportunity to spend the summer holidays travelling and sketching. With his sketches, and with the publication in 1792 of the *Three Essays* ('On Picturesque Beauty', 'On Picturesque Travel', and 'On Sketching Landscapes') he is said to have created a new approach to travelling.

**XXV.6  Thomas Hardy (1840-1928)** was brought up in Dorset, and his novels are mainly set there and in the neighbouring counties, which he described with fictional place names as 'Wessex'. He had an architectural training. Like John Clare, he was the son of a traditional musician, and traditional music and dancing play a part in a number of his poems and stories; the loss of such local arts in the process of 'modernization' is a theme which recurs in his work. In middle life, Hardy turned his main energy from the writing of novels to poetry; and his verse has had a growing influence on twentieth-century poets.

**XXI.5, XXV.1  Gerard Manley Hopkins (1844-89)** was educated at Highgate School, and Balliol College, Oxford. He was influenced there by Newman and the Oxford Movement, becoming a Roman Catholic, and in 1868 a Jesuit. At this stage in his life particularly, he felt a conflict between the demands of his faith and his work as a poet, and he burned his early poems. But when he later felt that the two demands could be reconciled he began writing again. His long poem 'The Wreck of the Deutschland' was rejected by a Jesuit newspaper, and although a few of his poems were published in anthologies, he was little known or appreciated in his lifetime. Hopkins went to Dublin in 1884 as Professor of Classics, and died there of typhoid fever. It was only when his friend Robert Bridges the Poet Laureate published his *Poems* in 1918 that the quality of his poetry was widely recognized. The publication of his Notebooks including some of his drawings, has further added to his reputation.

**XX.3  Ford Hueffer (Ford Madox Ford) (1873-1939).** Son of a German music critic, Francis Hueffer, Ford Hueffer was the grandson of Ford Madox Brown, the Pre-Raphaelite painter. He met Joseph Conrad in 1897 and collaborated with him on *The Inheritors* (1901) and *Romance* (1903). He founded and edited *The English Review* and among the writers he published early in their careers were Wyndham Lewis, Ezra Pound, and D. H. Lawrence. His finest work was probably the tetralogy *Parade's End* which depicts characters he fought with in the First World War.

**I.2  Samuel Johnson (1708-84)** was the son of a bookseller who managed to send him to Oxford. For financial reasons, Johnson was forced to leave before he received his degree, and became a schoolmaster; but when he came to London, poor and without patrons, he achieved solid fame for his poetry, his criticism, his essays, and for his Dictionary, while he was also perhaps the most celebrated conversationalist of his time.

**IV.10,11, XIII.3  John Keats (1795-1821)** was born in Moorfields, London, son of a livery-stable keeper, and was apprenticed to an apothecary; he qualified as a surgeon but gave up the idea of this career for literature. Together with his brother Tom he read deeply in the poetry of Spenser and the other Elizabethans, and evolved a rich personal style in the poems of 1819. In contrast to the meticulous style of his poetry, his letters are characterized by a lively carelessness, even when he is expressing his most deeply felt convictions. Keats's poems were attacked by critics on their publication; Byron said he was 'snuffed out by an article', but although adverse criticism had depressed him, he was killed by the consumption which had earlier destroyed his brother. Keats died in Rome at the age of twenty-six.

**XXIII.4  Zoltán Kodály (1882-1967)** was a Hungarian composer who also, like his compatriot Béla Bartók, and partly in collaboration with him, made an important contribution to the collecting and editing of Hungarian folk-song. Like Bartók, he developed a style of his own which was heavily influenced by folk-music. He was also responsible for influential new methods of teaching music in schools.

**XXV.7  David Herbert Lawrence** (1885-1930). The son of a Nottinghamshire miner, he had a more intimate knowledge of industrial life than most nineteenth-century commentators, and was a harsh critic of its debasement of human potential. His novels and essays are filled with a prophetic sense that he must warn his own generation about how it is imperilling life for the future.

**XXIII.1  Franz Liszt** (1811-86). Hungarian born, Liszt became a complete cosmopolitan, the greatest piano virtuoso of his time, and one of its leading 'progressive' composers. He moved in the most 'bohemian' circles and expressed radical social and artistic views, but his musical interests were wide—embracing Hungarian 'gipsy' music and the music of many past periods—and he befriended, as well as influencing, many of his contemporaries, including Richard Wagner.

**XXIV.5,6  A. L. Lloyd** (b. 1908) is one of the leading scholars associated with the recent (the 'second wave') revival in English folk-music. He is also a singer of folk-songs and has worked on radio productions involving the use of folk-music. His collecting and writing have been particularly important in the relatively new field of industrial folk-song, and his *Folk Song in England* (1967) has probably become the standard work on the subject.

**XVI.2  Thomas Babington Macaulay** (1800-59) was the son of Zachary Macaulay, once governor of Sierra Leone, and an ardent philanthropist. He went to Cambridge, and was called to the Bar in 1826. His wit and an early essay published in the *Edinburgh Review* won him fame. He entered Parliament in 1830 and his speeches in favour of the Reform Bill were praised highly by Sir Robert Peel. In 1834 he went to India, to a seat on the Supreme Council of India, where he applied 'sound liberal principles' in its government. He returned to England in 1838 and subsequently published his *Lays of Ancient Rome*, his collected *Essays*, and his *History of England*, all of which were highly popular in his lifetime.

**XII.3  Thomas Robert Malthus** (1766-1834). Educated at Cambridge, Malthus took holy orders but passed most of his life as Professor of Political Economy at the East India Company's College at Haileybury. His speculations on population, the result of a debate carried on in the 1790s about whether Britain's population was rising or falling, had a pervasive effect on economic and social policy, particularly in the first half of the nineteenth century.

**V.4, XVII.3,4, XVIII.2  Karl Marx** (1818-83) was the son of a Jewish lawyer with a keen interest in philosophy, and was educated at a time of strong Hegelian influence in the German universities. He began as a poet, turned to philosophy and the study of the material conditions of life, and became a journalist. He moved to Paris when the paper he was writing for in Cologne was suppressed, and met Friedrich Engels, with whom he later wrote the *Communist Manifesto*. He returned to Germany in the revolutionary atmosphere of 1848, but was expelled in 1849, and moved to London. Here, in spite of some journalistic work for the *New York Tribune*, and financial help from Engels, he lived in poverty. It was in London that he wrote most of his later works including *Das Kapital*, and from London he took part in the direction of some of the main revolutionary movements of his time in Europe.

**X.8   Henry Mayhew** (1812–87) was born in London, and educated at Westminster School. He became a dramatist and was one of the founders of *Punch*. *London Labour and the London Poor* was his most important work. It originally appeared in the *Morning Chronicle*; and it made a considerable impact on public opinion when published in book form, beginning in 1851.

**XVII.5, XVIII.3,4, XIX.5   John Stuart Mill** (1806–73). The son of James Mill and a follower of Jeremy Bentham, John Stuart Mill was perhaps the most outstanding British philosopher of the nineteenth century. His most substantial works were his *System of Logic* (1843) and *Principles of Political Economy* (1849). He was an active political reformer, being a Member of Parliament from 1865 to 1868, during which time he attempted to introduce a Bill giving women the right to vote. He wrote a number of shorter works, including *On Liberty* (1859), *Representative Government* (1861), *Utilitarianism* (1863), and *The Subjection of Women* (1869). He also wrote an essay on Bentham and Coleridge which traced the relationships between some of the ideas represented in this anthology; and an autobiography in which he records his revulsion against his early abstract and systematic education, and his sense that only poetry could fill the void it had left.

**XXV.4   William Morris** (1834–95) was born at Walthamstow, Essex, the son of a London broker who made a fortune in Devon copper-mining shares when Morris was a boy. He went to Marlborough College, then in 1853 to Exeter College, Oxford, where he met Edward Burne-Jones, his lifelong friend. Originally destined for the church, he read Ruskin's chapter 'The Nature of Gothic' in *The Stones of Venice* (XVII.7) when it first came out, visited Gothic cathedrals in France with Burne-Jones, and decided, with him, to become an artist. He started with architecture, then turned to painting under the influence of Dante Gabriel Rossetti. In time Morris took to a great range of crafts, including wall-paper designing, tapestry weaving, calligraphy, printing, and dyeing. He had started writing poetry at Oxford, and became one of the leading poets of his time, writing also prose romances, and translations of Norse sagas. Like Ruskin, who had influenced him when he was young, Morris became increasingly preoccupied with social questions as he grew older. A reading of John Stuart Mill's presentation of the case for and against socialism converted him to socialism, and he became one of the earliest members of the Social Democratic Federation, one of the sources of the present Labour Party.

**X.3   Richard Oastler** (1789–1861). The Tory-radical steward of an estate near Huddersfield, in 1830 Oastler set himself up as the champion first of the factory children, then of the factory labourers against their free-trading, largely Liberal employers, and of the Northern poor against the workhouse system introduced by the New Poor Law of 1834.

**XXIV.3   Sir Hubert Parry** (1848–1918) was an English composer—one of the first in the nineteenth century to suggest in his music that a distinctively English style was possible—whose choral works are the ones best remembered today. In the final decades of his life he was a very influential figure in English musical life.

**XIV.2   Thomas Love Peacock** (1785–1866), son of a London merchant, started working in trade. He gave it up and lived off private income, producing some verse, and satirical romances such as *Nightmare Abbey* in which he made fun of many of the fashions of his day—the ideas of Malthus, Bentham, the canal enthusiasts and many others. Scythrop is supposed to be a caricature of Shelley.

**II.2,3** Alexander Pope (1688–1744) was the son of a Roman Catholic linen-draper. At the age of twelve a serious illness ruined his health and left him stunted and disfigured. His disability is generally held responsible for the characteristic bitterness of much of his satirical writing. His talent was precocious, and his output prodigious. His poetry combines a frequently barbed wit with exquisite expression. He was a virulent enemy of bad taste and poor writing.

**VI.1** Joseph Priestley (1767–1852) was the son of the accountant to the Leeds and Liverpool Canal, and a canal manager who directed the affairs of the Aire and Calder Navigation from 1817 to 1851. His *Navigable Rivers and Canals* was a straightforward shipper's guide to the facilities offered by British canals and railways at the height of the canal age.

**XX.2** Dante Gabriel Rossetti (1828–82) was the son of an Italian liberal, and brother of the poet Christina Rossetti. He was a poet as well as a painter. He admired the paintings of Ford Madox Brown, and a chance meeting with Millais and Holman Hunt led him to suggest the forming of the 'Pre-Raphaelite Brotherhood'.

**I.3** Jean-Jacques Rousseau (1712–78) was born in French-speaking Switzerland, and died as the most famous French philosopher of his time. The *Discourse on Inequality*, an early work, is perhaps the first in the history of modern Europe seriously to question the value of civilization as a whole, and to accuse men's relationships in society of estranging them from nature and from their own inner life. Rousseau's best-known work is probably *Du Contrat Social*. Besides his political philosophy, Rousseau also wrote an opera and highly original lyrical prose.

**III.3, IX.2,3, XVII.7,8, XX.1** John Ruskin (1819–1900) was the son of a wine merchant. He went to no school but was taught by his mother and tutors and travelled extensively. In 1836 he went to Christ Church, Oxford, and won the Newdigate Prize for poetry in 1839. In his first book, *Modern Painters* (1843–52), he championed the painting of Turner; *The Stones of Venice* followed in 1851–3. He became the most famous art critic of his day. From the 1860s onwards, he wrote increasingly on economic and social questions. His marriage failed. He was always mentally unstable. An unreturned love for a young girl (who herself went mad) was followed by a permanent disturbance of his mind, although at intervals in the last decades of his life he wrote his remarkable autobiography *Praeterita*.

**IV.7** Walter Scott (1771–1832), author of the Waverley Novels, was born in Edinburgh. His father's profession, that of a Writer to the Signet, combined legal and antiquarian work, and Scott followed him at first in the law. He was called to the Bar, but began translating from the German of Goethe and collecting ballads and folk-songs. He took a part-time legal job as clerk to a quarter sessions from 1805 to 1806 in order to have more time for writing, and he also invested money unwisely in literary ventures. Debt added to his urge to write, and from 1805 onwards he turned to the novel, beginning with *Waverley*. His works brought him fame throughout Europe, and he was seen as a central figure in the Romantic movement. Felix Mendelssohn, for example, regarded it as an essential part of his tour of Scotland in 1829 to visit Sir Walter Scott at Abbotsford, as well as Fingal's Cave on Staffa.

**XXIV.4** Cecil Sharp (1859–1924) was an English musician who became the leader of the English folk-music revival. From 1893 he devoted himself mainly to the collection and editing of folk songs, publishing many collections and a classic study, *English Folk Song: Some Conclusions* (1907).

**XIII.4, XV.1   Percy Bysshe Shelley** (1792–1822) was born near Horsham, Sussex, eldest son of a rich family, and educated at Eton and at University College, Oxford. He was sent down from the University for publishing a pamphlet on 'The Necessity of Atheism'. Besides poetry, Shelley wrote political and philosophical pamphlets. Deeply influenced by the reformer Godwin, he wrote a revolutionary Declaration of Rights in 1812 and wrote his first long poem *Queen Mab* in the same year. He lived with Godwin's daughter Mary after the breakdown of his first marriage, and they shared a house with Byron in Switzerland. Shelley died by drowning at Lerici in the Bay of Spezia.

**XVII.6   Samuel Smiles** (1812–1904), the eldest son of a poor Scottish family, went to Edinburgh University, where he studied medicine. He soon abandoned medicine for journalism, and became editor of the *Leeds Times*. He published a series of biographies of industrialists; but his most successful book was *Self-Help*.

**XII.1,2, XVIII.1, XIX.1,2, XXII.1   Adam Smith** (1723–90) was born at Kirkcaldy, Fife, and educated at Glasgow University and at Balliol College, Oxford. He taught Moral Philosophy at Edinburgh, then Logic and Moral Philosophy as a professor at Glasgow University. His first book, *The Theory of Moral Sentiments*, was published in 1759. He left his professorship to travel in France as tutor to a nobleman, and there met the leading French economists of the day. On his return he retired to Kirkcaldy, and developed his earlier teaching and his new experience into his most famous work, *An Inquiry into the Nature and Causes of the Wealth of Nations* (1776). He was revising his first book at the time of his death, and those early essays and lectures which he did not destroy shortly before he died were published in 1795.

**XXI.1,4   Alfred Tennyson** (1809–92) was born at Somersby, a Lincolnshire parish, of which his father was rector. He was educated by his father and at Trinity College, Cambridge, where he won the prize for English verse. His first book, *Poems Chiefly Lyrical* (1830), was attacked by the critics, as the poems of Keats had been a few years before. At Cambridge Tennyson met Arthur Hallam; they became close friends, and on Hallam's death in 1833 Tennyson began *In Memoriam* which was published in 1850. In that year he was made Poet Laureate by Queen Victoria, who felt affinities between the author and herself as a widow. She later made him a peer. The four *Idylls of the King* were published in 1859, and established Tennyson's popularity with a wide public. Tennyson belonged to a circle of friends which included Gladstone and many of the leading scientific and philosophical thinkers of the late Victorian Age. His poems express not only his own lyrical feelings but some of the doubts about religion and the nature of the universe which affected many Victorians.

**XII,1   James Thomson** (1700–48) was born at Ednam on the Scottish–English border, the son of a minister, and educated at Edinburgh University. He moved to London and there under the stress of poverty wrote 'Winter', the first of *The Seasons* (1726). His poems are held to have been the first in English to challenge the artificiality of the followers of Pope; their feeling for nature foreshadowed much that was to come in the later Romantic movement.

**VIII.1    Alexis de Tocqueville** (1805–59), political writer and historian, was born in France of an aristocratic family. He read law in Paris, then went to America to study the prison system. After he had returned to France in 1832, he was elected a deputy. During the revolution of 1848 he was a member of the assembly's constitutional committee, and foreign minister for a few months in 1849. He protested against Louis Napoleon's *coup* in 1851, was imprisoned at Vincennes, and on his release forced to retire. His two most famous works are *Democracy in America* and *L'Ancien Régime*.

**XXV.3    Arnold Toynbee** (1852–83) was a young Oxford don, the disciple of Ruskin and the Hegelian philosopher T. H. Green, who took an active role in politics as a Poor Law Guardian. He was also an advocate of co-operation, as well as being a pioneer historian of the industrial revolution. After his early death his university commemorated him by the foundation of Toynbee Hall in Bethnal Green in the East End of London, where young Oxford men could instruct and live among the working classes. He was the uncle of Arnold J. Toynbee, the historian.

**V.2    Andrew Ure** (1778–1857). Born in Glasgow, Ure was educated in Scotland and from 1804 to 1830 was Professor of Chemistry and Physics at Anderson's College, Glasgow (now Strathclyde University). He was a notable popularizer of scientific discovery through his *Dictionary of Chemistry* (1821) and his *Dictionary of Arts, Manufactures and Mines* (1839).

**VI.2    Francis Whishaw** (1804–56) was an engineer during the early railway age in Britain, who turned his hand to publicizing—and criticizing—the lines which were currently in operation or under construction. His business affairs do not seem to have been successful and he died in the Marylebone Workhouse.

**XXV.5    Oscar Wilde** (1854–1900). Wit, essayist, editor, and playwright, Oscar Wilde became the leading figure of the aesthetic movement in the late nineteenth century. Yet he had been greatly influenced by John Ruskin while at Oxford, and his essay 'The Soul of Man under Socialism' (1891) explores some of the main concerns of the English social critics—in much the same tone of irony and fantasy with which he played on English manners in comedies like *The Importance of Being Earnest* (1895).

**IV.2,3,4, X.1,5, XI.3, XIII.2    William Wordsworth** (1770–1850) was born in the Lake District, son of an attorney at Cockermouth, and was educated at Hawkshead Grammar School and St. John's College, Cambridge. He travelled in France as a young man, had an illegitimate daughter with a French girl, and witnessed the early stages of the French Revolution. A friend left him a small income for life. With Coleridge he published *Lyrical Ballads* in 1798. The prefaces and postscripts to later editions of this book, especially the second edition of the *Lyrical Ballads* (1800), include some of his finest prose reflections on literature and on life. Though he was considered 'radical' when young, his political and social views changed as he became older. He was made Poet Laureate in 1848.

# Index